William Gifford Palgrave

Personal Narrative of a Year's Journey Through Central and Eastern Arabia, 1862-63

Vol. II.

William Gifford Palgrave

Personal Narrative of a Year's Journey Through Central and Eastern Arabia, 1862-63
Vol. II.

ISBN/EAN: 9783337011130

Printed in Europe, USA, Canada, Australia, Japan

Cover: Foto ©Andreas Hilbeck / pixelio.de

More available books at **www.hansebooks.com**

NARRATIVE

OF

A YEAR'S JOURNEY THROUGH

CENTRAL AND EASTERN ARABIA

(1862–63)

BY

WILLIAM GIFFORD PALGRAVE

LATE OF THE EIGHTH REGIMENT BOMBAY N.I.

Not in vain the nation-strivings, nor by chance the currents flow;
Error-massed, yet truth-directed, to their certain goal they go

TEY'YEEYAT EL KOBRA', BY EBN-EL-FÂRID

فلا عبثا والخلق لم يخلقوا سدى — وإن لم تكن افعالهم بالسديدة

IN TWO VOLUMES

VOL. II

THIRD EDITION

London and Cambridge

MACMILLAN AND CO.

1866

LONDON
PRINTED BY SPOTTISWOODE AND CO.
NEW-STREET SQUARE

CONTENTS

OF

THE SECOND VOLUME

CHAP.		PAGE
X	LIFE AT RIAḌ	1
XI	HISTORY OF THE WAHHABEE DYNASTY	38
XII	COURT OF RIAḌ—JOURNEY TO ḤOFHOOF	88
XIII	FROM HOFHOOF TO ḲAṬEEF	141
XIV	BAḤREYN AND ḲAṬAR	198
XV	'OMĀN	254
XVI	THE COASTS OF 'OMĀN	300
XVII	A SHIPWRECK—MASCAT	338

PLANS

Plan of the Palace . . . . . . *To face page* 81

" Hofhoof . . . . " 141

8.

JOURNEY AND RESIDENCE

IN

CENTRAL AND EASTERN ARABIA

CHAPTER X

LIFE AT RIAḌ

> But there's Morality himsel'
> Embracing all opinions:
> Hear, how he gi'es the t'ither yell
> Between his twa companions;
> See, how she peels the skin an' fell
> As ane were peeling onions!
> Now there—they're packed aff to hell,
> And banished our dominions,
> Henceforth this day.—*Burns*

OUR FIRST PATIENT DJOWHAR—HIS POSITION, CHARACTER, AND INFLUENCE—'ABD-EL-KEREEM—HIS HISTORY AND CHARACTER—VISIT TO HIS HOUSE—AN 'AAREḌ DINNER—FUMIGATION—HIS FAMILY—DISCUSSION ON THE DIVISION OF SINS IN MAHOMETAN THEOLOGY—GENERAL BELIEF—POLYTHEISM AND TOBACCO SMOKING—REASONS ALLEGED BY 'ABD-EL-KEREEM—QUALITIES OF ARAB TOBACCO—FURTHER REASONS—'ABD-EL-KEREEM'S MANŒUVRES TO AVOID PAYMENT—HIS SERMON—'ABD-ER-RAḤMÂN THE MEṬOW'WAA'—HIS ROOMS, STUDIES, AND PUPILS—STORY OF MAHOMET AT DAMASCUS—INDIGNATION OF 'ABD-EL-ḤAMEED—'ABD-EL-LAṬEEF THE WAHHABEE—HIS HISTORY AND CHARACTER—HIS SERMON—ANECDOTES OF DIVINE JUDGMENT ON TOBACCO SMOKERS—RIGORISM OF THE WAHHABEES AND ITS RESULTS—ARAB PUNISHMENTS—MOḤAMMED, BROTHER OF 'ABD-EL-LAṬEEF—OTHER INDIVIDUALS—A DIGRESSION ON ARAB NOSOLOGY—HYGIENIC CONDITION OF ARABIA IN GENERAL—ABSENCE OF CERTAIN MALADIES—EPIDEMICS—SCROFULA—ITS FORMS—RHEUMATISM—CARDIAC DISEASE AND DROPSY—ARAB REMEDIES—DYSENTERY—FEVER—APOPLEXY—PARALYSIS—CHOREA—TETANUS—MANIA—HYDROPHOBIA—ASTHMA—BRONCHITIS—LEPROSY AND CUTANEOUS MALADIES—OPHTHALMIA AND EYE-DISEASE—WANT OF NERVOUS SENSIBILITY AMONG ARABS—

AN OPERATION—DIFFERENCES OBSERVABLE ON THE PERSIAN SEA-COAST AND IN 'OMÂN—RECOVERY OF DJOWHAR—OUR POSITION AT THE PALACE—INTRODUCTION TO THE HISTORY OF THE WAHHABEE DYNASTY.

ACCORDING to promise, Aboo-'Eysa played his part and employed all his powers of amplification, vulgarly called "puffing," to bring us in patients and customers. His praiseworthy endeavours found their due success, and the very second morning that dawned on us in our new house, ushered in an invalid who proved a very godsend.

This was no other than Djowhar, treasurer of Feyṣul, and of the Wahhabee empire. My readers will be somewhat startled on learning that this great functionary was jet-black, a negro, in fact, though not a slave, having obtained his freedom from Turkee, the father of the present king. He was tall, and, for a negro, handsome, about forty-five years of age, splendidly dressed, a point never neglected by wealthy Africans, whatever be their theoretical creed, and girt with a golden-hilted sword. But, said he, gold, though unlawful if forming a part of apparel or mere ornament, may be employed with a safe conscience in decorating weapons. Many preachers have, I believe, wasted time and eloquence in attempting to persuade the ladies to moderation in dress. I would gladly consent to see them try their chance with a congregation of upper-class negroes; what might be the result I know not, but certainly Gabriel and the Wahhabee have both made a complete failure in this respect. In all other points Djowhar was an excellent fellow, good-humoured, rather hot-tempered, but tractable and confiding, like most "people of his skin," in Arab phrase.

The disease he was actually suffering under annoyed him much, especially as Feyṣul desired to send him without delay on a government errand to Baḥreyn (where we afterwards met him), a business which his bad state of health rendered him wholly unfit for. Thus, bettering his condition might be almost looked on as a national service. Aboo-'Eysa, an old acquaintance and friend of the chief treasurer's, introduced him, and placed him in great dignity on a carpet spread in the courtyard, where, with two or three other individuals of wealth and importance, he seated himself beside the patient, and launched out into an eulogium of my medical skill which would have required some qualification if applied to Cullen himself; but it served wonderfully to encourage Djowhar, and thus predispose him for a cure.

After ceremonies and coffee, I took my dusky patient into the consulting room, where by dint of questioning and surmise, for negroes in general are much less clear and less to the point than Arabs in their statements, I obtained the requisite elucidation of his case. The malady, though painful, was fortunately one admitting of simple and efficacious treatment, so that I was able on the spot to promise him a sensible amendment of condition within a fortnight, and that in three weeks time he should be in plight to undertake his journey to Baḥreyn. I added that with so distinguished a personage I could not think of exacting a bargain and fixing the amount of fees; the requital of my care should be left to his generosity. He then took leave, and was reconducted to his rooms in the palace by his fellow-blacks of less degree.

The ice was now broken; and the confidence displayed by our first patient towards his physician, joined with his high rank and important office, produced the best effect at court and in the town. It was for me a singular piece of good fortune that my first customer was a negro. The black race, much inferior to the Arab in intellectual power and in steadiness of will, are at the same time free from the sceptic distrustfulness and deep jealousy so common among their white fellow-citizens. Envy is indeed the plague-spot of Arabs, and whoever lives long among them will understand by his own experience whence the frequent mention and unavailing condemnation of that unlovely passion in the literature of the land. But nowhere have I found envy so venomous and so universal as in the 'Aareḍ.

The next individual worthy of note whom we took in hand was of a very different stamp from Djowhar; less pliable, less grateful, but in some respects even more to the purpose of our sojourn in Riaḍ. This was 'Abd-el-Kereem, son of Ibraheem, nearly allied by marriage with the great Wahhabee family, and claiming descent from the oldest nobility of 'Aareḍ. Himself a bitter Wahhabee, and a model of all the orthodox vices of his sect, he had figured conspicuously in the first band of Zelators at the epoch of their foundation in 1855, and the cruel death of Soweylim, the late minister, was by popular rumour ascribed to this man's personal jealousy and private aims, thinly disguised under the mask of religious zeal. Other acts of the same description were attributed to him, and he had during a brief exercise of power become so universally unpopular, that his fellow-Zelators had been compelled to avail themselves of the pretext of his weak health to remove him from office. Honoured by those who considered him a victim of his own virtues, hated by ordinary mortals, he now led a retired life in the third quarter of the town, whence a chronic bronchitis, no uncommon ailment in this climate, brought him to our door.

He presented himself with an air of cheerful modesty, and before stating his case entered, by way of introduction, into a discourse which proved him a master of Islamitic lore. Under our roof he affected a special tenderness for the Damascene school of doctrine, took care to remind us that the son of 'Abd-el-Wahhāb had learned the true faith in the capital of Syria, and insinuated that we ourselves were doubtless of equal orthodoxy and learning. It was a pleasure to converse with him on topics in which he was thoroughly at home, and a few encomiums soon led him to instruct us on many points of Wahhabee doctrine and manners. At last, from abstract, he descended to practical regions, and begged me to examine his chest. I prescribed what seemed requisite, and he took his leave, but not till after exacting a promise of our honouring his house with our presence at an early dinner next day. All this familiarity pleased yet alarmed Aboo-'Eysa. Pleased, because admittance to the domestic circle of so high a character in the orthodox world was, in common phrase, a feather in our cap, and a ticket of respectability elswhere; and alarmed when he considered the treacherous and evil heart of our future host. Indeed, this latter feeling so far predominated, that he advised us not to stand to our engagement; but I did not think fit to comply with this over-cautious admonition.

Next day, a little before noon, 'Abd-el-Kereem, in a long white robe, modest guise, and staff in hand, came to our abode in person, and claimed the fulfilment of our promise. We rose and accompanied him across the market-place and behind the palace, through neat streets where decorum and gravity were manifestly the order of the day, till we reached his dwelling.

It was a large one; he ushered us into the courtyard, and thence up a long flight of steps to the second storey, where we entered a handsome and well-lighted divan. Above its door was inscribed, in the large half-Cufic characters usual throughout Nejed, the following distich of the celebrated poet 'Omar-ebn-el-Fariḍ:—

> Welcome to him of whose approach I am all unworthy,
> Welcome to the voice announcing joy after lonely melancholy:
> Good tidings thine; off with the robes of sadness; for know
> Thou art accepted, and I myself will take on me whatever grieves thee.

Words bearing an ascetic, almost a Christian import, where they stand in the exquisite piece whence they are extracted, but here designed to express the feelings of hospitality and of ready friendship. Like all Nejdean inscriptions, they were simply painted not carved. Within the room sat Ibraheem, the aged father of our friend and master of the house, and with him another of his sons; several books treating of law and divinity, sections of the Coran, and inkstands, with good supply of writing paper; some of these objects strewed on the divan, others inserted in the little triangular niches which represent bookcases in Arabia, announced a haunt of learning and study.

Capital towns suppose more polished manners and greater elegance of life than elsewhere, nor does Wahhabee severity prevent Riaḍ from following the general rule. A very courteous greeting and honourable reception was made us by Ibraheem and his family, and one of the children brought in without delay a select dish of excellent dates, as a gage of good will and esteem. When in due time the dinner made its appearance, after many excuses for its simplicity—"You Damascenes would treat us better were we your guests, but Nejed is poor, the means want us, not the will," and the like—it included, among other delicacies, a dish which I was equally surprised and pleased to see, because it was a clear indication of our approach to the eastern coast. But were my readers, even though of East Norfolk, to guess for an hour together what was this well-omened platter, they would hardly, I think, hit on dried shrimps, the article now before us. My Syrian companion, who had never seen these crustaceæ before, did not know what to make of them; for me, I welcomed old friends, though under disadvantageous circumstances—less fresh and less correctly prepared than they might have been on the bonny banks of Yare. On inquiry, I was informed that these delicacies formed a regular item of importation from Ḥaṣa, and that the fishery itself belonged to Baḥreyn. But of the copious marine produce of that island nothing else arrives thus far; possibly from want of skill in salting and curing.

After dinner we washed our hands with potash or ḳalee (whence our own "alkali"), the ordinary cleanser of Nejed, and then took place the ceremony of fumigation. Not that we here underwent it for the first time, since even in Djebel Shomer it is sometimes practised, and in Sedeyr is of daily occurrence; but I forgot to describe it before, and this may be a suitable occasion. Indeed, here, in orthodox 'Aareḍ, perfuming has scarcely less of a religious than of a genteel character, the Prophet having declared himself in express terms almost as much a lover of sweet odours as of women, wherein he left an example to be imitated by zealous followers. Accordingly after meals, or even at the conclusion of a simple coffee-drinking visit, appears a small square box, with the upper part of its sides pierced filigree-wise, while its base offers a sort of stalk or handle, long enough to lay hold of without danger of burning one's fingers; the apparatus is of baked clay, and looks much like an overgrown four-petaled flower. Above, it is filled with charcoal or live embers of Ithel, and on these are laid three or four small bits of sweet-scented wood, identical with that which in the last chapter bribed the ministry on our behalf; or, in place of wood, fragments of benzoin incense, till the rich clammy smoke goes up as from a censer. Everyone now takes in turn the burning vase, passes it under his beard (which, I should say, is generally but a scraggy one in Nejed), next lifts up one after another the corners of his head-gear or kerchief, to catch therein an abiding perfume, though at the risk of burning his ears if he be a new hand at the business, like myself; and lastly, though not always, opens the breast of his shirt too, to give his inner man a whiff of sweet-smelling remembrance. For the odour is extremely tenacious, and may be perceived for hours after. Twice or thrice only did I see incense of the kind commonly employed in Europe brought in on these occasions; it had been imported, said the Nejdean, from Ḥadramaut. But to return to our host.

His father, old Ibraheem, could remember the Egyptian invasion and the siege of Ḍerey'eeyah. He told us many tales regarding those events, of which he had been an eyewitness; I shall insert some of them in my chronicle of the Ebn-Sa'ood dynasty a few pages further on. The name of Aboo-Noḳta, mentioned by the companions of Lascaris in his highly magnified description of the Wahhabee northern invasion, was not unknown to our narrator, but he assigned much greater military prominence to another negro hero, entitled Ḥārith: we shall hear more of this warrior hereafter. When the old man was on these topics, he kindled up, and looked as though he could swallow all the infidels on earth alive, nor do I suppose that he was in reality scant of courage; cowardice is no faul of Nejdeans.

'Abd-el-Kereem continued to pay us almost daily visits, and we occasionally to return them, till his ailment was sufficiently relieved, and he had no further need of us. He was not, I think, "clear," to borrow a Quaker phrase, touching our religious opinions, and in his attempts to draw us out, laid himself very open on many points, to my especial satisfaction.

During an intimate conversation, I enquired of him one day, what, according to the Wahhabee code, were the great sins, or "Kebēy'ir-eḍ-ḍenoob," in Arab terms, and what the little ones, or "Ṣeghey'ir." My readers may perhaps know that Mahometans divide sins into classes—the "great," to be punished in the next world, or at least deserving it; and the "little" sins, whose forgiveness is more easily obtained, and whose penalty is remissible in this life. Somewhat analogous to the division widely received among Christians between mortal and venial transgressions. To hold them all of equal gravity never occurred to a Mahometan, nor in consequence to a Nejdean.

The fact of a real and important distinction is admitted. But here comes a main difficulty, namely, which is which? Every one knows the infinite variety of opinion existing on this subject among Christian doctors or casuists. Nor are Mahometan divines less at variance. Some hold infidelity, polytheism, or non-Mahometanism, to be the only mortal sin—want of faith, in short. This seems to have been Mahomet's own decision, and is countenanced by several texts of the Coran. Others insisting on certain expressions contained in the "Book," add wilful homicide and usury; others again run the total number up to seven, perhaps in imitation of the seven deadly sins specified among Christians; others carry it on to fifty, to seventy; and in a learned manuscript perused by myself in the town of Ḥamah, I was alarmed to find no less than four hundred entitled to this "bad eminence." Lastly, some cut the knot after their fashion by declaring that God alone knows how to distinguish between mortal and venial, and that his Will is the only basis and measure of culpability and punishment.

I should add, though perhaps this point is almost too well known for a special notice, that, in the common credence of Islam, the chastisements of the next world, be they what they may, are eternal for non-Mahometans only; Mahometans will all ultimately escape from the fiery regions, whether by the intercession of Mahomet, as many hold, or by process of time, or by God's free mercy; but anyhow they will all sooner or later enter Paradise, leaving infidels and polytheists alone behind. A very consolatory dogma, after which the future state admits of two partitions: purgatory for Mahometans, hell for all else. For whatever interpretations may be given by commentators more merciful than exact, Christians, Jews, idolators, and whatever besides, all are certainly comprehended under one or other of the fatal titles, polytheist or infidel. So much the worse for them; yet no blame, since in the teaching of the Coran "God guides aright whom He chooses, and leads into error whom He chooses."

What a terrific prospect! my readers may say. However, I must notice, as a sort of apology for our Mahometan, and above all for our Nejdean friends, that this belief is in their ideas not quite so savage as it looks at first sight. For in their glorious ignorance of geography and statistics, they very commonly imagine the Mahometan religion almost universal throughout the world, while other creeds are supposed to number in comparison but very few followers. Europe, for instance, they know to be Christian, but then they conceive it to be but one town, neither more nor less, within whose mural circuit its seven kings—for that is the precise number, count them how you please—are shut up in a species of royal cage to deliberate on mutual peace or war, alliance or treaty, though always by permission and under the orders of the Sultan of Constantinople. An admirable geographical and political lesson, which has been inculcated to me not once but twenty times or more, at Ḥoms, Bagdad, Moṣool and even Damascus. In Arabia, however, knowledge, it was to be expected, makes a yet further retrogression, and I was often asked with the utmost seriousness "whether any Christians or other infidels yet existed in the world?" But no one doubts that among the sons of Adam three-fourths at the very least are Mahometans. Hence, while in fact sentencing a luckless majority of full ten to one to unquenchable fire, they are only, so far as their own intention and imagination are concerned, sending to hell an insignificant, an almost imperceptible flock of perverse unbelievers, who have maliciously shut their eyes against the bright Coran dawn, which has long since overspread the human horizon from east to west. A reflection not anywise novel, but at least forcibly brought home by similar absurdities: well for mankind that their Judge will be not man but God. "Man is man's worst devil," says a Hindoo proverb; and were the Great Assizes entrusted to an earthly arbitrator, of whatever country, religion or race, the best not excluded, heaven would run risk of great emptiness, hell the reverse.

However, many, very many, among what I may rightly call "nominal" Mahometans, and especially those who have travelled a little farther than others, and seen somewhat of the "more things in earth" than are dreamt of in correct Mahometan philosophy, hold, but in the secret of their thought, very different and mayhap more reasonable opinions. To them must be added the numerous disciples of the mystic Arab school, who, in concert with Ebn-Fariḍ, opine that "if the mosque be illuminated by the verses of the Coran, the church is nowise darkened by the words of the Gospel;" and, a few lines farther, "it is no jesting matter, and God did not create all these beings to throw them away, even though their actions and-ways be not always exactly the best." Nay, I have heard Eastern logicians go so far as to explain the phenomena which puzzle or drive to unintelligibility narrower heads and hearts, by saying that, "after all, judgment must be proportioned to knowledge, nor can positive laws and creeds be binding on those who never knew them; that a man's obligations are to be measured by his means, and that whoever acts well will be treated well hereafter;" with more to the same purport. But such tenets are in direct opposition to Mahometan orthodoxy and Coranic teaching, and they who hold them must not be taken for samples of Islam, but for exceptions, or rather antagonists.

Knowing the variety of opinion among ordinary Mahometans regarding the bipartition of sins, I was desirous to learn where Wahhabees thought fit to draw the contested line. My readers cannot fail to understand that the answer to this query must throw considerable light on the moral character of the sect; the most important point, perhaps, where national creeds are concerned. Accordingly I expressed to my learned friend the great anxiety which I lay under, and how uneasy my conscience was, from the fear of committing "great" sins, while deeming them only "little" ones; that I had found the doctors of the north diffident and unsatisfactory in their replies; but that now, in the most pious and orthodox of towns, and in the society of the most learned of friends (modestly looking towards him), I hoped to set my mind at rest, and settle once for all a matter of such high importance.

'Abd-el-Kereem doubted not that he had a sincere scholar before him, nor would refuse his hand to a drowning man. So, putting on a profound air, and with a voice of first-class solemnity, he uttered his oracle, that "the first of the great sins is the giving divine honours to a creature." A hit, I may observe, at ordinary Mahometans, whose whole doctrine of intercession, whether vested in Mahomet or in 'Alee, is classed by Wahhabees along with direct and downright idolatry. A Damascene Sheykh would have avoided the equivocation by answering, "infidelity."

"Of course," I replied, "the enormity of such a sin is beyond all doubt. But if this be the first, there must be a second; what is it?"

"Drinking the shameful," in English, "smoking tobacco," was the unhesitating answer.

"And murder, and adultery, and false witness?" I suggested.

"God is merciful and forgiving," rejoined my friend; that is, these are merely little sins.

"Hence two sins alone are great, polytheism and smoking," I continued, though hardly able to keep countenance any longer. And 'Abd-el-Kereem with the most serious asseveration replied that such was really the case. Before quitting this topic, I must add a word of explanation.

As to the answer given respecting the first of these two deadly crimes, "Sherk" (literally "association," or putting the creature on a level with the Creator), Wahhabee doctrine, which is none other than the genuine spirit of the Coran, renders all plain. I have in a former chapter explained at length the genuine notion of the Deity conveyed by the text-book of Islam, and that all-absorbing theocracy which would render God the most tyrannical of tyrants, and His creatures the most debased of slaves. A portentous conclusion, yet the unavoidable result of a pantheistic merging of all act, all responsibility, in God alone. Now, in this system, what the creature may do, how he may pass his time, whether he kills, steals, perjures himself, or the contrary, matters little to the Great Autocrat, so long as the sacred right of His supreme monarchy is left untouched and duly acknowledged. The tyrant is content with the slave, if the slave but avow himself for such, and He asks no more. In accordance with this theory is the practice. A sort of compromise is made between God and man: "I," says man, "will acknowledge you, and you alone, with undivided reverence and allegiance, for my Creator, Preserver, Master, Lord, everything. And in quittance of this obligation, I will make You five prayers a day, consisting of thirty-four prostrations, seventeen chapters of the Coran, and an equal number of inclinations, not forgetting previous ablutions, partial or total, with frequent 'La Ilāh illa Allāh's,' and the like. On your side, you will in consequence let me do what I like for the rest of the twenty-four hours, nor be over inquisitive about my private and personal conduct; and after this, you cannot do less than admit me into Paradise and there provide me with 'the flesh of birds exactly what men relish' (the words are from the Coran), shady trees, rivers of nectar, and goblets of wine, in return for my life-long adorations; and even should they have been now and then defective, my belief in You and You alone, with a good 'La Ilāh illa Allāh' on my death-bed, ought to be quite sufficient." This is the abridgment, the compendium of orthodox Islam, when rendered in plain English. And of the ratification of this pact by the Deity himself, the Muslim is assured by the heaven-sent promise conveyed in the Coran, "God will assuredly not pardon the association of others with Him, but He will pardon whatsoever else to whom He wills;" that is, to those whom His will has directed on the "straight path" of the true faith.

But ordinary Mahometans might well be surprised to find here, alongside of the first, a second deadly sin, the sister and the rival of the former. And why smoking in particular? The more so, since (in this system of the universe) whatever man does, it is God that does it, and consequently smoking is no less the result of Divine decree and irresistible impulse than theft or murder.

Here again a summary, if not a satisfactory answer, might be supplied by "God has willed it so." And who shall deny the right of the Autocrat to place guilt where He chooses, and then to punish it as He chooses?

Some other reason must, however, be given in ordinary enquiry, above all when the question is proposed by one not fully imbued with the doctrines of the sect. On this ground I proceeded humbly to entreat 'Abd-el-Kereem to explain to me the especial wickedness inherent in tobacco leaves, that I might the more detest and eschew them hereafter. I shall repeat his arguments, and then add what I myself consider to be a reason more conclusive on this point in the Wahhabee theory, than any suggested by 'Abd-el-Kereem himself.

He now proceeded to instruct me, saying that, Firstly, all intoxicating substances are prohibited by the Coran; but tobacco is an intoxicating substance; Ergo, tobacco is prohibited.

I insinuated that it was not intoxicating, and appealed to experience. But, to my surprise, my friend had experience too on his side, and had ready at hand the most appalling tales of men falling down dead drunk after a single whiff of smoke, and of others in a state of bestial and habitual ebriety from its use. Nor were his stories so purely gratuitous as many might at first imagine. The only tobacco known, when known, in Southern Nejed, is that of 'Omān, a very powerful species. I was myself astonished, and almost "taken in," more than once, by its extraordinary narcotic effects, when I experienced them, in the coffee-houses of Baḥreyn and the K'hāwahs of Ṣoḥar. It were no exaggeration to represent its strength by the analogous symbols of XX, or even XXX.

However, I would not subscribe to his argument; besides, I had not yet tried the sort of tobacco which he had in mind. So I rejoined that, without questioning in the least the accuracy of the facts he stated, they were after all to be looked on as exceptions, or unfortunate idiosyncracies; and that, in a general way, the depraved wretches whom we Damascenes, in the less enlightened regions of the north, daily saw with deep regret indulging in the use of the "shameful," did not exhibit any notable symptoms of ebriety, or incur such tragic catastrophes, at least in their outward man.

But my preceptor turned the tables on me by boldly asserting intoxication to be the rule and non-intoxication the exception. "Just so," added he, "some men will drink wine without being sensibly affected by it, yet their example nohow exempts the liquor from the absolute prohibition, founded on its natural and ordinary effect." Whereto I thought it wisest to make no reply, for fear of a too comprehensive major in my syllogism, which might have brought me under suspicion of advocating wine also, and so made bad worse.

Still 'Abd-el-Kereem, like most sophists, felt inwardly that his first reason was not entirely conclusive, and now brought forward a second, founded on tradition. That authority teaches us that Mahomet, why or when I do not remember, declared to his followers the unlawfulness of employing in food whatever had been burnt or singed with fire. Perhaps this is one reason for the universality of boiled meat in Nejed, to the total exclusion of roasted, grilled, or fried, unless ignorance of cookery be the only practical cause. Any way, there stands the prohibition, and it only remained to show that tobacco smoke was included in it. The Arab equivocation between "drinking" and "smoking"—for the word "shărebă" is applied to either—sufficed for this.

To this argument I opposed the use of fumigations, so common in Nejed, and so dear to the Prophet. But in vain, for the word "shărehă" was inapplicable here. Whereon I sought refuge in the "Mellah," or bread, baked or rather burnt, under the glowing cinders, of which comestible a former stage of our narrative has afforded frequent example, and which is equally in use throughout Nejed. This was really to the point; and 'Abd-el-Kereem fell back on the intoxicating properties of the herb.

But what, my readers may well ask, is in truth the real motive for the seemingly arbitrary ban laid by Wahhabeeism on tobacco? We need not go far to seek it; the passion for sectarian discrepancy fully explains all.

The early history of the Wahhabee sect, narrated in my first volume, may have, I think, sufficiently shown my readers that the idea of aggression and conquest was no less present to Moḥammed-ebn-'Abd-el-Wahhāb and his disciple the Chief Sa'ood, than that of dogma or proselytism; both of these men, and the latter perhaps even more than the former, had in view not only to found a sect, but an empire; not only to convert their neighbours, but to subdue them. The Wahhabee and Sa'ood were the joint apostles of Islam, and with Islam is necessarily associated the sword. Now, to embark on such a career, some decent pretext was wanted, while a visible and unequivocal badge was equally required to counterdistinguish their party from all others. The profession of the Unity of God, the regular performance of prayers almost identical with those of all other Mahometans, a little more simplicity in dress, a few canting phrases or downcast eyes, would not suffice for either one or the other end, would neither warrant the sword, nor enough distinguish those who unsheathed it from those against whom it was unsheathed. The greater number of the populations assaulted by the Wahhabee might justly reply, "In fine, we are equally good Mahometans with yourselves, there is no essential difference between us; by what right, under what pretext, do you attack, kill, and enslave your brethren?"

Something additional was requisite, and tobacco stepped in conveniently for the Wahhabee.

That its usage was universal was certain; that it was somehow opposed to the genuine spirit of the Islamitic code was no less sure. Men often judge right, even while they argue wrong. The arguments alleged by 'Abd-el-Kereem are, even in a Mahometan point of view, plainly inadequate to support his thesis. Yet it is more than probable, that had Mahomet known of tobacco, he would have forbidden its employment no less than that of the grape, and for precisely analogous reasons. Smoking is a social, a civilizing habit, it draws men together (I am sorry that it should have the opposite effect on ladies; but if they will have it so, we can only regret it), and disposes them, whatever Cowper may say to the contrary, to conversation, good humour, and friendly interchange of ideas. It has, moreover, though in the main a sedative, yet just enough of a stimulating effect also, to bring it on this score within the circle of wine and spirits. Lastly, it is not comprehended in the only relaxation allowed by Mahomet to his followers for the intervals of fighting and prayer. The Wahhabees are accordingly self-consistent and logical in their antipathy to this luxury; and we must also admit, that few more comprehensive pretexts for interference, and few more prominent marks of distinction, could have been chosen in the tobacco-smoking East. In fact, most natives of Syria, of Egypt, nay, of the outlying provinces of Arabia itself, when questioned about these sectaries, have little or nothing definite to say of them, except that they detest tobacco at home and abroad. Not that they are absolutely without imitators in this aversion, though in a lesser degree; many strict or half ascetic Mahometans among the ordinary Sonnees, and above all those belonging to the Mâlekee school, disapprove the use of tobacco, and hold it for a thing unseemly in a true believer, though without ascribing to it the diabolical origin or the extreme sinfulness which stigmatize it in Nejed. In Wadi Dowâsir the fanaticism on this point is, if possible, even fiercer than in 'Aared, and the like may be said, if my information be correct, of Djebel 'Aaseer.

Such was the upshot of my conversation that day with 'Abd-el-Kereem; I give it by way of a specimen of many others held at different times. However, I cannot omit what passed between us on occasion of his entire recovery, an event in which my readers, I hope, take a charitable interest; it was pre-eminently significative alike of the man and of the people.

In about three weeks' space the symptoms which had previously annoyed him had so far disappeared, that he felt and declared himself perfectly well. At the outset of the treatment we had fixed the fee to be paid on cure, and now that the time came, I gently reminded him of his engagement. The first hint having not taken effect, a second and a third followed, each broader than its predecessor, but all to no purpose. Meanwhile several of the most respectable inhabitants, for we had by this taken our place among the citizens, joined in urging the ex-Zelator to the acquittance of the stipulation. And since the whole sum in question did not exceed eleven shillings English, 'Abd-el-Kereem's backwardness was no less ridiculous than shabby. Ashamed, yet reluctant, he bethought himself of an expedient for getting off, ingenious, but hardly creditable.

I was seated alone in my Ḳ'hâwah, somewhat late in the afternoon, when a brisk knock at the door warned me to stop my note-writing and to undo the latch. In came three or four of my town friends, with the merry faces of men who have a good jest to tell, and had hardly seated themselves before they began to relate what they had just witnessed. They had arrived from the daily afternoon sermon at the Great Mosque or Djāmia'. While yet at Ḥā'yel I mentioned this kind of discourse; here there is no essential difference, unless that the ceremony is much longer, the audience more numerous, and the lecture or sermon turns twice out of three times on some peculiarity of the sect. On the present occasion, when the reader, a Meṭow'-wa', had finished his part, 'Abd-el-Kereem came forward to deliver the *vivâ voce* commentary, here never omitted. Our friend took for theme of his discourse, the inefficacy of created means, and the obligation of placing one's confidence in the Creator alone, to the exclusion of the creature. Thence coming to a practical application, he inveighed against those who put their trust in physic and physicians, not in God solely, and declared such trust to be, firstly, heretical, and, secondly, a sheer mistake, inasmuch as the only effective cause of health or sickness, life or death, is simply the Divine will; doctors and medicine being for nothing in the matter from beginning to end. Whence he deduced a second and a very legitimate consequence, that such useless things and beings could nohow merit any recompense either in money or in thanks from a true believer. Nay, added he, should even a sick man really seem to be bettered by medical means, and while employing them recover his health, such a recovery would be a mere coincidence, no matter of cause and effect, and the doctor would in consequence be entitled to absolutely nothing, since the cure was due not to him, but to God alone, La Ilāh illa Allāh, &c.

Probably, at another moment and from another mouth, these lessons of theologico-practical wisdom would have passed without other comment than silence or approbation. But unluckily 'Abd-el-Kereem was a conspicuous character, and so was I. Every neighbour knew the whole history of his ailment, his physicking, and his cure, by heart. The result was, that his holding forth, although perfectly orthodox in itself, lay under the imputation of private nor over-honourable feelings, and everyone suspected the preacher to be engaged rather in knotting his own purse-strings than in untying the plexus of a doctrinal question. Winks and nods went round; and, when the auditors were once out of the mosque, followed comments and what laughter might be compatible with Nejdean decorum. My friends enjoyed the joke heartily, and in conclusion promised to bring 'Abd-el-Kereem by one means or another to our house next day, while we agreed together on what should then be said and done.

They kept promise, and in the following forenoon 'Abd-el-Kereem appeared with an embarrassed look, and surrounded by several companions, amongst whom were those of the preceding evening. After the preliminaries of courtesy, and conversation having reached the desired point, "'Abd-el-Kereem," said I, "there can be no doubt that health and recovery come from God alone, and small thanks to the doctor. In the same manner, neither more nor less, I expect that God will give me so much" (naming the stipulated sum) "by your passive instrumentality, and when I have got it, small thanks to you also." Every one laughed, and fell on our poor ex-Zelator, till he became thoroughly ashamed of himself. He left the house with promise of speedy payment, and before sunset his younger brother had brought the money in question, thus preventing further sarcasms. But 'Abd-el-Kereem never crossed our threshold again, nor did we much regret him.

I had a much more favourable specimen of the learned or semi-learned class in a third patient of note, 'Abd-er-Raḥmān, the Meṭow'waa' or chaplain of the palace. For years past he had been subject to attacks of severe nervous headache, and he was actually labouring under a paroxysm which confined him to his room, and rendered him incapable of performing his clerical functions. Djowhar, who already felt and acknowledged an amelioration in his health, had by this time established the good reputation of his doctor in the palace; and at his suggestion the Meṭow'waa' sent for me, with a message of uncommon urgency.

His apartments, directly opposite to those of Maḥboob, were spacious and well-furnished, and contained, among other articles, about forty volumes, printed or manuscript, on various subjects; a very fair library for Arabia. In spite of pain, he mustered up all the elegant pedantry of grammar in the exposure of his case; and when, after two or three days, a proper treatment had relieved him of his tortures, he proved a very interesting acquaintance, infinitely more amiable and open than 'Abd-el-Kereem. In his rooms I learnt much of the history of Moseylemah, of the Wahhabee, of the religious state of Nejed in old times, and many similar topics; some of these particulars have already been recorded in my narrative, some are yet to come. Nay, the worthy chaplain knew by heart many chapters of Moseylemah's burlesque Coran, and would recite them with full appreciation of their coarse humour. Hither, as to a common centre, resorted many of the young students in law and divinity already alluded to, and would discuss before me moral questions or points of dogma after their fashion, for 'Abd-er-Raḥmān was not only learned, but agreeably communicative, and a good speaker, and drew these pale thin lads around him, till most regarded him as their guide and master.

One morning I was seated on the "Belas," or coarse-spun Nejdean carpet, by his side, and many of the palace were present in mixed conversation. Somehow the discourse fell on Damascus, or "Shâm," whereon all, in politeness bound, began to praise what they fancied to be my native city, and to cite the well-known tradition of Mahomet's visit to that city. A mere fable, according to which the Prophet, on whom be salutation and the blessings of God, had purposed entering the Syrian capital, and had already half-alighted from his camel near the southern gate; when just as one of his blessed feet reached the ground, and the other was about to follow it, lo! Gabriel the archangel by his side, to inform him that God left him his choice between the Paradise of this world and that of the next; and that consequently if he persisted in entering Damascus, it must be on condition of renouncing the gardens and houris of heaven. Whereon the Prophet very properly changed his design, preferred the enjoyments of eternity to the groves and waters of Barada, replaced his leg over his saddle, and returned by the way he came. However, to the confusion of all sceptics and infidels, the print of the prophetic foot which had already touched the rocky soil, remained ineffaceably imprinted there, and I myself have had the happiness of seeing it in the pretty little mosque commemorative of the vision and the choice, near the town-gate on the road from Ḥauran. Though indeed some contend that the five-toed mark belongs not to Mahomet but to Gabriel, who, in human form, but with angelic agility, alighted on one foot only. Far be it from me to attempt deciding so weighty a controversy; my readers may settle it for themselves.

Whosesoever the footprint may be, the story is gospel among Mahometans, and it was now recited for the thousandth time, in compliment to us the supposed "Showâm," or Damascenes. But 'Abd-el-Ḥameed, the Peshawuree, already described, was present, and could not bear this in silence. Besides the jealous ill will that he bore us, and which alone might have sufficed to move his choler, he was himself a native of the fair regions of Cachemire, and brought up amid groves far lovelier than the gardens of Damascus, and by the side of rivers to which the Barada were a mere gutter. Lastly, he was a true

Shiya'ee at heart, and the praises of the most Sonnee of all cities, the old capital of Beni-Ommeyah, and the centre even now of hostility and antagonism to his sect, were gall and wormwood to his soul. So "fierce he broke forth": "What nonsense you here are talking. Paradise of the earth! Paradise of the earth! and all for a few stunted trees and a little muddy water! Why! do you not understand that the Prophet and his companions were nothing but Bedouins, accustomed all their life to the arid sterilities of Ḥejāz, and the desert? so when at Damascus they came for the first time on a cluster of gardens and running streams, they straightway concluded this to be Paradise, and so named it! Guess, had they seen my country they would have changed their mind."

All eyes stared, all jaws dropped, and "Astaghfir Ullah," (I beg pardon of God,) and "La Ilāh illa Allāh" went largely round, while 'Abd-el-Ḥameed, now red-hot with excitement, and worked up into recklessness of results, glared anger and scorn, and muttered Cabul curses. Had he not been a personal favourite of Feyṣul's, matters might have gone ill for him. But 'Abd-er-Raḥmān prudently hastened to turn the conversation, and this outbreak of Affghan vehemence passed without further comment.

Needs not weary my non-medical readers with a detail of cases, here more numerous and luckily more successful than elsewhere. Some of my patients were townsmen, others strangers on business in Riaḍ; some were rich, some poor; many visits and meals were given and returned. Thus, at times we found ourselves cushion-reclined in a well-carpeted K'hāwah, before an ostentatious pile of coffee-pots, two for use and ten for show; at others in the low, ill-lighted rooms on the ground floor, the dwellings of the poor; sometimes in a garden a mile or more out of town, on a call of friendship or duty. The days passed rapidly; and I am much mistaken if some London practitioners would not have envied us our want of leisure, and a popularity which they would better have deserved.

However, I cannot leave in silence 'Abd-el-Laṭeef, the great-grandson of the famed Wahhabee, and now Ḳaḍee of the capital—a very, indeed remarkably handsome and fair-spoken man, and bearing in his manners a sensible dash of Egyptian civilization. While yet a mere child he was carried to Egypt with the rest of his family by the conquering Basha, and there educated. Cairo society, and the intercourse of men more learned and less exclusive than those of Nejed and Ḍerey'eeyah, have taught him an ease and variety of conversation surprising in a Ḳaḍee of Riaḍ; and thus enabled him to assume on occasion a liberality of phrase free from the cant terms and wearisome tautology of the sect which he heads. But such liberal semblance is merely a surface whitewash; the tongue may be the tongue of Egypt, but the heart and brain are ever those of Nejed. Nor do I believe that the central mountains of Arabia contain a more dangerous man than 'Abd-el-Laṭeef, or one who more cordially hates the progress he has witnessed, and in which he has to a certain degree participated. Nameeḳ Basha, 'Alee-Basha, or any other Basha, returning to the Bosporus after years by the Seine or the Danube, with the intense bitterness of envy at the prosperity and civilization there witnessed, and which they feel above or beyond their own reach, hating acknowledged superiority and fully determined to employ the personal advantages there acquired in thwarting and injuring those whom they cannot or will not imitate, are types of 'Abd-el-Laṭeef the pupil of Cairo and the head of Wahhabee Zelators. It is the embodied antipathy of bad to good, at least equal to that of good to bad.

We were not unfrequently together, though the knowledge of whom I had to deal with made me rather hold back, in spite of his great courtesies. That his house was a palace, his gardens of the widest, his slaves a throng, need hardly be said; next after the king, he was unquestionably the first personage in the capital, and even in the empire; nay, in many respects, he was more powerful than Feysul himself. Nor was the oft-repeated lesson of the Coran, "O ye who believe, why should you deprive yourselves of the good things which God sets before you?" lost on one whose family, rank, office, and influence gave him the fairest occasion for enjoying all that was enjoyable. I was again and again his guest to a cup of coffee: from I know not what intonation of my voice, he believed me not a Damascene but an Egyptian, and conversed willingly about the Ḳaṣr-el-'Eynee and the Djāmia'-el-Azhar. But he also knew me to be a Christian, and in due time showed what were his real feelings towards me as such.

I was often present at his public lectures and comments, whether delivered in his own elegant mosque, close by his house in the third quarter of the town, or in the great Djāmia' of the city. On these occasions he was surrounded by numerous and earnest auditors, besides a select body of especial disciples; and I must give him the deserved credit of being a clear and elegant speaker, possessed also of the range of learning suitable to his position. But narrower and sourer sectarianism than what formed the groundwork and key-note of his teachings, it was never mine to hear.

I well remember one lovely November afternoon, when the great mosque was full of hearers, then highly excited by fresh news from 'Oneyzah, and a victory gained by the "Muslims" over the infidel Zāmil and his crew. 'Abd-el-Laṭeef was the orator that day, and his theme the obligation of strict orthodoxy, and the danger of modern innovations. To confirm his thesis, he recounted a celebrated tradition, wherein Mahomet is reported to have given his companions the consolatory news, that, "as the Jewish body had been divided into seventy-one different sects, and the Christians into seventy-two"—(perhaps the unhistorical prophet had in mind some confused idea about the seventy-two disciples sent by our Lord to preach)—"even so his own co-religionists would separate into seventy-three sects, while of these numerous ramifications seventy-two were destined to hell-fire, and one only to paradise." Here the preacher paused, much like Massillon after his "Remnant of Israel, pass to the right!" and a devout thrill of pleasing horror ran through the audience. He then resumed, raising his voice, and recounted how the Ṣaḥḥābah, on receiving this alarming announcement, had eagerly demanded, "And what, O messenger of God, are the signs of that happy sect to which is ensured the exclusive possession of Paradise?" Whereto Mahomet had replied, "It is those who shall be in all conformable to myself and to my companions." "And that," added 'Abd-el-Laṭeef, lowering his voice to the deep tone of conviction, "that, by the mercy of God, are we, the people of Riaḍ."

The old and somewhat broad jest, "Orthodoxy means my

doxy, heterodoxy another man's doxy," occurred to my mind —could it be otherwise? One of the Nā'ib's Bagdadees was at my side; on hearing this precious specimen of Riaḍ theology, he rose and pushed his way out of the mosque, almost trampling the crowded ranks in the excess of ungovernable anger. But the Nejdeans were much too absorbed in the words of their instructor to take heed either of my smile or of Ḥaṣan's frown. One deep "Ashedŭ un la Ilāh illa Allāh" went through the mosque, and every forefinger was raised to attest that undivided all-devouring unity which ensures the salvation of true believers, while it justifies the damnation of the incredulous and the polytheist.

What I have just described is a tolerable sample of Nejdean instruction. Of morality, justice and judgment, mercy and truth, purity of heart and tongue, and all that makes man better, I never heard one syllable during a month and a half of sermon frequentation in this pious capital. But of prayers, of war against unbelievers, of the rivers of Paradise, of houris and bowers, of hell, devils, and chains, also of the laws of divorce, and of the complicated marital obligations of polygamy, plenty and to spare. Nor should I omit a very frequent topic, the sinfulness of tobacco, ay, and that confirmed by visible and appalling judgments, curiously resembling those which a spirit less Christian than Judaical introduces occasionally into European books of edification. Thus, for example. A man, supposed of correct life and unquestionable Islam, died and was buried at Sedoos, the same little frontier town which we passed not long since. Prayers were said over him, and he was duly laid in his grave, reclining on his side, his face toward the Ca'abah, like any other good Muslim. Now it chanced that a neighbour, while assisting at the funeral ceremonies, had let fall, unperceived by himself, a small purse of money exactly into the pit, where it remained covered up with earth alongside of the dead man. On returning home, the owner of the purse discovered his loss; he searched everywhere, but to no purpose, and at last rightly concluded that his money must have found an untimely grave. What was to be done? To disturb the repose of the dead is an action no less abhorred among Mahometans than among ordinary Christians. But *quid non mortalia pectora cogis Auri sacra fames?* The peasant consulted the village Ḳaḍee, who assured him that in such a case digging up a corpse was no crime, though he wisely advised him to await nightfall, for fear of scandal and gossip. Night at last came, and the excusable "resurrection man" set to work, and soon released his purse from the cold grasp of death. But what was his amazement and horror to see his deceased townsman now laid with his face turned away from the Ca'abah, and shifted to a position exactly the opposite of that in which they had but lately placed him. Hastily covering up the grave, he returned to give the Ḳaḍee information of the portent. Both agreed that the defunct, to merit this ominous transposition, must have died in infidelity or some equally grievous sin, and an official search of his quondam domicile was set on foot, to discover the traces or indications of his wicked ways. High and low they ransacked, and at last detected, where it had been carefully hidden in a crevice of the wall, a small bone pipe, whose blackened tube and diabolical smell too plainly denoted its frequent use, and revealed the infamous hypocrisy of its owner. The crime was evident, the visible chastisement explained, and no doubt but that the amateur of "shameful" smoke had already gone to unquenchable fire—"*sarve him right!*" Another had rotted piecemeal, a rock had fallen on the head of a third, &c. Bigotry and its tales are the same under every climate, and in every tongue *mutato nomine—fabula narratur.*

Meanwhile poor morality fares little better in this pharisaical land than in Burns's Kilmarnock, or Holy Fair. True, lights are extinguished an hour or so after sunset, and street-walking rigorously inhibited; while in the daytime not even a child may play by the roadside; not a man laugh out. True, profane instruments of music disturb not the sacred hum of Coranic lectures, and no groups of worldly mirth offend serious eyes in the market-place. But profligacy of all kinds, even such as language refuses to name, is riper here than in Damascus and Seyda themselves, and the comparative decency of most other Arab towns sets off the blackness of Riaḍ in stronger and stranger contrast. "A government which, not content with repressing scandalous excesses, demands from its subjects fervent and austere piety, will soon discover that, while attempting to render an impossible service to the cause of virtue, it has in truth only promoted vice," is one of the many just remarks of a well-known modern author. In fact, most of what Macaulay observes on this very topic in his "Critical and Historical Essays," whether his theme be the Rump Parliament and Puritan austerity, or the hideous reaction of immorality under the reign of the latter Stuarts, may be almost literally applied to the present condition of the Arab kingdom of saints, while it foretells a future inevitably not remote.

It is a singular fact, and worth mentioning before we leave an odious subject, that crimes hateful to all, because condemned by nature herself, were the only ones punished in Nejed by anything like torture during the epoch preceding the Wahhabee administration. I have noticed at an earlier period of this work, that while Turks and Persians have become a horror among nations by the barbarity of their penal executions, among which impaling may seem almost a mercy, the Arabs, in the few cases where death was to be inflicted, have always contented themselves with simple decapitation by the sword, deeming it unlawful for man to embitter the last moments of his fellow-man, however criminal, by superfluous agony. Few are the exceptions recorded, and then only to stigmatize. But in the cases just hinted at, outraged society embodied its detestation in a cruel but a significant procedure, and the offenders were hung up by the heels head downwards, till they expired. Under the present rule, the leniency of the Coran in behalf of such culprits is appreciated and observed. Such is the model state of Islam.

'Abd-el-Laṭeef is not the only representative of his family; he is the eldest of several brothers, but all notably inferior to him in talent. The youngest among them, Moḥammed, was a very original character. He had just returned from Egypt, where he had figured for two years among the medical students of the Ḳaṣr-el-'Eynee, and exemplified in his person the Arab proverb, "went a donkey and came back a jackass." Narrow-minded, narrow-hearted, as avaricious at twenty as ever Sir John Cutler at sixty, with the exotic vices of Cairo engrafted on the indigenous stock of Riaḍ, and a dialect confused like his who in his travels "lost his own language, and acquired no more," it was most amusing to hear his Egyptian experiences, and his comments on the race of Pharoah, as he impolitely styled the inhabitants of the great Delta. He had followed the preliminary lectures of the medical college, but little understood them; at last, time came to attend the anatomical course, and witness the mysteries of the "dead room," when, said he, his orthodoxy could not stomach practices so contrary to correct Islam, and he had abandoned college and capital in disgust. So ran his version of the matter; I much suspect that hopeless stupidity, perhaps ill-conduct, held the larger part with an expulsion veiled under the more respectable title of retirement. He was in truth one of the most thorough brutes I ever had the bad fortune to meet; and I was honoured by his especial hatred, and peculiar calumnies.

Were I not deterred by the fear of abusing my reader's patience, I might add some account of the Bedouin chief Ṭoweel, of the 'Oṭeybah clan, whom I counted among my patients, and who, Bedouin-like, availed himself of returning health to run away from Riaḍ without settling his bill; of the wealthy 'Abd-er-Rizzaķ, and his handsome dwelling in the genuine style of an old Nejdean chief; of the good-humoured Abyssinian Fahd, whose sprightly off-hand manner contradistinguished him from his Arabian neighbours; of the young Ḥamood, wounded in 'Oneyzah warfare, and thus half a martyr, with many other patients and friends who enlivened our stay, while they filled now our note-book and now our purse. But we have much yet to narrate ere we can leave the capital, much after we shall have left it; and I must without further delay hasten to pay a debt due to those of my readers who possess medical science, or at least physiological curiosity. To have played the doctor for a twelvemonth in Arabia, and then give no sanitary report on that country, would be unpardonable; I will therefore state, however cursorily, the leading features of Arab nosology: a few pages will suffice. This duty accomplished, I will return to our first patient Djowhar, and let him open the way to more important matters of past or present life—to the ruling dynasty, the Riaḍ court, and what befel us there.

Of Arabia in general, I may say that the whole central

plateau, comprising the space occupied by Djebel Ṭoweyḳ on the east, Wadi Dowāsir on the south, the desert margin of the Ḥajj or pilgrim route to the west, and the Nefood or sand-stream above Djebel Shomer to the north, with whatever lies within these four limits, is one of the healthiest countries, and in consequence affords the fewest nosological varieties, in the world. In its pure keen atmosphere, dry climate, and moderate temperature, we should hardly expect to add greatly to our observations on "Bright's kidney," or "Addison's supra-renal capsules." Nor do its sober inhabitants offer much predisposition to the gout, of which I never witnessed or heard mentioned a single example. Cancer too, in all its varied and loathsome forms, seems banished from these regions, nor has hysteria a better chance with the very unromantic and coarse-nerved ladies of the land. In a word, most classes of disease which seem—for seeming must be in these matters the common limit of assertion—to depend on impure atmosphere, want of light and air, high living; or, on the other hand, on life over "cribbed and cabined," and, again, on overwrought nervous temperament, are, to the utmost of my knowledge and research, almost absent from these districts of the Peninsula; nor have its inhabitants any specific names for such. Of intermittent fever also, though I heard of it and witnessed one or two cases, I should say that it is extremely rare, whether tertian, quartan, or other. Measles I neither saw nor heard of; but that proves little, since the inaccurate observation of my informants may have confounded it with small-pox, perhaps with scarlet fever, which certainly exists here. Typhus and typhoid are wholly unknown throughout Nejed, taking that term in its widest geographical acceptation. Nor have I heard anything to intimate that the plague, whether imported from Egypt or from Persia, has ever found its way to the up-hill country.

It is, however, clear, that in spite of these gaps in the ranks of disease, other, and to some extent supplementary forms must exist, since the threescore and ten to fourscore rule is no less applicable to Arabia than to any other country of the world; only more have here, I think, the full benefit of the allotted vital term than is proportionately the case elsewhere. Were birth and death registers kept, one might obtain a correct approximation on this head; but even in the absence of official data, my companion and myself, after much observation and discussion, agreed that while infant mortality was perhaps greater here than in lands where better housing, better clothing, and greater variety of domestic or hygienic means exist, the longevity of those who escape the dangers of early childhood seems decidely above even that of the Syrian mountains, where also matters are on a good footing in this respect.

But, sooner or later, men must die, and death unushered in by any direct morbid change, or in other words what is called dying of mere old age, is a rare phenomenon, if indeed it does not belong only to popular belief. The particular causes of death may be latent, but they are not less real and definite, though at times unobserved. What then are the ordinary paths by which the human race finds its way from Arabia to man's common home?

And firstly, that this land is occasionally visited by epidemic or contagious diseases, may be collected from what has been already said. Thus the cholera, late indeed, and far from universal in its range, made an inroad in Nejed, where it seems to have been attended by all its well-known symptoms and horrors, though the disease did not cross the high ground that divides Ḳaseem from Djebel Shomer, which latter district, by the account of its inhabitants, enjoyed entire exemption from the Asiatic scourge, while the low though isolated valley of Djowf suffered severely. The Nejdeans trace its advance from Egypt, and assign it a regular march from west to east. The small-pox has been known in Arabia from time immemorial, and inoculation is still in use throughout Nejed, though no one could tell me the date of its introduction. I hardly see how it could have been imported from Constantinople, nor does any Arab Lady Mary Wortley Montague lay claim to that honour. Damascene adventurers have brought vaccination so far as the Djowf, and Ṭelāl quite lately encouraged its extension throughout Djebel Shomer; but in the Wahhabee dominions prejudices analogous to those once found among the uneducated classes in England have hitherto impeded its use. I have mentioned scarlet fever a few lines back; the cases I witnessed were not malignant.

A very common source of varied disease is the scrofulous diathesis, remarkably frequent in the Arab race. The stress of this constitutional mal-assimilation falls sometimes on the pectoral and sometimes on the abdominal cavity, but more frequently on the latter, owing perhaps to the comparative mildness of a climate where the exciting causes of this fatal deposit bear much less on the respiratory organs than in cold damp Europe, while, on the other hand, irritating and often hardly digestible food may readily predispose the lower viscera to the development of latent evil. Hence I was at first startled by the number of cases where abdominal phthisis was the leading feature, and pectoral only the secondary, or even absent altogether, at least in the manifest indications of its existence. But of the former variety, instances were frequent and unequivocal, both among men and women. Its ordinary period of attack seems to lie between the ages of twenty and forty, though I remember a case where the victim, a wealthy female, could not have been much under fifty; but this is rare. Scrofula, too, affecting the glands of the neck, and rachitis, producing the distortions witnessed in Europe, are diseases often to be seen in Southern Nejed; in Shomer, Ḳaseem, and Sedeyr I did not come across them. Pure pulmonary phthisis, or rather that which offers no other prominent symptoms, is comparatively unfrequent; I saw a case at Riad. Of course Arabs have not the faintest idea of a treatment for the sufferers, unless we call it one to make the individual eat as much as possible. In small-pox and other eruptive complaints they still, like European physicians in a former age, do their best to suffocate their helpless victim with clothes, fire, and closed window-shutters. Of their cholera regimen I have spoken in the former chapter, nor had they any other.

Rheumatism of all possible forms and degrees, sciatica, lumbago, with kindred diseases, are perhaps the commonest complaints, more especially among the Bedouins and the poorer villagers. Nor is cardiac affection, its ominous sequel, at all rare; I witnessed many instances of heart disease, traceable to no other cause. This latter malady often terminates in dropsy; I have seen it again and again both among young and old. The disease was evidently of cardiac origin. I may remark that on the supervention of anasarca, Arabs give up all hope of recovery. Heart-disease in its earlier stages they sometimes make an attempt to remedy by bleeding and purgatives, thus obtaining temporary alleviation at the cost of ulterior damage. Sometimes, too, the breast of the patient (no idle name in Arabia) is seared all over with hot irons, a proceeding worse than useless, but authorised by prophetic tradition. A similar treatment awaits rheumatic individuals, though they sometimes obtain the benefit of friction; sudorifics are never used. Of renal dropsy I do not remember a single instance.

Dyspepsia and chronic gastritis are hardly less the fashion than rheumatism. No wonder, where dry dates and ill-baked unleavened bread, with an occasional gorging of badly cooked mutton, is all the diet for eight or nine months of the year, at least among the lower and the middle classes. Ulceration of the stomach appears nowise rare; it attacks women by preference, and I am convinced, that were autopsy here introduced, one female at least out of every six would exhibit traces of it. In my short and limited practice I had two cases where sudden and violent peritonitis, followed by speedy dissolution, succeeded long gastric derangement, and was, I have little doubt, the result of perforation. One of the victims, a young woman, was further tortured amid the agonies of such a death by extensive branding on the abdomen at the hand of a farrier, in spite of all I could protest to the contrary.

Colic is not rare, not even total occlusion of the intestine. Here again Arab pharmacy has nothing to suggest. Dysentery and chronic diarrhœa, though they sometimes occur, are considerably less frequent than in India. Opium, unknown to Arabs as a medicine, was here my sheet-anchor, and it did wonders. Hemorrhoids and fissures are of daily occurrence in the doctor's path; the latter discomfort is most often complained of in Shomer and Nejed, the former towards the shores of the Persian Gulf. Arab practitioners treat hemorrhoids with extirpation when they can, with a homily on patience when they cannot. But for dysentery they have neither specific nor diet, and hence it sometimes proves fatal.

I said before that intermittent fever is rare. That statement applies to the disease considered as indigenous: but in an imported form, hanging for months and even years about individuals returned from Basrah, Ḥasa, or Ḳaṭeef, it is often met with. It commonly induces enlargement of the spleen. I had several cases of this nature to treat, even in Riaḍ. After putting a stop to the fever itself, where it still existed, by quinine, I found sulphate of zinc singularly efficacious in reducing the tumid gland. How far that drug is employed in Europe I do not know; I myself picked it up in India, and it did me yeoman's service in Nejed.

A remittent fever of a simple type, and seldom severe, exists here and there throughout Nejed, including Shomer; it is a milder form of the remitting fever of India. Sometimes it drags on for two or three weeks together; but if properly treated soon yields. A half-empirical receipt of Marriott's, where tartarized antimony is administered in small but repeated doses, never failed to procure me a fee, and the patient a recovery.

Be it remarked, that although quinine is wholly unknown in Arabia, and no wonder, the use of other tonics is not equally a stranger. The natives employ to this effect decoctions of Sheeaḥ, an extremely bitter plant which grows everywhere in the uplands, or of Ṭhemām, a slender aromatic herb peculiar, I believe, to Nejed. In slight cases I found them efficacious.

A disease which I need not name is frightfully common. Like all other nations, Arabs assign it a foreign origin, and declare it to have been unheard of among them till imported from Persia and by Persians. Yet the designative name of the malady, "Belegh," is a pure Arabic word, and hence I fear that the disease itself may have been not less indigenous, though the especial profligacy of Persian visitors, and the frequent passage of their pilgrim-caravans through Nejed to and from Mecca—itself a hot-bed of vice and its loathsome consequences—may have contributed to spread it. Now it is in full possession of domicile, and by its rapid and uncontrolled progress proves a great scourge. The virus is supposed by the natives no less communicable from one to another, and in no less comprehensive a way, than that of small-pox or scarlet fever. Whether this be true, I cannot venture to affirm; yet I have seen cases where the phenomena hardly admitted any other explanation.

Mercury is known and employed as a specific, but only in one form, namely, its sulphate, the ordinary cinnabar of commerce; other preparations, calomel for instance, ointment, or bichlorure, are not to be found. I did my best to introduce them, as a real benefit to the country. A peculiar treatment, consisting mainly in diet, and in Europe called "Arab," does not appear deserving of its name; at least, I heard nothing of it in Arabia. In the present state, or rather dearth, of the native pharmacopœia, my readers will hardly expect to hear of iodine; the very name has never reached these lands, unless during the transient exception of my journey.

I had forgot to say that ovarian dropsy is not rare in Nejed. The inhabitants ignorantly mistake it for protracted gestation, and will talk to you about women four and five years with child. When such patients were brought before me, I declined meddling, and expressed my hopes of a speedy delivery.

Apoplexy finds a conspicuous place on the list of Adam's sad heritage to his Arab children; so too paralysis, both hemiplegia, paraplegia (I saw a curious example at Ḥă'yel, and suspect that caries was at work in the spine), and paralysis of a single limb or nervous branch. Tic douloureux and hemicrania surpassed my expectations by their frequency, nor were exclusively confined to the "beaux esprits," or to the brunettes who here replace the "fair sex." Chorea, and very bad cases too, came under my hands; but it is not ordinary. Of tetanus I heard, but, thank Heaven, did not witness it. Epileptic patients were occasionally brought before me, but I never stayed long enough in a locality to think of seriously treating the Arab form of this strange malady, not a whit less appalling here than in Europe, and terminating at last in the same melancholy consequences. Mania, raving madness, I had the pain of contemplating at Riaḍ, and heard of it elsewhere. All these forms of disease, and especially the two last, find, like rheumatism, their Arab medicament, or, to speak more truly, their additional torture, in the actual cautery—branding, in short. I have seen an ill-starred epileptic lad seared from head to foot, of course to no good purpose; and the unfortunate madman of Riaḍ, a young man of high birth, had received on his head a circular burn going down to the very bone, and resembling that of the iron-crowned Luke in Bohemia. Had he not been already mad, this alone would have sufficed to make him so.

Hydrophobia, resulting from the bite of some rabid dog, is known in all parts of the Peninsula; and I heard wonderful stories about a remedial herb, after the internal use of which one patient in particular had discharged—I beg pardon of my readers—several little dogs! and then recovered. Nay, the narrator professed to have seen these extraordinary puppies, and described their size, colour, form, &c. with great circumstantiality. But in vain I enquired after the wonder-working plant, it was nowhere forthcoming. Tænia and other parasitical worms are extremely rare in Arabia; when suspected, a decoction of wild pomegranate root is the sole but unfailing remedy.

Asthma is, I think, proportionately more frequent than in Europe; the keen air of Ṭoweyḳ seems to give a predisposition towards this troublesome complaint. Stramonium grows everywhere, but is not much employed as a remedy; though it occasionally plays the part of a poison in malicious hands, sometimes that of a love philtre; a curious one, certainly, nor, I should think, much to the point.

Of the stone I heard and saw nothing, yet hardly suppose Arabia fortunate enough to claim an entire exemption from it.

Bronchial affections, from a simple cold and sore throat to chronic and wearing disease, will frequently afford the Arab doctor employment. They are as common as pulmonary maladies are rare. Pleurisy is neither frequent nor wholly absent; here the cauterising regimen comes into full force.

About hooping-cough, thrush, and other ills ordinary to European childhood, I say nothing; because my medical practice was confined to individuals of riper age. But of the first-named disorder no report was made me anywhere; the second was perhaps included in the generic title of Khanaḳ, or "strangulation," whereby many Arab little ones are said to anticipate the cares of life.

But the list of cutaneous disorders is long and loathsome, much more so than in Europe, from *lupus exedens* down to simple *impetigo*. Leprosy, as is well known, abounds:

sometimes it assumes the blotchy and not dangerous form called "Baraṣ;" sometimes it is the hideous Djedām, under which the joints first swell, then break out into sluggish yet corroding ulcers, and at last drop piecemeal, while frightful sores open in various parts of the body, especially about the back and loins, till death comes, though after too long delay. The "Baraṣ" also, though never fatal, may lead to superficial ulceration. However, neither of these diseases corresponds exactly with what we read of in Numbers, so that the leprosy of the Jews remains distinct from that of the Arabs. Nor does this latter, however disgusting, render its victim legally impure, nor does any one believe it to be contagious. The natives have in this case hit on a vigorous though too often an unsuccessful specific in the sulphate of arsenic, or "yellow arsenic," for so they call it; and now and then they cure with it, occasionally killing by an overdose or smearage. Common arsenious acid is not used, except by way of poison.

The itch, and its best remedy sulphur, abound from one end of Arabia to the other; but the unskilfulness of the Arabs themselves in the application of the mineral often thwarts its effect, or leaves it only partial. This unseemly affection is common among camels, and from them is frequently communicated to men.

Ophthalmia is fearfully prevalent, especially among children, and goes on unchecked in many or most instances to its worst results. It would be no exaggeration to say, that one adult out of every five has his eyes more or less damaged by the consequences of this disease. Yet the uninventive Arabs have never bethought themselves of a remedy, even the most simple—much less of lunar caustic, and whatever else meets with great success in the neighbouring land of Egypt. Cataract too is the order of the day. Amaurosis is not seldom met with: sometimes it has come on quite suddenly; the natives often attribute it to exposure in the cold night air; certainly it is not the result of over study. That peculiar and capricious-seeming species of blindness which supervenes from sunset to sunrise only, exists here as in India. Chronic inflammation and granular thickening of the *conjunctiva* will frequently exhaust the Arab practitioner's patience. In fine, I know not any item on the catalogue of ocular affections of which one or more samples may not be found in any middle-sized town of Nejed.

I regret that I cannot, from my own experience, confirm the statements of several travellers regarding the extraordinary keenness of sight and hearing among Arabs in general. Both Bedouins and townsmen seemed to me average in the use of their senses with the rest of human race—longer sighted, for instance, than most Germans, and of shorter visual range than is common among Greeks. What is really remarkable among them is a great obtuseness in the general nervous sensibility. On more than one occasion I had to employ the knife or caustic, and was surprised at the patient's cool endurance. While at Riad, a young fellow presented himself with a bullet lodged deep in the forearm; it gave him some annoyance, and he insisted on having it cut out. The operation was, for my inexpertness, a difficult one; the muscular *fasciæ* had to be divided down to the bone. Meanwhile the Nejdean held out the limb steady and inflexible, as though it belonged to a third party, and never changed colour, except it were a flush of excited pleasure on his face when I finally drew out the ball through the incision and placed it in his hand. After a short interval of bandaging and repose he got up and walked home, carrying his leaden trophy along with him. Much similar I saw and heard; the Arabs are not a nervous or excitable race.

Of many rarer or occult forms of disease I say nothing, not only because such have no particular bearing on climate or physiology, but also from the difficulty of precision in statements unaccompanied by satisfactory and minute inspection during life, and anatomical investigation after death. The preceding enumeration may suffice for a summary sketch of the Nejdean "lazar-house." I subjoin a few words on the far east and south of the Peninsula, and on the islands and coasts of the Persian Gulf, willing thus far to anticipate our visit thither, and to avoid the necessity of recurrence to a less grateful subject, on which I have perhaps already dwelt too long for the majority of my readers.

Accordingly, when we descend eastwards from the extreme verge of the great plateau, and enter the warm moist atmosphere of Ḥasa, several diseases almost or wholly absent from Nejed appear in great frequency. Foremost stands intermittent fever, often pernicious and always serious; its head-quarters are amid the oozy shores of Ḳaṭeef, but it extends more or less throughout the entire coast province from Koweyt to Ḳaṭar, and is not rarely fatal. Typhoid fever (not typhus, which I believe a stranger from the land) never wholly quits the population, and becomes at times a real epidemic. Its symptoms differ in nothing from those noted in Europe. Dysentery is often met with; hæmorrhoids, alike painful and tedious, may be called universal. On the other hand, scrofula in all its forms, pectoral disease, and ophthalmic affections, are comparatively rare; so is also rheumatism. These brief remarks hold good, with very slight local exceptions, for Ḥasa, Ḳaṭeef, the islands of Baḥreyn, Ge's, Djishm, and Ormuz, with the coast of Linja, and the sea-line of 'Omān. But the mountainous regions of the last-named province may rival in healthiness with Sedeyr or Shomer. Ḳaṭar, too, is not insalubrious; and, having said thus much on nosology, we will resume our tale, interrupted at the first visit received from the chief treasurer, Djowhar.

With negro docility, he forgot his high position so far as to come and seek treatment morning and evening at our modest domicile, though movement was in his case accompanied by much pain. At the end of three weeks his cure was far advanced, and he could without serious inconvenience undertake his journey to the coast. His joy was unbounded, and a present handsome for Nejed—it amounted to about forty shillings of our own money—with abundance of hearty encomiums, testified his gratitude. Our position at court was now excellent, and 'Abd-Allah himself, the heir-apparent, and the active administrator of the kingdom, was decidedly in our favour. But Maḥboob, the prime minister, had hitherto looked coldly on us; and it was to his father's recovery that we at last owed his patronage, and, for a certain period of time, his intimacy. Our visits at the palace became more and more frequent, and we could talk of sultans of Nejed, princes and ministers, "as maids of thirteen do of puppy-dogs." However, before entering on the details of what befel us at court, it may be well to give some account of the Sa'ood dynasty, and the history of its principal personages and events. The subject is of great interest in itself, and may also serve to elucidate some of the ensuing scenes which diversified the weeks passed at Riad.

In the following sketch of the Wahhabee dynasty, its wars and revolutions, its fall and its restoration, I shall simply and exactly follow the account given me by the people of the land. That such an account may contain several discrepancies in dates, and even in persons, from what has been by others reported or published on these topics, I well know; nor yet do I intend to claim for it the merit of superior accuracy, though it seems to me in some points clearer, and possessed of greater intrinsic probability. As to certain particular facts or conversations recorded on such or such occasion, they can have still feebler title to unreserved belief; imagination has doubtless done here the work of memory, and conjecture is not document. Yet I should do wrong to omit them; they are lively representations of men and manners, and the formula, so to speak, of more abstract and of more critically historical truths. The speeches of Germanicus and of Otho form no impeachment against the veracity of Tacitus, nor do we throw aside the account of the Corcyræan revolution because Thucydides has embodied Athenian, perhaps personal feelings, in discourses which assuredly were never pronounced word for word as they stand in his astonishing history. The complete divorce between the truth of fact and the truth of imagination, between the map and the landscape, the historical essay and the historical novel, which characterizes this branch of literature in our days, has been noticed by Lord Macaulay, and he notices it with regret bordering on censure. In fact, if the ancients were rather too facile on this point, may not we moderns have become squeamish to excess? But, to sum up, in the following historical digression I shall merit in a critical point of view neither blame nor praise, giving merely what I have heard, without attempt at examination, analysis, or distinction.

CHAPTER XI

HISTORY OF THE WAHHABEE DYNASTY

I read the history of man, age after age
And little find therein but treachery and slaughter.
No pestilence, no fiend could inflict half the evil
Or half the desolation that man brings on man.—Arab Poet

RISE OF THE EBN-SA'OOD DYNASTY — LATTER YEARS OF SA'OOD II. — HIS DYING ADVICE—REIGN OF 'ABD-EL-'AZEEZ — HIS CONQUESTS — THE SHI-YA'EE DAGGER — ASSASSINATION OF 'ABD-EL-'AZEEZ — REIGN OF 'ABD-ALLAH—HIS EXPEDITION AGAINST MESHID ḤOSEYN—CONQUEST OF MECCA AND MEDINAH — EXPEDITION AGAINST SYRIA — REVOLT OF ḤAREEḲ — MASSACRE OF THE INHABITANTS — PREPARATIONS OF MOḤAMMED 'ALEE AGAINST THE WAHHABEES—TARSOON BASHA—HIS DEATH—IBRAHEEM BASHA IS APPOINTED GENERAL—MEASURES TAKEN BY 'ABD-ALLAH—HIS LETTER TO IBRAHEEM BASHA—ITS RESULT—A SKILFUL ENVOY—MARCH OF IBRAHEEM THROUGH ARABIA—HIS POLITIC CONDUCT—BATTLE OF ḲOREYN—SIEGE OF ḌEREY'EEYAH—ITS CAPTURE—CONDUCT OF IBRAHEEM BASHA TOWARDS THE ROYAL FAMILY AND NOBILITY—COUNCIL OF RIAḌ—ITS ABRUPT TERMINATION—IBRAHEEM AS CONQUEROR IN NEJED—HE RETURNS TO EGYPT — ADMINISTRATION OF ISMA'EEL BASHA—HIS CRUELTIES—TURKEE EBN-SA'OOD—HIS REAPPEARANCE—REVOLT OF NEJED—TURKEE REGAINS THE THRONE—HIS FIRST MEASURES AS KING—EXPEDITION OF HOSEYN BASHA—ITS FAILURE—LATTER YEARS OF TURKEE—FEYṢUL KING—HIS EXPULSION BY KOURSHEED BASHA—HIS WANDERINGS—VICEROYALTY AND RESIGNATION OF KHĀLID—FEYṢUL A PRISONER IN EGYPT—VICEROYALTY OF EBN-THENEY'YĀN — HIS DOWNFALL AND DEATH—RETURN OF FEYṢUL — LATTER EVENTS OF HIS REIGN — HIS OLD AGE—HIS FAMILY—SUMMARY VIEW OF THE PROVINCES OF HIS EMPIRE—THEIR DISPOSITIONS—'AASEER—AFLĀJ—OUR VISIT THITHER—WADI DOWĀSIR—WADI NEJRĀN—NUMERICAL CENSUS—REVENUE—CENSUS OF THE KINGDOM OF SHOMER—ITS REVENUE.

THE circumstances to which this dynasty owed its rise, have been already stated in the sketch, two chapters back, of Moḥammed-ebn-'Abd-el-Wahhāb, and of his position at the castle and court of Sa'ood, the first independent prince of that name at Ḍerey'eeyah. We find special mention of Ḍerey'eeyah in Arab annals, previous to the importance conferred on it by its Wahhabee rulers. Riaḍ had been the capital of the 'Aareḍ in the time of Moseylemah and later; 'Eyānah had taken that rank under the Ma'ammer family; while Manfooḥah long remained the head town of Yemāmah. Sa'ood, a chief of 'Anezah extraction, and in consequence of kindred blood to Wā'il, Ṭaghleb, and Shomer, had obtained mastery of the village destined to rule Arabia, and held it in vassalage from the Benoo-Ma'ammer. This was about fifty years before the accession of his grandson, the first of the family who assumed the title of king. But Sa'ood the First is regarded in Nejed as the founder of the family. At his death he was succeeded by his son 'Abd-el-'Azeez, and who was in his turn followed by Sa'ood the Second, the disciple and the patron of the great Wahhabee. How this prince was converted to the Wahhabee sect, and with what zeal and success he exerted himself in its propagation, I have already described with sufficient minuteness. His reign was long, occupying from first to last nearly fifty years, and before he died he saw his authority acknowledged from the shores of the Persian Gulf to the frontiers of Mecca. The dynasty of Ebn-Ṭāhir in Ḥasa, of Da'ās in Yemāmah, of the descendants of Dārim in Ḳaseem, had each in their turn disappeared before the conqueror, and his empire had already attained an extent equal to that which it covers at the present day. But Sa'ood, no less cautions than enterprising, carefully avoided any encroachment on the limits of the great powers in contact with his new empire. The supremacy of Persia in Baḥreyn, and its protectorate in Ḳaṭeef, were respected by the Nejdean; Ebn-Sa'eed, the monarch or sultan of 'Omān, could complain of no aggression, nor had the sacred frontiers of the Meccan Ḥaram been as yet violated, or any risk incurred of Turkish and Egyptian animosity. Sa'ood himself seems to have been not only victorious abroad, but popular at home; he was a patron of learning and study so far as compatible with the tenets of his own sect; and while he cooperated vigorously in the propagation of Wahhabee doctrines, he did not neglect to adorn his capital with religious and national monuments calculated to feed the pride and to augment the veneration of his subjects. The ruins of an enormous palace, and of a scarce less enormous mosque at Ḍerey'eeyah, even now remain to attest the magnificence of the monarch who reared them, and the old capital displays amid all its present desolation traces of much greater regularity and ornament than Riaḍ can boast. Sa'ood was also averse to unnecessary bloodshed, and humane even in war. His campaigns were regulated by Minerva rather than Bellona; timely pacification often turned the edge of his sword; nor do Nejdean chronicles record any wasting massacres or wholesale devastation in most of the provinces annexed during his reign, not even in Ḳaseem, where we might have expected the worst. The Benoo-Khālid alone, in Ḥasa, resisted fiercely, but they were unseconded by the majority of the inhabitants, and were soon subdued.

On his death-bed Sa'ood called before him his two elder sons, 'Abd-el-'Azeez and 'Abd-Allah; named the first his successor, assigned to the other an honourable position in the government, and, lastly, recommended them most earnestly to follow his own line of policy, and, to quote the expression attributed to him by popular tradition, "not to undermine the cliff;"—words denoting the danger they lay under of being some day overwhelmed by the hostility of their more powerful neighbours, and especially of the Ottoman government, seemingly weak, yet crushing by the mere dead weight of its immense resources.

In 1800 or near it (my readers will call to mind what I have more than once said about Arab dates) 'Abd-el-'Azeez ascended the throne. His reign was short, but full of events equally glorious and pernicious.

Restless and bold, but much less prudent than his father, 'Abd-el-'Azeez at once turned his arms against the East, stormed Ḳaṭeef, where he made great slaughter of the inhabitants, occupied Baḥreyn and the adjacent islands of the Persian Gulf, attacked the eastern coast or Barr-Fāris, which he detached irrecoverably from Persian rule, and lastly assailed the kingdom of 'Omān. This last expedition was headed by his younger brother, the impetuous 'Abd-Allah. The success of the Nejdeans was complete; after several battles, each a victory, 'Abd-Allah reached the heights above Mascat, and turned the fort batteries against the town below. The Sultan Sa'eed yielded to the storm, consented to the payment of an annual tribute, admitted a Wahhabee garrison in the more important localities of his kingdom, and permitted the erection of mosques of orthodox fashion in Mascat and elsewhere.

But these very conquests were fatal to 'Abd-el-'Azeez, who had by them provoked a foe much more dangerous than any hitherto known to the Wahhabee empire. Ḳaṭeef and Baḥreyn were both of them dependencies of Persia, and had been even more closely linked to the latter kingdom by religious than by civil ties. 'Omān was also in intimate connection with Persia. The court of Ṭeheran resolved to avenge its allies on the Arab brigand. To hazard a Persian army amid the wilds of Arabia would have been a measure equally dangerous and unprofitable; but there remained an easier way through an instrument familiar to Shiya'ees in all ages and climes, namely, the murderer's dagger.

Numerous and dissident as are the sects sprung from the quarrels of 'Aleo with his more successful rivals, they all of them agree on one point,—the traditional approbation and frequent practice of assassination. Shiya'ees of the original stock, Ismaileeyah (assassins *par excellence*, and from whom all others have derived the name), Druses, Carmathians, Khāri-jeeyah, Metāwelah, in a word, the entire kith and kin from the earliest Rāfeḍee down to the Bābee of our own time, have and do sanction the assassin's knife, wherever a purpose is to be attained or a rival to be got rid of; it is a part of their practical no less than of their theoretical code. Muslim and Christian, Sonnee and polytheist, each in his day has, an Arab would say, "tasted" the dagger of the multiform Shiya'ee, the prototype "carbonaro" of the East. 'Abd-el-'Azeez was now to learn at his own cost that the "secret sects" of Asia are not to be trifled with.

A fanatic, native of the province of Ghilān, the land where 'Abd-el-Ḳadir had six centuries before made the enthusiasm of his disciples a pedestal to almost divine honours, offered himself for the work of blood. He received suitable instructions in Ṭeheran, whence he journeyed to Meshid Ḥoseyn, the authentic Mecca of Shiya'ee devotion. There he procured a written pardon of all past or future sins, and a title-deed duly signed and sealed, assuring him the eternal joys of paradise, should he rid the earth of the Nejdean tyrant. With this document carefully rolled up and secured in an amulet round his arm, he took his way under mercantile disguise to Ḍerey'eeyah, and there awaited an occasion for meriting the reward promised to the deed of treachery.

'Abd-el-'Azeez, a sincere Wahhabee, never failed to be present in person at the public prayers held in the great mosque of the town. Then it was that, without arms, and wholly taken up by the scrupulous exactness of devotions which permit no backward or sideward glance, he might prove an easy victim to the meditated crime. This the Persian knew; and when weeks of intercourse and strict outward orthodoxy had acquired him the full confidence of the townsmen, he one day took his stand in the ranks of evening prayer immediately behind 'Abd-el-'Azeez, went through the first two Reḳa'as of Islamitic devotion, and at the third, while the sultan of Nejed was bowed in prostrate adoration, plunged his sharp Khorassān dagger in his body. The blade penetrated between the shoulders, and came out at the breast; and 'Abd-el-'Azeez lay dead without a groan or struggle.

His attendants caught up their swords where they lay ungirded for prayer, and unsheathed them on the assassin. The Persian, courageous from despair, defended himself awhile with the weapon yet dripping royal blood; at last he fell, and was literally hewn to pieces on the ground of the mosque, but not till he had sent three of his assailants to follow their king in death. The written engagement, countersigned by the governor of Meshid Ḥoseyn, was found on the corpse; and 'Abd-Allah, who was now Sultan of Nejed, swore that his first vengeance for his brother's death should be on the city that had harboured his assassin.

These events took place, so far as my informants could supply a date, about 1805 or 1806. 'Abd-Allah henceforth reigned alone; his younger brother Khālid, and Theney'yān, the son of 'Abd-el-'Azeez, with the other members of the family, had no share in the royal power. Khālid left a son, by name Meshāree, the future assassin of Turḳee, and already mentioned in this narrative, in which Ebn-Theney'yān and another Khālid, also nephew of 'Abd-Allah, will find subsequent mention.

'Abd-Allah had inherited all his father's skill and superior force of character, but to these better qualities he joined the ordinary vices of one born in the purple; despotic, cruel, perfidious, haughty to a degree rare even in the East, and bigoted beyond measure for the sect in which he had been himself brought up. The odious features seldom wanting in the portrait of a Mahometan autocrat—pride, reckless bloodshed, contempt of human suffering, lavish prodigality linked with unsparing oppression, capricious cruelty and equally capricious mercy—all found a full development in the Wahhabee despot, and marked each measure of his reign.

Scarcely had he buried his brother than he prepared to accomplish his sworn revenge on Meshid Ḥoseyn and the Shiya'ees of the Persian frontier. To this intent he put himself at the head of a powerful army, and directed his march towards the western bank of the Euphrates. On his way he threatened to swallow up the little municipality of Koweyt, then first rising into commercial importance, but a seasonable submission and large presents averted the dangerous honour of a Nejdean visit. Carrying all opposition before him, 'Abd-Allah scattered the forces assembled to check his onset at Zobeyr, at Sooḳ-esh-Sheyookh, and at Samowah, till he arrived before the large town of Meshid 'Alee, to which he immediately laid siege. But whether a miraculous interposition of the stepson of Mahomet threw confusion among the Wahhabee assailants, as the Shiya'ees affirm to this day, or whether the besiegers wanted the requisite skill and strength for storming the fortifications, 'Abd-Allah was repulsed with considerable loss, and had to give up his projects against Meshid 'Alee. Leaving it to its defenders, he marched northward with new rage against Meshid Ḥoseyn or Kerbelah, the main object of his hatred. Here the impetuosity of his onset overcame all resistance, the town was stormed, and a promiscuous massacre of garrison and inhabitants appeased the manes of 'Abd-el-'Azeez. The tomb, real or supposed, of the son of Faṭimah was destroyed, the rich mosque plundered and desecrated. I myself have seen at Riaḍ different objects then carried off from the sanctuary of Persian devotion; all agree that the carnage was merciless, and that the inhabitants armed or unarmed were alike put to the sword.

Thus far successful, 'Abd-Allah, in defiance of his father's dying advice, resolved to complete his projects of conquest by an invasion of the Meccan territory on the west. Gathering a second time the whole force of Nejed, he crossed the frontiers of the Ḥaram at Meghasil, and within a few days encamped before Mecca, too weak for effectual defence. The sacred town, which since the days of Ḳarmooṭ-ebn-Ṭāhir had been respected by all factions, and protected from every invader, was now taken, the garrison massacred, and along with the Turkish soldiers many of the oldest and most honoured Shereefs and Sey'yids fell among the slain. Every ornament, every vestige of un-Arab devotion or superstition was taken away or destroyed; and the Ca'abah, now restored to the naked purity of Islamitic worship, was protected against future contamination by the refusal of access to all except the orthodox, that is, the conquering sect. However, a slight relaxation from this comprehensive prohibition was accorded to pilgrims whom the payment of a suitable tribute and pecuniary homage furnished with a satisfactory testimonial to the correctness of their religious views; on no other terms was Mecca under her new lords approachable by Sonnee or Shiya'ee. Even then a fit of fanatic zeal would occasionally prevail over all the charms of gold, and 'Abd-Allah atoned for his purchased compromises by an absolute refusal of passage thrown every now and then in the path of Turkish pilgrims, whatever might be their rank or station. On one such occasion the sister of the Sultan himself was sent back "with sorrow and shame" from the Meccan frontier, before she had kissed the black stone, or thrown a single pebble in the valley of Mina. More than once the plunder of wealthy heretical caravans gratified the Wahhabee guardians of the holy place by a happy union of principle and interest, of zeal and gain. Golden times, though of brief duration, but long to live in the affectionate memory of 'Aareḍ and Riaḍ, where I heard many a sigh after the good old days of conquest, intolerance, and 'Abd-Allah.

His next enterprise was against Medinah. This was due, if we may trust the Meccan account of the event, to a singular political manœuvre effected in the upper regions. The surviving Shereefs and Sheykhs of Mecca, seeing that the Almighty did not appear to take sufficient notice of the wrongs done to His house and servants at the capital, bethought themselves of seeking more effectual aid, by interesting the Prophet himself in their cause. To this end it was necessary that 'Abd-Allah should do that all-potent personage some signal wrong, and thus provoke his private and personal resentment. Now although respect for their great countryman Mahomet would not allow them to cooperate directly in such a deed, it might yet be managed indirectly, nor yet a whit less effectually. Accordingly one morning all the venerable greybeards of Mecca betook them in a body to the despoliated Ca'abah, and there earnestly entreated God to move the Wahhabee monarch to the desecration of Medinah and the Prophet's grave, that he might thus fill up the measure of wrath, and draw down on his head the vengeance of the Beloved, Mahomet to wit. Their prayer was heard, and 'Abd-Allah with the Wahhabee army marched on Yathreb, otherwise Medinah, there to consummate his crimes. My readers will, I trust, remember that I am for the present a narrator—not an historian.

Medinah fell an easy prey, and the Wahhabee victor proceeded to put in practice the well-known maxim of his sect, "Kheyr-ol-Ḳeboor' id-dowāris," "the best tombs are those of which no trace is left," by outraging the sepulchre of the Prophet, and those of his two great successors Aboo-Bekr and 'Omar. After he had levelled every construction of memorial import, his attention was attracted to the rich offerings suspended by the devotion of ages in the sepulchral mosque. "Mahomet is dead, I am alive, and such wealth is safer in the guard of the living than of the dead," was 'Abd-Allah's impious jest, as he caused sixty camels to be laden with the trophies of his profane triumph, and sent them off to the treasury of Ḍerey'eeyah.

With whatever indifference the Prophet may have regarded the wrongs of the Ca'abah, he could not certainly but be deeply moved by this last and personal insult. But whether he was for the moment, with Baal, "on a journey," or perhaps "sleeping, and must be awakened," he let it go by for five years more. Meanwhile the Wahhabee conqueror, now master of the entire Peninsula, a corner of Yemen and Ḥaḍramaut alone excepted, directed his locust bands on the northern frontier. Shomer and

Djowf had already submitted, but from Carac to Palmyra all that lay in the open country was ravaged, burnt, or slaughtered; fortified towns and castles could alone protect the helpless inhabitants from the swords of their too orthodox brethren. The 'Anezah of the north were not, however, in general, disposed to make common cause with the southern plunderers, and some skirmishes took place which gave occasion to the tremendous fiction of a seven days' conflict between armies headed, the one by Benoo-Sha'alān, the other by Aboo-Nokṭa and his compeers, recorded in M. Lamartine's well-known work on the East. But for all enquiries I could make, whether among the Benoo-Sha'alān themselves, the Ru'ala, the Sebaa', and the Ḥasinah of the north, or the Nejdeans and Benoo-Tameem in the south, I could discover no trace of an event which, had it occurred in the gigantic proportions given it by the narrator, would have been immortalized by at least fifty poets of desert and town.

While the main body of Nejdean troops were thus employed on the different frontiers, the Wahhabee pressure on the interior of the empire was of necessity somewhat lightened. Discontent had opportunity to manifest itself, and a formidable revolt broke out in Nejed, where the tyranny of 'Abd-Allah had rendered him scarce less odious to his own subjects than to his foreign enemies. This was especially the case in the provinces to the south of 'Aareḍ; the centre of the reaction was in Ḥareeḳ, that great outpost of Yemāmah, whose remote position renders it even now a frequent brood-nest of disaffection against the Wahhabee government. Foremost in the revolt stood the townsmen of Ḥooṭah, and with them many of the old nobles of the land, now reappearing to claim their own.

But 'Abd-Allah was ready also, and his yoke was too strong to be shaken off by a partial rising. He collected the reserve troops of 'Aareḍ and Sedeyr, his trustiest vassals, and without awaiting the onset of the revolt was himself the first to attack them in Yemāmah. After much slaughter—for the war was civil and internecine—he reached the province of Ḥareeḳ and wasted it far and wide. But the full weight of his vengeance was reserved for the town of Ḥooṭah—not a house but was burnt, not a man or child but was butchered. Of all the male inhabitants soever, reckoned at nigh ten thousand, only one hundred and thirty are said to have escaped his sword.

Then, while the conqueror rode through the bloodstained ruins, attended by his fierce companions, a woman childless and husbandless from the massacre, met him midway, and called out, "'Abd-Allah." "Here I am," replied the king. "Pronounce the name of God," said the woman. "O God," exclaimed 'Abd-Allah. "O God," continued she, completing the sentence thus begun, "if 'Abd-Allah has done well in what he has here done, reward him with good. But if it be injustice and cruelty, requite him accordingly." 'Abd-Allah, conscience-struck and downcast, turned silently away, and returned to Derey'eeyah, leaving Ḥareek a desert behind him. But the curse followed him close at heels.

The government of Constantinople enjoined Moḥammed 'Alee, the viceroy of Egypt, to take in hand the expulsion of the Wahhabees from Mecca, and to inflict on them a suitable chastisement. The first military operations to this end were conducted under the command of Tarsoon Basha, son of Moḥammed 'Alee, and elder brother of Ibraheem Basha. How Tarsoon and his troops landed in Ḥejāz, what circumstances of success and reverse occupied from two to three years of fighting and negotiation; the plague that broke out in the Egyptian army, Tarsoon's death, and the other events of this expedition, are sufficiently, even minutely described, if I remember rightly, in Burckhardt's narrative. Mecca was indeed reconquered, but the Egyptian armies made little further progress and had no settled idea of reaching Nejed itself. Moḥammed 'Alee had, on the contrary, already formed the bold design of not only putting an end to Wahhabee insolence in the Ḥejāz, but, moreover, of precluding the possibility of its future recurrence by the capture of Derey'eeyah, so to smother the hornets in their nest.

But first (my readers remember that I am giving them the Nejdean version of the story) he summoned in Cairo a general meeting of all his generals, ministers, officers, and statesmen, to deliberate on the matter. After explaining at length to those present why he had called them together, and what was his desire, Moḥammed 'Alee pointed to an apple which lay on the floor of the divan; it had been placed exactly at the centre of the large carpet spread in the hall before them. "Now," said he, "whichever of you can with his hand reach and give me that apple, but without placing his foot on the carpet where it lies, he shall command the expedition against Nejed." Many a lithe Bey sprawled his full length on the ground, with his heels just out of the carpet rim, and his arm outstretched to the fruit; but the distance was too great, and the apple remained ungrasped. One after another each tried some new devices, but all in vain, and ended by giving it up in despair. At last the short stout Ibraheem, Mohammed 'Alee's adopted son, rose, bowed to his father, and offered to execute the difficult manœuvre. All laughed, not doubting of his failure. But their scorn was soon changed for admiration when Ibraheem Basha quietly set to work rolling up the carpet from its rim inwards, till the apple stood within an easy reach; he then took it up and handed it to his father, who understood the figurative enigma and forthwith named him commander-in-chief of the Egyptian army.

Fable or fact, the idea herein contained regarding the nature of the country to be invaded, and the likeliest means to ensure success, is by no means bad or inadequate. The whole difficulty of the proposed expedition lay in conveying a regular army across the broad desert margin that fences in Nejed on every side. Over this many a conqueror's arm has proved too short to reach, while the attempt has led more than one Crassus to detach his heels,—in this case his rearward military communications,—from their necessary communication with a secure basis. But the central plateau itself, if once attained, could offer no more resistance than an apple to the fingers which clutch it. But how did Ibraheem Basha intend to fold up the carpet and reach the prize? His campaign itself will soon afford us the practical solution of this riddle: meanwhile I must transport my readers for a few moments to the Arab soil, there to see what preparation 'Abd-Allah made to meet the coming foe.

Whilst Ibraheem remained yet awhile in Egypt, collecting troops and ammunition, the first shadows of this formidable war cloud reached 'Abd-Allah in his capital. The Nejdean troops had been as yet but little called upon for active duty in the war of Tarsoon Basha, during which the main brunt had fallen on the numerous and warlike inhabitants of Djebel 'Aseer, under the command of the chief Ebn-Sa'adoon. A reference to the map will show my readers that the mountainous province of 'Aaseer lies immediately to the south of the Meccan territory; its fighting men are reckoned by Nejdean exaggeration at seventy thousand; should we allow them a third of this number we may perhaps be near the average truth. The inhabitants of 'Aaseer are fanatic Wahhabees of the strictest observance, and are besides allies, though not subjects, of Nejed. They accordingly formed the first serious barrier against Egyptian invasion. But 'Abd-Allah had now reason to fear lest 'Aaseer alone should prove too weak to bar out the advancing tide of war.

He wrote a letter of encouragement and promised support to Ebn-Sa'adoon, and then occupied himself with military preparations on an unusual scale. But meanwhile he chose out from among the inhabitants of Ḍerey'ecyah one whom he deemed best fitted to act the part of spy, and sent him in disguise to Egypt, there to find out what was really on foot, charging him to leave nothing unobserved; but in all secrecy. After a certain lapse of time the emissary returned. Then 'Abd-Allah held a public audience in front of the palace gate, called forth the messenger, and bid him recount before the assembled multitude all that he had seen and heard. The unlucky man, on whose Arab imagination the military force and organized display of Egypt and its armies had made the deepest impression, proceeded to set forth before the eyes of his fellow-countrymen an appalling picture of the mighty Basha and his troops, his cannons and regiments, horse and foot, and all to invade Nejed Every cheek grew pale, but 'Abd-Allah cut short the recital by ordering the too-faithful narrator to be led off and beheaded on the spot for "weakening the hearts of the Muslims."

But though the king had thus somewhat silenced the apprehensions of the multitude, he could not so easily get rid of his own. He would fain have sent an ambassador to the Egyptian to treat of peace and avert the danger ere it should be too late, but he could no longer find anybody willing to take on him such a charge; every one drew back, fearing for himself, and not unreasonably, the fate of the first envoy. At last a man came forward to the task, but on condition that he himself should be allowed to read beforehand the letter of which he was to be the bearer—a wise precaution, all things considered.

On a small square scrap of dirty brown paper, 'Abd-Allah

had written, Wahhabee fashion, a short and most unceremonious note to Ibraheem Basha. It contained, after due mention of the divine Name: "We, 'Abd-Allah-ebn-Sa'ood, salute you, Ibraheem Basha," without title, compliment, or further preface; then followed a dozen lines of sage admonition, garnished by citations from the Coran, and a cool proposal of friendship, on the terms that each party should remain where they were. Wahhabee pride would not permit of opening negotiations in any other way. But when the messenger had demanded and read this rather undiplomatic note, he threw it aside, saying, "To take that with me were as much as my head is worth. You must let me myself write the letter in your name; thus I can go, but not otherwise." 'Abd-Allah, who knew that envoys were likely to prove scarce, reluctantly answered, "Write." "But do you," added the future ambassador, "first pledge me your solemn oath and promise of personal safety, write I what I may." 'Abd-Allah swore accordingly. Hereupon the Nejdean, who had travelled far, and knew more of the world and its usages than his palace-nursed master, demanded a large sheet of white paper, and nibbed an excellent pen. He then in a large and ornamental hand traced several lines of compliment, the customary Eastern exordium to state letters, wherein the titles of "Master, Lord, Ruler," and so forth—all sheer idolatry in Wahhabee estimation if applied to any other save the Supreme Being alone—were thickly lavished on the Egyptian infidel. Followed an offer of friendship and alliance, but couched in terms breathing submission and concession, not equality and menace; and last, a humble request that "our Lord" (Ibraheem Basha) would condescend to accept the presents which, so he wrote on his own authority, accompanied the letter.

His composition finished, he handed it to the king. "By God," exclaimed the despot, "had I not sworn to your personal safety, your life had paid these blasphemies." However, there was no help for it, and 'Abd-Allah sealed the abhorred document, adding besides, the offering of six handsome Nejdean horses, mentioned in the letter. Thus equipped, the ambassador set out on his westerly way.

From Djiddah he crossed to Koseyr in Egypt, where he had

not gone far inland when he met the army, and Ibraheem Basha at their head, already on their seaward march from Cairo. Three days had 'Abd-Allah's envoy to wait for his audience. On the fourth he was admitted.

"Well, man," said Ibraheem Basha in that genuine slang Cairo dialect which to the end of his life he never laid aside, "what have you brought us from that dog of Nejed your master?" The ambassador presented his letter. The Basha took it, glanced his eyes over the contents, and burst out into a horse-laugh.

"So—'Master, Lord! your humble servant!' Boy" (turning to an attendant), "bring the letter which we received four days since from Sa'adoon, that dog of 'Aaseer."

The document was brought. It was a protestation of submission and allegiance, while within it, as a pledge of his sincerity, the 'Aaseer chieftain had forwarded the very note sent him not long before by 'Abd-Allah son of Sa'ood.

"Hear this, you pig," said Ibraheem, and proceeded to read aloud the second Wahhabee document, interspersing his lecture with curses on Nejdean calligraphy: "In the name of God the Merciful, We, 'Abd-Allah-ebn-Sa'ood, salute you Ebn-Sa'adoon, and peace be on you and the mercy of God and his blessings. Next we say: be not deceived by that ass of Egypt and all his brayings, for he cannot avail you or injure you in aught, and we by God's permission are the victorious party; and beware, I say, beware of the boasting of the infidels; may God put them to shame, for assuredly they are the losers, and we are ready with horse and foot to your aid, and the victory is from God, and the triumph near at hand, and peace be with you."

"Thus he writes to his friends," continued Ibraheem; "and thus," pointing to the fair-spoken document on the ground before him, "does he write to us. Your master, Ebn-Sa'ood, is a humbug. Tell the pig," added the Basha, "that I will give him his answer in person at Ḍerey'eeyah. And now get you gone, you and your presents; were it not for your character of ambassador I had put you to death."

The Nejdean saw that there was no room left for apology or diplomacy. He attempted neither, but taking his horses along with him, he re-embarked at once from Koseyr, and was soon at Djiddah.

Once there, he began to think how he should show his face at Ḍerey'eeyah after such an exit, and with such an answer: there was enough in it to forfeit not one but a hundred heads. However, a true Arab is seldom long at a loss for expedients. He sold his horses, the intended peace-offering, at a good price, and with their money bought a dozen Nubian slaves, whom he dressed in the handsomest style possible, and then took them with him on the road to the interior, giving out everywhere on his way that they were a present sent from Ibraheem Basha to the Sultan of Nejed, and a token of alliance and friendship, nay even of fear.

In this guise he arrived at Ḍerey'eeyah, and entered the city in the afternoon, just at the moment when the Mu'eḍḍin's voice was summoning the inhabitants to the prayers of 'Aṣr. Accompanied by his gorgeously dressed blacks he made straight for the great mosque, then crowded with worshippers; 'Abd-Allah was in the first rank, and prayers were about to begin. As the envoy entered the place, all eyes were directed towards him and his dusky band, while the wish proved father to the thought, and all, 'Abd-Allah included, drew mentally the very identical conclusion intended by the cunning Dromio. "La Ilāh illa Allāh! God is with the Muslims, God alone is great, praise be to God," ran in one deep murmur like the sea through that vast assembly. 'Abd-Allah, though himself more elate of heart than any at the anticipated good tidings, imposed silence with a gesture, and prayers were said. No sooner were they ended than the monarch called on his envoy to relate before the gathered multitude the progress and issue of his mission.

A courteous reception made him by the Egyptian potentate, the alarm of Ibraheem Basha on learning the warlike vigour of Nejed, his glad acceptance of the offered presents, their requital by the gift of the slaves now present, with protestations of friendship, alliance, and what not, formed the enormous but seasonable lie now passed off by the wary messenger on king and people. "Now let us see the infidel's letter," said 'Abd-Allah, when the ear-pleasing narrative had ended amid the "Allāho Akbar's" of the townsmen. But the messenger answered that the letter contained matters to be read in private council only, and begged 'Abd-Allah to defer its perusal till then. The monarch, who was in an unusually good humour, consented after some demur, took the envoy with him, and at once moved off to the palace, attended by his ministers and court, with the negroes in the rear.

Once in the private divan, 'Abd-Allah a second time demanded the supposed letter. "It is of a very confidential nature," replied the discreet impostor, "and can be entrusted to no eyes or ears but your own." And 'Abd-Allah, somewhat surprised, had to send his councillors away.

"There is no answer to your proposals except what Ibraheem Basha will give you himself in person here at Ḍerey'eeyah; and now, if you are a man, prepare to fight it out," said the envoy, obliged at last to take the bull by the horns. He then exposed to 'Abd-Allah all that he had seen and heard, and apologized for the momentary deception he had practised to prevent discouragement and alarm from finding their way to the capital. "But," concluded he, "the danger is imminent, and you must expect a campaign in Nejed itself."

The monarch could not otherwise than praise the dexterity of his servant, and dismissed him with his head on his shoulders. He then applied himself to call forth and concentrate the whole force of his empire, and determined, thus strengthened, to await the enemy at the entrance of the inner Nejdean passes near Kowey', where the Meccan road first enters the labyrinthine valleys of Ṭoweyḳ, before reaching Wadi Ḥaneefah and the heart of Nejed. His own troops, fresh and undiminished, would thus fight for their country on their own native soil against an enemy who, thought 'Abd-Allah, can only arrive weary and harassed by the passage of the intervening desert, and perhaps after having his impetuosity still more broken and his numbers thinned by the guerilla war from the Bedouins and villagers scattered over his way. Nor can there be any doubt that 'Abd-Allah's calculations were skilful, and might have been followed by success with a less wary assailant.

But Ibraheem Basha now put in practice his project of rolling up the Arab carpet, and showed, not by theories but facts, how the sadly famous expeditions of a Cambyses, a Crassus, and a

Napoleon might well have been rendered, if not wholly successful, at least far less disastrous to those who undertook them, even in Lower Scythia, in the Syrian desert, or amid the Russian snows. The manner in which he did it deserves attention; it is a good lesson for military operations in Asia, above all when conducted on a large scale and carried deep inland.

After landing at Djiddah, where be received the submission of Ebn-Sa'adoon and Djebel 'Aaseer, he advanced with the main body of his troops up the long and sandy valley that leads from Mecca to Nejed, having the Nefood of Ḳaseem on his left, and the low arm of Ṭoweyḳ (sometimes, but improperly, denominated Djebel 'Aarod) on his right, thus keeping his line of march clear of Wadi Dowāsir and its fanatic population. On this road he had no enemy to encounter except the ill-armed inhabitants of scattered villages, and the Bedouin tribes of Ḥarb, 'Oṭeybah, 'Anezah, and Ḳaḥṭān; while water, if not to be met with daily, was at least sure in the wells situated along the track from every forty to fifty hours of route.

But Ibraheem advanced not as a conqueror but as a friend. Every bucket of water that the inhabitants or the Bedouins drew for his army, every date the soldiers gathered, every stick of firewood they consumed, was at once and handsomely paid for; while officers and men were alike strictly and efficaciously prohibited from offering the slightest insult or outrage to the unarmed and unresisting inhabitants. Village after village, tribe after tribe, overawed by military display, and attracted by the hope of profit, nor unmoved by the favourable contrast of civilized order and protection with Wahhabee insolence and ferocity, tendered allegiance to the Egyptian and renounced Nejdean rule. The suppliants, whatever their quality or clan, were at once received on the most advantageous terms. A minority still refused to exchange the government of the "Muslims" for the sovereignty of the "Ass of Egypt." No direct violence was employed even against them, no blood was shed; with calculating clemency Ibraheem only obliged them to quit their abodes, and to precede him on his way to Central Nejed, there, said he, with bitter sarcasm, "to swell the armies of the faithful," but in reality to exhaust 'Abd-Allah's means and depress his courage by the burden of a mixed and useless multitude. A tender of pecuniary interest and abundant tobacco to all Bedouins who could supply camels for water carrying and guides for the road, drew the nomade clans without exception under the standard of the Basha. Thus "folding up Nejed," in Arab phrase, step after step, and approaching by easy marches to the central heights, untired, and provided with all requisites for his men, without losing or shedding a single drop of blood on the way, Ibraheem left behind him safe communications with the coast and well-disposed allies, while he sent before him famine, an unavailing crowd, and the terror inspired by strength combined with and held in by perfect discipline, and the moderation of conscious power.

Near Kowey' he first fell in with the advanced posts of the Nejdean army or outlying garrison. 'Abd-Allah had already sent messenger after messenger to appease or avert the invader; but to all offers he received only one answer, "at Ḍerey'eeyah." With all his faults Ebn-Sa'ood was no coward; he determined to stand at bay before his own mountains, and to sell their entrance dearly.

His outposts were soon driven in by the Egyptian columns, and some skirmishes brought Ibraheem to Shaḳra', a town then as now unwarlike and commercial; she readily opened her gates to the Basha. But a few leagues farther on at Ḳoreyn lay gathered the great force of Nejed with 'Abd-Allah at its head; second in command was the invincible Ḥārith, described by tradition as the fiercest among all Wahhabee leaders of old or of recent times.

A tremendous battle, recalling that of Khālid and Moseylemah, here took place. It is said to have lasted two days, and to have been only decided by the Egyptian field-pieces on the afternoon of the second. Ḥārith with his lancers broke through the enemy's lines, and reached the Basha himself; but just as the sword of the Nejdean was raised to put an end to the war at one blow, a Circassian came behind him in the mêlée, and with a drawing stroke of his sabre cut through the Arab's loins. Ḥārith fell dead from his horse, but his companions undiscouraged continued the fray till night parted the combatants. The dreams of Ibraheem Basha are reported to have been long haunted by the memory of his imminent personal danger on that day, and for years after he would often start from sleep exclaiming the name of Ḥārith.

At last the artillery, which had been dragged up a commanding height, did its work. 'Abd-Allah with his broken troops retreated to entrench himself in Ḍerey'eeyah, and Wadi Ḥaneefah lay open to the Egyptians. They advanced, but cautiously, and after dispersing a few troops left to check their way, came before the capital.

An assault was at once given, but was repulsed by the garrison. Ibraheem, whose far-sighted policy would gladly have spared unnecessary bloodshed, did not repeat the attempt, and contented himself with posting troops around the walls, to prevent all communications from without, while he summoned the townsmen to capitulate. No answer was returned. Twenty days did the Egyptians maintain the blockade without firing and without receiving a shot, for the Wahhabees, resolved to keep their whole strength ready for the decisive onset, made no sallies, nor replied otherwise than by silence to Ibraheem's repeated proposals for surrender. Meanwhile a reserve Wahhabee force gathered head in Sedeyr, and marched to relieve the capital. Ibraheem was informed of their movements, and sent against them a strong detachment, which met them at Sedoos, and by an easy victory scattered with the Sedeyrees 'Abd-Allah's last hopes of succour. Then, on the twenty-first day of the siege, the Basha sent the besieged his ultimatum of honourable capitulation or of storm, trusting that the late reverse of fortune would have abated the pride of the Nejdean monarch, and would bring him to accept the proffered clemency. But even then 'Abd-Allah would not submit, and the messenger returned without an answer. Ibraheem gave orders to range the artillery on the heights around the capital.

At sunset the bombardment began, and lasted without intermission till sunrise next day. Six thousand shot and shell are said to have been thrown during that night on the devoted town. Morning dawned on crumbling walls and heaps of ruin, on the dying and the dead whelmed beneath their falling dwellings, and on the helpless despair of the survivors.

Without parley, without opposition, Ibraheem entered Ḍerey'eeyah. His first care was to seize on the persons of 'Abd-Allah, his family, his court, and the other chiefs and nobles gathered within the capital. A few resisted, and were killed by the soldiers; the greater number bowed their heads to the will of God, and submitted. The religious teachers, the various representatives of the great Wahhabee family, the Ḳaḍee, Imām, the Meṭow'waa's, and all who formed the strength of the doctrinal party, were also taken prisoners and put under sure guard. A general amnesty included all the other inhabitants; and, except a few hours of plunder, no violence was permitted to the victorious army. Meanwhile the avenues leading from the town to the mountain were carefully watched. A few only of the citizens effected their escape during the first confusion of capture, but among those few was Turkee, the eldest son of 'Abd-Allah, and his destined successor.

When all was over, and a well-disciplined garrison of Egyptian soldiery secured the surviving townsmen equally against the licence of conquest and the dangers of their own fanaticism, Ibraheem retired to the plain without the walls, pitched his tent, and ordered 'Abd-Allah with all his kinsmen to be brought before him. Without reproach or menace, he simply said: "I am the servant of the Sultan of Constantinople, and he must be your judge, not I. Meantime, awaiting his further pleasure, you will accompany me to Egypt, where you shall be honourably treated; and when the Sultan's orders are known, you will comply with them." 'Abd-Allah had no reply except a phrase of the Coran and submission. Ibraheem acted with equal lenity towards the other prisoners belonging to the royal family and court, and towards all invested with civil or military character. None were put to death or anywise harshly used during the whole time that the Basha remained in Nejed.

But while he thus sought to attach the hereditary strength of the country to his own government, he was equally and for the very same reasons desirous of extirpating a fanaticism incompatible with the stability of that government. The nationality of Nejed might side with order, commerce, and advancement; the bigotry of Nejed never; it would always remain the pernicious seed of interminable retrogression and revolt. With this Ibraheem now determined once for all to make an end.

After dismissing the royal family and their retinue to guarded but honourable confinement, he called in the Meṭow'waa's, doctors, and teachers of the law: their number is said to have exceeded five hundred. He then informed them that he was desirous of having the religious differences which existed between them and ordinary Mahometans thoroughly sifted and examined; that to this end he had brought with him learned men of the most orthodox schools from Cairo, and that a conference would accordingly be held within the precincts of the great mosque, where he himself would attend to hear the issue.

A conqueror's invitation admits of no excuse, and the Council of Riaḍ began its sessions. They lasted, if report be true, three days; all the points in controversy were minutely discussed, and either party obtained, no doubt, the wordy victory in the opinion of its adherents. Ibraheem Basha, who in his heart cared less than Gallio about any of these things, presided with much patience, and for a while with the silence of an interested auditor.

But on the fourth day, whether his endurance had been fairly exhausted, or whether he thought that the controversy had reached a fit point for interference, he himself took up the word; and after obtaining from the Nejdean theologians the orthodox declaration, common to many beside, that "As there is only one God, so there is only one faith, and that faith is our faith," and that in logical consequence, salvation out of their pale was wholly impossible, he thus proceeded to argue in his customary Egyptian slang:—

"Well, you pigs, and what do you say about Paradise? what is its extent?" Now to this question there is only one answer admissible in the mouth of a Mahometan, namely, that contained in the words of the Coran, "a Paradise equal in extent to all heaven and earth, prepared for the pious." This was accordingly given.

"A Paradise equal in extent to all heaven and earth!" repeated Ibraheem Basha; "and meanwhile, should you Nejdeans by some incomprehensible act of God's mercy get admittance there, one single tree of its gardens would be well enough to shelter you all! And for whom, pray, is the rest of the enclosure?"

They were silent. "Fall on them and kill them," said Ibraheem, turning to the soldiers drawn up behind; and in a few minutes the mosque of Ḍerey'eeyah was the bloody tomb of Wahhabee theology.

I will not exactly say that Ibraheem Basha did well on this occasion; but I do say that, for those lands at least, he did wisely. Toleration for the masses is both right and wise; toleration for enthusiasts and agitators may be right, perhaps, but is not wise as certainly. One might add that in all cases positive encouragement of ways and doctrines opposed to quiet, stability, and national health and progress, is neither right nor wise; certainly not in the East. But to return to our subject.

After having, to borrow an Arab expression, made the inhabitants of Ḍerey'eeyah "taste his sweet and his bitter," Ibraheem proceeded to a work in which he was pre-eminent if not singular among all before or after him in the East, that of consolidation after conquest. He visited in person the adjoining provinces, everywhere pursuing the identical line of policy which he had observed during his march from Mecca, and when at the capital; conciliation and gentleness towards the national chiefs and common people, efficacious severity for religious dogmatizers, order and progress, payment and justice for all. My readers should observe that I am not here writing an imaginative panegyric of the great Basha, I am simply repeating what was told me in Nejed, in the conquered land itself. To one point of Ibraheem's wise administration I can indeed bear the testimony of an eye witness, having myself seen its abiding results. It was, that he took an especial care to observe and to fortify the strong points of the land, at the western entrance of Wadi Ḥaneefah, at Ḥoreymelah, on the central heights above Ḍerey'eeyah, and elsewhere. At the same time he laid the foundation for agricultural improvement, by causing new wells to be sunk wherever he surmised the existence of water hitherto unemployed. At 'Eyānah, as we have already seen, his efforts failed of success; we shall soon have to notice a similar memorial of Egyptian enterprise in Wadi Farooḳ. Meanwhile silk dresses, gold rings, and tobacco, had their day throughout Nejed; and it is a sad proof of human weakness, that succeeding years of orthodoxy and zeal have never been able wholly to eradicate the bad consequences of one short period of self-indulgent depravity.

Ibraheem remained some months thus employed in Nejed; on his return to Cairo he took with him 'Abd-Allah and the greater part of the Ebn-Sa'ood family, besides several hostages selected from among the principal nobles of the land. In this last measure he had a special object, namely, that of rearing for Nejed men of better education and wider views than what their own country could afford, and thus paving the way for real and lasting progress. His hopes were disappointed, more through the folly and incapacity of his own successors than through the resistance of the Nejdean character itself. Departing, he left behind him a feeling of confidence, attachment, and fear, blended into a respectful admiration, such as few conquerors bequeath to the nations whom they have subdued; and to this day his name and that of his family is popular throughout Central Arabia among all except the ultra-zealots, who might reasonably fear lest a second Egyptian visit should be followed by another dogmatical conference resembling the first held in the great mosque of Ḍerey'eeyah.

When he quitted Nejed, Ibraheem had left one of his officers, Isma'eel Basha by name, as vice-governor of the land. Isma'eel occupied this post for two years, during which he visited Ḥasa, overjoyed to be delivered anyhow from the Wahhabee yoke, besides Yemāmah, Ḥareeḳ, and Ḳaseem, placing Egyptian garrisons everywhere. But unlike the son of Moḥammed 'Alee, Isma'eel indulged, and permitted his officers to indulge themselves in all the licence of conquerors, till insolence and oppression revived old national antipathies, lulled awhile to sleep by the moderation of Ibraheem, and undermined the foundations of the Egypto-Arabian government.

No outbreak, however, of any importance occurred for the moment, and Isma'eel Basha, his two years ended, returned to Egypt, leaving Khālid Basha governor in his stead. The new ruler proved more overbearing and much more cruel than Isma'eel had been. The tortures of impalement and of burning alive, both of which Khālid introduced into Nejed, heightened the growing indignation of the inhabitants, now fully resolved to throw off the Egyptian tyranny. The means were not long wanting, nor the man.

I have said that Turkee, son of 'Abd-Allah, had (so runs the tale) contrived to escape from Ḍerey'eeyah at the very moment of its capture. He fled to Sedeyr, and, despairing of any return to his country and throne while Ibraheem Basha and his successor Isma'eel were still in Nejed, led for some years a wandering life on the outskirt frontiers. At last he reached Basrah, and there or in its neighbourhood remained disguised for a considerable time. Meanwhile what news reached him seemed to cut off all hope of the future. His father 'Abd-Allah, after a short captivity in Egypt (where, however, Moḥammed 'Alee had treated him well), had been summoned to Constantinople, and there put to death on his first arrival. His brothers and kinsmen, with the survivors of the old Wahhabee family, and many other chiefs of note, were, by order of the Sultan, close prisoned in Egypt. Nor had any general reaction yet declared itself in Nejed and its provinces; while the Egyptian government seemed on the contrary to be taking day by day firmer and more irrevocable hold on Central Arabia.

But at the news of the cruelty and injustice of Khālid, Turkee learned to hope in the revival of those deep Arab feelings which could in no case have slumbered for ever, though a wiser conduct on the part of the Egyptians might have rendered the outbreak less dangerous. Nejed was impatient to rise, and waited only for a leader. The son of her slaughtered monarch, the natural heir of the throne, was yet alive and free, though in exile. Messengers were sent to Turkee, who had already approached the frontiers of Sedeyr; nor did the banished prince hesitate for a moment to accept the invitation of his subjects. Soon bands of marauders descending from Djebel Ṭoweyḳ, and sudden attacks directed against the Egyptian outposts, announced the presence of Turkee on the verge of Wadi Ḥaneefah.

Khālid was bewildered by the change of affairs, and allowed his strength to be first divided and then wasted, in a guerilla war, where knowledge of the ground, the support of the peasantry and indigenous population, and an indomitable will, put all the advantages on the side of Turkee. The matter grew daily more and more serious, till at last it was one general uprising of the Nejdeans, who had now learnt not only to hate, but to despise, their Egyptian masters. From Ḳaseem to the shores of the

Persian Gulf all was in a blaze. The garrisons of Ḥasa, Yemāmah, and Ḥareeḳ were overpowered and massacred; a few soldiers only found safety in individual compassion, a few also escaped by flight. Khālid dreaded, nor without cause, to find himself before long isolated from Egypt and blockaded in Wadi Ḥaneefah. With all his surviving troops he retreated to Ḳaseem; Turkee descended into the great central valley, and was unanimously proclaimed Sultan of Nejed and restorer of the Wahhabee empire.

His first care was to select a capital. The bloodstained ruins and disastrous memories of Ḍerey'eeyah rendered that locality unsuited for a reviving dynasty and a better star. With politic good judgment Turkee fixed on Riaḍ, the ancient centre of Nejed in the days of Moseylemah, and safe guarded by heaven from the sword of even Khālid-ebn-Waleed. Besides it was a town advantageously situated in every respect, and placed amid a tract of unusual fertility; a slight deficiency in the healthiness of its climate was a circumstance likely to pass almost unnoticed in the calculations of an Arab statesman. Here accordingly he established his court, and began the construction of that great palace now inhabited by his son Feyṣul. Next the fortifications of the city, and the construction of the great mosque or Djāmia', occupied his attention. For Turkee, well aware that religious enthusiasm was at once the mainspring of his rule in Nejed, and the only decent pretext for attempting those foreign conquests which he already meditated, showed himself at all times the zealous restorer of his father's sect no less than of his empire.

His authority as Sultan (the title of Imām is very little used, because liable to equivocation, and suiting more the Mesjid than the throne) was from the outset acknowledged throughout 'Aareḍ, Woshem, Sedeyr, Aflāj, Yemāmah, Ḥareeḳ, and Dowāsir, in a word, in all the central provinces. But Ḳaseem, upper and lower, was yet held by Khālid Basha, while whatever lay beyond it, north or west, was of course lost to the Wahhabee. Ḥasa and Ḳaṭeef had indeed expelled their Egyptian oppressors, but with no intention of receiving Nejdeans in their place; native chiefs had once more resumed their ancestral power over those fertile lands. Lastly, 'Omān had long since returned to the undisputed sovereignty of her own sultan, Sa'eed-ebn-Sa'eed.

Turkee wisely began by reorganizing the civil and military administration of Nejed itself. But while he was thus occupied, and before he could attempt to reconquer his sundered provinces, a new storm burst upon him from the west, whence Moḥammed 'Alee now sent Ḥoseyn Basha with a numerous army, to retrieve the fortunes of Egypt in Arabia.

The son of 'Abd-Allah, unable to resist the first onset of well-disciplined troops, resolved to await the results of time and the blunders of his enemy. He fled his capital, and took refuge, with the main body of his adherents, in the heights of Ṭoweyḳ, behind Ḥoreymelah, thence to watch the proceedings of the Egyptians in the southern valleys. Ḥoseyn enjoyed a while the most entire success; towns and villages opened their gates, and the Nejdean garrisons submitted or dispersed themselves. Some of the fugitives rallied around Turkee in the mountains; others, in greater numbers, traversed Yemāmah, and concentrated their strength in Ḥareeḳ, where prevailed the bitterest hatred to Egyptian rule.

Meanwhile Ḥoseyn Basha, unopposed by Turkee, occupied Riaḍ and Wadi Ḥaneefah far and wide, and might long have done so, had he acted wisely. But his impatience urged him to crush all opposition at the very outset, and he rashly determined to march against the fugitives in Ḥareeḳ, leaving Turkee and Sedeyr for his return.

Then ensued one of those deeds of studied treachery nowise uncommon in Nejed, comparatively rare in the rest of Arabia, and hardly to be excused even by the cause of national independence and liberty. Before reaching Ḥareeḳ, the Egyptian army must needs cross an arm of the Great Desert, namely, that which separates Ḥareeḳ from Yemāmah, and terminates northward in Wadi Soley'. Ḥoseyn Basha sought guides for himself and his army; he found traitors.

Under the pretext of conducting the Egyptians by nearer and securer tracks, the Nejdeans led them astray amid the sand-hills south-west of Ḥareeḳ, and there left them to perish of thirst in the burning labyrinth. All, in fact, so perished; and when the villagers, who were only at a few hours' distance, crossed the sand-ridges to see the work of death, they found (the tale was told me by an eye-witness) nothing but corpses, convulsed in the death-agonies of drought and despair. They were counted, and their number was above four thousand. One tradition reckons Ḥoseyn Basha himself among the victims; another, and more probable, it seems, makes him escape along with a reserve left behind the main body in Yemāmah, whence he retreated to Ḳaseem, and soon after to Egypt.

Turkee, thus delivered from the invader, reappeared at Riaḍ, and took quiet possession of his kingdom, which he continued to hold for some years without fresh molestation from Egypt or elsewhere. What regards the expedition organized by him against Haṣa, his own assassination by his cousin Meshāree, the part taken by 'Abd-Allah-ebn-Rasheed in the chastisement of the usurper, and the instalment of Feyṣul on the throne left vacant by his father's death, I have already fully related in the third chapter of this work, and thither accordingly I refer my readers.

Feyṣul when thus unexpectedly raised to the supreme power was about thirty-three or thirty-four years of age. But though in a manner taken unawares by events, he possessed many qualities which rendered him equal to the difficulties of his new position. In personal character he resembled his father Turkee much more than his grandfather 'Abd-Allah. Of a naturally mild and not unamiable disposition, prudent and wary even to excess, moderate in his opinions, gifted with singular foresight and perspicacity, of a prepossessing exterior and a very eloquent tongue, there was much in him to conciliate the affection and the loyalty of his hereditary subjects, and to promise a ruler alike powerful and good. But Wahhabee education, sectarian bigotry, and the influence of what one may conveniently entitle, though without the most distant European allusion, the High Orthodox Nejdean party, conjoined with an innate turn for superstition and an overwrought devotion, went far to blight these fair hopes. Advancing age rendered the evil effects of Wahhabee bias more and more dominant; and in his last years Feyṣul has ended by becoming a mere tool in the hands of his narrow-minded counsellors and his violent son, who administer the kingdom in the old monarch's name, and obtain from his decrepitude an easy sanction for the grossest oppression and the blackest crimes. Still occasional gleams of a better nature pierce at times through the cloud of absolutism and fanatic perverseness thrown around his declining days; an evidence that, under other circumstances, and with a better education and counsel, the son of Turkee might have been an excellent king, at least for Nejed.

Hardly proclaimed sultan, Feysul applied himself to restore order in the central provinces, where all had been thrown into confusion by the death of Turkee, and the usurpation of Meshāree. Nor had he time to do more. For the Egyptian viceroy, deeming this a favourable occasion for avenging the late disaster of Ḥoseyn Basha, and re-establishing his own authority in Central Arabia, sent against Nejed a new commander, Khoursheed Basha by name, with considerable forces. Ḳaseem had throughout remained in the hands of the Egyptians, and furnished them a secure entrance into Wadi Ḥaneefah at short notice. Koursheed Basha pounced on the new sovereign almost unawares; Feysul had barely time to save himself by flight; several of the royal family were taken prisoners and sent anew to Egypt. The Basha then established Khālid, the grandson, not of 'Abd-el-'Azeez, but of one of his brothers, whose name I have lost, on the vicarious throne of Nejed, while he himself returned to Ḳaseem, where the climate suited him better than that of 'Aareḍ.

Feysul, driven from his capital, and not inclined to carry on, like his father, a guerilla war against the invaders, took the opportunity of seeing the world; and after a pilgrimage—of course under disguise—to Mecca, travelled northward to Damascus, besides visiting the Djāmia'-el-Aḳṣa at Jerusalem, and many towns of the Syrian coast. It is a pity that exiled monarchs seldom seem to derive much good from their foreign peregrinations: whether that their minds are too much preoccupied with their own real or supposed wrongs, or whether the evil genius that attended them on the throne accompanies them also on their travels, were hard to say, but such appears too often to be the fact; and neither Dionysius in old times, Charles II. in the seventeenth century, nor the Comte d'Artois in our own, appear to have returned to Syracuse, London, or Paris much wiser or better than when they left them. One only, more recent still, has turned the lessons of adversity so far to profit, that the exile has ripened into the emperor. A striking exception, and more striking from its rareness.

But to return to Feyṣul. Whatever may have been his early deficiencies on the score of bigotry, they were now amply made up by physical draughts from the brackish waters of Zemzem, and the spiritual irrigation of lectures delivered by the Ḥanbelee or Shāfi'ee fanatics of Damascus. This process, which effectually stunted the Nejdean into the Wahhabee, lasted about two years. Feyṣul then received information recalling him to the frontiers of Nejed. Khālid, long since dissatisfied with the false and odious position of an Egyptian tool—he an Ebn-Sa'ood and a born Wahhabee—had given signs of a desire to quit his insecure and unenviable viceroyalty. He was, indeed, a quiet and sensible individual, and though his countrymen respected him for his family's sake too much to rise against him, they sympathized in the uneasiness of his feelings, and seconded his proposal of abdication. Feyṣul reappeared; and Khālid withdrew to Ḳaseem, thence crossing over to Egypt, till after many years passed on the banks of the Nile he sought a retreat at Mecca, where he led a tranquil nor unrespected life, till he enjoyed in 1861 the privilege, rare in his family, of dying a natural death on his bed. The son of Turkee meanwhile reinstated himself in his father's palace at Riaḍ without difficulty or opposition.

But Khoursheed Basha was not disposed to remain a quiet spectator of changes so unfavourable to his own views. By a sudden manœuvre he surrounded the capital of 'Aareḍ, and forced Feyṣul to surrender at discretion, after which he sent him off without delay to Egypt, not this time a tourist, but a prisoner. Moḥammed 'Alee placed the fallen prince in a closely guarded fortress between Cairo and Suez, and there Feyṣul remained immured till the death of the great Basha.

Meanwhile Ebn-Theney'yān, cousin of Khālid, and, like him, grandson of 'Abd-el-'Azeez-ebn-Sa'ood, was installed by Khoursheed Basha in the viceregency of Nejed. Very different from Khālid, the new sovereign, or rather vassal, was a thorough Ebn-Sa'ood, and had inherited all the good qualities of the royal race, and all the bad. Handsome, generous, daring, keen-sighted, and long-handed, he belonged no less to that category of "bloody and deceitful men" who seldom, whether in David's time or our own, "live out half their days." Scarce enthroned, he began to administer the kingdom after his own fashion, and with very little dependence on his Egyptian patron. His first measure was, in itself, a good one, namely, the repression of the Bedouins, who during this troubled epoch had regained much of their old power and impertinence. Meṭeyr and 'Oṭeybah were the two most powerful clans among the Nejdean nomades; but they learned to dread the sword of Ebn-Theney'yān, and acknowledged their master. Victorious over the Bedouins, the prince next subdued a revolt broken out among the semi-barbarous inhabitants of Wadi Dowāsir. Pity that scenes recalling the horrors of Glencoe and Arcot should have sullied, it is said, enterprises otherwise alike necessary and beneficial to the land. Ebn-Theney'yān perfected also many of the architectural improvements commenced in the capital by Turkee; he enlarged the palace, and constructed within its precincts, and in a somewhat dangerous situation, the present powder-magazine and arsenal.

But success and power were poison to his haughty character, and he now became a tyrant to his own subjects; he renewed the odious cruelties of Khālid Basha, and often impaled those who incurred his displeasure without even the form of a trial, and on the slightest provocation. Hence the minds of his subjects, who had been awhile conciliated by his graceful appearance, his lavish generosity, great vigour, and the half-independence which he procured them from Egyptian rule, became at last wholly alienated from him; the cord was overstrained, and ready to snap under the first blow.

Ebn-Theney'yān had administered Nejed for about five years when Moḥammed 'Alee died, and was succeeded by his half-mad grandson 'Abbas Basha. I have already explained the projects of this crazy debauchee regarding Arabia; no sooner had he reached the throne than he took a first step in that direction, or at least in what he fancied to be such, by the liberation of Feysul and his companions from their captivity. Yet not daring to do this openly without a permission from Constantinople, scarce attainable and difficult even to ask, he performed his act of folly in an underhand manner, by lessening and removing the guard of the fortress, at the same time that he caused the prisoners to be secretly supplied with ropes and other means of escape. Of these they gladly availed themselves, climbed over the walls one dark night, and were soon in the open air at Koseyr, where, like true Wahhabees, they thanked God and laughed at 'Abbas Basha.

From Koseyr, Feysul sent spies to Nejed to feel out his way back to the throne. He had not long to wait; scarce was it known in Nejed that Feysul was once more at liberty, than invitations and proffers of allegiance crossed the water to Koseyr. Khoursheed, Basha, said they, and Ebn-Theney'yān were alike detested; let Feysul but come over, and all will gather round his banner. Meanwhile the unlucky Basha became aware of the impending danger, and in vain implored aid and supplies from his master, who was determined to betray his own cause and servant. Khoursheed, having nothing to hope from Cairo, wisely evacuated Ḳaseem before the general rising of the province; and thus ended the Egyptian rule in Arabia, after about twenty-seven years of interrupted duration.

Left to themselves, the inhabitants of Ḳaseem, great and small, chiefs and people, heartily tired of the long residence of foreigners in their land, sent new and pressing messages to Feysul, praying him to become their lord and master. This proved, as my readers already know from the events recorded in the preceding chapters, the old story of the trees and the bramble. Our Arab Abimelech hesitated no longer; from Koseyr he embarked for Yambo, and suddenly with a few attendants showed himself in Ḳaseem. The over-hasty enthusiasm of its inhabitants surrounded him with subjects and a numerous army. Feysul arrayed them, advanced towards Shaḳra', and sent messengers to Riaḍ, summoning Ebn-Theney'yān to surrender the crown to its legitimate owner.

Ebn-Theney'yān was not a man to give up his claims at a first asking. He called together the local chiefs of Nejed, and demanded their support. But they answered him to his face that no man would raise a finger in his cause, and proved their words by setting off one after another to join Feysul in Ḳaseem.

Still a chosen band of followers remained true to the usurper, and with these he marched on Shakra' to meet the foe. But when the son of Turkee drew nigh, defection began its work even among the staunchest retainers of Ebn-Theney'yān, and he was fain to fall back without fighting on Riad, where, despairing of the town, he fortified himself in the palace, along with the few who yet continued faithful to their unfortunate though guilty master.

Feysul entered Riad, and called his cousin to an honourable capitulation, promising him life and liberty. But Ebn-Theney'-yān refused to surrender his post, the more so that the only artillery of Nejed was in his possession within the castle. Deprived of these engines of siege, Feysul and his Arabs would not venture an assault on the massive and well-guarded walls; nothing remained but blockade. For a whole month there were two kings in Nejed, one within the palace, the other without. The son of Turkee renewed day after day his summons and offers of pardon, but without effect; and Ebn-Theney'yān declared himself resolved to quit the throne only with his life.

One evening, a little after sunset, the besieged usurper, while roaming dispirited through the corridors and apartments of the castle, came on a side wicket opening into a small chamber, where were seated some of his own retainers in deep conversation. Ebn-Theney'yān approached to listen, and, like most listeners, heard no good. The discourse ran thus—that God had abandoned the grandson of 'Abd-el-'Azeez, that it was high time for themselves to second the designs of Providence, to open the palace gates to give entrance to Feysul, and obtain pardon and reward by presenting him with the head of his rival. Ebn-Theney'yān saw that he could trust his own no more—all was lost; under cover of the night he passed through the secret door and fled the place. But bewildered by despair, instead of seeking safety in some distant retreat, he went right to the house of a wealthy noble, by name Ebn-Soweylim, the very same whom the Zelators beat to death some years later, and entering the K'hāwah sat him down in silence, with his head-dress drawn over his face.

His astonished host recognised the unbidden guest, and exclaimed, "Ebn-Theney'yān?" Silence supplied affirmation.

"Came you seeking protection?" said Ebn-Soweylim. For so sacred in Arabia is the character of a suppliant or "Mujeer," that had Ebn-Theney'yān even then claimed it for himself, his host could neither have denied nor given him up. But the wretched man, reckless from the excess of misery, answered, "No." "What brought you here then?" asked the master of the house. A word would have ensured his safety; Ebn-Theney'yān remained silent. A third interrogation was put, but in vain.

Hereon Ebn-Soweylim gave news to Feyṣul that his competitor was now in his power. Soldiers were at once sent; the fallen usurper was taken where he still sat motionless, and brought before the rightful king. "Do you come to throw yourself on my protection?" asked Feyṣul. A "yes" would have disarmed all vengeance; whether from pride or conscious guilt, or the stupefaction of ruin, Ebn-Theney'yān again replied "No." "Be all of you witness," said Feyṣul, turning to those around, "that God has delivered him up to me without condition or stipulation." He then took peaceable possession of the now open castle, and cast his ill-starred cousin into the "dungeon of blood," where he died a few days after, of despair say some, of poison administered by order of Feyṣul say others; either report is probable. His grave is close by that of Turkee in the Great Cemetery; some of his children yet live in Aflāj, not many days distant from the capital.

Feyṣul was now the sole and undisputed master of Central Arabia. But Ḥaṣa refused to recognise his sceptre, and 'Omān had been long since freed from Wahhabee interference. The numerous and warlike tribe of the Ajmān were in open revolt on the north-eastern frontier, and had called in to their aid the scarce less warlike Benoo-Hājar and Benoo-Khālid. Their combined forces menaced Nejed with a nomade invasion, nor could any of the native chieftains be trusted with forces sufficient to meet the peril. In short, Feyṣul had come into possession of an empire curtailed in extent, and shaken to its very foundations by frequent and protracted revolutions.

Nor was the sultan himself much of a warrior, more skilled in the use of diplomatic than of military weapons; besides, his eyesight had suffered from ophthalmia contracted in Egypt, and the progressive disease threatened him with total loss of vision. This misfortune had already befallen some of his companions in captivity, and was by the gratuitous suspicion of the Nejdeans ascribed to occult poison, administered by order of the Cairene viceroy.

But Feysul had at hand in the person of his eldest son 'Abd-Allah a full supplement to his own martial deficiencies. Whatever vices this prince might have, and we have already alluded to some of the blackest dye; however proud, immoral, treacherous, and cruel he might be, the praise of great courage, and a degree of skill in war-tactics extraordinary in an Arab, cannot be justly denied him. To 'Abd-Allah accordingly, the military department was confided, while Feysul remained in his capital to organize and administer the empire.

'Abd-Allah's first expedition was directed against the Ajmān Bedouins. Their army, formidable from its number and excellent equipment, had gathered head near Koweyt, and was about to march on Nejed, where they confidently expected a ready victory. But while in their presumptious security they imagined 'Abd-Allah far off in 'Aared, he was already upon them. With only three hundred horsemen he attacked their advanced division, and threw it back in confusion on the main body. Next day both parties collected their whole strength to a decisive battle. The Bedouin army was, according to custom, preceded by a Hadee'yah, that is, a maiden of good family and better courage, who, mounted amid the fore ranks on a camel, has to shame the timid and excite the brave by satirical or encomiastic recitations. I have heard but forgotten the name of the damsel who figured on this memorable day; she is reported to have been remarkable for stature and eloquence, worthy of a place among those whose lofty bearing drew on them from the Princess of Tennyson's poem the wondering remark, "What! are the ladies of your land so tall?" However, cruel Mars would not spare this Arabian Bellona, and her death by a Nejdean lance is said to have decided the rout of the Ajmān army. 'Abd-Allah followed up his advantage by an exterminating pursuit, and a campaign in which two-thirds of the male Ajmān population were destroyed, and the northern clans reduced to lasting submission. The conqueror then turned his arms against the nomades of the West—

Meṭeyr, 'Anezah, and 'Oṭeybah, and did to them as he had done to the Ajmān.

Ḥaṣa was next subdued, though after fierce fight, and Ḳaṭeef once more received a Nejdean garrison. Successful everywhere, 'Abd-Allah longed for a visit to 'Omān. But of the occasion of that great campaign, its progress, its result, and what else concerns the relative position occupied by the governments of Riaḍ and 'Omān, I shall have to speak in detail afterwards, nor will I now anticipate a recital which my readers will better understand when the course of our mutual journey has rendered them more familiar with south-eastern Arabia.

At what time Wadi Seley'yel was annexed to the extreme south-west of the Wahhabee empire, and whether peaceably or by war, I could not learn. But I should hardly imagine that so small a province, occupying too a middle position between Wadi Dowāsir on one side, and Djebel 'Aaseer on the other, both districts no less fanatical than 'Aareḍ itself, can ever have caused much anxiety at Riaḍ. Perhaps it merely followed the fortunes of Wadi Dowāsir, of which valley it is indeed a sort of appendage, sharing in its territorial character and ungenerous fame.

The events thus briefly related occupied about ten years, during which period Feyṣul, absorbed in civil or religious cares and reforms, took little or no active part in the wars of his impetuous son, though he visited the provinces thus acquired after their submission, and settled their taxes, tribute, and local administration. Almost immediately after 'Abd-Allah's return from Omān, began in Ḳaseem the fatal series of events already described in the fourth chapter. But Feyṣul's attention was never wholly diverted from the Persian Gulf, where commerce and civilization had accumulated on its shores wealth well calculated to stimulate his greedy ambition. After the simulated pacification brought about in 1855-6 between the Nejdean autocrat and Zāmil, the chief of 'Oneyzah, a Wahhabee expedition was assembled by order of Feyṣul at Ḳaṭeef, and for the first time under the new empire the warriors of Nejed embarked in a fleet destined to the conquest of Baḥreyn, with what result I leave to a future chapter.

Djebel Shomer and the provinces thereon dependent had been practically detached from Nejed by the vigour and prosperity of the vicarious dynasty there established in the person of 'Abd-Allah-ebn-Rasheed. There, however, Feyşul has long laboured to sow discord among the inhabitants, and even between the members of the royal family, by means of his hypocritical agents, till some fitting opportunity may present itself for armed intervention; no improbable event, if matters go on their present course.

Meanwhile age advanced, and Feyşul became stone blind, while increasing corpulence, a rare phenomenon in Arab physiology, rendered him more and more incapable of active exertion. Timidity also, and superstition its frequent follower, grew on him daily, till for the last three or four years he has almost wholly resigned the direction of affairs to his son 'Abd-Allah, dividing what time yet remains to him between the oratory and the ḥarem. He never appears in public, except for an early visit every Friday morning to his father's tomb, or when some extraordinary event induces him to show himself to the populace for a few minutes and no more. Without the palace walls 'Abd-Allah governs supreme, while within Maḥboob and some negro slaves, privileged in their access to the person of the old despot, lead him at their will. The only other human beings freely admitted to his presence are the bigoted Zelators, whose moral and even material influence he is unable to withstand, nor dares reject whatever they may impose on him, however injurious to the better interests of the empire. Avarice, "that good old-gentlemanly vice," has claimed over Feyşul the dominion which she too often extends over better men at a similar period of their existence, while dissimulation and treachery have been perfected by long practice into a second nature. In short, it may be feared that what good was in him has almost if not totally vanished, while heart and head, intellect and will, are alike sinking into a dotage well befitting a tyrant of seventy.

Of 'Abd-Allah his eldest son the past sketch may suffice. It is, however, worth adding that his mother (the Book of Kings always notices the mothers of the Jewish monarchs) belongs to the Sa'ood family. Not so the mother of the second son, named after the first founder of the race Sa'ood, but born from a woman of the Benoo-Khālid clan, and verifying a known Arab saying, by presenting much more of the maternal than of the paternal resemblance. For whereas 'Abd-Allah is, like his father, short, stout, large-headed and thick-necked, a very bull in appearance, Sa'ood is tall, slender, handsome, and with a strong trace of the careless Bedouin expression in his countenance. Open and generous, fond of show and horsemanship, he is a great favourite with the "liberal" party, who entitle him "Aboo-'hala," literally, "father of welcome," from the "Ya-'hala," or "welcome" with which he is wont to greet whoever approaches him. Whereas 'Abd-Allah stands forth the head of the orthodox party, who look up to him as their main support and future hope.

Of course the two brothers, almost equal in age, are at daggers drawn, and cannot even speak peaceably to each other. Feysul, to prevent frequent collision, has appointed Sa'ood regent of Yemāmah and Ḥareeḳ, with Salemee'yah for chief residence, thus putting him at a distance from Riaḍ, where 'Abd-Allah resides in quality of special governor over the town. Meantime Sa'ood, by his easy access and liberal conduct, has won the hearts of his immediate subjects, and of all opposed to rigorism in the other provinces. Hence it is universally believed that the death of Feysul will prove the signal for a bloody and equally matched war between the Romulus and Remus, or, if you will, between the Don Henry and Don Pedro, of Nejed. So far as two despots and two evils admit of a choice, my own good wishes go with Sa'ood. Fesul, however, from orthodoxy and perhaps sympathy, favours the elder brother, and tries to keep the second in the background. Once only, on occasion of some troubles in Wadi Dowāsir, he appointed Sa'ood leader of the armament about to be sent thither. But he soon repented him of having thus given him an opportunity for public display, when Sa'ood, after a brief but brilliant campaign, reappeared at Riaḍ accompanied by two hundred picked men, all richly dressed in handsome scarlet uniform, with gold broidery, silvered swords, costly housings, and "each man mounted on his capering beast," in a splendour unknown even to the days of the first 'Abd-Allah, and equally offensive to paternal bigotry and fraternal jealousy. Sa'ood was ordered back with speed to Salemee'yah, whence, however, we shall soon see him return, and I will then duly relate what passed on the meeting of the family trio—Sa'ood, 'Abd-Allah, and Feyṣul.

A third son, Moḥammed, offspring of a Nejdean dame, and much resembling his father and eldest brother in appearance, was now at the siege of 'Oneyzah, where we left him a few chapters back. The fourth and last, 'Abd-er-Raḥmān, is a heavy-looking boy, who as yet inhabits his father's harem. He appeared to me between ten and twelve years old: a Lavater would not gather from his features much promise for the future. I have mentioned the old maid, Feyṣul's only unmarried daughter and private secretary. She is, I trust, very beautiful, but I have never been blest with a peep behind the black veil wherein she sits muffled up, looking more like a heap of clothes than a king's daughter. And thus much for the royal family of Nejed.

But before we return to our narrative and relate what passed between us and them, it may not be amiss to take a brief view of the actual condition of this empire, whether considered within its own limits, or relatively to its neighbours, allies, or enemies.

And firstly, within the empire itself. It presents two elements, very diverse and often sharply opposed to each other: the first consists of the real staunch Wahhabees, men who, in the words of old Oliver, "bring a conscience to their work;" the second, of those who are only Wahhabees by subjection, and because they cannot help it. German idiom might class them into Wahhabees and "muss," or "*must-be*-Wahhabees."

The former class predominates in the six oft-named provinces, 'Aared, Woshem, Sedeyr, Aflāj, Dowāsir, and Yemāmah. Not that disaffected individuals are here wholly wanting, but they form a decided minority, composed chiefly of old chieftain families dispossessed by the present government, and of their immediate retainers. The rest of the inhabitants are all sincerely attached to the Sa'ood dynasty and system, though the reason and degree of their attachment are nowise the same. It is strongest in the 'Aared, where religious sympathy is reinforced by national bonds: the Sa'oods are natives of the land, and its long-honoured chieftains, so that the government is here eminently popular, or, to speak more exactly, upheld by the people. Besides, a restless and warlike disposition, joined to poverty at home, renders the character and consequences of the prevalent system especially well pleasing to the highlanders of 'Aareḍ. However, even here exists a reactionary party, men who would gladly see more tobacco and fewer prayers. Yet even these do not precisely desire a change of dynasty, though in case of Feyṣul's death they would prefer a Sa'ood to an 'Abd-Allah. But in general the partisans of the latter and of strict orthodoxy are at least seven to one throughout 'Aareḍ. In a political and moral point of view this province is, and always has been, of the highest importance.

In the Yemāmah popular feeling is not much dissimilar, though it assumes a somewhat mitigated form. Here too there prevails the deepest hereditary respect for the reigning family, though the well-wishers of Sa'ood outnumber those of 'Abd-Allah, wherein Yemāmah contrasts with 'Aareḍ. The personal presence of Sa'ood, and the less deep-grained dye of fanaticism in the southerly province explain this difference. Both 'Aareḍ and Yemāmah are meanwhile essentially Wahhabee.

In Ḥareeḳ, old discord, cruel wars, and unplea ing memories have left their traces, and there may be found many families discontented not only with Wahhabeeism in general, but with the family of Ebn-Sa'ood in particular. This was yet more the case a few years back; at the present day Sa'ood, by frequent visits to Ḥooṭah, and a peculiar courtesy to its citizens, seems to have won over the majority of hearts; and when the inevitable contest shall ensue between the two brothers, 'Abd-Allah can hardly reckon on a single sword or dagger in his behalf from Ḥareeḳ.

Aflāj, barren and savage, resembles 'Aareḍ in its inhabitants, unless that here religious motives form a stronger tie of attachment than political feeling.

This is above all the case in Wadi Dowāsir, where enthusiasm darkens into positive fanaticism of the worst kind, and where the love of plunder comes in to aid even more than in 'Aareḍ itself. The most contemned and the most contemptible among all the Arab race, if history, poetry, and satire (with my own personal experience to boot) hold true, the denizens of Wadi Dowāsir, or Âal-'Aamār, to give them their genuine name, perpetuated by the biting verses of Motenebbi, rank the highest in the Wahhabee and the lowest in the national scale. For ages nothing, they are now, to the misfortune of their neighbours, something by their incorporation with the great Wahhabee body; and no better exemplification of a certain vulgar proverb touching a beggar on horseback, and whither he will ride, can be found anywhere than among the Khodeyreeyah and Âal-'Aamār of Wadi Dowāsir. Needs not say that where pillage is to be had, their ragged troops can always be counted on, be it for Sa'ood or be it for 'Abd-Allah.

Woshem is a very different province. Here predominates the commercial, or at least the shopkeeper spirit, and "it is the cause, it is the cause, my soul," finds a fainter echo in Woshem hearts than anywhere else throughout Djebel Ṭoweyḳ. But their quiet, unmartial disposition hinders them from being otherwise than good subjects of a government on whose existence mainly depends their substantial profit, while it trebles and quadruples the caravans of pilgrims on the Mecca road, and fills the warehouses of the wayside towns and villages, especially Shaḳra', with whatever merchandise passes from the West to Nejed. In war this province supplies the commissariat rather than the ranks; however, its inhabitants are good Wahhabees, and if they furnish few "Zelators," produce also few malcontents.

Sedeyr is in extent the largest, and in reputation the highest of all these districts. Here Nejdean generosity, courage, perseverence, and long patience, are animated by somewhat of that enterprising spirit so distinctive of the Shomer population; and in physical qualities the men of Sedeyr have decidedly the advantage over all their neighbours. Here also are those old towns, almost the oldest on Arab records, old families, old and honourable memories. The Sedeyr is the nobleman of Nejed. The greater proportion of the inhabitants are genuine Wahhabees, and sincerely attached to the tenets of the sect, especially in the southern tracts of the mountain; in the northern districts, their intercourse with Koweyt, Zobeyr, and Djebel Shomer has somewhat unsettled their opinions. On the other hand, there is less political attachment to the Ebn-Sa'oods here than elsewhere in Nejed; many of the chiefs regret their former independence, and the people hanker after an indigenous government. It would require no very violent shock to detach them from the Riaḍ dynasty; but not so from Wahhabee doctrines.

The Bedouins of these six provinces are comparatively few in number, scattered up and down the immense plateau and its varied valleys. They are one and all sincere lovers of civil and religious anarchy, being easily gained and easily lost, in proportion to the strength or weakness of the governing hand; creatures of the day, and a ready tool for invasion or insurrection, disturbance and disorganisation, whoever be the bidder.

Thus much for Nejed proper, with Ḥareeḳ and Dowāsir. Next follow three great provinces, subject to Nejed for one only sufficient reason, that they cannot free themselves from her; I mean Ḥaṣa, Ḳaṭeef, and Ḳaseem.

Of the inhabitants of Ḳaseem we have already said enough to explain their tendencies, whether political or religious. The 'Oneyzah war may suffice for a sample. Gladly would they, and perhaps some day will, ally themselves to the first power, be it what it may, that shall show itself their protector, whether in the name of Ḥejāz or Cairo, Ottoman or Egyptian. The majority here are Mahometans, nowise Wahhabees; some, perhaps a fourth, have no settled religion either in theory or in practice.

Ḥaṣa and Ḳaṭeef remain to be more minutely described hereafter. It will then appear that their union with Nejed is even more unstable and compulsory than that of Ḳaseem. Farther on we shall see the influence also of Wahhabeeism and of Nejed on Baḥreyn, on the opposite Persian coast or Barr-Fāris, on Koweyt to the north, and on 'Omān to the South—an influence of fear not of love, with three local and limited exceptions; namely, Barr-Fāris a strip of Ḳaṭar, and the coast of the Djowāsimah.

'Aaseer is ever the constant ally, though not the tributary, of Nejed. I myself have not visited its mountainous district where it lies to the south of Mecca, not far from the shores of the Red Sea, as my readers know. But I have often heard it described by natives both before and during my journey in Inner Arabia. The fanaticism of its inhabitants seems at least equal to that of the Nejdeans, with whose doctrines and ways they are said to harmonize in every respect. In military qualities, what I have heard would lead me to suppose them less constant in war and less tenacious in purpose than the

Nejdeans—in a word, more nearly resembling the races of Ḥejāz, on whose boundaries they dwell. But at all events their number, and the geographical importance of their position, so close to Mecca, and exactly on the flank route of an Egyptian invasion, render them useful allies of a useless cause.

In order not to interrupt the subsequent continuity of our Riaḍ narrative, I will here insert a few words about a short excursion made by Barakāt and myself to the Aflāj. That province, which in most maps is, I know not why, thrown to a distance of two or three hundred miles from the 'Aareḍ, is in reality contiguous, and separates it from Wadi Dowāsir. It is, if I may be allowed the half-metaphor, a buttress standing out from the great wall of Ṭoweyḳ; its altitude is however lower than that of the principal chain; and behind it the whole land-level slopes gradually down—so said Arab travellers, and what I saw confirmed their report—to within three or four days' distance (sixty or seventy miles) from Ḳela'at Bisha'. Hence it again rises towards Djebel 'Aaseer. My companion and myself left Riaḍ during the second week of November by a south-western track, and crossing Wadi Ḥaneefah, reached the same evening the village of Ṣafra' on the frontiers of 'Aareḍ. Our guide was a native of Nejrān, by name Bedaa', or "Heresy," an unlucky denomination for a visitor to the most orthodox of lands; however, the person who bore it was a lively good-natured fellow, broad faced and broad shouldered, a travelling merchant by profession, and a great lover of diversion and pleasure. He had often drunk coffee and smoked pipes in our Ḳ'hāwah at Riaḍ; the present trip was his proposal; and medical practice furnished me as usual with a convenient pretext.

Once out of Wadi Ḥaneefah we found the southerly plateau more broken and uneven than the northern; in other points it resembles it, being of the same limestone or calcareous formation. The road, or rather track, mounted and descended amid whitish cliffs, where, however, occasional trees, Sidr or Markh, and herbage sufficient for tolerable sheep pasture, preserved the landscape from the reproach of barrenness. The course of the winter torrents lay for several miles towards Wadi Ḥaneefah, then changed to take a southerly direction.

At Ṣafra' we were well received in Nejdean fashion. The

smallness of the village, scarce sixty dwellings, gave a decent excuse for not overstaying next morning. Some of the houses were of palm branches and thatch, marks of a warm climate; the surrounding walls (I can hardly call them fortifications) were of unbaked brick, and ruinous. In compensation, the Mesjid, whither all repaired with edifying punctuality, was neat and new.

Next day we remounted our camels, and wound for several hours amid what an east-country Englishman might entitle "denes," with occasional sand valleys, and on a gradual but perceptible descent to the south-west. We were now in Aflāj; about noon we passed the large village of Meshallaḥ (literally, "the stripping-place"—an ominous sound for travellers; but shirts excepted, we had all three little fit for the purpose), and here we abode during the heat of noon in a small house, with whose tenants Bedaa' claimed a pedlar's acquaintance. The population appeared decidedly poor; the gardens and palm-groves, though extensive, were thinly set, and the wells far from copious. Cotton is more grown here than in 'Aareḍ, and fields of white millet replace the lentils abundant around Riaḍ. In dress and in other respects men and women resemble those of 'Aareḍ, save that here the shirt is shorter, and the heavy straight knife at the girdle or "Bereem" more common.

From Meshallaḥ to Kharfah the way lies mostly in a gorge of some depth; its stony bottom bears traces of a winter torrent, but at this time of year it was yet dry; on either side above are excellent pastures and flocks in plenty; below a few palm-groves with gardeners' huts beside; the district is but scantily peopled, especially when compared with Yemāmah or even Sedeyr. Night fell before we reached Kharfah, and we took our rest in the sandy palm-sprinkled plain beside the walls. The governor of the province, who resides here, is a native of 'Aareḍ, and a zealous Wahhabee. Bedaa' declined visiting him, nor did we think it advisable to present ourselves unintroduced. The town, for it may be so called, owns eight thousand citizens or rather more; water is here abundant, and the gardens better than elsewhere in Aflāj. The Khoḍeyreeyah, or mulattoes, almost equal in number the white population; like their negro relatives, they often repudiate the Arab shirt, content with a

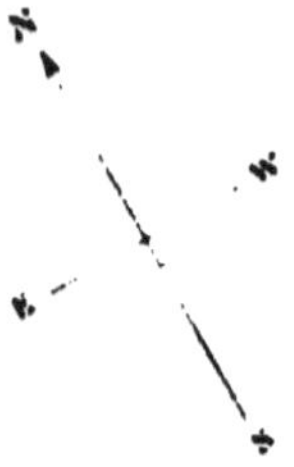

1. Court of the Harem
2. Feysul's private Divan
3. Apartments of the Harem
4. Inner Court for audience
5. K'hawah
6. Prisons
7. 7 Apartments of Mahbub
8. Apartments of Saood
9. 10 Court yard with small

[illegible] London

ragged cloth round the waist. Hospitality was meagre, and I observed a want of sociability and a coarseness of manners reminding of Wadi Dowāsir, whose first limits are in fact only fifteen or twenty miles hence to the south. We remained till the afternoon, and then returned homeward by the road we had come.

Of course conversation at Ṣafra', Meshallaḥ and Kharfah, turned principally on the 'Oneyzah war, whither a third of the male fighting population had already gone. But another, and to me a more interesting subject, was the country and the traffic between Aflāj and Yemen, a topic to which the presence of Bedaa' gave occasion. I collected the following data, and give them on hearsay, not doubting of their general correctness, nor yet vouching for their accuracy of detail.

They were: firstly, that in a moderate day's journey to the south of Kharfah, the Yemen-bound merchant or traveller enters on Wadi Dowāsir, described as a long, monotonous, and sandy valley, bordered on its northern side by Ṭoweyḳ (here sometimes called, after its central point, Djebel 'Aareḍ or Djebel Nejed; but neither name is geographically correct), and on the south by the Dahnā. The length of the Wadi is stated to be ten days' journey; say about two hundred miles. Villages, consisting mainly of palm-leaf huts, and of a straggling character, lie along the way; water is met with everywhere. I should think this district a kind of southerly Wadi Serḥān. On reaching the farther extremity of Wadi Dowāsir, the wayfarer enters the Ḳora, a large but thinly peopled district, half desert: it is placed behind the Ṭā'if and Djebel 'Aaseer. Its principal locality is Ḳela'at Bisha', about two days (or forty miles) distant from Wadi Dowāsir. Three more days of southerly road conduct through Wadi Seleyyel; I was unable to learn the name of its capital, if indeed it has one. Bedaa' spoke of it as a wretched district, full of sandhills, and with little water. Two more days give entrance to Wadi Nejrān; if Bedaa's account be true, the fertility of this district has the character rather of Yemen than of Nejed: well cultivated, well inhabited by a numerous and civilized population, with excellent dates and cornfields, a land of peace and plenty. Here passes the main road of Ṣanaa', on whose Emeer Wadi Nejrān depends.

The inhabitants of Wadi Nejrān call themselves Shiya'ees; by the Nejdeans they are stigmatized with the comprehensive denomination of "Keffar" or infidels. Bedaa', once out of Wahhabee hearing, made no secret of his own sect and that of his countrymen. Like the natives of Ḥaṣa and 'Omān, they belong to the great Carmathian school, akin to the Persian, and subdivided into Biaḍeeyah, Druses, Ismaileeyah, and many more. No other Carmathian colony exists to my knowledge in Western Arabia. Wadi Nejrān is the only abiding memorial of the outbreak in the third century of Islam. The route by Wadi Dowāsir and Seley'yol is much frequented by the merchants of Yemen on their way to Nejed; it is tolerably direct, and avoids the mountain passes and intolerance of Djebel 'Aaseer.

For the well-known route leading through Wadi Ḥaneefah to the north of Aflāj, and passing through Shaḳra', and thence south of Ṭoweyḳ to Mecca, I heard its marches and halts repeatedly detailed by the many who had travelled it in either direction. Their account corresponded very exactly with what appears in the German map published in Gotha, 1835, after the researches of Niebuhr, Ehrenberg, and Rüppell. This is the high road of Central Arabia. At Shaḳra' goes off a cross-cut to 'Oneyzah and Ḳaseem.

From Riaḍ north there is only one ordinary track, the same by which we ourselves arrived; but at Zulphah it undergoes a triple division, leading to Ḳaseem on the west, to Djebel Shomer on the north-west, and to Zobeyr on the north-east. Eastward from Riaḍ there is only one frequented road from the centre to the circumference; we shall soon follow it. Hence it appears that Nejed proper has four lines of communication with the outlands and coast, corresponding in some degree with the four points of the compass, and having all at some part of their course to traverse a strip of desert, though the two which lie south-west and west have less sand to encounter than the others. The path we had trod in coming hither was precisely the longest, the most difficult, and the least frequented, and for these very reasons the safest and best for us.

To the south of Wadi Dowāsir and to the east of Nejrān lies the Great Desert. It extends also from beyond the last lines of Yemāmah and Ḥareeḳ, untracked and untrodden, an impassable barrier, to which much said regarding the ocean in the concluding stanzas of Childe Harold may be suitably applied. But more of it when we visit it.

To sum up, we may say that the Wahhabee empire is a compact and well organised government, where centralization is fully understood and effectually carried out, and whose mainsprings and connecting-links are force and fanaticism. There exist no constitutional checks either on the king or on his subordinates, save what the necessity of circumstance imposes or the Coran prescribes. Its atmosphere, to speak metaphorically, is sheer despotism, moral, intellectual, religious, and physical. This empire is capable of frontier extension, and hence is dangerous to its neighbours, some of whom it is even now swallowing up, and will certainly swallow more, if not otherwise prevented. Incapable of true internal progress, hostile to commerce, unfavourable to arts and even to agriculture, and in the highest degree intolerant and aggressive, it can neither better itself nor benefit others; while the order and calm which it sometimes spreads over the lands of its conquest, are described in the oft-cited *Ubi solitudinem faciunt pacem appellant* of the Roman annalist. We may add that its weakest point lies in family rivalries and feuds of succession, which, joined to the anti-Wahhabee reaction existing far and wide throughout Arabia, may one day much disintegrate and shatter the Nejdean empire, yet not destroy it altogether. Ibraheem Basha alone saw the true means of delivering Arabia and her neighbours from this upas of tyrannic fanaticism, and began the work which the caprice and folly of his successors left incomplete or thwarted. But so long as Wahhabeeism shall prevail in the centre and uplands of Arabia, small indeed are the hopes of civilization, advancement, and national prosperity for the Arab race.

In conclusion, I here subjoin a numerical list, taken partly from the government registers of Riad, partly from local information, and containing the provinces, the number of the principal towns or villages, the population, and the military contingent, throughout the Wahhabee empire. A second list supplies something analogous for the Bedouins existing within its territory.

Provinces	Towns or villages	Population	Military muster
I 'Aared	16	110,000	6,000
II Yemâmah	32	140,000	4,500
III Hareek	16	45,000	3,000
IV Aflâj	12	14,000	1,200
V Wadi Dowâsir	50	100,000	4,000
VI Seley'yel	14	30,000	1,400
VII Woshem	20	80,000	4,000
VIII Sedeyr	25	140,000	5,200
IX Kaseem	60	300,000	11,000
X Hasa	50	160,000	7,000
XI Kateef	22	100,000	—
	316	1,219,000	47,300

Two remarks are here necessary. Firstly, we may notice an occasional disproportion between the number of the inhabitants and that of the villages. This is caused by the varying size and importance of the latter, according to the political and other conditions of the respective provinces. Thus, for example, in Wadi Dowâsir, where no considerable town exists, and the ordinary centres of population are mere hamlets, their number almost equals that assigned to Kaseem, where however the existence of large towns, like 'Oneyzah, Bereydah, Henâkeeyah, Rass, and so forth, together with the general fertility of the country, raises the total of the inhabitants to the triple of what Wadi Dowâsir supplies.

Secondly, the military quota is subject to no less striking inequalities. This again depends in great measure on the character of the districts on the list. Thus Kateef, though thickly peopled, furnishes absolutely nothing to the army, for reasons which will afterwards be explained; while 'Aared, with a scarce higher cipher for its inhabitants, fills the ranks of the Nejdean combatants. Most of these anomalies find their solution in what we have already said in the detail of our journey.

I will now sum up the Bedouin population, a much diminished element of Central Arabia.

Tribes	Population
I Ajmân	6,000
II Benoo-Hâjar	4,500
III Benoo-Khâlid	3,000
IV Meteyr	6,000
V 'Oteybah	12,000
VI Dowâsir	5,000

Tribes	Population
VII Sebaa'	3,000
VIII Kahtân	6,000
IX Harb	14,000
X 'Anezah	3,000
XI Aâl-Morrah	4,000
Scattered Families	10,000
Total	76,500

The military force of a Bedouin tribe is reckoned at about one-tenth of its entire sum. This calculation gives us 8,000 for the utmost number of nomade warriors under the white and green banner of Ebn-Sa'ood.

I would here recall to my readers' memory, though explained before, that the Benoo-Khâlid of this catalogue are identical in origin with the homonymous tribe in Syria: that the 'Anezah and Sebaa', on the contrary, are not; that Kahtân and 'Aâl-Morrah are clans much more numerous in reality than they stand here, where only those among them who depend more or less on the beck of the Wahhabee are noticed; lastly, that Ajmân, Benoo-Hâjar, and Benoo-Khâlid, are those among whom the sword of 'Abd-Allah has made most havoc.

Thirdly, I subjoin the amount of annual tribute furnished by the several provinces to the treasury of Riad, exclusive of extraordinary contributions. The estimation is given after the lists in Djowhar's charge, and set down in rials or Spanish dollars, which are employed here, and not unfrequently elsewhere in the East, for a standard of monetary summation; they may, in the Nejdean exchange-market, be roughly reckoned equivalent to about five shillings and sixpence of our own money.

Provinces	Tribute
I 'Aared	5,000 Rials
II Yemâmah	6,000
III Hareek	10,000
IV Aflâj	2,000
V Wadi Dowâsir	4,000
VI Seley'yel	3,000
VII Woshem	6,000
VIII Sedeyr	7,000
IX Kaseem	120,000
X Hasa	150,000
XI Kateef	50,000
Total	363,000
	= about 100,000*l.* sterling

To this must be added: firstly, an annual tribute or black-mail of 8,000 rials, or about 2,200*l.* exacted from Baḥreyn. Secondly, a similar contribution levied on the western provinces of 'Omān, and amounting to 20,000 rials = 5,500*l.* sterling. These when added to the former sum, give a total 391,000 rials = 107,000*l.* sterling.

Extraordinary contributions, fines, presents, spoils of war, and the like, are calculated at an almost equal income; nor would the entire revenue of the year be overrated at 160,000*l.* sterling, or even more. And since there is no standing army, no fleet (except two or three miserable vessels at Ḳaṭeef), and no court retinue of any consequence, to be kept up in Nejed, we may conclude that the Wahhabee government is not much exposed to the danger of incurring a national debt, and that it may even be held wealthy for the country and circumstances.

I will now add by way of appendix an approximative estimate of the like elements in the kingdom of Ṭelāl-ebn-Rasheed. This I might have given before; but I prefer putting the two states side by side; that my readers may have better occasion for remarking several important diversities in population and other respects between the territories of Nejed and Djebel Shomer:—

	Provinces	Towns or villages	Population	Military muster
I	Djebel Shomer	40	162,000	6,000
II	Djowf	12	40,000	2,500
III	Kheybar	8	25,000	2,000
IV	Upper Kaseem	20	35,000	2,500
V	Teyma'	6	12,000	1,000
	Total	86	274,000	14,000

Follow the Bedouin tribes subject to Ṭelāl:—

	Tribes	Total
I	Shomer	80,000
II	Sherarat	40,000
III	Ḥoweytat	20,000
IV	Benoo-'Āteeyah	6,000
V	Ma'āz	4,000
VI	Ṭā'i	8,000
VII	Waḥhidee'yah	8,000
	Total	166,000

Military muster, about 16,000.

Total of population, 430,000; of military force, 30,000.

My readers will not fail to notice the far greater proportion of nomades in the north. Of Ṭelāl's revenues I was unable to obtain any exact statement; but, judging by the state and character of agriculture and commerce in his dominions, I should estimate them at about one fourth of what Feysul receives yearly.

CHAPTER XII

Court of Riaḍ—Journey to Hofhoof

Let me have
A dram of poison, such soon-spreading gear
As will disperse itself through all the veins,
And that the trunk may be discharged of breath
As suddenly as hasty powder fired
Doth hurry from the fatal cannon's womb.—*Shakespeare*.

FIRST ACQUAINTANCE WITH 'ABD-ALLAH—HIS FAVOUR—CHARACTER OF THIS PRINCE—A VISIT TO THE ROYAL STABLES—THE NEJDEE HORSE—DETAILS ON THE BREED—THE PRIME MINISTER MAḤBOOB—HIS HISTORY, CHARACTER, AND CONDUCT—EGYPT AND NEJED—RECEPTION OF THE PERSIAN NĀ'IB AT COURT—HIS ANNOYANCE—A MORNING VISIT FROM THE ZELATORS—RESULT—MANŒUVRES OF THE NĀ'IB WITH THE RIAḌ GOVERNMENT—CONCLUSION OF THE NEGOTIATION—PREPARATIONS AGAINST 'ONEYZAH—OFFICIAL CORRESPONDENCE—ARRIVAL OF SA'OOD WITH THE SOUTHERN CONTINGENT—THEIR RECEPTION AT RIAḌ—QUARRELS OF SA'OOD AND 'ABD-ALLAH—INTERVIEW WITH SA'OOD—HIS CHARACTER—RELATIVE POSITION OF THE TWO BROTHERS—'ABD-ALLAH BECOMES COLD AND SUSPICIOUS—PROPOSAL OF A RIAḌ ESTABLISHMENT—HOW EVADED—THE STRYCHNINE CURE—DEMAND MADE BY 'ABD-ALLAH—OUR REFUSAL—A NIGHT-SCENE AT THE PALACE—CRITICAL POSITION—A LULL—ESCAPE FROM RIAḌ—FAREWELL TO THE CAPITAL—THREE DAYS IN WADI SOLEY'—JOURNEY WITH ABOO-'EYSA AND EL-GHANNĀM—UPLANDS OF EASTERN ṬOWEYḲ—LAḲEY'TĀT—LAST RANGE OF ṬOWEYḲ—LANDSCAPE—WELLS OF OWEYSIṬ—THE DAHNĀ, OR GREAT DESERT—A DANGEROUS MOMENT—NEJMAT ABOO-'EYSA—THE AÂL-MORRAH—SEPARATION OF ABOO-'EYSA FROM EL-GHANNĀM—DESERT ROUTE—WADI FAROOḲ—THE HEIGHTS OF GHĀR AND GHOWEYR—DESCENT TO THE COAST-LEVEL—LOCUSTS—NIGHT ARRIVAL AT HOFHOOF.

The first storm had blown over, and all seemed to promise us a quiet and secure residence in the capital, so long as we should choose to abide there. Djowhar had won us a fair outset reputation, and every day brought new consultations and acquaintances, most of a favourable character. Feysul, whose apprehensions were now somewhat calmed, had returned to his palace, and after some delay mustered up courage enough to accord the Nā'ib a private audience in the inner divan. Moḥammed-'Alee was not however over-pleased with his reception, and could not understand the coolness with which the "Bedouin" (the only title avouched by the Shirāzee to the Nejdean monarch) received his long list of grievances; nor did Maḥboob display much zeal in the furtherance of his cause. We, for our part, had agreed with Aboo-'Eysa not to request any special interview with Feyṣul; the old man was a mere tool in the hands of his ministers and of the "Zelator" faction; and while no useful result could be expected from our presence in his divan, it might on the other hand give rise to jealous suspicions and to idle conjecture.

But 'Abd-Allah, exempt from the senile fears which agitated his father's breast, was not disposed to let us remain long without the favour of his personal acquaintance. We had, as my readers are aware, already opened and perused 'Obeyd's letter to this prince, nor had it much increased our desire of intimacy with either correspondent. Besides, whatever fame and hearsay had thus far given us to know regarding the personal character and dispositions of the heir-apparent, was no loadstone to draw us to his embrace. 'Abd-Allah, in quality of administrator, gave public audiences twice a day; nor was he said to be of difficult access even in the interior of his palace. But we studiously avoided that part of the adjoining street where an assembled crowd announced the prince's visibility, and contented ourselves with a distant perspective of his attendants and person.

However, many days had not gone by, when we received a message requesting our appearance before him. The bearer of his highness's invitation was also by name 'Abd-Allah, a Nejdean of the Nejdeans, belonging to the sourest and the most bigoted class; lean limbed, sallow featured, and wrinkled; intelligent indeed and active, but by no means an agreeable companion. This worthy informed us that the health of his uncle (polite style for 'Abd-Allah), was something deranged, and that he in consequence desired a doctor's visit. He concluded by recommending us not to delay compliance with the royal wish.

We put on clean over-dresses and went to 'Abd-Allah's palace. There we had to pass two outer courts before we reached a vestibule, just at the other end of which was the prince's private Ḳ'hāwah. He had also another one, but public; this was situated in the second court; it was of large dimensions, and full twice the size of Feyṣul's guest-chamber. The private apartment was, on the contrary, small, and capable of containing from twenty to twenty-five individuals only; well furnished, but not equally well lighted. The morning was far advanced, and the heat within doors oppressive. 'Abd-Allah had taken his seat on a carpet spread in the vestibule, with three or four attendants at his side. Many others, some white, some black, plainly dressed, but all armed, stood or sat by the portal, and in the outer courts; an ungenial-looking set they were, especially the true-born Nejdeans.

Were it not for a haughty, almost an insolent, expression on his features, and a marked tendency to corpulency—an hereditary defect, it would seem, in some branches of the family—'Abd-Allah would not be an ill-looking man. As he is, he resembles in a degree certain portraits of Henry VIII., nor are the two characters wholly dissimilar. On our approach, he mustered up a sort of rough politeness, and gave us a tolerably encouraging reception, though I soon found that the story of his bodily indisposition was a mere pretext for gratifying his curiosity. Of course no mention of 'Obeyd or his letter crossed our lips. 'Abd-Allah made some general enquiries about Djebel Shomer, for he had been already informed of our visit there, manifested much ill-will against Ṭelāl, railed at the defenders of 'Oneyzah, and cursed Zāmil. Then began a series of unscientific medical queries about temperaments—bilious, lymphatic, sanguine, and the like. He was particularly anxious to know what his own temperament might be, and I rose considerably in his estimation by assuring him it was a happy combination of all four. He next made us repeated assurances of protection and good will, nor do I believe that they were for the moment hypocritical, since he had not yet any particular suspicions on our score. Lastly, he ordered rather than requested our attendance at an early hour next morning, and wished us to bring our medical books along with us, professing himself very desirous to learn the healing art: "a promising pupil," thought I, and so doubtless will my readers.

He was, however, in earnest, and when next day we were introduced into the little or private Ḳ'hāwah, and honourably treated with coffee and perfumes, he kept us for a full hour reading and being read to, partly from my own Boulac-printed volume, and partly from a dateless manuscript belonging to his highness's library, wherein therapeutic traditions of the Prophet (proving him, alas! to have been a very poor medical authority), old definitions and receipts stolen from second-hand translations of Galen, and spoilt by the way, were jumbled together, with Persian names of plants and botany of Upper Egyptian idiom, till "a Daniel, yea, a Daniel," would have been puzzled to find out the interpretation thereof. Of course we treated the work with great deference, and tried to engraft on it somehow or other more authentic explanations; with what success I hardly know. But at any rate we succeeded in securing a large share of the royal confidence, and now, when we passed by the palace attendants, if white they smiled on us, if black grinned, till we felt quite at home.

For about three weeks matters continued on this amiable footing. Almost every day came a general or a special invitation to visit the prince, and pass two or three hours of the forenoon or night amid the atmosphere of royalty. Nor was his highness at all reserved. He talked politics, and with all the insolence of ignorance would scoff at those very powers which had only a few years before annihilated the empire of his ancestors, beheaded one of his predecessors, driven another to years of exile, and shut up his own father in long captivity. However, Constantinople and Cairo were nothing in 'Abd-Allah's sight, and when on one occasion I asked him casually if he had been to Mecca, "I will go there," answered he, "but on horseback;" with an implied meaning that we may perhaps see realised in our own day. Then followed the wildest plans for storming 'Oneyzah, how the walls were to be breached by cannon, or might better still, seeing that they are of unbaked brick, be melted down by a gigantic water-engine; how he would cut off Zāmil's head, &c. A series of successes over marauding Bedouins and unwarlike neighbours, had led the prince to believe the Nejdeans the first army, and himself the first general, on earth. Yet take it all in all, it was not mere brag, for within the limits of the Peninsula 'Abd-Allah stands a fair chance of overriding be it who it may; and Egypt has not every century an Ibraheem Basha to command her armies.

During this time I got a sight of the royal stables, an event much desired and eagerly welcomed. For the Nejdean horse is considered no less superior to all others of his kind in Arabia, than is the Arabian breed collectively to the Persian, Cape of Good Hope, or Indian. In Nejed is the true birthplace of the Arab steed, the primal type, the authentic model. Thus at any rate I heard, and thus, so far at least as my experience goes, it appears to me; although I am aware that distinguished authorities maintain another view. But at any rate, among all the studs of Nejed, Feysul's was indisputably the first; and who sees that has seen the most consummate specimens of equine perfection in Arabia, perhaps in the world.

It happened that a mare in the imperial stud had received a bite close behind the shoulder from some sportive comrade; and the wound, ill-dressed and ill-managed, had festered into a sore puzzling the most practised Nejdean farriers. One morning while Barakāt and myself were sitting in 'Abd-Allah's Ḳ'hāwah, a groom entered to give the prince the daily bulletin of his stables. 'Abd-Allah turned towards me, and enquired whether I would undertake the cure. Gladly I accepted the proposal of visiting the patient, though limiting my proffer of services to a simple inspection, and declining systematic interference with what properly belonged to the veterinary province. The prince gave his orders accordingly; and in the afternoon a groom, good-natured as grooms generally are, knocked at our door, and conducted me straight to the stables.

These are situated some way out of the town, to the north-east, a little to the left of the road which we had followed at our first arrival, and not far from the gardens of 'Abd-er-Raḥmān the Wahhabee. They cover a large square space, abut 150 yards each way, and are open in the centre, with a long shed running round the inner walls; under this covering the horses, about three hundred in number when I saw them, are picketed during night; in the daytime they may stretch their legs at pleasure within the central courtyard. The greater number were accordingly loose; a few, however, were tied up at their stalls;

some, but not many, had horse-cloths over them. The heavy dews which fall in Wadi Ḥaneefah do not permit their remaining with impunity in the open night air; I was told also that a northerly wind will occasionally injure the animals here, no less than the land wind does now and then their brethren in India. About half the royal stud was present before me, the rest were out at grass; Feyṣul's entire muster is reckoned at six hundred head, or rather more.

No Arab dreams of tying up a horse by the neck; a tether replaces the halter; and one of the animal's hind-legs is encircled about the pastern by a light iron ring, furnished with a padlock, and connected with an iron chain of two feet or thereabouts in length, ending in a rope, which is fastened to the ground at some distance by an iron peg; such is the customary method. But should the animal be restless and troublesome, a fore-leg is put under similar restraint. It is well known that in Arabia horses are much less frequently vicious or refractory than in Europe, and this is the reason why geldings are here so rare, though not unknown. No particular prejudice that I could discover exists against the operation itself; only it is seldom performed, because not otherwise necessary, and tending of course to diminish the value of the animal.

But to return to the horses now before us; never had I seen or imagined so lovely a collection. Their stature was indeed somewhat low; I do not think that any came fully up to fifteen hands; fourteen appeared to me about their average; but they were so exquisitely well shaped that want of greater size seemed hardly, if at all, a defect. Remarkably full in the haunches, with a shoulder of a slope so elegant as to make one, in the words of an Arab poet, "go raving mad about it;" a little, a very little, saddle-backed, just the curve which indicates springiness without any weakness; a head broad above, and tapering down to a nose fine enough to verify the phrase of "drinking from a pint-pot," did pint-pots exist in Nejed; a most intelligent and yet a singularly gentle look, full eye, sharp thorn-like little ear, legs fore and hind that seemed as if made of hammered iron, so clean and yet so well twisted with sinew; a neat round hoof, just the requisite for hard ground; the tail set on or rather thrown out at a perfect arch; coats smooth, shining, and light; the mane long, but not overgrown nor heavy; and an air and step that seemed to say "look at me, am I not pretty?" their appearance justified all reputation, all value, all poetry. The prevailing colour was chestnut or grey; a light bay, an iron colour, white, or black, were less common; full bay, flea-bitten, or piebald, none. But if asked what are, after all, the specially distinctive points of the Nejdee horse, I should reply, the slope of the shoulder, the extreme cleanness of the shank, and the full rounded haunch, though every other part too has a perfection and a harmony unwitnessed (at least by my eyes) anywhere else.

Unnecessary to say that I had often met with and after a fashion studied horses throughout this journey; but I purposely deferred saying much about them till this occasion. At Ḥā'yel and in Djebel Shomer I found very good examples of what is commonly called the Arab horse: a fine breed, and from among which purchases are made every now and then by European princes, peers, and commoners, often at astounding prices. These are for the most part the produce of a mare from Djebel Shomer or its neighbourhood, and a Nejdean stallion, sometimes the reverse; but never, it would seem (although here I am, of course, open to correction by the "logic of facts"), thorough Nejdee on both sides. With all their excellences, these horses are less systematically elegant, nor do I remember having ever seen one among them free from some one weak point; perhaps a little heaviness in the shoulder, perhaps a slight falling off in the rump, perhaps a shelly or a contracted hoof, or too small an eye. Their height also is much more varied; some of them attain sixteen hands, others are down to fourteen. Every one knows the customary divisions of their pedigrees: Manaḳee, Siḳlawee, Ḥamdanee, Ṭoreyfee, and so forth; I myself made a list of these names during a residence some years previous among the Sebaa' and Ru'ala Bedouins, nor did I find any difference worth noting between what was then told me and the accounts usually given by travellers and authors on this topic. Nor did the Bedouins fail to recite their oft-repeated legends about Solomon's stables, &c. But I am inclined to consider the greater part of these very pedigrees, and still more the antiquity of their origin, as comparatively recent inventions, and of small credit, got up for the market of Bedouins or townsmen. Nor is a Koḥlanee mare by any means a warrant for a Koḥlanee stallion; crossing the breed is an everyday occurrence, even in Shomer. Once arrived at this last district, I heard no more of Siḳlawee, Delhamee, or any other like genealogies; nor were Solomon's stables better known to fame than those of Augeus. In Nejed I was distinctly assured that no prolonged lists of pedigrees were ever kept, and that all enquiries about race are limited to the assurance of a good father and a good mother; for Solomon, added the groom, he was much more likely to have taken horses from us than we from him; a remark which proved in him who made it a certain amount of historical criticism. In a word, to be a successful jockey in Nejed requires about the same degree of investigation and knowledge that it would in Yorkshire, and no more; perhaps even less, considering the stud-books.

The genuine Nejdean breed, so far as I have hitherto found, is to be met with only in Nejed itself; nor are these animals common even there; none but chiefs or individuals of considerable wealth and rank possess them. Nor are they ever sold, at least so all declare; and when I asked how then one could be acquired, "by war, by legacy, or by free gift," was the answer. In this last manner alone is there a possibility of an isolated specimen leaving Nejed, but even that is seldom; and when policy requires a present to Egypt, Persia, or Constantinople (a circumstance of which I witnessed two instances and heard of others), mares are never sent, and the poorest stallions, though deserving to pass elsewhere for real beauties, are picked out for the purpose.

'Abd-Allah, Sa'ood, and Moḥammed keep their horses in separate stables, each one containing a hundred or thereabouts. After much enquiry and remark, my companion and I came to the conclusion that the total Nejdean horse-census would not sum up above five thousand, and probably falls short even of that number. The fact that here the number of horsemen in an army is perfectly inconsiderable when compared to that of the camel riders, may be added in confirmation, especially since in Nejed horses are never used except for war or parade, while all travel work and other drudgery falls on camels, sometimes on asses.

Pretty stories have been circulated about the familiarity existing between Arabs, Bedouins in particular, and their steeds; how the foal at its birth is caught in the hands of bystanders, not allowed to fall on the ground, how it plays with the children of the house, eats and drinks with its master, how he tends it when indisposed, whilst it no doubt returns him a similar service when occasion requires. That the Arab horse is much gentler, and in a general way more intelligent than the close-stabled, blinkered, harnessed, condemned-cell-prisoner animal of "merry England," I willingly admit; matters, alas! cannot be otherwise. Brought up in close contact with men, and enjoying the comparatively free use of his senses and limbs, the Arab quadruped is in a fair way for developing to full advantage whatever feeling and instinct good blood brings with it, nor does this often fail to occur. If, however, we come to the particular incidents of Arab horse-life just alluded to, they certainly form no general rule or etiquette in practice, nor would any Arab be the worse thought of for rapping his mare over the nose if she thrust it into his porridge, or for leaving nature to do the office of midwife when she is in an interesting condition. Still I do not mean to say that the creditable anecdotes immortalised in so many books may not perhaps take place here and there, but, to quote an Arab poet, "I never saw the like nor ever heard." For my own personal experience, it goes no farther than feeding Arab horses out of my hand, not dish, and prevailing on them, better than the spirits of the vasty deep, to come when I did call for them; the rest I cannot help classing, though reluctantly, with many other tales of the Desert.

After a delightful hour passed in walking up and down among these beautiful creatures, attended by grooms professionally sensible to all the excellences of horseflesh, I examined the iron-grey mare in question, saw another whose appetite was ailing, prescribed a treatment which if it did no good could certainly do no harm, and left with longing lingering look behind, the stables, whither however I subsequently paid not unfrequent visits, befitting to a doctor.

Farther on, when we cross the eastern and southern limits of Ṭoweyḳ, we find the Arab breed rapidly losing in beauty and perfection, in size and strength. The specimens of indigenous race that I saw in 'Omān considerably resembled the "tattoes" of India; but in the eastern angle of Arabia the deficiency of horses is in a way made up for by the dromedaries of that land.

Nejdee horses are especially esteemed for great speed and endurance of fatigue; indeed, in this latter quality none come up to them. To pass twenty-four hours on the road without drink and without flagging is certainly something; but to keep up the same abstinence and labour conjoined under the burning Arabian sky for forty-eight hours at a stretch is, I believe, peculiar to the animals of the breed. Besides they have a delicacy, I cannot say of mouth, for it is common to ride them wthout bit or bridle, but of feeling and obedience to the knee and thigh, to the slightest check of the halter and the voice of the rider, far surpassing whatever the most elaborate manège gives a European horse, though furnished with snaffle, curb, and all. I often mounted them at the invitation of their owners, and without saddle, rein, or stirrup set them off at full gallop, wheeled them round, brought them up in mid career at a dead halt, and that without the least difficulty or the smallest want of correspondence between the horse's movements and my own will; the rider on their back really feels himself the man-half of a centaur, not a distinct being. This is in great part owing to the Arab system of breaking in, much preferable to the European in conferring pliancy and perfect tractability. Nor is mere speed much valued in a horse unless it be united with the above qualities, since whether in the contest of an Arab race, or in the pursuit and flight of war, "doubling" is much more the rule than "going ahead," at least for any distance. Much the same training is required for the sport of the Djereed, that tournament of the East, and which, as I witnessed it in Nejed, differed in nothing from the exhibitions frequent in Syria and Egypt, except that the palm-stick or "Djereed" itself is a little lighter. I should add that in the stony plateaus of Nejed, horses are always shod, but the shoe is clumsy and heavy; the hoof is very slightly pared, and the number of nails put in invariably six. Were not the horn excellent, Nejdean farriery would lame many a fine horse.

I quit the subject with regret; yet enough for my present

limits of what Cowper calls on some occasion, and in comparison with its biped master, "the nobler beast." Noble, not nobler; in this the poet erred; for bad as man may sometimes be, and low as he may sink, he has always in him human good, much to love, something even to respect. The Wahhabees are in no way a model people, still less their court a model court; yet man remains ever God's likeness, though occasionally but the ground-plan, physical be it or moral.

While we advanced in 'Abd-Allah's good graces, and prescribed now for his four-legged and now for his two-legged servants, Maḥbooh, moved by the encomiums of his father, Djowhar, condescended to pay us a visit, which prudence had prevented us from the courtesy of anticipating. Prime minister Maḥboob, and what a prime minister! Luckily for me, Aboo-'Eysa had so often given me his excellency's portrait, that I did not mistake him at his first entrance, but my companion Barakāt did, and could hardly believe when told that the individual before him was the main column of Nejed and of the whole Wahhabee empire.

Born of a Georgian slave-woman, herself a present from 'Abbas Basha to Feyṣul at his first accession, Maḥboob, now about twenty-five years of age, presented so very boyish, so un-Nejdean, so un-Arab an appearance, that I was utterly startled. His father is Djowhar, our black patient—I mean his legal father; for so white a complexion, such smooth streaky hair, such blue eyes, such symmetrically proportioned limbs, never owned a black for physical parent, unless indeed my study and my books be false, and my observation too. The fact is, that while the official tongue, with a prudence which I shall imitate throughout my narrative, designates Djowhar as father of the prime minister, no one high or low entertains a doubt of Feyṣul's own better right to that endearing title. Needs not enter into the details of court mysteries or scandal, if scandal can find place in Nejed; my readers may take it on my word that so sure as the Georgian woman is Maḥboob's mother, so sure Feyṣul, her first master and possessor, is Maḥboob's father.

The youth is clever, of that there could be no doubt; that he is daring is equally certain. A taste for general literature, and a spirit of research indicative of Caucasian origin, may also be remarked in him. But vanity, imprudence, overbearing pride, despotic cruelty, and a levity of manner strangely contrasting with the gravity customary at Riaḍ, are equally the share of Maḥboob, nor any wonder, considering his origin and palace education. These faults are however in a measure veiled, nay, rendered almost becoming, by a manly independence of thought and manner, an outspoken tone, and a hearty cheerfulness at times, not generally found in the Nejdeans round him; qualities certainly due to his mother rather than to his father, whoever that may be. Last, not least perhaps, he is remarkably handsome, almost beautiful, a thorough Georgian; in a word, Byron's Arnold in the strange dream of the "Deformed Transformed," came often in my mind while conversing with the graceful but bloodstained Maḥboob. Thus endowed in mind and body, this half-caste Caucasian stripling, at an age when well-born Englishmen are being plucked in the Schools, or serving as cornets or midshipmen, leads by the nose the old tyrant of Nejed, browbeats his terrible son, commands the servility of courtiers, chiefs, and Zelators, and wields almost alone the destinies of more than half the Arabian Peninsula.

Maḥboob's first visit to us was very characteristic. Little ceremony, much familiarity, a second question asked before the first was answered, everything rapidly examined—books, drugs, dress, and all; a cup of coffee hastily swallowed, a word of encouragement and patronage, a very European shake of the hand, and then farewell till next meeting.

Aboo-'Eysa, whose main prop at court was no other than Maḥboob, and whose lot was now in a way bound up with our own, was extremely anxious that this first interview should be followed up by a closer intimacy, nor was I at all reluctant to study more at leisure so exceptional and at the same time so important a personage. To this end I returned the call next day, in company with Aboo-'Eysa.

Maḥboob was seated in Djowhar's divan. To Aboo-'Eysa he showed all the familiarity of an old patron, and extended much of the same hand-in-hand manner to myself. But this time he pushed his interrogations farther than before, and I discovered that the minister did me the honour of supposing me of similar origin with himself, namely, an Egyptian by country, and born of a Georgian or Circassian. Such a supposition had in Riaḍ a very peculiar bearing, and influenced not a little the events which followed.

Egypt had been for Nejed by times a friend and an enemy; feared when the latter, suspected, not without cause, when the former. At the present moment suspicion predominates over fear, yet both exist. From Persia Nejed has little to dread, the armies of the Shah would hardly cross the Gulf, nor need she apprehend direct attack or invasion from Constantinople itself. Turkish troops would find an effectual barrier in the intervening sands; and should they attempt it, few would probably reach Djebel Ṭoweyḳ. For more distant nations, one only excepted, their very names are shrouded in misty indistinctness, and frequent experience, if not their own, at least that of their neighbours, has taught Nejdeans that an occasional thunder-growl from the West is seldom if ever followed by a serious storm. Alone the Persian Gulf, opening a way on the Indian Sea, and thus bringing the coast-line of the Wahhabee territory somewhat too near that great empire on which the sun never sets, causes a certain and a justifiable anxiety to Feyṣul, from those who at first the merchants, have at last become the conquerors and the rulers of India. But a nearer and continual cause of fear is in Egypt: "what man has done man can do;" the banner of St. George might indeed possibly wave on the coast, but the victorious standards of Egypt have already fluttered in the gales of Wadi Ḥaneefah. Hence an Egyptian, be he physician, pilgrim, or merchant, is looked on at Riaḍ with some respect and with more suspicion, one not to be either trifled with or trusted, a dangerous and unwelcome guest, yet of whom one may not lightly get rid in the off-hand way sometimes adopted for others.

Maḥboob was inwardly convinced that we were in reality more or less spies, sent by the Egyptian government, probably with reference to the Ḳaseem war and the siege of 'Oneyzah. This was no bad conjecture; the route we had traversed, the books in our possession, the very fact of (comparatively) superior medical knowledge, my own pronunciation, all tended to justify this idea. Not that Maḥboob said it in so many words, but it was easy to perceive the drift of his thought, the more so from his careless and desultory manner. Meanwhile Moḥammed, 'Abd-el-Laṭeef's younger brother, had got up an enormous lie of his having personally known me while in Egypt, of all my past history and present intentions; a series of fictions readily contradicted, but not to be with equal readiness effaced.

After this first meeting in Djowhar's K'hāwah, Maḥboob opened to me his own, and there I often passed several hours of the succeeding days. His library was the most copious that I had yet seen in Arabia; it consisted of the works of many well-known poets, among whom were Ebn-el-'Āṭiheeyah, Motenebbi, Aboo-l-'Ola, besides the Divan of Ḥariri, the Ḥamāsa, and other works of classic Arab literature; along with these, treatises on law and religion by Mālekee and Ḥanbelee authors, commentaries on the Coran, books of travels, touching whose authenticity least said were soonest mended; geographical treatises, dividing the world into seven regions, of which Arabia was of course the first and by far the greatest, and much else of like manufacture. The most interesting work for me was a manuscript history of the Wahhabee empire, preceded by a general sketch of Arab annals; the ante-Islamitic portion closely resembled that given by Aboo-l-Feda, perhaps was copied from him; the space intervening between the wars of Khālid-ebn-el-Waleed and the rise of the Sa'ood dynasty, related to Nejed alone; it was ill filled up, and most of what it told has been already embodied in this narrative; the little which remains will be inserted in its turn. Account books, muster rolls, official correspondence and the like, were stowed away in a large side cabinet; but the folding doors were frequently left open, and I was able to get an occasional look at the documents, of which my Arab census in the last chapter is in great measure an extract. Maḥboob raised hardly any difficulty to my taking notes or copying passages, especially out of the literary works; I regret that some of the papers then written were lost in the subsequent casualties of my journey.

The prime minister promised much and did something. He took care that we should be duly supplied from the palace with the entire list of Nejdean luxuries—butcher's meat and coffee—

besides making me a handsome present of ready money, which I accepted in hopes of thereby lessening his preconceived suspicions. But his eye was always on me with the restless unsatisfied expression of one who pries into deep water for something at the bottom and cannot quite distinguish it; however, a supposed sympathy of race inclined him to be friendly.

Meanwhile both Maḥboob and 'Abd-Allah made fun of the old Nā'ib to their hearts' content; and he too in his turn fleered at them. The Persian, finding Feysul hopelessly cold in his cause, resolved on a visit to his son and heir, and having arrayed himself in all his finery, called at the prince's palace. When introduced into the Ḳ'hāwah, he found 'Abd-Allah stretched out on the carpet Bedouin-fashion, back uppermost, with a cushion under his elbows to prop him up, and much in the position of a dog when he puts his muzzle on his fore-paws and looks at you. "Welcome," said the gracious prince to the approaching ambassador, and motioned him to sit down, without the while changing his own unceremonious posture. Then, after a minute of staring, "Is your beard dyed?" was the first princely question. I should say that staining the hair is looked on by Wahhabees as an unlawful encroachment on the rights of the Creator to bestow on His creatures whatever colouring He chooses. The Nā'ib in a grave but somewhat vexed tone allowed that his beard was dyed, and asked what was the matter even if it were? "Because," replied 'Abd-Allah, "we consider such a practice to be highly improper." Whereto the Nā'ib drily answered, that the Persians thought otherwise. "Are you a Sonnee or a Shiya'ee?" next enquired the reclining majesty. The Nā'ib's patience, always scant, was now at an end. "I am Shiya'ee, and my father was a Shiya'ee, and my grandfather was a Shiya'ee, and we are all Shiya'ees," answered he, in a tone of downright passion; "but you, 'Abd-Allah, what are you, a prince or a chaplain?" The whole in that broken Arabic which rendered anger impossible. "A prince," replied 'Abd-Allah, looking very big. "Because," rejoined the Persian, "I thought from your questions you were a chaplain; and if you are indeed so, get you off to the mosque; that is the place, not a palace, for one who talks in your style." 'Abd-Allah burst out laughing, and made an apology worse than the fault, by pretending ignorance of diplomatic usages and the respect due to ambassadors, and then changed the discourse. All this was nohow real levity or clownishness in the Nejdee; his insolence was the result of cool and deliberate calculation, designed to bring the Persian down to the right point for the bargain already resolved on by Feysul and his son. The Nā'ib came away in a fury against the Bedouin, and Aboo-'Eysa had much ado to prevent his leaving the capital in a huff that very day.

Nor was he more successful with Maḥboob, to whom he paid many ceremonious visits, in hope of gaining his influence with the old king, and never without hearing something premeditatedly offensive on the score of Persians and Shiya'ees. These last, among their many other fancies, have an excessive and superstitious reverence for the written names of holy personages, and hold the wilful destruction of such words to be an atrocious crime. On one occasion, while the Nā'ib was present in the divan, Maḥboob received some letters bearing the customary heading "In the name of God." These letters the minister read, and then, before the Persian's face, tore them across and threw them into the fire burning on the hearth. Not Elnathan, Delaiah, and Gemariah made more intercession to Jehoiakim that he would not burn the prophecy-written roll, than Moḥammed-'Alee on this occasion to Maḥboob, or with less effect. He nearly fainted with horror. But worse followed. The Shirāzee had with him a silver drinking-cup of Persian workmanship, and beautifully embossed, with the five names so venerated by Persians—Moḥammed, 'Alee, Faṭimah, Ḥasan, and Ḥoseyn—worked on the rim. This goblet he one day brought with him to the palace, with the view of "astonishing the natives." Maḥboob took it in his hand, turned it round, and on reading the characters round the edge exclaimed, "What are these abominable inscriptions?" and flung the cup on the ground. The Nā'ib's feelings may be better imagined than described. During the quiet evening hours that we often passed in his cool upper apartments, smoking his Nargheelahs and talking over the events of the day, we had the advantage of hearing from his own mouth all these incidents, and many more of like tenor, sometimes in mutilated Arabic, sometimes in elegant Hindoostanee.

A comical event which occurred about this time brought matters, as they say, to a crisis, and by its pre-eminent absurdity rescued the Nā'ib from further outrages to his Shiya'ee feelings. I have already said that morning and evening roll-calls were daily read in the mosques belonging to the several quarters of the town, and that absentees were liable to very practical admonitions towards better attendance in future. Of course neither the Nā'ib and his men as Shiya'ees, nor Barakāt and myself as Christians, troubled ourselves much with Wahhabee congregational attendance. One morning the "Zelator" superintendent of the mosque, to which according to our place of residence we were supposed to belong, took it into his head that infidels or not we were bound in common decency to act like orthodox Muslims: "cum Romæ fueris, Romano vivitur usu." Accordingly our two names, with those of the Nā'ib and his posse, were read out among the rest, but there was no voice nor any that answered. Hereon the indignant Zelator collected a pious band armed with sticks and staves; and a little before sunrise presented himself at our door, the nearest on his rounds. Luckily the door was bolted from within, while Barakāt, Aboo-'Eysa, and myself were, in place of prayers and ablutions, smoking our morning pipes over a very excellent cup of coffee. When Aboo-'Eysa heard the knock, which his bad conscience at once interpreted, he was terribly frightened, knowing by experience that Wahhabee fanaticism when once up is no trifling matter. Turning quite pale, he begged us to return no answer to the summons, but to hide ourselves within an inner chamber. Barakāt, on the contrary, with all the courage of a Zaḥlawee, determined to face the danger, went right to the door, opened it suddenly, and stepping out slammed it to as suddenly behind him, without giving the visitors time to enter. Next ensued the following parley in the street: —

"Why did you not come to prayers this morning?" "We have already said our prayers; what kind of atheists do you take us for?" "Why then did you not answer when your names were called over?" enquired the Zelator, supposing from the other's ready equivocation that we must have been somehow or other at the mosque. "We imagined that you Wahhabees had some peculiar ceremony of your own which did not concern us foreigners; how are we to know all your customs?" replied the unabashed Barakāt. "Who was your right-hand man when you stood up to prayer?" enquired the doubting cross-questioner. "Some Bedouin or other; is it my business to know all the Bedouins in Riaḍ?" answered my companion. "And who was on your left?" "The wall." Which last was said with such an air of innocence and unconcern, that the stick-bearers knew not what to make of it. So, like good Arabs, they allowed us the benefit of doubt, and passed on after an admonition to be regular in our religious duties. "If God wills it," was the vague but orthodox answer.

From our door the holy squadron passed to that of the Nā'ib. Here a thundering knock was at once answered by 'Alee, the younger servant, who with unsuspecting rashness flung the entrance wide open. No quarter to Persians: "Throw him down, beat him, purify his hide," was shouted out on all sides, and the foremost laid hold of the astonished Shiya'ee to inflict the legal chastisement. But 'Alee was a big strapping lad, and not easily floored; he soon tore himself away from his well-intentioned executioners, and rushed into the interior of the house calling madly for aid on his brother Ḥasan. Out came the elder with a pistol in either hand, while 'Alee having picked up a dagger brandished it fearfully; and the old Nā'ib, aroused from sleep in his upstairs bedroom, leaned over the parapet in his dressing-gown, like Shelley's grey tyrant father, and screamed out from above Persian threats and curses. The Zelators turned tail and fled in confusion; 'Alee and Ḥasan ran after, sword and pistol in hand, half-way down the street, beating one, kicking another, and leaving a third sprawling in the dust.

Without delay the Nā'ib donned his clothes and went to the palace, there to demand justice for the housebreaking aggression thus committed, and to protest very reasonably this time against the absurdity of compulsory attendance on divine worship. We did not think it necessary to accompany him, since our affair had at any rate ended smoothly. But Aboo-'Eysa, who had gone with the Nā'ib, played the orator in our behalf. The result was a royal order issued to the Zelators not to trouble themselves further about us and our doings; while, in compensation for past insults, the Persian ambassador was henceforth treated at the palace with greater decency by Maḥboob and his crew.

It may be well to recount at once the remainder of Moḥammed-Alee's fortunes at Riaḍ. After a month of veering and tacking, speeding to-day, put back to-morrow, and never getting nearer to the point, Aboo-'Eysa told him plainly what he had already suggested more than once, but without effect—that in the Wahhabee capital it was money, and money alone, that could make the mare to go, and that if he desired a speedy and a favourable solution of his difficulties, he had only to make some judicious offerings, and all would be well.

Sad news this to Moḥammed-'Alee, close-fisted as Persians usually are; however, he had no other course open. Next day the double-barrelled fowling-piece went to 'Abd-Allah, the tea-making machine to Maḥboob, a beautiful ruby found its way to Feyṣul's inner chamber; and I believe that the king's fair daughter, the she-secretary of the cabinet, obtained her share of the gifts. The effect was magical. Instantaneously, a magnificent letter of apology for "past accidents" was drawn up, addressed to the Shah, and signed by Feyṣul, wherein all the blame of whatever had befallen the caravan was safely thrown on the luckless Aboo-Boṭeyn, now a refugee among the "infidels" at 'Oneyzah; but no sooner should God have delivered him up to the vengeance of the faithful, than the wretch should be put in irons and sent to Ṭeheran to anwer for himself before the majesty of Persia, unless indeed he were killed first, as might be hopefully anticipated. Not a word about Mohanna. Nor a word either (I read the document myself) about costs and damages, except what Aboo-Boṭeyn was to refund—when the hare was caught, which, please God, should soon be the case.

In conclusion, the better to stop the Nā'ib's mouth, and to prevent too urgent representations on the score of his plundered followers, some presents were offered him. An elderly horse, which might at Bombay have brought two hundred rupees or thereabouts; a camel, worth in Nejed from six to seven rials, somewhat less than two pounds English; three or four cloaks of Ḥaṣa manufacture, and of second-rate quality, were thrown as a sop to Cerberus, and greedily swallowed. The Nā'ib was no judge of horse-flesh or camel-flesh either; the cloaks too were new to him, and he very properly supposed the gift-horse and raiment to be each the very best in their kind. In return he pledged his word that the Persian pilgrims should continue to pursue the route of Nejed, and pay for it also. It was a scoundrelly business from beginning to end, and did little honour either to the merchandising Sultan of Nejed and his subordinates, or to the Persian who deliberately sold his country-men's rights and the interests of his government for an old horse, an old camel, and some old cloaks.

As a corollary to these manœuvres, Aboo-'Eysa procured for himself a royal patent naming him head conductor from the Persian coast to Mecca of all future pilgrim bands, to the permanent exclusion of competitors; a measure which had at least the advantage of ensuring to the unlucky Shiya'ees a certain amount of good treatment while on their road, and of putting our friend in possession of emoluments sufficient to meet even his own extravagant habits and ostentatious generosity.

One question yet remained to be settled by Moḥammed-'Alee, namely, by what road he should return to Meshid and thence to Bagdad and Ṭeheran. Winter was setting in, and the land route, leading mainly over high ground, might prove disagreeably cold, even in Arabia. This and other valid reasons would have led him to prefer the easier and warmer line of journey through Ḥaṣa, and thence by ship up the Persian Gulf and the Shaṭṭ-el-'Aarab to Meshid 'Alee, instead of the weary track by the mountains of Sedeyr, Zulphah, and the up-country. But Moḥammed-'Alee was a devout Shiya'ee, and as such must needs first consult his luck by counting his beads. Thrice his computation notified to him the heaven-sent warning to adopt not the former, but the latter path, and this he accordingly did, with much loss of time and increase of expense and trouble.

My readers perhaps know (if they do not, it is worth remarking) that a Persian, and in fact a Shiya'ee in general, even though not by birth a Persian, can do nothing, not so much as drink a cup of coffee or light a Nargheelah, without counting his luck on his rosary; a ridiculous custom, and justly reprobated by the Wahhabees, whose hatred of magic, spells, charms, and the rest of that category, extends also to divinations and omens of whatever sort, dream-interpretations, lucky or unlucky days, and the like; a favourable piece of witness which I am glad to be able to render the Wahhabees.

In the last week of November, just before our own departure, Moḥammed-'Alee with all his attendants set off for Sedeyr, and in the following spring I was rejoiced on learning at Bagdad that he and his had arrived in safety at their journey's end.

The two Meccan beggars, our companions from Ḥā'yel hither, got a shirt and two rials apiece, with which munificent present one of them went to Baṣrah, where he passed himself off for a Sey'yid, and invested in a huge turban; the other set his face westward, and went—I know not whither. We will now resume the actual course of events.

During these forty days active preparations were making in Nejed for the decisive blow to be struck at 'Oneyzah. What had hitherto been sent against that town were little more than mere skirmishing parties, and consisted of a certain number of men from Aflāj and Sedeyr, from Zulphah and Shaḳra', with a few warriors of 'Aared and Yemāmah to keep up the spirits of the rest, and a younger son of Feyṣul's to command. The intention of the Wahhabee council was, that when occasional attacks, joined with the half-blockade, should have sufficiently weakened their enemy, the whole force of Central and Southern Nejed, with that of the great eastern provinces, should be brought to bear. The entire expedition was to be entrusted to the invincible and murderous 'Abd-Allah.

The appointed time now drew on, and Yemāmah and Ḥareeḳ were ordered to send in their contingent, Soley' and Dowāsir were called on for their rude militia, while the levy from Ḥaṣa with the artil,ery of Ḳaṭeef was to come, and along with the dreaded battalions of 'Aareḍ itself, to complete the besieging army. What chance could be left to one isolated town, however strong, against such a concentration of assailing force?

Zāmil and his adherents felt that their ruin was not only planned, but certain. No hope remained them from the Shereef of Mecca, and Egypt was for them, no less than for the Israelites of old, a broken reed. Accordingly, they sent submissive, nay suppliant, letters to Feyṣul, offered allegiance, tribute, and obedience, renewed their protestations of orthodoxy, appealed to the brotherhood of Islam, and, lastly, summoned the Sultan of Nejed to answer before the judgment-seat of God for all the evils of war and a city taken by storm. Feyṣul was moved, relented of his purpose, and would gladly have accepted a submission so humbly tendered, and the refusal of which must draw after it such awful responsibility. But Maḥboob looked forward with all the ambition of rising power to the great extension of Wahhabee prerogative consequent on the fall of 'Oneyzah; while 'Abd-Allah, ferocious in the anticipation of success, was no more disposed to let slip a lesson in his art, or a laurel leaf from his garland, than he whom history or libel reports to have fought the battle of Nimwegen with the treaty of Utrecht in his pocket. The Zelators also, on their side, besieged the old and vacillating monarch, and urged him to the unsparing severity enjoined by the Prophet in that famous chapter of the Coran, last in order of time, and entitled "Repentance," but of which Aboo-Bekr too justly remarked that the name of "Vengeance" had suited it better. Long consultations were held in the palace, and at last Feyṣul's ultimatum was sent. "Give up Zāmil, El-Khey'yāt, and the other ringleaders of revolt," so ran the document, "and then, not till then, will I treat of peace." Death was more tolerable to the men of 'Oneyzah than compliance on such terms, and no further answer was returned. I myself obtained, through Maḥboob, a sight of the letter from 'Oneyzah, and of the reply, though of course I was not admitted to the council itself, for my account of which I depend on current report.

'Abd-Allah made no secret of his joy, and prepared for a speedy departure. Meanwhile Feyṣul sent orders to his second-born Sa'ood, to bring up the troops of Ḥareeḳ, and to hand them over when in Riaḍ to his elder brother, whose special office as governor of the capital he, Sa'ood, was to fill during the absence of the latter at 'Oneyzah. Sa'ood speedily arrived, and with him about two hundred horsemen; the rest of his men, more than two thousand, were mounted on camels. When they entered Riaḍ, Feyṣul for the first and the last time during our stay, gave a public audience at the palace gate. It was a scene for a painter. There sat the blind old tyrant, corpulent, decrepit, yet imposing, with his large broad forehead, white beard, and thoughtful air, clad in all the simplicity of a Wahhabee; the gold-hafted sword at his side his only ornament or distinction. Beside him the ministers, the officers of his court, and a crowd of the nobler and wealthier citizens. 'Abd-Allah, the heir of the throne, was alone absent. Up came Sa'ood with the bearing of a hussar officer, richly clad in Cachemire shawls and a gold wrought mantle, while man by man followed his red dressed cavaliers, their spears over their shoulders, and their swords hanging down; a musket too was slung behind the saddle of each warrior; and the sharp dagger of Ḥareeḳ glittered in every girdle. Next came the common soldiers on camels or dromedaries, some with spears only, some with spears and guns, till the wide square was filled with armed men and gazing spectators, as the whole troop drew up before the great autocrat, and Sa'ood alighted to bend and kiss his father's hand. "God save Feyṣul! God give the victory to the armies of the Muslims!" was shouted out on every side, and all faces kindled into the fierce smile of concentrated enthusiasm and conscious strength. Feyṣul rose from his seat, and placed his son at his side. Another moment and they entered the castle together, whilst the troops dispersed to their quarters, chiefly in the Khajiḳ.

I have noticed that 'Abd-Allah did not appear. Much though he rejoiced at an event tending to forward his own aims, yet personal jealousy and hatred would not allow him to bear part in his brother's reception. Next day Feyṣul, while seated in his private divan with Sa'ood, enquired of him whether he had yet seen his elder brother, and, on his negative answer, ordered him to pay 'Abd-Allah the first visit. "I am the stranger guest, while he is an inhabitant of the town," replied Sa'ood, "and it is accordingly his duty to call first on me." Feyṣul urged his orders, but in vain; Sa'ood persisted in refusal. The old king at last lost his wonted self-command, and, supported by two negro slaves, rose to strike his son. "Strike," said Sa'ood, bending his shoulders to receive the blow; "you have me before you, but I will not go to my brother's house." The slaves now interfered, and Feyṣul, abashed at the indecorum of his own conduct, permitted Sa'ood to retire without further comment.

A few hours after, the blind monarch, mounted on a led horse, was seen traversing the street which conducts to the palace of 'Abd-Allah. Arrived there, he related what had just occurred, and entreated his son to fulfil the obligation of a first visit. But the elder son proved no less intractable than the younger, though less excusably. Finally, "It is all my fault, I have treated your brother ill," said Feysul; "he was in the right, and we are in the wrong. The error must be repaired somehow. Do you come along with me to the palace, and we will both together call on him in his lodgings; your visit will thus be coloured by mine, and matters will resume their proper course." 'Abd-Allah could no longer refuse; the customary ceremonies of politeness were exchanged between the brothers, and the dangers of a gross and public scandal so far avoided. But Mahboob had been informed of all. "Do you now understand the true state of affairs?" said he to Feysul. "By God! you will hardly be in your grave when the clash of swords will be heard from 'Aared to Sedeyr." Feysul sighed deeply; but what remedy where the rivalry of the mothers, inherited by the children, is heightened by the rivalry of a kingdom?

Sa'ood had not been three days in his new quarters within the palace, when a tall and handsome attendant came with extreme courtesy of demeanour to call me into the presence of his master, who, said he, was suffering from a toothache or a headache, I forget which, and required my professional help without delay. On entering the prince's apartments I was met by a hearty welcome in the good-humoured style customary to Sa'ood, and a loud laugh when I enquired after his ailment. "As well as yourself," he replied; "all I wanted was a pretext for having you here." He then entered freely into conversation, and expressed, or at least professed, much sympathy for Egypt. The fact is that being a mortal enemy to 'Abd-Allah, and feeling the certainty of a not distant struggle, he would gladly seek support from a government whose feelings he can anticipate to be on the whole unfriendly to his ultra-Wahhabee brother. During the rest of my stay here he repeatedly sent for me, showed much good will, possibly sincere, under the idea that I was an emissary of Egypt, and thereby contributed to set 'Abd-Allah against me, in the manner which now remains to relate.

At first we have seen that everything went on very smoothly

and even favourably with the heir-apparent. But time advanced, success provoked jealousy here and there, while closer observation awakened suspicions, till the fair sky began to overcloud, and there appeared indications of a gathering storm, enough to have put us on our guard had we been more cautious than, I regret to say, we were. Truth here obliges me to the recital of more than one imprudence, for which I trust that my European readers will bear more indulgence than his royal highness at Riaḍ. I put down the circumstances in order to render clearer the cause and connection of events.

Thus, one evening 'Abd-Allah importuned me for a prophylactic against a toothache which from time to time gave him annoyance. I proposed one or two, but he did not approve them. At last I suggested that there yet remained one sovereign remedy, but that he must keep it a profound secret. "What is it?" eagerly enquired the prince. "It consists in tobacco, chewed and applied to the tooth, with a lighted pipe to promote its action," answered I. The Wahhabee said nothing, but his frown spoke much, and I felt I had gone too far.

Another time he wanted me to pay more regular and specific attention to his horse's ailments. For awhile I tried, but without use, to make him understand that a physician was one thing, and a veterinary surgeon another: the truth was that I was seriously afraid of committing some real blunder with his mares and colts. But 'Abd-Allah would hear no excuse, till finally I cut matters short by saying, "Your highness will please to remember that here in your capital I am a doctor of asses, not of horses." He understood the hit, and was not over-pleased; then laughed a sour laugh, and changed the discourse.

But worse followed. One night we were at the palace, and 'Abd-Allah, as often, was for keeping me up till midnight, pestering me with medico-scientific enquiries, and exacting for himself a regular course of pharmaceutical lectures, but without the fees. I was sleepy and tired, and should much have preferred going home to bed. Desirous of bringing matters to a crisis, I now remained silent, and let his highness's questions go by without an answer. "What are you thinking of?" said he. After one or two evasive answers, I replied that I was thinking of a story regarding the Caliph Haroon-er-Rasheed and his well-known-jester and boon companion Aboo-Nowas. 'Abd-Allah, who, like all Arabs, relished nothing so much as a story of kings and caliphs, eagerly enquired what the tale might be. So I informed him that the celebrated caliph had a bad habit of sitting up very late, and that he used to keep Aboo-Nowas for companion of his vigils at hours when the latter would willingly have been at rest. One night Haroon was talking at a great pace, and Aboo-Nowas remained silent as though wrapped in thought. "What are you thinking about?" asked the caliph. "Of nothing," answered Aboo-Nowas, and relapsed into silence. A second time the same question was put, and met with the same reply. But on a third interrogation Aboo-Nowas raised his head, looked the majesty of Bagdad hard in the face, and said, "I am thinking of this" (the Arab word is, I regret to say, that most "unpleasing to a married ear," we will render it by) "brute, who will neither go himself to bed nor let me go."

'Abd-Allah stared, and hesitated a moment between anger and laughter. At last the latter prevailed. "You are at liberty," said he, and I took my leave.

By this time he was ripe for serious displeasure, and the Ḳaḍee 'Abd-el-Laṭeef, as I was afterwards informed, with some others of like strain, took the opportunity of putting his suspicions on the alert. The first intimation that we received was curious enough.

For a foreigner to enter Riaḍ is not always easy, but to get away from it is harder still; Reynard himself would have been justly shy of venturing on this royal cave. There exist in the capital of Nejed two approved means of barring the exit against those on whom mistrust may have fallen. The first and readiest is that of which it has been emphatically said, *Stone-dead hath no fellow*. But should circumstances render the bonds of death inexpedient, the bonds of Hymen and a Riaḍ establishment may and occasionally do supply their office. By this latter proceeding, the more amiable of the two, 'Abd-Allah resolved to enchain us.

Accordingly, one morning arrived at our dwelling an attendant of the palace, with a smiling face, presage of some good in reserve, and many fair speeches. After enquiries about our health, comfort, well-being, &c., he added that 'Abd-Allah thought we might be desirous of purchasing this or that, and begged us to accept of a small present. It was a fair sum of money, just twice so much as the ordinary token of good will, namely, four rials in place of two. After which the messenger took his leave. Aboo-'Eysa had been present at the interview: "Be on the look-out," said he, "there is something wrong."

That very afternoon 'Abd-Allah sent for me, and with abundance of encomiums and of promises, declared that he could not think of letting Riad lose so valuable a physician, that I must accordingly take up a permanent abode in the capital, where I might rely on his patronage, and on all good things; that he had already resolved on giving me a house and a garden, specifying them, with a suitable household, and a fair face to keep me company; he concluded by inviting me to go without delay and see whether the new abode fitted me, and take possession.

Much and long did I fight off; talked about a winter visit to the coast, and coming back in the spring; tried first one pretext and then another; but none would avail, and 'Abd-Allah continued to insist. To quiet him, I consented to go and see the house. For the intended Calypso, I had ready an argument derived from Mahometan law, which put her out of the question, but its explanation would require more space than these pages can afford. Suffice that it was peremptory, and the "proposal" came to a premature end. However, the offered house and income remained behind. On these points 'Abd-Allah hoped to meet with a less efficacious resistance, and indeed I doubt if any legislation in the world can supply a valid pretext for declining a good revenue. So he told one of his attendants to show me over the premises, and I for my part promised him a categoric answer next morning.

The house was really good, well situated, with a small garden adjoining, nor could any reasonable demur be made on its score. A real vagrant Arab physician would, in vulgar phrase, have snapped at the offer. But in the question was really "to be or not to be," and difficulties when they cannot be turned, must be faced.

On our ensuing meeting I told 'Abd-Allah that we were fully sensible of the honour done us, but that we had previously made all our engagements for going on to Ḥasa, that we could no longer break them, that a return to Riaḍ in the following spring might suffice, and that since 'Abd-Allah himself was to head in person the expedition against 'Oneyzah, we might well await his return before taking up our settled residence in the capital, where difficulties might possibly occur during his absence; in short, that we could not pass the winter in Nejed, but that we hoped for a second and a longer visit next year. However palliated, the refusal could not but be disagreeable; 'Abd-Allah admitted it with evident reluctance and concealed mistrust.

The winter season was now setting in; it was the third week in November; and a thunder-storm, the first we had witnessed in Central Arabia, ushered in a marked change for cold in the temperature of Wadi Ḥaneefah. Rain fell abundantly, and sent torrents down the dry watercourses of the valley, changing its large hollows into temporary tanks. None of the streams showed, however, any disposition to reach the sea, nor indeed could they, for this part of Nejed is entirely hemmed in to the east by the Ṭoweyḳ range. The inhabitants welcomed the copious showers, pledges of fertility for the coming year, while at 'Oneyzah the same rains produced at least one excellent effect, but which I may well defy my readers to guess. The hostile armies, commanded by Zāmil and Moḥammed-ebn-Sa'ood, were drawn up in face of each other, and on the point of fierce conflict, when the storm burst on them, and by putting out the lighted matchlocks of either party, prevented the discharge of bullets and the effusion of blood. When this piece of news reached Riaḍ, Aboo-'Eysa said to me, "Do not forget on your return to mention this in Europe, it may serve to give an idea of Arab warfare."

The affairs of the Nā'ib were nearly terminated, and Aboo-'Eysa had received his patents. We now prepared to start eastwards, but the day of our departure from Nejed was yet to fix, when a sudden explosion of royal ill-will put an end to our indecision, and necessitated more promptitude than we had hitherto intended for our movements.

In one of my medical cases, the nature of the malady had led me to try a powerful though dangerous therapeutic agent, namely, strychnia, and its employment had been followed by prompt and unequivocal amelioration. Not that the amendment was, I should think, of a permanent character, but of this point the Nejdeans, who saw no farther than the present effect, were and could be no judges, while the high rank of the patient himself, an old town chief, drew special attention to the fact. Everybody talked about it, and the news reached the palace.

'Abd-Allah had just paid his compulsory visit to Sa'ood, and the mutual rivalry of the brothers, now the more exasperated by vicinity, was very thinly concealed, or rather not concealed, under the formalities of social politeness. Intrigues, treasons, violence itself, were hatching beneath the palace walls, and assassination, whether by the dagger or the bowl, I had better said the coffee-cup, would have been quite in keeping, nor likely to cause the smallest surprise to any one. Maḥboob, too, always odious to 'Abd-Allah, was at this moment more so than ever, and the minister himself could not fail to foresee his own personal peril when time should place undivided and autocratic power in the hands of one whom he had so often browbeaten and kept in abeyance. Hence he sided with Sa'ood, and by so doing heated the furnace of 'Abd-Allah's evil passions one seven times more than it was wont to be heated. The nobles of the town, the very strangers, all sided with the one or the other of the half-brothers, and though Feyṣul's life, like the silken thread round the monsters in Triermain's "Hall of Fear," yet held the tigers back, it might not suffice to restrain some sudden and especially some secret spring.

Now 'Abd-Allah in the course of his amateur lectures had learnt enough to know the poisonous qualities of various drugs, and of strychnine in particular; and though probably unacquainted with the exploits of European criminals, was fully capable of giving them a rival in the East. The cure, or at least the relief, just alluded to, had occurred about the 16th of November, exactly at the time when I had given him to understand our definite refusal of his offers, and when he was in consequence somewhat uncertain what course next to follow. A day or two after he sent for me, expressed his regret at our resolution to quit the capital, and begged that we would at least leave behind us in his keeping some useful medicines for the public benefit, and above all that we would entrust him with that powerful drug whose sanitary effects were now the subject of general admiration.

All that I could say about the uselessness, nay, the great danger, of pharmacy in unlearned hands, was rejected as a mere and insufficient pretext. At last, after much urging, the prince ended by saying that for the other ingredients I might omit them if I chose, but that the strychnine he must have, and that though at the highest price I might fancy to name.

His real object was perfectly clear, nor could I dream of lending a hand, however indirect, to his diabolical designs, nor did I see any way open before me but that of a firm though polite denial. In pursuance, I affected not to suspect his projects, and insisted on the dangerous character of the alkaloid, till he gave up the charge for the moment, and I left the palace.

Next day he renewed his demands, but to no purpose. A third meeting took place; it was the 19th or 20th of the month. Beckoning me to his side, he insisted in the most absolute manner on having the poison in his possession, and at last, laying aside all pretences, made clear the reasons, though not the person for whom he desired it, and declared that he would admit of no excuse, conscientious or otherwise.

He was at the moment sitting in the further end of the Ḳhāwah, and I was close by him; while between us and the attendants there present, enough space remained to prevent their catching our conversation, if held in an undertone. I looked round to assure myself that we could not be overheard, and when a flat denial on my part had been met by an equally flat rejection and a fresh demand, I turned right towards him, lifted up the edge of his head-dress, and said in his ear, " 'Abd-Allah, I know well what you want the poison for, and I have no mind to be an accomplice to your crimes, nor to answer before God's judgment-seat for what you will have to answer for. You shall *never* have it."

His face became literally black and swelled with rage; I never saw so perfect a demon before or after. A moment he hesitated in silence, then mastered himself, and suddenly changing voice and tone began to talk gaily about indifferent subjects. After a few minutes he rose, and I returned home.

There Aboo-'Eysa, Barakāt, and myself immediately held council to consider what was now to be done. That an outbreak must shortly take place seemed certain; to await it was dangerous, yet we could not safely leave the town in an over-precipitate manner, nor without some kind of permission. We resolved together to go on in quiet and caution a few days more, to sound the court, make our adieus at Feysul's palace, get a good word from Maḥboob (no difficult matter), and then slip off without attracting too much notice. But our destiny was not to run so smoothly.

On the evening of the 21st we were sitting up late, talking over the needful preparations of the journey, and drinking coffee with a few good-natured townsmen, who had no objection to a contraband smoke; a practice for which our dwelling had long since become famous or infamous, when a rap at the door announced 'Abd-Allah—not the prince, but his namesake and confidential retainer. "What brings you here at this hour of the night?" said we, not overpleased at the honour of his visit.

"The king" (for such is in common Riaḍ parlance the title given to the heir-apparent) "sends for you; come with me at once," was his short and sharp answer. "Shall Barakāt come with me?" said I, looking towards my companion. "The king wants you alone," replied the messenger. "Shall I bring one of my books along with me?" "There is no need." "Wait a few minutes while we get a cup of coffee ready for you."

This last offer could not in common decency be refused. While the ceremony was in performance, I found time to exchange a few words with Aboo-'Eysa and Barakāt. They agreed to dismiss the guests, and to remain on the alert for the result of this nocturnal embassy, easily foreseen to be a threatening one, perhaps dangerous. Yet the fact of my companion's not being also sent for, seemed to me a guarantee against immediate

The royal messenger and myself then left the house, and proceeded in silence and darkness through the winding streets to the palace of 'Abd-Allah. Arrived there, a short parley ensued between my conductor and the guards, who then resumed their post, while the former passed on to give the prince notice, leaving me to cool myself for a minute or two in the night air of the courtyard. A negro then came out, and beckoned me to enter.

The room was dark, there was no other light than that afforded by the flickering gleams of the firewood burning on the hearth. At the further end sat 'Abd-Allah, silent and gloomy; opposite to him on the other side was 'Abd-el-Lateef, the successor of the Wahhabee, and a few others, Zelators, or belonging to their party. Mahboob was seated by 'Abd-el-Lateef, and his presence was the only favourable circumstance discernible at a first glance. But he too looked unusually serious. At the other end of the long hall were a dozen armed attendants, Nejdeans or negroes.

When I entered, all remained without movement or return of greeting. I saluted 'Abd-Allah, who replied in an undertone, and gave me a signal to sit down at a little distance from him but on the same side of the divan. My readers may suppose that I was not at the moment ambitious of too intimate a vicinity.

After an interval of silence, 'Abd-Allah turned half round towards me, and with his blackest look and a deep voice said, "I now know perfectly well what you are; you are no doctors, you are Christians, spies, and revolutionists ('mufsideen') come hither to ruin our religion and state in behalf of those who sent you. The penalty for such as you is death, that you know, and I am determined to inflict it without delay."

"Threatened folks live long," thought I, and had no difficulty in showing the calm which I really felt. So looking him coolly in the face, I replied, "Istaghfir Allah," literally, "Ask pardon of God." This is the phrase commonly addressed to one who has said something extremely out of place.

The answer was unexpected; he started, and said, "Why so?"

"Because," I rejoined, "you have just now uttered a sheer absurdity. 'Christians,' be it so; but 'spies,' 'revolutionists,'—as if we were not known by everybody in your town for quiet doctors, neither more nor less! And then to talk about putting me to death! You cannot, and you dare not."

"But I can and dare," answered 'Abd-Allah; "and who shall prevent me? you shall soon learn that to your cost."

"Neither can nor dare," repeated I. "We are here your

father's guests and yours for a month and more, known as such, received as such. What have we done to justify a breach of the laws of hospitality in Nejed? It is impossible for you to do what you say," continued I, thinking the while that it was a great deal too possible after all; "the obloquy of the deed would be too much for you."

He remained a moment thoughtful, then said, "As if any one need know who did it. I have the means, and can dispose of you without talk or rumour. Those who are at my bidding can take a suitable time and place for that, without my name being ever mentioned in the affair."

The advantage was now evidently on my side, I followed it up, and said with a quiet laugh, "Neither is that within your power. Am I not known to your father, to all in his palace? to your own brother Sa'ood among the rest? Is not the fact of this my actual visit to you known without your gates? Or is there no one here?" added I, with a glance at Maḥboob, "who can report elsewhere what you have just now said? Better for you to leave off this nonsense; do you take me for a child of four days old?"

He muttered a repetition of his threat. "Bear witness, all here present," said I, raising my voice so as to be heard from one end of the room to the other, "that if any mishap befalls my companion or myself from Riaḍ to the shores of the Persian Gulf, it is all 'Abd-Allah's doing. And the consequences shall be on his head, worse consequences than he expects or dreams."

The prince made no reply. All were silent; Maḥboob kept his eyes steadily fixed on the fireplace; 'Abd-el-Laṭeef looked much and said nothing.

"Bring coffee," called out 'Abd-Allah to the servants. Before a minute had elapsed, a black slave approached with one and only one coffee-cup in his hand. At a second sign from his master he came before me and presented it.

Of course the worst might be conjectured of so unusual and solitary a draught. But I thought it highly improbable that matters should have been so accurately prepared; besides, his main cause of anger was precisely the refusal of poisons, a fact which implied that he had none by him ready for use. So I said "Bismillah," took the cup, looked very hard at 'Abd-

Allah, drank it off, and then said to the slave, "Pour me out a second." This he did; I swallowed it, and said, "Now you may take the cup away."

The desired effect was fully attained. 'Abd-Allah's face announced defeat, while the rest of the assembly whispered together. The prince turned to 'Abd-el-Laṭeef and began talking about the dangers to which the land was exposed from spies, and the wicked designs of infidels for ruining the kingdom of the Muslims. The Ḳaḍee and his companions chimed in, and the story of the pseudo-Darweesh traveller killed at Ḍerey'eeyah, and of another (but who he was I cannot fancy; perhaps a Persian, who had, said 'Abd-Allah, been also recognized for an intriguer, but had escaped to Mascat, and thus baffled the penalty due to his crimes), were now brought forward and commented on. Maḥboob now at last spoke, but it was to ridicule such apprehensions. "The thing is in itself unlikely," said he; "and were it so, what harm could they do?" alluding to my companion and myself.

On this I took up the word, and a general conversation ensued, in which I did my best to explode the idea of spies and spymanship, appealed to our own quiet and inoffensive conduct, got into a virtuous indignation against such a requital of evil for good after all the services which we had rendered court and town, and quoted verses of the Coran regarding the wickedness of ungrounded suspicion, and the obligation of not judging ill without clear evidence. 'Abd-Allah made no direct answer, and the others, whatever they may have thought, could not support a charge abandoned by their master.

What amused me not a little was that the Wahhabee prince had after all very nearly hit the right nail on the head, and that I was snubbing him only for having guessed too well. But there was no help for it, and I had the pleasure of seeing, that though at heart unchanged in his opinion about us, he was yet sufficiently cowed to render a respite certain, and our escape thereby practicable.

This kind of talk continued awhile, and I purposely kept my seat, to show the unconcern of innocence, till Maḥboob made me a sign that I might safely retire. On this I took leave of 'Abd-Allah and quitted the palace unaccompanied. It was now near midnight, not a light to be seen in the houses, not a sound to be heard in the streets, the sky too was dark and overcast, till, for the first time, a feeling of lonely dread came over me, and I confess that more than once I turned my head to look and see if no one was following with "evil," as Arabs say, in his hand. But there was none, and I reached the quiet alley and low door where a gleam through the chinks announced the anxious watch of my companions, who now opened the entrance, overjoyed at seeing me back sound and safe from so critical a parley.

Our plan for the future was soon formed. A day or two we were yet to remain in Riaḍ, lest haste should seem to imply fear, and thereby encourage pursuit. But during that period we would avoid the palace, out-walks in gardens or after nightfall, and keep at home as much as possible. Meanwhile Aboo-'Eysa was to get his dromedaries ready, and put them in a courtyard immediately adjoining the house, to be laden at a moment's notice.

A band of travellers was to leave Riaḍ for Ḥaṣa a few days later. Aboo-'Eysa gave out publicly that he would accompany them to Hofhoof, while we were supposed to intend following the northern or Sedeyr track, by which the Nā'ib, after many reciprocal farewells and assurances of lasting friendship, should we ever meet again, had lately departed. Mobeyreek, a black servant in Aboo-'Eysa's pay, occupied himself diligently in feeding up the camels for their long march with clover and vetches, both abundant here; and we continued our medical avocations, but quietly, and without much leaving the house. At the palace all were busy about the departure of the Ḥareeḳ contingent, which now set out on its 'Oneyzah way by Shaḳra', but marched, contrary to expectation, without 'Abd-Allah, that prince reserving himself for the arrival of the artillery, which was daily expected from Ḥaṣa, under the charge of Moḥammed es-Sedeyree. Amid all this movement and bustle no particular enquiry was made after us; the tempest had been followed by a lull, and it was ours to take advantage of this interval before a new and a worse outburst.

During the afternoon of the 24th we brought three of Aboo-'Eysa's camels into our courtyard, shut the outer door, packed and laded. We then awaited the moment of evening prayer; it came, and the voice of the Mu'eddineen summoned all good Wahhabees, the men of the town-guard not excepted, to the different mosques. When about ten minutes had gone by and all might be supposed at their prayers, we opened our door. Mobeyreek gave a glance up and down the street to ascertain that no one was in sight, and we led out the camels. Aboo-'Eysa accompanied us. Avoiding the larger thoroughfares, we took our way by bye-lanes and side passages towards a small town-gate, the nearest to our house, and opening on the north. A late comer fell in with us on his way to the Mesjid, and as he passed summoned us also to the public service. But Aboo-'Eysa unhesitatingly replied, "We have this moment come from prayers," and our interlocutor, fearing to be himself too late and thus to fall under reprehension and punishment, rushed off to the nearest oratory, leaving the road clear. Nobody was in watch at the gate. We crossed its threshold, turned south-east, and under the rapid twilight reached a range of small hillocks, behind which we sheltered ourselves till the stars came out, and the "wing of night," to quote Arab poets, spread black over town and country.

We drew a long breath, like men just let out of a dungeon, and thanked heaven that this much was over. Then, after the first hour of night had gone over, and chance passers-by had ceased, and left us free from challenge and answer, we lighted our camp-fire, drank a most refreshing cup of coffee, set our pipes to work, and laughed in our turn at 'Abd-Allah and Feysul.

Yet I slept little that night. Many and serious, nay saddening thoughts, crowded the mind on looking back to that huge dark outline of wall and tower amid the shades of the valley; we remembered those whom it encircled, we thought of what influence it had already exercised and might yet exercise over the entire Peninsula; how stern yet how childish a tyranny; how fatal a kindling of burnt-out fanaticism; a new well-head to the bitter waters of Islam; how much misdirected zeal; what concentrated though ill-applied courage and perseverance; and what might be in the end! And here we had just passed fifty days, under the roofs and at the tables of those who, had they known but for one hour what we really were, and what our purport, that hour had ended our journey and our lives; still more, suspected, accused, judged, almost convicted; yet escaping from the very clutches where others had perished, we were now almost in safety, and without those dreaded walls—and when to see them again?

But further difficulties remained before us. It was now more than ever absolutely essential to get clear of Nejed unobserved, to put the desert between us and the Wahhabee court and capital; and no less necessary was it that Aboo-'Eysa, so closely connected as he was with Riaḍ and its government, should seem nohow implicated in our unceremonious departure, nor any way concerned with our onward movements. In a word, an apparent separation of paths between him and us was necessary, before we could again come together and complete the remainder of our explorations.

In order to manage this, and while ensuring our own safety to throw a little dust in Wahhabee eyes, it was agreed that before next morning's sunrise Aboo-'Eysa should return to the town, and to his dwelling, as though nothing had occurred, and should there await the departure of the great merchant caravan, mentioned a few pages back, and composed mainly of men from Ḥaṣa and Ḳaṭeef, now bound for Hofhoof under the guidance of Aboo-Ḍahir-el-Ghannām. This assemblage was expected to start within three days at latest. Meanwhile our friend should take care to show himself openly in the palaces of Feyṣul and 'Abd-Allah, and if asked about us should answer vaguely, with the off-hand air of one who had no further care regarding us. We ourselves should in the interim make the best of our way, with Mobeyreek for guide, to Wadi Soley', and there remain concealed in a given spot, till Aboo-'Eysa should come and pick us up.

All this was arranged; at break of dawn Aboo-'Eysa took his leave, and Barakāt, Mobeyreek, and myself, were once more high perched on our dromedaries, their heads turned to the south-east, keeping the hillock range between us and Riaḍ, which we saw no more. Our path led us over low undulating ground, a continuation of Wadi Ḥaneefah, till after about four hours' march we were before the gates of Manfooḥah, a considerable town, surrounded by gardens nothing inferior in extent and fertility to those of Riaḍ; but its fortifications, once strong, have long since been dismantled and broken down by the jealousy of the neighbouring capital. Manfooḥah long belonged to Yemāmah, not to 'Aareḍ, and owned the vale of Da'ās, the early rival of Ebn-Sa'ood. In point of climate this town is preferable to Riaḍ, because situated on higher ground, and above the damp mists which often gather in the depths of the Wadi; but in a military view it is inferior to the capital, because in a more exposed and less easily guarded position. Passing Manfooḥah without entering it, our road dipped down again, and we found ourselves in Wadi Soley', a long valley, originating in the desert between Ḥareeḳ and Yemāmah, and running far to the north, till lost amid the uplands of Ṭoweyḳ above the level of Ḥoreymelah, close behind Djebel 'Aṭālah. But, unlike Wadi Ḥaneefah, it presents few wells, and none but small and unimportant villages. The Ḥaneefah valley itself goes no farther eastward than Manfooḥah, and the low cross-range which we had just traversed forms a geographical and territorial demarcation.

After winding here and there in the broad valley of Soley', we reached the spot assigned by Aboo-'Eysa for our hiding-place. It was a small sandy depth, lying some way off the beaten track, amid hillocks and brushwood, and without water: of this latter article we had taken enough in the goat-skins to last us for three days. Here we halted, and made up our minds to patience and expectation.

Two days passed drearily enough. We could not but long for our guide's arrival, nor be wholly without fear on more than one score. Once or twice a stray peasant stumbled on us, and was much surprised at our encampment in so droughty a locality. Sometimes leaving our dromedaries crouching down, and concealed among the shrubs, we wandered up the valley, climbed the high chalky cliffs of Ṭoweyḳ, on its eastern side, and gazed around to acquire a clearer idea of the land, of its ups and downs, its fertility or barrenness, to gain a distant glimpse of the blue sierra of Ḥareeḳ in the far south, and the white ranges of Ṭoweyḳ north and east. Or we dodged the numerous nor over-shy herds of gazelles, not for any desire of catching them, but merely to pass the time, and distract the mind weary of conjecture. So the hours went by, till the third day brought closer expectation and anxiety, still increasing while the sun declined, and at last went down; yet nobody appeared. But just as darkness closed in, and we were sitting in a dispirited group beside our little fire, for the night air blew chill, Aboo-'Eysa came suddenly up, and all was changed for question and answer, for cheerfulness and laughter.

He now related, amid many jokes and congratulations, how on the very day he had left us, he had called on 'Abd-Allah, and to his question, "What is become of those two Christians?" had answered by a gratuitous supposition of our being somewhere on the road to Zobeyr; how Maḥboob had also enquired after us, and met with a similar answer; how comments had been passed on us, some favourable, others unfavourable; what wild suppositions had circulated concerning our origin and our purposes; how some had opined us to be envoys from Constantinople, and some from Egypt (good luck that no one hit on Europe), with much of like tenor, now matter of mirth. Ḍahir-el-Ghannām was halting a little farther on with his band; we were to join them next morning.

Early on November 28th we resumed our march through a light valley-mist, and soon fell in with our companions of the road. They were numerous, but I spare my reader a minute description, since they presented nothing very different from what we have already met. The most original men of the party, and whom Barakāt and myself studied with some curiosity, were three individuals, natives of Wadi Dowāsir; one a blind "Meṭow'waa'" ignorant, fanatic, and avariciously mean beyond all imagination; the other, a countryman from the same district, and not much better than his associate and pastor; the third, his son, who, like Falstaff's page, had doubtless a good angel about him, but the devil outbid him too. Most of the others were ordinary merchants, with nothing special to say for themselves; this time we had no Bedouins in our company, and no regret for their absence.

The first day led us out of Wadi Soley'. We traversed the outskirting plantations of Salemee'yah, a large fortified village, indeed a town in size, and once the capital of Yemāmah and residence of the Da'ās family. It is often known by the name of the Khorj, no less than the district around it. The practice of using the same denomination indifferently for the head town of a province and the entire province itself, is a frequent source of confusion in Arab geography. Thus, "Shām" is at once Damascus and the whole of Syria. Teyma', Nejrān, Djowf, Ḥasa, are words of like ambiguity. This, with the constant recurrence of the same descriptive appellations, like "Rowḍah" "a garden," "Ḳela'at" "a castle," "Theneeyat" "a pass," "Djowf" "a hollow," "Akhaf" "sand-hills," and the like, renders Arab local nomenclature one of the poorest, and at the same time one of the obscurest, in the world. The whole system is bad, and seems expressly calculated to render difficult the identification of places.

In this Khorj or Salemee'yah is the ordinary abode of Sa'ood, our former friend, and second son of Feysul, when not absent, which is often the case, in Ḥooṭah and the Ḥareeḳ. The country around is the most fertile of the Yemāmah, and the paradise of Nejed; but the vegetation, trees, or plants, differ little from that of Wadi Ḥaneefah, except in greater continuity of extent and depth of green. Cotton alone by its frequency forms an exception to the uniformity of palm-groves, maize, and millet, more than elsewhere. Of the character of the population and their politico-religious tendencies I have spoken already; I may add that they are generally considered gentler and more amiable than the inhabitants of Riaḍ and Ḍerey'eeyah. But they are, with few exceptions, sincere Wahhabees; they were once the most devoted followers of the hapless Moseylemah.

Much to my regret, our caravan passed on without halting, and soon after, turning a little to the north, we entered a long gorge cleft in the limestone wall of Ṭoweyḳ, and mounted for about three hundred feet till we came on a high broad steppe, where a scanty pasturage, just enough to brown the chalky soil here and there, maintained a few herds of sheep-like goats, or goat-like sheep; while the dreary ascents and descents reminded me of scenes in Scotland, save that fir and pine were here wanting. We were long in traversing this waste, until towards evening we came on a patch of greener soil, and a cluster of wells, the Laḳey'yāt by name, and here we encamped for a very cold night.

Next morning the whole country, hill and dale, trees and bushes, was wrapped in a thick blanket of mist, fitter for Surrey than for Arabia. So dense was the milky fog, that we fairly lost our way, and went on at random, shouting and hallooing, driving our beasts now here, now there, over broken ground and amid tangling shrubs, till the sun gained strength, and the vapour cleared off, showing us the path at some distance on our right. Before we had followed it far, we saw a black mass advancing from the east to meet us. It was the first division of the Ḥaṣa troops on their way to Riaḍ; they were not less than four or five hundred in number. Like true Arabs, they marched with a noble contempt of order and discipline—walking, galloping, ambling, singing, shouting, alone or in bands, as fancy led. We interchanged a few words of greeting with these brisk boys, and they informed us that their general of brigade, Moḥammed-es-Sedeyree, with the main *corps d'armée* and the artillery, had already set out, but were a day or two in the rear. For themselves, they avowed without hesitation or shame, that they should much have preferred to stay at home, and that enforced necessity, not any military or religious ardour, was taking them to the field. We laughed, and wished them Zāmil's head, or him theirs, whereon they laughed also, shouted, and passed on.

Whilst hereabouts, we caught a magnificent southward view of the Ḥareeḳ, to which we were now opposite, though separated from it by a streak of desert. Its hills, seemingly granite (but I beg my readers, once for all, expressly to remember that I am no more of a geologian than I am a botanist, "the more's the pity"), lie east and west in a ragged and isolated chain, which was apparently sixty miles or more in length. Thus girdled by the desert, Ḥareeḳ must needs be a very hot district; indeed, its name (literally, "burning") implies no less, and the dusky tint of its inhabitants confirms the fact. We could not at such a distance distinguish any towns or castles in particular; only the situation of the capital, Ḥooṭah, was pointed out to us by the knowing ones of our band. It was curious also to see how suddenly, almost abruptly, Djebel Ṭoweyḳ ended in the desert, going down in a rapid series of precipitous steps, the last of which plunges sheer into the waste of sand. Ṭoweyḳ is here mainly limestone, but in some spots iron-ore is to be found, in some copper; Aboo-'Eysa pointed out to us a hill, the appearance of which promised the latter metal, with the remark that Europeans, were they here, would make good use of it.

On we went, but through a country of much more varied scenery than what we had traversed the day before, enjoying the "pleasure situate in hill and dale," with pretty little groves of Sidr, and clumps of wide-branched Markh, till we arrived at the foot of a high white cliff, almost like that of Dover; but these crags, instead of having the sea at their foot, overlooked a wide valley full of trees, and bearing traces of many violent winter torrents from east to west; none were now flowing. Here we halted and passed an indifferent night, much annoyed by "chill November's surly blast," hardly less ungenial here than on the banks of Ayr, though sweeping over a latitude of 25°, not 56°.

Before the starlight had faded from the cold morning sky we were up and in movement, for a long march was before us. After a little parleying, so to speak, with the mountain, we climbed it by a steep winding path, hard of ascent to the camels, of whom Arabs report that when asked which they like best, going up hill or going down, they answer, "A curse light on them both." "Maledetto l'ottimo," an Italian might render it. At sunrise we stood on the last and here the highest ledge of Ṭoweyḳ, that long chalky wall which bounds and backs up Nejed on the east; beyond is the desert, and then the coast. The view now opened to us was very extensive, and the keen air made all the more sensible our elevation above the far-off plains, that hence showed like a faintly-ribbed sea-surface to the west. Neither man nor beast, tree nor shrub, appeared around; marl and pebbles formed the plateau, all dry and dreary under a cold wind and a hot sun.

After about three hours of level route we began to descend, not rapidly, but by degrees, and at noon we reached a singular depression, a huge natural basin, hollowed out in the limestone rock, with tracks resembling deep trenches leading to it from every side. At the bottom of this crater-like valley were a dozen or more wells, so abundant in their supply that they not unfrequently overflow the whole space and form a small lake; the water is clear and good, but no other is to be met with on the entire line from hence to Ḥaṣa. At these wells (whose geographical position has earned them the name of Oweysiṭ, the diminutive of Owseṭ, or centre) meet several converging roads; that of Ḥareeḳ, from the south; that of Yemāmah and Southern Nejed—our own route—from the west; that of Djebreen and Wāb, leading down Wadi Soley', from the north-west; a narrow mountain track, frequented by few but shepherds, follows the entire length of the ridge northwards till it falls in with the road of Koweyt and Zobeyr; last is the eastward path, leading to Ḥaṣa and Hofhoof; by this we were now to travel. All the flocks and herds of the adjoining mountain region resort hither to drink.

We now rested awhile, prepared a cup of coffee, filled our water-skins almost to bursting, and then with the briskness of men who have made up their minds to a hard pull, remounted our dromedaries and emerged from the crater by its eastern outlet. For the rest of the day we continued steadily to descend the broad even slope, whose extreme barrenness and inanimate monotony reminded me of the pebbly uplands near Ma'ān on the opposite side of the Peninsula, traversed by us exactly seven months before. The sun set, night came on, and many of the travellers would gladly have halted, but Aboo-'Eysa insisted on continuing the march. We were now many hundred feet lower than the crest behind us, and the air felt warm and heavy, when we noticed that the ground, hitherto hard beneath our feet, was changing step by step into a light sand that seemed to encroach on the rocky soil. It was at first a shallow ripple, then deepened, and before long presented the well-known ridges and undulations characteristic of the land ocean when several fathoms in depth. Our beasts ploughed laboriously on through the yielding surface; the night was dark, but starry; and we could just discern amid the shade a white glimmer of spectral sand-hills rising around us on every side, but no track or indication of a route.

It was the great Dahnā, or "Red Desert," the bugbear of even the wandering Bedouin, and never traversed by ordinary wayfarers without an apprehension which has too often been justified by fatal incidents. So light are the sands, so capricious the breezes that shape and reshape them daily into unstable hills and valleys, that no trace of preceding travellers remains to those who follow; while intense heat and glaring light reflected on all sides combine with drought and weariness to confuse and bewilder the adventurer, till he loses his compass and wanders up and down at random amid a waste solitude which soon becomes his grave. Many have thus perished; even whole caravans have been known to disappear in the Dahnā without a vestige; till the wild Arab tales of demons carrying off wanderers, or ghouls devouring them, obtain a half credit among many accustomed elsewhere to laugh at such fictions. However, will they nill they, merchants, travellers, messengers, armies—in a word, all who pass to and fro between the populous Ḥasa and the imperial Nejed—must cross this desert, and that by one especial line, for in all other directions the Dahnā is, with hardly any exception, impracticable. On either side, indeed, of this sand-river, the roads are clearly indicated nor liable to mistake, the whole difficulty consists in the intermediate space. To lessen its risks, Aboo-'Eysa, with a degree of public spirit very rare in the East, had two years before laden several camels with a prodigious quantity of large stones, which he had thus conveyed midway across the sands, and there piled them up in what Arabs style a "Rejm," namely, a stone-heap, or rough pyramid, between twenty-five or thirty feet high, forming a most desirable landmark in the pathless desert. The changes effected in the sand by winds and tempests are seldom enough to overwhelm so large a pile; and should it even be covered up for a day or two, a second gale soon blows the light mantle off again from the stony nucleus. Many a blessing had been bestowed on Aboo-'Eysa for his Rejm, and much aid had been thereby afforded to travellers. Better still, Aboo-Ḍahir-el-Ghannām, the same in whose company we now were, and whose business often obliged him to cross this dreary space, had been seized by an honourable emulation, and had constructed a second stone-heap farther on, known by the name of Rejmat-el-Ghannām, as the former by that of Rejmat Abee-'Eysa. But, in spite of these rude direction-posts, the way of the Dahnā continues always a hazardous one, and our own caravan was not far from adding another page to the long chapter of accidents.

For, after about three hours of night travelling, or rather

wading, among the sand-waves, till men and beasts alike were ready to sink for weariness, a sharp altercation arose between Aboo-'Eysa and El-Ghannām, each proposing a different direction of march. We all halted a moment, and raised our eyes heavy with drowsiness and fatigue, as if to see which of the contending parties was in the right. It will be long before I forget the impression of that moment. Above us was the deep black sky, spangled with huge stars of a brilliancy denied to all but an Arab gaze, while what is elsewhere a ray of the third magnitude becomes here of the first amid the pure vacuum of a mistless, vapourless air; around us loomed high ridges, shutting us in before and behind with their white ghost-like outlines; below our feet the lifeless sand, and everywhere a silence that seemed to belong to some strange and dreamy world where man might not venture. Aboo-'Eysa stretched his arm to point out one way, El-Ghannām another, and either direction appeared equally devoid of pass or outlet. After awhile, however, Aboo-'Eysa cut the matter short by raising his voice, shouting to all to follow him, and, spite of the resistance which Ghannām persisted in making, led us all off at a sharp angle on the left, till at last we floundered down into a sort of valley where a few bushes diversified the sand, and dismounted for a few hours of repose; warmer at any rate than that of the preceding night.

Next morning we resumed our course, but now under the sole guidance of Aboo-'Eysa, to whom our band, confiding in his superior conversance with this wild region, had unanimously agreed to entrust themselves till we should reach the opposite bank. How our leader contrived to direct his steps would be hard to tell; the faculty of keeping one's nose in the right direction when neither eyes nor ears can afford any assistance, is, I suppose, one of the many latent powers of human nature, only to be brought out by circumstance and long exercise. When not far from the midmost of the Dahnā, we fell in with a few Bedouins, belonging to the Aāl-Morrah clan, sole tenants of this desert; they were leading their goats to little spots of scattered herbage and shrubs which here and there fix a precarious existence in the hollows of the sands. The flocks themselves can, by special privilege of endurance, pass four or five days at a time without watering; and when at last even they must drink, their shepherds conduct them to the Oweysiṭ or some other brackish well on the verge of Ṭoweyḳ, unknown to ordinary mortals. More savage-looking beings than these Aāl-Morrah Bedouins I never saw; their hair was elf-locks, their dress rags, their complexion grime, their look wildness personified. But in speech, that distinctive countersign of the human animal, they proved themselves not only men, but men of eloquence also. Their dialect was wholly different from that of the north, or even of Nejed; it puzzled me at first; when I came to master it, I found it belonging to that ancient, or indeed primeval, form of Arabic for which I must once more refer my readers to such specimens as those preserved in the Proverbs of Meidanee, and rendered into uncouth Teutonic Latin by the learned Freytag. This form of language is richer in variety of words and turns of speech than the cast-iron dialect of the Coran, whose geometrical accuracy and monotonous cadence have assigned the boundary-lines of more modern Arabic; its terminations are of the archaic modification already alluded to in a former chapter; and its roots less seldom coincide with those of Hebrew or Syriac; peculiarities which harmonize with the anterior and southern, perhaps African, origin assigned it by historical tradition, before the epoch of Ismael and the immigration of the northerly tribes of Ḥejāz. The Aāl-Morrah themselves are a very widely spread tribe; a small portion of them only acknowledge the Wahhabee influence by an occasional tribute and a mangled prayer; the greater number pass for sheer infidels, and in matters of religion and manners much resemble our old friends the Sherarat, as they figure in the first chapter of this work. Their duskiness verges almost on blackness; their weapons spears and knives, for the musket has made little progress among them. Eloquence alone remains to them of all the heritage of Ḳaḥṭān; in other respects they are mere savages, but not barbarous; I found them even good-natured, though impudent and predatory, like all their Bedouin brethren.

Theirs is the great desert from Nejed to Ḥaḍramaut. Not that they actually cover this immense space, a good fourth of the Peninsula; but that they have the free and undisputed range of the oases which it occasionally offers, where herbs, shrubs, and dwarf-palms cluster round some well of scant and briny water. These oases are sufficiently numerous to preserve a stray Bedouin or two from perishing, though not enough so to become landmarks for any regular route across the central Dahnā. From the main sand-waste runs out the long and broad arm which we were now traversing; it presents like features with the southern desert, till, after pushing on to the north between Djebel Ṭoweyḳ and the coast-range of Ḥaṣa, it ends in the plain of Zobeyr behind Koweyt, nearly parallel with the northern extremity of the Persian Gulf.

From our Aāl-Morrah friends Aboo-'Eysa now took indications for the way we had to follow, and thus procured us five minutes of standing still, but without alighting from our camels. About an hour after, we came in sight of his Rejm, a work of much labour and cost. Reassured by its eloquent silence that we were certainly on the right track, we hastened on, very weary from the intense heat, yet unwilling to halt in this region of danger. When the afternoon was somewhat advanced, we saw coming up from the east, and not far on our left, what seemed a troop of black ants; it approached, and we discerned in it the main army of Ḥaṣa, slowly dragging along with them through the sands two heavy guns sent from Ḳaṭeef for the siege of 'Oneyzah. The number of this division, much larger than the former, could not have been less than seven or eight hundred men; but we did not meet them, as they kept about a quarter of a mile aside of us to the north; and no one in either party had curiosity enough to take him a circuitous scamper through the sands for the sake of gossip.

After sunset we reached the second Rejm or cairn, if cairn may be called a heap of stones with no one buried under it; this is Rejmat-el-Ghannām. Here the desert-scene began to change; the sands were henceforth mixed with gravel, and gave firmer footing to our beasts. We alighted for supper; I might entitle it breakfast, for we had taken nothing all day. Every one rejoiced at our leaving the Dahnā in our rear. But the success of Aboo-'Eysa, who had piloted the caravan better than their original leader, aroused in the breast of El-Ghannām and his partisans the feeling which "does merit as its shade pursue," and nowhere more than in Arabia. I must allow that the prevalence of this unamiable passion somewhat vitiates my parallel between the Arabs and the English—not that Englishmen or other Europeans are wholly and absolutely free from it, yet Western envy bears no comparison with Eastern. However this may be, an open rupture now took place between the rival chiefs, and as the rest of the way was easy to find, Ghannām could all the better afford the quarrel. Some travellers sided with the one, some with the other; high words were interchanged, and we seemed on the point of having a regular "Yowm" or "day," as Arabs term a fight. Whereon Barakāt and I interposed, by suggesting to Aboo-'Eysa that he had best push on with us and whoever else might choose to follow, and by arriving the first at Hofhoof complete his triumph over El-Ghannām. *Detto, fatto*, and off we started with two or three in our suite, leaving our mortified competitors to their coffee and humiliation.

The ground, for it now deserved that name, being about equal parts of pebble, marl, and sand, sloped down to the east, and glistered to the far horizon in barren whiteness, interrupted here and there by dark streaks of low and thorny thicket. Sheltered by one of these clusters, we snatched a few hours of brief rest, followed by another day of most monotonous plain, in level and character just like that of the preceding evening. A few travellers whom we met coming up from Djoon in Ḥasa, and who took us for robbers and almost died of fear, so fierce did we look, made the sole variety for fourteen hours of road. Villages, shade, and wells, of course there were none; fortunately the heat was much more supportable here than it had been amid the sand.

Another night's bivouac, and then again over the white down-sloping plain. At last a change ensued, abruptly chalky hills and narrow gorges bounded our way, till at the bottom of a hollow we came on a large solitary tree with more thorns than leaves, and in hermit loneliness. "Here," said Aboo-'Eysa, "Ibraheem Basha caused a well to be sunk for at least sixty feet in depth, in hopes of finding water, but to no purpose." The dry pit, now half filled up with stones and sand, remained a witness of the attempt. Had it succeeded, the difficulty of the communications between Nejed and the eastern coast would have been much alleviated.

A little farther on we entered the great valley, known by the name of Wadi Farooḳ. This valley, like all other leading geographical features of this region, whether mountain or plain, runs from north to south; its general type resembles the Dahnā, of which it is in a manner a parallel offshoot. Deep and wide, it contains a labyrinth of sand-hills, among which, hardly less than in the Dahnā, travellers often lose their way, and occasionally their lives. But what gives Wadi Farooḳ an especially bad reputation, is the infesting presence of marauders, sometimes belonging to Aāl-Morrah, sometimes to the Menāseer Bedouins, a tribe whose fuller acquaintance we shall make farther east; and "You dogs, your lives or purses," is the frequent alternative propounded by some "bold thief" to the honest men of this road. The Wahhabees, who most properly abhor all robbers but themselves, have again and again tried to put down the brigands of Farooḳ, though hitherto without much success, and the Aāl-Morrah still hold their own—and sometimes their neighbours'.

We descended into the valley about noon, crossed it not altogether without anxiety, and near sunset climbed the opposite bank, and began to thread the coast-range of Ḥasa. For here too the desert is separated from the sea by that barren and rugged line of hills which passes round the entire, or almost the entire, circumference of Arabia, beginning at 'Aḳabah on the north-west, then down the whole length of the Red Sea, round by 'Aden and Naḳab-el-Ḥajjār fronting the Indian Ocean, till it comes up to Rās-el-Ḥaḍḍ, and lastly follows the coast of 'Omān and the Persian Gulf almost to its northern extremity. Occasionally, but very seldom, it leaves a gap; its height is for the most part inconsiderable, hardly exceeding a thousand feet; but sometimes, in 'Omān for instance, it reaches an elevation of six thousand feet above the sea, while the chain broadens out at the same time into a wide mountain district. Opposite Wadi Farooḳ the hills attain, after my very rough observations, about fourteen hundred feet above the sea-level, and about four hundred above the desert on the west, which would thus be itself bout a thousand feet higher than the coast. The mountains of Ḥasa contain here and there limestone, but their main components are, I believe, granite and sandstone, with occasional quartz and basalt. Their sides are often eaten out into caverns, and their whole look is fanciful and desolate in the extreme.

It was now three days and a half since our last supply of water, and Aboo-'Eysa was anxious to reach the journey's end without delay. Similar reasons had acted no less powerfully on El-Ghannūm and his companions, who by dint of forced marches here overtook us; we all made peace, and pushed on together over hills that shone like gold in the rich mellow rays of the setting sun. As darkness closed around we reached the furthermost heights, entitled Theneeyat-Ghūr, from a small village hidden among the mountain clefts. Hence we overlooked the plains of Ḥasa, but could distinguish nothing through the deceptive rays of the rising moon; we seemed to gaze into a vast milky ocean. After an hour's halt for supper, we wandered on, now up, now down, over pass and crag, till a long corkscrew descent down the precipitous sea-side of the mountain for a thousand feet or near it, placed us fairly upon the low level of Ḥasa, and within the warm damp air of the sea-coast.

The ground glimmered white to the moon, and gave a firm footing to our dromedaries, who by their renewed agility seemed to partake in the joy of their riders, and to understand that rest was near. We were in fact all so eager to find ourselves at home and homestead, that although the town of Hofhoof, our destined goal, was yet full fifteen miles to the north-east, we despised whatever repose the neighbouring hovels of Ghoweyr, at the foot of the pass, or the village of Sha'abah, about five miles distant on our right, could offer, and pressed on for the capital. And there, in fact, we should have all arrived in a body before day-dawn, had not a singular occurrence retarded by far the greater number of our companions.

Soon after the crags in our rear had shut out, perhaps for years, perhaps for ever, the desert and Central Arabia from our view, while before and around us lay the indistinct undulations and uncertain breaks of the great Ḥasa plain, when on a sloping bank at a short distance in front we discerned certain large black patches, in strong contrast with the white glister of the soil around, and at the same time our attention was attracted by a strange whizzing like that of a flight of hornets, close along the ground, while our dromedaries capered and started as though struck with sudden insanity. The cause of all this was a vast swarm of locusts, here alighted in their northerly wanderings from their birthplace in the Dahnā; their camp extended far and wide, and we had already disturbed their outposts. These insects are wont to settle on the ground after sunset, and there, half stupefied by the night chill, to await the morning rays, which warm them once more into life and movement. This time our dromedaries did the work of the sun, and it would be hard to say which of the two were the most frightened, they or the locusts. It was truly laughable to see so huge a beast lose his wits for fear at the flight of a harmless, stingless insect; of all timid creatures none equal the "ship of the desert" for cowardice.

But if the beasts were frightened, not so their masters; I really thought they would have gone mad for joy. Locusts are here an article of food, nay, a dainty, and a good swarm of them is begged of Heaven in Arabia no less fervently than it would be deprecated in India or in Syria. This difference of sentiment is grounded on several reasons; a main one lies in the diversity of the insects themselves. The locust of Inner Arabia is very unlike whatever of the same genus I have seen elsewhere. Those of the north are small, of a pale green colour, and resemble not a little our own ordinary grasshoppers. They are never, to my knowledge, eaten by the Bedouins or villagers of Syria, Mesopotamia and 'Irāk, nor do I believe them eatable under any circumstances, extreme hunger perhaps alone excepted. Like bees, they have a queen, whose size is proportioned to her majesty; but, like bees in this point also, locust queens do not lead the swarms, but keep retired state. The locust of Arabia is, on the contrary, a reddish-brown insect, twice or three times the size of its northern homonym, resembling a large prawn in appearance, and as long as a man's little finger, which it equals also in thickness. Among these locusts I neither saw nor heard of any queen, a deficit which tends to class them with the species "Arbah" of the Bible, as described by Solomon, if Solomon it be, in the penultimate chapter of the Proverbs. The names "Djandeb" and "Djerād" are applied indifferently by the Arabs to this insect, but I think that the former is more common. The long hind-legs bear the name of "Keraa'."

This locust when boiled or fried is said to be delicious, and boiled and fried accordingly they are to an incredible extent. However, I could never persuade myself to taste them, whatever invitations the inhabitants of the land, smacking their lips over large dishes full of entomological "délicatesses" could make me to join them. Barakāt ventured on one for a trial; he pronounced it oily and disgusting, nor added a second to the first; it is caviare to unaccustomed palates.

The swarm now before us was a thorough godsend for our Arabs, on no account to be neglected. Thirst, weariness, all was forgotten, and down the riders leapt from their starting camels; this one spread out a cloak, that one a saddle-bag, a third his shirt, over the unlucky creatures destined for the morrow's meal. Some flew away whirring across our feet, others were caught and tied up in cloths and sacks; Cornish wreckers at work about a shattered East-Indiaman would be beaten by Ghannām and his companions with the locusts. However, Barakāt and myself felt no special interest in the chase, nor had we much desire to turn our dress and accoutrements into receptacles for living game. Luckily Aboo-'Eysa still retained enough of his North Syrian education to be of our mind also. Accordingly we left our associates hard at work, turned our startled and still unruly dromedaries in the direction of Hofhoof, and set off full speed over the plain.

Thirteen or fourteen miles we rode on together, and passed the little village of 'Eyn-Nejm, or Fountain of the Star, where the shadows of its houses darkened the moonshine on the white cliffs under Ghoweyr. Here was not long since a hot and sulphurous spring, famous for the cure of cutaneous diseases, a fact easily understood, and for that of paralysis also, though on the correctness of this point I am rather doubtful; perhaps some coincidences may have occurred, and been set down for healings. In popular belief 'Eyn-Nejm was a panacea for all ruined constitutions. An open cupola had been erected by former generations over the source, and bath receptacles constructed around. Hither crowds repaired, and often found the health they sought, till the place became a point of resort and meeting for all around, and attracted the suspicious attention of the Riaḍ government. Order was given in consequence, about three years before the date of our visit, to destroy the cupola and the baths, and to choke up the mouth of the fountain with stones, lest, to quote the words of Feyṣul's orthodox firman, "the people should learn to put their trust in the waters rather than in God, which would be idolatry." The imperial decree was executed, and the ruins of the "Ḳubbah" or dome, with the hot stream that yet escapes from between the piles of rubbish, remain to attest the bounty of the Creator, the stupid narrow-mindedness of the Wahhabee, and the ill fortune of a land governed by bigots. It is an old tale, and not peculiar to Arabia.

Farther on we sighted another small village, whose name I forgot to note. But it was not till near morning that we saw before us in indistinct row the long black lines of the immense date-groves that surround Hofhoof. Then, winding on amid rice-grounds and cornfields, we left on our right an isolated fort (to be described by daylight), passed some scattered villas with their gardens, approached the ruined town walls and entered the southern gate, now open and unguarded. Farther on a few streets brought us before the door of Aboo-'Eysa's house, our desired resting-place.

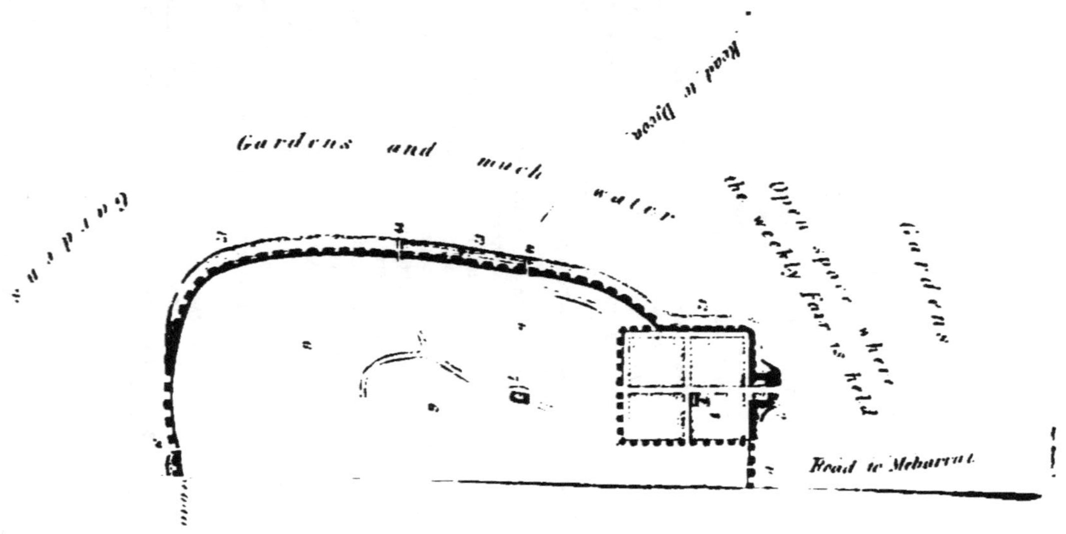
Gardens
Gardens and much water
Road to Djeon
Open space where the weekly fair is held
Gardens
Road to Meharrat

CHAPTER XIII

FROM HOFHOOF TO ḲAṬEEF

Hardly the place of such antiquity
Or note, of these great monarchies we find;
Only a fading verbal memory;
An empty name in writ is left behind.—*Fletcher*

ABOO-'EYSA'S HOME—GENERAL CHARACTER OF THE INHABITANTS OF ḤAŞA—THEIR AVERSION FROM THE WAHHABEES—RISE AND PROGRESS OF THE CARMATHIAN MOVEMENT IN ARABIA—ITS CHARACTER AND RESULTS—SUBSEQUENT FORTUNES OF ḤAŞA—OUR LODGINGS AT HOFHOOF—DESCRIPTION OF THE TOWN—THE KÔT—THE ḲEYSAREEYAH—THE RIFEY'-EEYAH—THE NA'ĀTHAR—FORTIFICATIONS—THE KHOṬEYM—NEIGHBOURHOOD OF HOFHOOF—HOT SPRINGS—EARTHQUAKES—NATURE OF THIS DISTRICT—VEGETATION—DECLINE OF AGRICULTURE, MANUFACTURE, AND COMMERCE—CLIMATE—NABṬEE VERSIFICATION—THE NABATHÆANS—WHO THEY WERE—REMARKS ON THE MISAPPLICATION OF NAMES—LITERATURE IN ḤAŞA—DRESS—ORNAMENT—PLEASURE PARTIES OF MOGHOR—OUR OWN LIFE AT HOFHOOF—EVENINGS IN SOCIETY—DISAFFECTION AGAINST ISLAM AND THE WAHHABEE GOVERNMENT—ANTI-WAHHABEE CONSPIRACY—ITS RAMIFICATIONS AND PROGRESS—NEJDEAN SPIES—A FAIR AT HOFHOOF—VISIT TO MEBARRAZ—THE CASTLE AND TOWN—INTERIOR OF A HOUSE—GARDENS AND PLANTATIONS—THE KHALĀŞ DATE—VISIT TO OMM-SABAA'—DESCRIPTION OF THE FOUNTAIN—AN ARAB PICNIC—THE WATERS OF ḤAŞA—WOMEN—ARAB CURRENCY—THE ḤAŞA COINAGE—PLANS FOR VISITING 'OMĀN—DEPARTURE FROM HOFHOOF—AN INCIDENT—KELĀBEEYAH—THE NORTH ḤAŞA ROAD—CHARACTER OF THE COUNTRY—DJEBEL-MUSHAHHAR—BEDOUINS—'AZMIAH—HILLS OF ḲAṬEEF—THE PLAIN—AN AQUEDUCT—TOWN OF ḲAṬEEF—THE CASTLE—THE SEA—DESCRIPTION OF THE HARBOUR—FEYŞUL'S NAVY—FARḤĀT, GOVERNOR OF ḲAṬEEF—PALACE OF ḲARMOOṬ—FARḤĀT'S Ḳ'HĀWAH—NEIGHBOURHOOD OF ḲAṬEEF—RUINS—A SEMI-PERSIAN SUPPER—LIFE OF NEJDEANS AT ḲAṬEEF—WE EMBARK FOR MOḤARREḲ.

IT was still night. All was silent in the street and house at the entrance of which we now stood; indeed, none but the master of a domicile could think of knocking at such an hour, nor was Aboo-'Eysa expected at that precise moment. With much difficulty he contrived to awake the tenants; next the shrill voice of the lady was heard within in accents of joy and welcome, the door at last opened, and Aboo-'Eysa invited us into a dark passage, where a gas-light would have been a remarkable improvement, and by this ushered us into the K'hāwah. Here we lighted a fire, and after a hasty refreshment all lay down to sleep, nor awoke till the following forenoon.

Our stay at Hofhoof was very pleasant and interesting, not indeed through personal incidents and hairbreadth escapes—of those we had had a fair traveller's portion at Riad and elsewhere—but in the information here acquired, and in the novel character of everything around us, whether nature, art, or man. Aboo-'Eysa was very anxious that we should see as much as possible of the country, and procured us all means requisite for so doing, while the shelter of his conscious roof, and the precautions which he adopted or suggested, obviated whatever dangers and inconveniences we had experienced in former stages of the journey. Besides, the general disposition of the inhabitants of Hasa is very different from that met with in Nejed and even in Shomer or Djowf, and much better adapted to make a stranger feel himself at home. A sea-coast people, looking mainly to foreign lands and the ocean for livelihood and commerce, accustomed to see among them not unfrequently men of dress, manners, and religion differing from their own, many of them themselves travellers or voyagers to Basrah, Bagdad, Bahreyn, 'Omān, and some even farther, they are commonly free from that half-wondering, half-suspicious feeling which the sight of a stranger occasions in the isolated desert-girded centre; in short, experience, that best of masters, has gone far to unteach the lessons of ignorance, intolerance, and national aversion. Free intercourse with other races has indeed in all lands, unless I am much mistaken, this excellent effect, that, while it nowise lessens, nay even strengthens, national and patriotic feelings, it encourages at the same time a kindlier and a more generous way of thought and action towards other branches of the great human family, and renders men more social to all, without disuniting them among themselves. The history of commercial nations and sea-port cities, whether chronicled in records or read by observers in the great book of life whose pages are countries, affords a constant proof of this.

In Ḥaṣa also, independently of the external and circumstantial causes just alluded to, the character of the inhabitants themselves is little predisposed to exclusiveness and asperity. Wahhabeeism exists indeed, but only among the few who form the dominant and hated class; while its presence serves by natural reaction to render the main bulk of the inhabitants yet more averse from a system whose evils they know not only by theory, but more by frequent and bitter experience. Nay, Mahometanism itself, though varnished over most of the surface, is scarce skin-deep, and numbers who hate Islam no less in its ordinary than in its Wahhabee form, are devoid of even this superficial coating. What then is here the prevalent tone and tendency of belief and usage? The question is not easy to answer, nor the answer perhaps more easy to understand, without a certain amount of previous knowledge and research, involving too much minute and lengthy detail for the limits of this work. I will, however, do my best, though in a summary manner, to unravel for the benefit of my readers a skein which cost my own mental fingers no little trouble.

From the period of the great schism which in the first century of Islam divided the Mahometan world into two distinct sections —namely, the Sonnee or orthodox, and the Shiya'ee or the faction of 'Alee and his family, a faction including all attached to that race, and imbued with their peculiar and mystic doctrine —Ḥaṣa, with the adjoining lands that reach northwards along the banks of the Euphrates and the Tigris, had joined herself to the latter or Shiya'ee party, and partook, in a measure, of all the vicissitudes of fortune and phases of mind through which the Fatemite family and their partisans were destined to pass. But while the armies of the Ommiade dynasty, and above all the cruelties of the bloodthirsty and infamous Ḥejjāj, repressed the Shiya'ees of Coufa and Baṣrah, Ḥaṣa, more fortunate in the protection of the intervening desert, was comparatively left to herself, and her inhabitants maintained their distinctive ways and tenets without much molestation from the victorious Sonnees. In Ḥaṣa accordingly, the exiled disciples of Moseylemah, the broken troops of Aboo-Na'āmat-el-Ḳaṭaree, the soldiers of the heroic Shebeeb-Aboo-eḍ-Ḍoḳḥāk, the scattered survivors of the prodigies and castle of 'Áta-el-Khorassānee (more famous by his title of Moḳannaa', or the "Veiled" Prophet) —all these, and many others of analogous belief and fortunes, took secure refuge, while each successive band brought with it fresh enmity to Islam, and bitterer hatred against the Mahometan system and rule.

The separation of Ḥaṣa from that great body of which the Ḥejāzee Arabs were at once the framers and the backbone, was further encouraged by difference of national origin. The first known colonists of these coasts had been Benoo-Khālid and Benoo-Hājar, both of them Ḳaḥṭānic tribes, and hence unsympathizing with the Arabs whom history or mythos designates by the symbol of Ismael. To the two clans already mentioned had been added the numerous family of Fezārah, Nejdean indeed in origin, but banished by long wars and an enmity of almost fabulous bitterness from Nejed, nor more disposed to fraternize with the Ḥejāzees and their caliphs than the Ḳaḥṭānees themselves. Last, the clans of Kelb (mortal enemies they of Ḳoreysh), of Belee, of Tenookh, and all the countless branches of Ḳoḍaa', the noblest and most high-spirited among the children of Ḳaḥṭān, had overspread the whole eastern coast from Ḳaṭar to Baṣrah, and reached even farther north. Of all the Arab race these were the last to take Islam, and the first to lose it. Finally, the neighbourhood of Persia, and the intoxicating atmosphere of her strange mysticism, were here strongly felt; and this appears to have been the case even in the remotest times on which the doubtful glimmer of legend throws just enough light to redeem them from absolute obscurity. In short, Ḥaṣa, formerly, like 'Omān, a stronghold of Sabeeism, and now a subject, rather than a convert, to Islam, was anything but a favourable soil for Mahometan orthodoxy and allegiance.

Much fermentation of opinion, many partial, and for that very reason ineffectual, movements, took place in this province during the first two centuries of Islam; but I pass them by to arrive at the great outbreak headed by Aboo-Sa'eed-el-Djenābee, popularly known as El-Ḳarmooṭ, a name of which the world-wide celebrity equals the obscurity of its origin, and whence our own European term "Carmathian." In vain did the Caliph of Bagdad, Ma'teḍad-b-'Illāh, in the year 287 of the Hejirah, send his most numerous troops and bravest generals to trample out the rising flame; the armies of Islam were cut to pieces in the battle of Djebel Moghāzee by the infuriated Carmathians, whose hatred of Mahometanism led them so far as to burn all their surviving prisoners alive, reserving from the flames one officer alone, whom they dismissed to announce at Bagdad the fate of his companions. Aboo-Sa'eed-el-Ḳarmooṭ, no longer held in check by fear of the Abbaside soldiery, burst forth with his followers from Ḥasa, and extended his ravages far and wide over Mesopotamia and Syria itself. To this prince is ascribed the erection of the great fort and palace at Ḳaṭeef, for more than eight hundred years after the stronghold of his race. But the exploits of his son and successor Aboo-Ṭāhir Soleymān threw those of his father into the shade.

Now followed those tremendous and devastating wars which sealed the downfall of Mahometanism throughout two-thirds of Arabia, while they menaced its very existence in the rest of the Eastern world. With the sword of his predecessor Dja'oonat-el-Ḳaṭaree (first chief of the Khowarij in the sixtieth year after the Hejirah) in his hand, and with his verses in his mouth—those verses of which Ebn-Khallikān has said that "they would impart courage to the greatest coward that God Almighty ever created"—Aboo-Ṭāhir-el-Ḳarmooṭ now held the trembling caliph a prisoner in Bagdad, now menaced the citadel of Aleppo, and now filled the precincts of the Ca'abah and the well of Zemzem with Mahometan corpses. In a former chapter I gave, or attempted to give, a faint English echo of Arabian love-song. A few lines from the war-cry of Dja'oonat-el-Ḳaṭaree and Aboo-Ṭāhir Soleymān may not be unacceptable to my readers; the more so as historical is here added to poetical interest:—

I said to my soul, when a moment struck with dread
In presence of the hostile squadrons, Shame on thee, why dost thou fear?
Wert thou to do thy utmost to prolong thy being for but one day
Beyond the destined term allotted thee, 't were all in vain;
Bear up, then, amid the eddies of death, bear up,
An eternity of life were an unattainable desire.
Length of days is no mantle of honour to the wearer,
Be it then a robe to wrap the faint-hearted, the coward;
Death is life's goal, and all our paths lead thither;
Death is king, and his herald summons one and all;

And he who ends not in blood must bear wrong and decrepitude,
Till he too is cut off by death from life and being.
Life is no blessing to a man, nor worth possessing,
When old age classes him among things no longer of use or value.

But the wars, the successes, the reverses of the mighty sect named after El-Ḳarmooṭ, belong to general history, and may be sufficiently studied in the annals of the East. It was a strong effort of the human mind to break the bonds of formalism and theocratic fatalism, and to reassert its own native liberty and unfettered action; like most such efforts, too, it overshot its mark. But when after a struggle of more than a century the fortunes of Islam had prevailed, when the Black Stone had been washed in rose-water and restored to the Ca'abah, when the great Unitheist Creed had triumphed over its fierce Rationalistic antagonist, much had been undone during the strife that could not be subsequently replaced, and there were ruins which no legislation or authority could repair. Above all, the original focus and centre of the outbreak remained, as always happens in such cases, irretrievably lost to the second restoration. The mountains of the Valais, the forests of Bohemia, northern Saxony, and the neighbourhood of Paris, might be cited as examples of a more recent date and nearer home. In Arabia the provinces of Ḥaṣa and Ḳaṭeef acknowledged the same common law of events. This district remained permanently estranged from Islam, a heap of moral and religious ruins, of Carmathian and esoteric doctrines, where naturalism, to use a modern phrase for a very old thing, and materialism were mixed up and confused with Shiya'ee transmigrations and incarnations, with the now reviving relics of old Sabeeism, and with the fetichism common among the lower and uneducated classes all over the globe, though it may vary in form and name. Christianity had never gained much footing on the mainland of Ḥaṣa, though it once predominated in the adjoining islands of Baḥreyn; and but slight traces of it are discernible in what we know of the subsequent history of this coast, or among the actual population.

Meanwhile industry, commerce, agriculture, and art, all of them favoured by the geographical position and the local resources of Ḥaṣa, flourished in their turn, and occupied the minds of the inhabitants, well content to remain separated from Mecca and Bagdad, and enjoying the undisturbed advantages of political and religious independence. Relics, some of early, many of later date, but mostly remarkable as monuments of power and skill, cover the land of Ḥaṣa, and attest the material prosperity of past times. When Wahhabeeism first appeared in Nejed, its earliest and most far-sighted opponents were, as we have already noticed, the rulers of the Eastern coast. But unable long to cope with superior numbers and military skill, they were at last vanquished, and those of the native chiefs who escaped the sword of Ebn-Sa'ood sought a refuge, some in Persia, some in the desert adjoining Koweyt, and not a few in the remote province of Ḥareeḳ, while their country remained a helpless spoil to the hardy mountaineers of the interior. Islam now became compulsory throughout Ḥaṣa and Ḳaṭeef, mosques were built everywhere, and prayers were said by men who turned their faces to Mecca, and raised their voices in the formulas of the Coran, while their hearts were full of curses against the Prophet, his book, and his religion ;—and whispers denied what words asserted.

No sooner had Ibraheem Basha shattered the overgrown colossus of Nejed, than Ḥaṣa reasserted her civil and religious freedom. Shortly after the inhabitants, trusting to find a guarantee for either liberty in the Egyptian protectorate, offered themselves ready allies to Isma'eel Basha when on his eastward visit. But the new rulers, elated by success, forgot in Arabia the lessons of moderation inculcated at Cairo, and set up in Ḥaṣa a system more resembling that of the old Memlooks than that of Moḥammed-'Alee. They treated the population as conquered slaves, not as voluntary subjects, laid on them arbitrary exactions, ransacked the houses of the wealthy, imprisoned the nobles on frivolous pretences; nor content with this, made it a boast to impose the public performance of menial and degrading offices on the most respectable citizens of Hofhoof, and even insulted the women in the streets of the city. This could not last. A murderous insurrection drove the Egyptians for ever from the lands over which they had begun to tyrannize, and Ḥaṣa regained for a short space her past independence.

A few years later the Wahhabee dynasty, re established by

Turkee, and restored to something of its first energy by the cautious despotism of Feysul, once more projected, and ultimately accomplished, the subjection of Ḥasa, though not without a long and bloody war, in which, if I remember rightly, Feysul seconded in person the military operations conducted by his son 'Abd-Allah. The walls of Hofhoof and of other towns were in part pulled down, the fortresses dismantled, some villages were utterly destroyed. In recompense, old mosques were restored, new built, and a whitewash of orthodoxy was spread over the religious nakedness of the land. Thus matters have remained ever since. Meanwhile, like a fire the hotter for a good covering of ashes, the Carmathian reaction burns secretly on, and waits but an occasion to break out afresh into a blaze, sufficient to consume, perhaps for the last time, the superstructure of Wahhabeeism and Islam. But separated by the whole breadth of the Peninsula from Egypt, unsympathizing with the Turkish rule of Bagdad, and hopeless of aid from the decrepit anarchy of Persia, the chiefs of Ḥasa can for the present only bide their time, ready to welcome a deliverer whom they know not exactly whence to expect, and meditating plans of revolt and liberty which the overwhelming weight of Nejed renders it impossible to execute unassisted. Thus much may suffice for a general view of the province in its national bearings; the details afforded by our stay will complete the picture.

On awaking to an excellent breakfast of—O luxury unheard of since Gaza—roasted fowl, rice, and pastry, prepared by the culinary skill of our Abyssinian hostess, Aboo-'Eysa's wife, a good-natured thoughtless dame, like most of her country-women, we began to look about us, and found ourselves in a comfortable dwelling, well adapted to the quiet tenor of life which we proposed here to lead for a few weeks. The Ḳ'hăwah was small and snug, not admitting above twenty guests at a time; alongside was a second and larger apartment, set apart by Aboo-'Eysa for our more especial habitation, and opening on the courtyard; two spacious rooms communicated with this on either side; the one was at our disposal, the other answered the purposes of a nursery, and was the ordinary abode of the dusky lady, with her mulatto son and heir. A kitchen and two secluded chambers, into which the rougher sex might not indiscriminately venture, completed the ground storey; while above were three empty and unfurnished rooms, and a large extent of flat roof, whereon it was very pleasant to sit morning and evening. In the courtyard below we might at our leisure contemplate "the patient camels ruminate their food," as Southey has it in a well-known poem where the vivacity of the author's imagination almost retrieves his want of personal experience in many an Eastern scene. Lastly, the neighbourhood out of doors was particularly tranquil, and less liable than elsewhere to suspicion.

The town of Hofhoof, whose ample circuit contained during the last generation about thirty thousand inhabitants, now dwindled to twenty-three or twenty-four thousand, is divided into three quarters or districts—namely, that of the Kôt, or fortress (my Bombay or Madras readers will recognize the exotic word, imported hither from the shores of the Kishna and the Taptee), where resides the Wahhabee governor, along with his retinue and adherents; that of the Rifey'eeyah, inhabited by a large proportion of the older and nobler families; and thirdly, the Na'āthar, the largest in extent, and containing a mixed body of townsmen, rich and poor, merchants and artisans. In this last quarter was our present home; moreover, it stood in the part farthest removed from the Kôt and its sinister influences, while it was also sufficiently distant from the over-turbulent neighbourhood of the Rifey'eeyah, the centre of anti-Wahhabee movements, and the name of which alone excited distrust and uneasiness in Nejdean minds.

The general form of the town is that of a large oval. The public square, an oblong space of about three hundred yards in length by a fourth of the same in width, occupies the meeting-point of the three quarters just mentioned; the Kôt lies on its north-east, the Rifey'eeyah on the north-west and west, and the Na'āthar on the east and south.

The Kôt itself is a vast citadel, surrounded by a deep trench, with walls and towers of unusual height and thickness, earth-built with an occasional intermixture of stone, the work of the old Carmathian rulers; it is nearly square, being about one-third of a mile in length by one quarter in breadth. Three sides of this fortress are provided each with a central gate; on the fourth or northern side a small but strong fortress forms a sort of keep; it is square, and its towers attain more than forty feet in elevation, or about sixty, if we reckon from the bottom of the outer ditch. Within dwells the Nejdean governor, formerly Moḥammed-es-Sedeyree, but at the present day a negro of Feyṣul's, Belāl by name, a good slave and a bad ruler, if the disaffection of the town say true. Here too is the model orthodox Mesjid, where all is done after the most correct Wahhabee fashion; here abide the Meṭow'wan's and Zelators sent hither from Riaḍ, and other Nejdeans of 'Aareḍ, Woshem, and Yemāmah. Within the Kôt dwells also a population in number between two and three thousand souls; for the whole space, even up to the inner line of the walls, is thickly inhabited; it is divided by rectangular streets running from gate to gate, and from side to side.

The towers, fifteen or sixteen on each side of the Kôt, are mostly round, and provided with winding stairs, loopholes, and machicolations below the battlements; the intervening walls have similar means of defence. The trench without is for the greatest part dry, but can be filled with water from the garden wells beyond when occasion requires; the portals are strong and well-guarded.

On the opposite side of the square, and consequently belonging to the Rifey'eeyah, is the vaulted market-place or "Ḳeysareeyah," a name by which constructions of this nature must henceforth be called up to Mascat itself, though how this Latinism found its way across the Peninsula to lands which seem to have had so little commerce with the Roman or Byzantine empires, I cannot readily conjecture. This Ḳeysareeyah is in form a long barrel-vaulted arcade, with a portal at either end; the folding doors that should protect the entrances have here in Hofhoof been taken away, elsewhere they are always to be found. The sides are composed of shops, set apart in general for wares of cost, or at least what is here esteemed costly; thus weapons, cloth embroidery, gold and silver ornament, and analogous articles, are the ordinary stock-in-hand in the Ḳeysareeyah. Around it cluster several alleys, roofed with palm-leaves against the heat, and tolerably symmetrical; in the shops we may see the merchandise of Baḥreyn, 'Omân, Persia, and India exposed for sale, mixed with the manufactured produce of the country; workshops, smithies, carpenters' and shoemakers' stalls, and the like, are here also. In the open square itself stand countless booths for the sale of dates, vegetables, wood, salted locusts, and small ware of many kinds. Tobacco, however, once a common article of purchase, is now prescribed by Wahhabee disciplinarians, and no longer offends the eye; its store and traffic are in private, where, after the over-true principle that "stolen waters are sweet," the supplies are copious and the purchasers active. Public auctions are frequently held in the square; here too barbers ply their trade, and smiths and shoemakers abound, though these latter callings number also many followers in other parts of the town. Even yet, in spite of the deadening influences of tyranny and bigotry, much activity prevails among this naturally clever and industrial population.

The Rifey'eeyah, or noble quarter, covers a considerable extent, and is chiefly composed of tolerable, in some places of even handsome dwellings. The comparative elegance of domestic architecture in Hofhoof is due to the use of the arch, which after the long interval from Ma'ân to Ḥasa now at last reappears, and gives to the constructions of this province a lightness and a variety unknown in the monotonous and heavy piles of Nejed and Shomer. Another improvement is that the walls, whether of earth or stone, or of both mixed as is often the case, are here very generally coated with fine white plaster, much resembling the "chunam" of Southern India; ornament too is aimed at about the doorways and the ogee-headed windows, and is sometimes attained. The streets of the Rifey'eeyah are, for a hot country, wide and very clean; those of Damascus and even of Beyrouth are not one quarter so well kept. This quarter is very healthy; it stands on a slightly rising ground, implied by its name "Rifey'eeyah," or "elevation," and is exposed to the sea-breeze, here distinctly perceptible at times.

The Na'âthar is the largest quarter; it forms indeed a good half of the town, and completes its oval. In it every description of dwelling is to be seen—for rich and poor, for high and low, palace or hovel. Here too, but near the Kôt, has the pious policy of Feysul constructed the great mosque, where Moresco arches, light porticoes, smooth plaster, and a mat-spread floor, presented an appearance much surpassing in decency the naked cathedral, so to speak, of Riaḍ. In this quarter, however, the Wahhabee sect, as such, numbers but few partisans. Many merchants, traders, and men of business here reside; here strangers from Persia, 'Omān, Baḥreyn, from Ḥareeḳ also, and Ḳaṭar, take up their dwelling; here weavers and artisans live and carry on their business. My readers may be interested to know that the ill-fated Darweesh traveller, whose death-scene at Ḍerey'eeyah I have before described, occupied for a few weeks a house in the Na'ūthar, the locality was pointed out to us by Aboo-'Eysa. The unfortunate man had already betrayed himself in his choice of dwelling, for a genuine Darweesh should know no lodging but the mosque—

I am a stranger, and I seek no one for my host;
I am a stranger, nor pass a night within the walls of a dwelling.
I am a stranger, and know nor family nor child,
Nor own I any one to bring me within the shelter of man.
The narrow Mesjid, that is my resort and that my resting-place,
That is the choice of my heart, its portion and its lot for ever,

—sings the true religious mendicant of Islam.

In the Na'ūthar more frequently than the other two quarters we find a small garden enclosed here and there amid the houses, and an occasional tree enlivens the roadside by its overspreading foliage. The fig and the citron-tree are the most common.

The fortifications of the town were once strong and high, but are now little better than heaps of ruins, of broken towers and winding stairs that lead to nothing. They are girdled by a trench, which on the Na'ūthar side is full of water, but dry towards the Rifey'eeyah, where the conduits which connected it with the wells beyond have been cut across or filled up, perhaps purposely, perhaps from mere neglect. Without the walls lie the gardens and plantations, stretching away north and east far as the eye can reach; on the south and west they form a narrower ring. At no great distance from the southern gate stands the isolated fortress which we had passed on the night of our arrival; it is a small but well constructed building, and placed so as effectually to command and check all entrance from the south and west; its name, the "Khoṭeym," or "Bridle-bit," implies its object and its character. This fort is recent; the chief of Hofhoof erected it during the last century to serve as a "bridle" to the impetuous onset of the Wahhabees, when the hordes of Nejed poured down through the passes of Ghoweyr, and approached the capital of the province from this direction. Alas! that the "bit" should have been broken, the "bridle" unavailing. It now stands dismantled, a page from past politics, like the Drachenfels or Conway Castle.

Another smaller fort, a watch-tower in fact, rises close by. Like the Khoṭeym it is built of unbaked bricks, hardened by process of time into the semblance of stone. For seventy or eighty years these unroofed walls have braved winter rains and spring blasts without losing an inch of their height or opening a fissure in their sides.

Hence due south the view extends over a waste and desert space, interposed between the province of Ḥasa and that of Ḳaṭar, a natural boundary dispensing with artificial limits between the rival domains of Nejed and 'Omān. Did an exact frontier-line exist, it would run about twenty miles south of Hofhoof. On the south-east low sand-hills shut out from view the Gulf of Baḥreyn and the harbour of 'Ajeyr, not far distant; to the south-west rise the heights of Ghoweyr, and below them 'Eyn-Nejm and another village. Sha'abah itself is out of sight, but above it we can discern the last steep buttress of the coast-range, which then sinks down to a low undulation and inclines eastward to join at some distance the hills of Ḳaṭar, which will carry it on with little interruption to 'Omān.

Turning westward, we have before us a multitude of water-courses, no longer the wells of Nejed, but living running streams amid deep palm-groves, and a vegetation of that semi-Indian type peculiar to this part of Arabia. Many little villages stud the plain, till at a north-westerly distance of five or six miles the cavernous cliffs of Djebel-el-Moghāzee, or "Mountain of military expeditions," where perished the armies of 'Abbas, chief general of the caliph El-Ma'teḍad-b-'Illah, in the days of Aboo-Sa'eed-el-Djenābee, the first Carmathian monarch, close in the prospect. But the mountain-chain extends for at least a hundred miles further north, and ends beyond Wāb and its copious waters. North and east of Hofhoof is one green mass of waving foliage, save where occasionally the overflowing water-channels present that phenomenon specially dear in reminiscences to an east-country Englishman, namely, a real genuine marsh, with reeds, rushes, and long-legged waterfowl. Heaven bless them all! I cannot say how glad I was to see them after so long a separation; while around the rim of the swamps and pools rise stately palm-trees, laden with the choicest dates of Arabia, or rather of the entire world. A solitary conical hillock, the freak of nature, rises alone on the north-east from the level of this well-watered plain; its summit bears the vestiges of Carmathian fortification. These details have, I trust, given my readers a tolerable idea of the town of Hofhoof and its immediate neighbourhood. Its general aspect is that of a white and yellow onyx, chased in an emerald rim; the name of "Hofhoof," like the Winchester of our own island, implies glitter and beauty.

But perhaps my reader, after accompanying me thus far, may feel thirsty, for the heat, even in December, is almost oppressive, and the sky cloudless as though it were June or July. So let us turn aside into that grassy plantation, where half a dozen buffaloes are cooling their ugly hides in a pool, and drink a little from the source that supplies it. When behold! the water is warm, almost hot. Do not be surprised, all the fountain sources and wells of Ḳaṣa are so, more or less: in some one can hardly bear to plunge one's hand; others are less above the average temperature, while a decidedly sulphurous taste is now and then perceptible. In fact, from the extreme north of this province at the limits of Koweyt, down to its southernmost frontier at Sha'abah, this same sign of subterranean fire is everywhere to be found. It is again absent in Ḳaṭar and along the coast up to Rās Mesandum, but reappears, as we shall afterwards find, in the Bāṭinah or lower district of 'Omān. I have already spoken of 'Eyn-Nejm and its hot baths. Omm-Sebaa', a scarce less remarkable source, we have yet to visit. The rocks too are here very frequently of tufa and basalt, another mark of igneous agency. Lastly, the inhabitants informed me that slight shocks of earthquake—a phenomenon wholly unknown, so far as I could gather, to the historical records or the living tradition of Upper Nejed—are here nowise uncommon. One of unusual severity, and to which the rents and clefts in the high walls and the upper storeys of several houses in the town yet bore witness, was said to have taken place about thirty years before. Perhaps it was coincident with the well-known catastrophe which in 1836 buried the inhabitants of Ṣafed under the ruins of their town, rolled the huge stones of Ḳela'at-Djish (Djiscala) down the valley, and shook the strong castle-walls of Aleppo. In fact Ḥaṣa, in its littoral position alongside of the Persian Gulf, belongs to that great valley which, partly sunk beneath the waters of the Gulf itself, partly rising to form the bed of the Tigris and the Euphrates, reaches from the shores of Beloochistan and 'Omān up to Kara Dagh and the mountains of Armenia, and at the upper extremity of which earthquakes are only too common. The continuity of this long valley is further attested by the remarkable uniformity of its climate; it forms a huge hot-air funnel, the base of which is on the tropics, while its extremity reaches 37 degrees of northern latitude. Hence it comes that the Semoom, unknown in the far more southerly regions of Syria and Palestine (my readers are, I trust, too well informed to fall into the popular error of confounding the specific and gaseous Semoom with the Shilooḳ or Sirocco of Syria, Malta, and even Italy), pays occasional visits to Mosoul and Djezeerat 'Omar, while the thermometer at Bagdad attains in summer an elevation capable of staggering the belief of even an old Indian, at least from the Bombay side. That an analogical uniformity of character should exist underground the valley as well as above, has nothing inconsistent with theory, and the facts above mentioned seem to confirm it. But this is the province of geologists, and to them I leave to follow out, perhaps to disprove, these indications; my own science or ignorance can carry me no further here.

The products of Ḥaṣa are many and various; the monotony of Arab vegetation, its eternal palm and ithel, ithel and palm, are here varied by new foliage, and growths unknown to Nejed and Shomer. True, the date-palm still predominates, nay, here attains its greatest perfection. But the Nabaḳ, with its rounded leaves and little crab-apple fruit, a mere bush in Central Arabia, becomes in Ḥaṣa a stately tree; the papay too, so well known in the more easterly Peninsula, appears, though seldom, and stunted in growth, along with some other trees common on the coast from Cutch to Bombay; I will give their catalogue in a following chapter. Indigo is here cultivated, though not sufficiently for the demands of commerce; cotton is much more widely grown than in Yemāmah; rice-fields abound, and the sugar-cane is often planted, though not, I believe, for the extraction of the sugar; the peasants of Ḥaṣa sell the reed by retail bundles in the market-place, and the purchasers take it home to gnaw at leisure in their houses. Corn, maize, millet, vetches of every kind, radishes, onions, garlic, beans, in short, almost all leguminа and cerealia, barley excepted (at least I neither saw nor heard of any), cover the plain, and under a better administration might be multiplied tenfold. But a heavy land-tax and arbitrary contributions have deeply discouraged the agriculturist no less than the merchant. I have myself repeatedly seen large tracts of ground, over which a few blows of the spade or shovel would have conducted a copious irrigation, but now left dry and infertile. On my enquiry why no one undertook a very slight labour in prospect of an abundant recompense, I heard for answer, "What would it profit us? All would go to the strong-box of Feyṣul;" or, "Better to leave the land to the God who made it, than to till it for those dogs the Wahhabees."

However, if the ploughman has reason to cry, the merchant may howl; for he is by far the greater sufferer of the two. For centuries Ḥaṣa had carried on a flourishing commerce with 'Omān, Persia, and India on the right, and with Baṣrah and Bagdad on the left, nay even with Damascus itself, in spite of political hostility and local distance. For the cloaks of Ḥaṣa manufacture, and the embroidery which adorns them, are alike unrivalled; such delicacy of work, such elegance of pattern, are unknown save in Cachemire alone. The wool employed is of exquisite fineness, and, when skilfully interwoven with silk, forms a tissue alike strong to wear and beautiful to the eye; while its borderings of gold and silver thread, tastefully intermixed with the gayest colours, may be envied, but never equalled, by Syria and Persia. In the workmanship of the precious metals, in the adornment of a sword-hilt or a powder-flask, of a dagger or a Nargheelah, the artisans of Ḥasa, though inferior in this respect to those of 'Omān, have nothing to fear from the competition of Damascus or Bagdad. In implements of copper and brass, also, they well know how to combine elegance with utility, and the coffee-pots of Ḥasa certainly outvie any to be met with north of Basrah. All these and similar objects were once regular articles of an advantageous exportation, and when added to the never-failing trade in those Khalās dates, peculiar to this district, and which make all mouths water from Bombay to Mosoul, besides a supplementary bale of sugar-cane or the like, formed an excellent outport trade. Cloth of more ordinary quality, cutlery, ironwork, swords, spears, crockery, silk, gold thread, silver thread, and a hundred analogous articles, came in return. Hence the great wealth of the Ḥasa merchants, and consequently of the local government, and hence the monuments whose relics yet attest that wealth. Now all is fallen away; the Nejdean eats out the marrow and fat of the land; while by his senseless war against whatever it pleases his fanaticism to proscribe, under the name of luxury—against tobacco and silk, ornament and dress—he cuts off an important branch of useful commerce, while he loses no opportunity of snubbing and discouraging the unorthodox trader, who prefers ships to mosques, and bales of goods to "Allah" and the Coran. To this praiseworthy end, whenever an expedition is ordered, or a levy made, the malignant policy of Mohanna, already mentioned in our chapter on Ḳaseem, finds a yet wider application in Ḥasa, where the first who receives the bidding to sling the musket and shoulder the spear is the wealthy merchant, the busy shopkeeper, and the hard-working artisan; and all to the detriment prepense of their affairs in hand. Such had been pre-eminently the system adopted by Feysul in the actual war; and when we reached Hofhoof we found full half of its better inhabitants thus forcibly absent on a war whose only result could be to rivet the hated Wahhabee yoke still more firmly on their own necks.

The climate of Ḥasa, as I have already implied, is very different from that of the uplands, nor equally favourable to health and physical activity. Hence a doctor, like myself, if my readers will allow me the title, has here more work and better fees, this latter circumstance is also owing to the greater amount of ready money in circulation, and the higher value set on medical science by men whose intellects are much more cultivated than those of their Nejdean neighbours. In appearance the inhabitants of Ḥasa are generally good-sized and well-proportioned, but somewhat sallow in the face, and of a less muscular developement than is usual inland; their features, though regular, are less marked than those of the Nejdeans, and do not exhibit the same half-Jewish type; on the contrary, there is something in them that reminds a beholder of the Rajpoot or the Guzeratee. They are passionately fond of literature and poetry, whether it be according to the known Arabic rules and metre, or whether it follow the Nabṭee, that is, the Nabathæan versification.

This latter form of composition, occasionally met with even in Nejed, but rare, becomes here common, more so indeed than the Arabic, from which it differs in scansion, metre, and rhyme. In Nabṭee verses scansion goes by accent, not by quantity; the metre is variable, even in the same piece; and the rhyme, instead of being continuous, is alternate. In a word, this class of poetry presents in form a strong resemblance to the ordinary English ballad, and, like it, is the popular style of the country.

But how it came by the title of "Nabathæan," what was the period or what the circumstances of its introduction into Arabia, who were these Nabathæans, and what they had to do in this part of the world, no one could tell me anything. A very common and unfortunate result of historical enquiry in the East. Meanwhile this peculiar and non-Arabic form of literature, just traceable in Nejed, frequent in Ḥasa, becomes entirely dominant in 'Omān, where nothing else but Nabṭee, to give it its country name, is employed by the poets of the Bāṭinah and Djebel-Akhdar.

"What are the inhabitants of Baḥreyn?" said the sanguinary Ḥejjāj to the ill-starred Arab chronologist, Eyoob-ebn-el-Ḳirreeyah, while holding him in suspense between life and death. "Nabathæans turned Arabs," replied the historian. "And what the inhabitants of 'Omān?" was the next enquiry. "Arabs turned Nabathæans." This dialogue, with much more of the highest interest, but too long for insertion here, took place, if Ebn-Khallikān say true, about the year A.D. 700, or the eighty-fourth after the Hejirah, and would consequently send back Nabathæan race and influence on these coasts to a tolerably ancient date. And if we recall to mind that these Nabathæans, or "Nabaṭ," be they whom they may, seem to have belonged to the class of astral or solar worshippers, and that on the other hand, Ḥaṣa and 'Omān were certainly at the time of Mahomet the main seat of that form of religion in Arabia, we have a further, though an indirect witness to Nabathæan influence here.

Everyone has his theory, and I trust that my readers will not deny me this universal privilege. These Nabathæans, of whom traces exist from the eastern bank of the Jordan to the Tigris, and from northern Mesopotamia, where the "Shemseeyah" or sun-worshippers of Mardeen yet represent them, down to Rās-el-Ḥaḍḍ, and even beyond, what race were they? and to what family of mankind did they belong? The ridiculous conjecture which would identify them with the "Nebajoth" of Scripture is sufficiently refuted by the first principles of Semitic etymology; the two words "Nabaṭ" and "Nebajoth" presenting a double difference in consonant and in vowel utterly irreconcilable with community of origin; not to mention other reasons self-evident to a calm enquirer. These hyper-Biblical theories—I know no better name for them—are worthy of intellects which would discover the children of Hagar, Abraham's concubine, in the Benoo-Hājar of Ḥasa, and read the entire Pentateuch on the rocks of the Sinai desert. Daydreams more creditable to the imagination than to the knowledge or judgment of those who indulge in them. Some investigators of a more learned and a more sober description incline to merge the Nabathæans in the Chaldæans; others make them a distinct people; Maḳreezee, in one of his works, seems to class them with the Persians.

For my own part, I should look upon the name Nabaṭ or Nabathæan as less national than conventional; a general denomination, in fact, under which the inhabitants of Syria, Palestine, and Arabia included the various populations inhabiting the regions of the Euphrates and Tigris, whether of Assyrian, Chaldæan, or Babylonian origin; thus "Nabaṭ" would comprehend several dynasties, governments, and races, distinct among themselves, yet sufficiently homogeneous to form one whole by opposition to those who looked on them from without. A few words will explain this.

The Eastern world may, I think, be spoken of without rashness as divided at a very early period, by blood, religion, and geography, into three main segments. To the west were the Syrians, the Jews, and the Arabs—nations near akin, and, in spite of marked differences, held together by several points of resemblance: "facies non omnibus una, Nec diversa tamen." To the far East dwelt the Persians and the Medo-Persians, destined before long to fuse into one powerful empire, and very dissimilar both in physical and moral type from the western races. Between these two confederations, taking the word in its widest sense, lay a great district, watered by the double branches of the Shaṭṭ, the Tigris, and the Euphrates, where dwelt a third family, unlike the former two, divided indeed internally, yet presenting in the broader lineaments of religion, institutions, politics, and manners, a certain community of outline enough to make them pass in the eyes of their westerly neighbours for one race, or at least for one generic whole. Diametrically opposed on almost every point with those who acknowledged Abraham for father or kinsman, their constant adversaries in war, in worship, in innate feeling, and in social organization, this very antithesis and the generalization of antipathy would overlook minuter discrepancies in the hostile whole, and assign one common name for those whom it classed under one common fear and hatred. In process of time, and thus much seems implied in the citation just made from Ebn-Khallikān, the term "Nabathæans," at first peculiar to some one particular branch of Chaldæan parentage with which the indwellers of Syria came in most frequent contact, and then extended to the entire Assyrian and Babylonian nationality, would be applied to all who by usages and customs, originating perhaps at Babylon, but afterwards widely spread over the mid-East, were in their measure brought under the first classification; and thus to become an imitator of Chaldæan planetary worship, or analogous practices, was tantamount in Arab mouths and ideas to becoming a Nabathæan. Apart from this, historical inference, even though unsupported by precise documentary testimony, will readily admit a Chaldæan, Casdee, or Cushite, perhaps Curdee colony in Baḥreyn, an island so intimately connected by position and by commerce with the mouths of the Shaṭṭ; nor is it hard to imagine how such colonists might find their further way to Ḥasa, and even penetrate into the interior of Arabia, while they overspread its eastern coast. An organizing people exercises an invariable ascendency over another richer in imaginative than in constructive faculties (Saxons on the one side, and Celts on the other, may afford us a familiar example in the West), and hence the predominance of Chaldæan or Nabathæan commerce and influence, perhaps of religion, would soon be followed by a corresponding modification in literature and poetry, now applied to new ends, or at least to the expression of new thoughts and turns of mind. "Poetry is the literature of the Arabs," said Aṣmaa'i, himself the most learned Arab of his day; and hence poetry would be the first to feel and the longest to record the impress of foreign or "Nabathæan" action, and retain a name, become at last almost a misnomer, though at first expressive of a fact.

We have frequent instances of a similar process of nomenclature at the present day, especially in the inaccurate East. Thus, for example's sake, these very same inhabitants of Syria and Arabia, after all the experience and knowledge acquired by centuries of intercourse, persist in assigning to all the Christian nations of the West, in common, the term "Afrānj," a denomination peculiar in its origin to the Franks or French of the Crusades. Yet certainly the citizens of Nineveh were hardly more diverse from the inhabitants of the Babylonian Shinar or Sena'ar, than are Frenchmen from Germans, Englishmen, or Italians. Never mind; all are "Afrānj" for the Arab. In requital, Westerns repeatedly lump together under one universal "Arabs," the races comprised by the whole region from Aleppo to Asowān, from the Mediterranean and the Nile to the Tigris and the Persian Gulf; though the lands thus included—Egypt, Syria, Mesopotamia, 'Irāḳ, Arabia, &c. &c.—be tenanted by tribes and populations differing from each other in almost every respect, lineal, historical, and national. Such sweeping classifications are common among men, and arise from many causes, prevalent in every age, the earliest and the latest. And such was, it is highly probable, the purport of the word "Nabathæan," a proper name, we may suppose, in its origin, a generic name in its application. Very similar to this is the classification adopted by the historian Shems-ed-Deen-el-Dimishkee, when he assures us that Chaldæans, Casdees, Djerāmihah, Ganbān, and Kenana'oon were all Sabæans, that is, adds he, were all worshippers of the stars. Now the term "Saba'i" or "Sabæan" had in its origin a much more local and restricted bearing, and was far from including the Chaldæans or the Chananeans, thus brought under it by popular usage at a later period.

More might be added on a topic which has deservedly occupied the attention of several distinguished Orientalists, and cost no little time and labour; but the page would grow into a chapter, and the chapter into a volume. Perhaps what has here been said, imperfect as it is, may suggest a clue to the solution of difficulties inseparable from an enquiry knotty in itself, and rendered yet knottier by the curiously uncritical character of Eastern memorials; nor should I wonder were it to prove ultimately a tolerable approximation to the truth.

A word or two may be subjoined upon a correlative instance of those technical confusions which are so often made, and give rise to strange inaccuracies and injurious misapplications. The European public is deluged with accounts of Arab customs, Arab ways, Arab qualities, houses, dresses, women, warriors, and what not; the most part from materials collected in Syria, Mesopotamia, Egypt, 'Irāk, perhaps Tunis, Algiers, and Morocco; or at the best in Djiddah and on the Red Sea coast. Sometimes a romantic spirit will furnish scenes among the hybrid Bedouins of Palmyra as portraits of Arab life; sometimes we are invited to study Arab society in a divan at Cairo or Aleppo. Such narratives, however accurate they may be for the localities and races they describe, have not an equal claim to the title of correct delineations of Arabs and of Arab customs. The case appears to me much as if the description of a backwoodsman of Ohio should be given for a faithful portrait of a Yorkshire farmer, or the ways and doings of Connaught for a sketch of Norfolk life and manners. Syria and Egypt, Palmyra and Bagdad, even less Mosoul and Algiers, are not Arabia, nor are their inhabitants Arabs. The populations alluded to are instead a mixture of Curdes, Turcomans, Syrians, Phœnicians, Armenians, Berbers, Greeks, Turks, Copts, Albanians, Chaldæans, not to mention the remnants of other and older races, with a little, a very little Arab blood, one in twenty at most, and that little rediluted by local and territorial influences. That all more or less speak Arabic is a fact which gives them no more claim to be numbered among Arabs, than speaking bad English makes an Englishman of a native of Connaught or of Texas. For the popular figure of the Bedouin, I must add, that even were he sketched, as he rarely is, from the genuine nomade of Arabia, it would be no juster to bring him forward as an example of Arab life and society, than to publish the "Pickwick Papers," or "Nicholas Nickleby," with "Scenes in High Life," or "Tales of the Howards," on the back. These unlucky and much-talked-of Bedouins in the Syrian, also miscalled Arabian, desert, are in fact only hybrids, crosses between Turcoman and Curdish tribes, with a small and questionable infusion of Arab blood, and that too none of the best, like a wine-glass of thin claret poured into a tumbler of water. In short, among these races, town or Bedouin, we have no real authentic Arabs. Arabia and Arabs begin south of Syria and Palestine, west of Basrah and Zobeyr, east of Kerak and the Red Sea. Draw a line across from the top of the Red Sea to the top of the Persian Gulf; what is below that line is alone Arab: and even then do not reckon the pilgrim route, it is half Turkish; nor Medinah, it is cosmopolitan; nor the seacoast of Yemen, it is Indo-Abyssinian; least of all Mecca, the common sewer of Mahometans of all kinds, nations, and lands, and where every trace of Arab identity has long since been effaced by promiscuous immorality and the corruption of ages. Mascat and Ḳaṭeef must also stand with Mokha and 'Aden on the list of exceptions.

But to return to Ḥaṣa, whence the Nabathæans have led us on a long and circuitous track. It was the form of poetry usual in Ḥaṣa which first set us on their trail. While at Hofhoof many pieces of Nabṭee, fewer of Arab versification, composed by authors still living, were sung or recited before me, some of remarkable originality and terseness. A lament on the destruction of 'Eyn-Nejm, a poem on the expedition against Baḥreyn, a third of the Ḳoṭrobee form, known to Arab scholars, struck me as compositions of real value; love-songs, and those pretty too, were not wanting. Barakāt and I took down seven or eight; but, alas! three months later the greedy waves of the Indian Ocean swallowed up my treasure. The standard of poetry in Ḥasa seemed to me decidedly higher than in Nejed. On the other hand, the language of common conversation is inferior in copiousness, purity, and flexibility to that of the inner uplands. The dialect prevailing on this coast is neither the Ismaelitic of Nejed nor the Ḳaḥṭānee of 'Omān, but a mixture of both to their mutual detriment; nor will a practised ear fail to detect a slight infusion of Persian, a vicious element of speech in Arab mouths, very perceptible in Ḳaṭeef and Baḥreyn. However, the inferiority of the Ḥasa tongue is compensated by superiority of Ḥasa intellect; and in what may be called rational conversation and in consecutive reasoning the men of Hofhoof surpass by far the inhabitants of Riaḍ and Ḥā'yel. Foreign intercourse, while debasing their grammar, has refined their wits; perhaps, too, their acuteness is intrinsic and hereditary, though favoured and fostered by local and other circumstances.

The dress here worn presented an agreeable variety to our eyes, wearied by the unparalleled monotony of costume, male or female, from Djowf to Yemāmah. In Hofhoof and the villages around, the wide white Arab shirt or smock is not unfrequently replaced by the closer-fitting, saffron-dyed, silk-embroidered vest of 'Omān, a garment which recalls to mind the Anghee or Anghurka common in Western India; instead of the eternal Ḳafee'yah, a turban, now large and white, now coloured and of narrower folds, adorns many a head; the light red cloak, peculiar, I believe, to the eastern coast, diversifies the blackness of the Arab mantle, while the shining red leather and elegant shape of Baḥreyn or 'Omān sandals protect the feet better and with more grace than the coarse brown-yellow productions of the Nejdean shoemaker. Lastly a crooked dagger, silver-hilted and mounted, may here be occasionally seen at the waist; it becomes universal when we enter the limits of 'Omān. All this pleased us much, for uniformity, even if genuinely simple and primitive, wearies at last.

Before the subjection of Hasa to the Wahhabee, ornament and display were the mode in the province, and even now silk and embroidery appear far more frequently than is consistent with the orthodoxy of Islam. At the period of the great Riad reform in 1856, described in the ninth chapter of this work, certain zealous preachers visited Hofhoof, and, deeming it highly probable that the iniquities of the inhabitants had borne a share in the late visitation of the cholera, preached copiously and emphatically against gay dresses and worldly vanity. But finding the ramparts of sin proof against all the batteries of pulpit eloquence, the hands of the missionaries achieved here as elsewhere what their tongues could not; and while the depraved wretches of Hasa yet hesitated to tear and cast aside their unrighteous gewgaws, orthodox Nejdeans lent them their friendly aid, till, as eyewitnesses assured me, torn silk and unravelled embroidery literally bestrewed the streets. A fierce campaign was of course simultaneously waged against tobacco, which henceforth retired into private life.

Another evil practice, common among the upper classes, was at this time somewhat subdued, though not entirely got under The merchants and traders of Hofhoof and Mebarraz, thinking themselves not to be mere beasts or automatons, and consequently capable of rather more refined and varied enjoyments than what the Prophet conceded to his followers, had from time immemorial been in the custom of organizing pleasure-parties, especially during the days of vacation from ordinary business. These intervals of social relaxation lasted often a week or two at a time, and were generally allotted to the autumn season. North-east of Hasa rises a long isolated ridge, basalt and sandstone, about four hundred feet in height; its cliffs are pierced in every direction by large natural caverns, and their name, "Moghor," or "caves," has become synonymous with the mountain itself. Within these caves the air is cool, even during the hottest months of the year; and fresh water flows in a perennial supply at the mountain foot. Hither accordingly the merchants and business-men of Hasa would repair when wearied of their accounts and ledger-books, and pass together a few days in the caverns of Moghor, amid the ease of familiar conversation, well-furnished tables, music, dancing, and whatever like diversions even thinking men often allow themselves when tired with hard and sedentary work. Now it is evident, and what has been before said may suffice for proof, that such pleasures are in direct opposition to the pure and orthodox spirit of Islam; and hence the Nejdeans regarded the pleasure-parties of Djebel Moghor with hardly less horror than what a fiddle heard in the public streets on a Sunday would excite in Glasgow. Feysul issued his orders to put down the abomination with a high hand; some of the culprits were arrested, others fined; and what yet remains of these diversions, for they continue even now, is managed by stealth, or at least by only a small number, and under due precautions. Our own stay at Hofhoof will furnish an example.

It were much to be wished that morality had at least been a gainer by these sumptuary laws and regulations. But, to judge by what I heard of private scandal and domestic mischief, the "saints" do not seem to have better attained their object in Ḥasa than did their elder brethren under Calvin in Geneva, or in London under the Rump. Such appears to be the general law; but to profit by experience is perhaps even more rarely the fortune of governments than of individuals.

I have already said that our great endeavour in Ḥasa was to observe unobserved, and thus to render our time as barren as might be in incidents and catastrophes. Not that we went into the opposite extreme of leading an absolutely retired and therefore uneventful life. Aboo-'Eysa took care from the first to bring us into contact with the best and the most cultivated families of the town, nor had my medical profession anywhere a wider range for its exercise, or better success than in Hofhoof. Friendly invitations, now to dinner, now to supper, were of daily occurrence; and we sat at tables where fish, no longer mere salted shrimps, announced our vicinity to the coast; vermicelli too, and other kinds of pastry, denoted the influence of Persian art on the kitchen. Smoking within-doors was general; but the Nargheelah often replaced, and that very advantageously, the short Arab pipe; perfumes are no less here in use than in Nejed. I need hardly say that domestic furniture is here much more varied and refined than what adorns the dwellings of Sedeyr and 'Aared; and the stools, low dinner-tables, cupboards, shelves, and bedsteads, are very like the fittings-up of a respectable Hindoo house at Baroda or Cambay. Wood-carving is also common; it finds its usual place on door-posts and window-frames; lastly, decorative figures painted on the walls, though not absolutely equal to the frescoes of Giotto or Ghirlandajo, yet suffice to give the rooms a more cheerful and, if I may be allowed the expression, a more Christian look than the unvarying brown and white daub of the apartments in 'Aared and Ḳaseem. After all, without the perceptions of art in some form or other, how many degrees are men, at any rate the most of men, above the brute? But I will not weary my reader with speculation, lest he should be as long in reading the journey as we were in making it.

What however gives to the houses of Ḥaṣa their most decided superiority over those of Central Arabia, is the employment of the arch, without which indeed there may be building, but hardly construction. The Ḥaṣa arch, whether large or small, contracted to a window or spanning the entire abode, is, I believe, never the segment of one circle, but of two; it is half-way between the form peculiar to Tudor Gothic, and the "lancet" of the Plantagenets. Neither did I witness here the horse-shoe curve characteristic of what is called Moresco architecture; it is a simple, broad, but pointed arch, within which an equilateral, sometimes an obtuse, but never an acute triangle, could be inscribed. The arch brings other improvements with it; the entire house becomes here much more regular, its apartments wider, its arrangement more symmetrical, light and air circulate with greater abundance and facility; while the roof, instead of remaining a mere mass of heavy woodwork, supported midway on clumsy pillars, assumes a something of lightness and spring, very refreshing to the eye of a traveller just arrived from Riaḍ.

Under these roofs, by these firesides, while coffee went round, and poetical recitations or tales of the land, interspersed with many a good joke and hearty laugh, hurried on the too-rapid hours of night, we had ample occasion to see what is sometimes called "the reverse of the medal," and what I might perhaps, in common with the Arabs, entitle even more expressively "the underside of the carpet." For every Nejdean blessing on Feyṣul, here were ten curses; for every good wish there bestowed on the

"Muslims," here were bitter imprecations. At Hofhoof for the first time in Arabia, though not the last, I heard the emphatic summing-up of anti-Mahometan feeling, in the words, "Bagḥaḍna Allah w'al Islam," literally, "hatred to Allah and Islam," equivalent to our own "Down with," or "Death to," coupled with the no less emphatic "T-foo 'ala 'l-Muslimeen" (in plain English, "d—n the Muslims"), phrases pronounced from between set teeth, and accompanied with no less meaning gestures. "La Ilāh illa Allāh" was here wholly out of fashion, and "Islam" a synonym of reproach; nay, *horresco referens*, often coupled with the uncourteous predicate of "dogs," or "Kelāb." Meanwhile lavish praise was given to the good order and prosperity of Bombay and Kurrachee, both of which towns many of our hosts had visited; a praise intermingled with comparisons far from advantageous to Wahhabee and Turkish rule. Journeys to Baṣrah and Bagdad have enabled a considerable number to become in some degree acquainted with the Ottoman administration, and to rate it at its just value.

Frequently, under cover of night and in houses out of the way, or round Aboo-'Eysa's ever-blazing hearth, were held meetings of the old chiefs and their partisans. I was twice present at such in the character of a seemingly casual guest, and in these assemblies I learnt how widespread are the ramifications of the anti-Wahhabee conspiracy, or rather confederacy. Ḥaṣa and 'Omān form its main force; Ṭelāl-ebn-Rasheed, and all who sympathize with him throughout Shomer, are ready to cooperate on the north; numerous partisans exist in Ḥareeḳ and Sedeyr; in Ḳaseem three-fourths of the population welcome the project. The Bedouins participate in the movement, with hardly any, if any, exception.

Those of my readers whom study or observation has given to know the immense extent and depth of clannish and hereditary feeling among the Arab race, will easily understand why a government which has everywhere dispossessed, banished, or killed the noblest of Arabia, is for that reason alone, not to mention others apparent from the course of this work, an object of unqualified hate, and the butt for the meditated vengeance of those over whom it tyrannizes: to the twentieth generation and beyond an Arab never pardons the wrongs of his ancestors. Add to this, national and hereditary antipathy, that "crasis" of the blood, to borrow a phrase—physiological indeed, but here not metaphorical; add the pressure of actual subjection and often positive misrule; add lastly the innate antipathy of the Arab to whatever is straitlaced and expressed by formulas and minute observances, and my reader may well wonder, not at the extent of the anti-Wahhabee reaction, but rather that it is not more widely extended; not at its intensity, but rather that it can hold an hour from breaking out into action. The Bedouins too, no less than the townsmen, have much blood to revenge, many rights to reassert; and if the love of liberty animate the more intelligent inhabitants of Ḥasa and Ḳaseem, that of licence inflames no less the Ajmān and the Benoo-Khālid. Hence in case of an insurrection these last can securely be reckoned on for the cause. But though an assured, they are not a very valuable accession, for reasons already explained at length, especially in the fifth chapter. Only could swaggering do the work, the Bedouins alone might suffice; I never heard fuller or fouler-mouthed abuse than theirs of Feyṣul and his government.

The men are come, to reverse the Kelpie's saying, but not the hour. In spite of all causes and elements of discontent, a justifiable dread of the concentrated force of Nejed, especially when in the hands of the terrible 'Abd-Allah-ebn-Sa'ood, so often attacked, so often attacking, and always victorious, assailant or assailed, restrains the desired outbreak, and the reactionary party remains waiting in silence the moment when weakness from within, or some new and powerful enemy from without, may divert for an instant the attention of their jealous tyrant, and lighten the weight of his arm. I have said it before, and here may say it again, Arabs are above all a prudent race, and undertakings of this nature require no ordinary prudence. In addition, the spies of Feyṣul, disseminated throughout Arabia from Djowf to Mascat, let no movement, no symptom, go by unnoticed and unreported. Hence nothing is left at present to the friends of freedom but hope, hatred, and submission.

We had passed about a week in the town when Aboo-'Eysa entered the side-room where Barakāt and I were enjoying a moment of quiet, and copying out "Nabṭee" poetry, and shut the door behind him. He then announced to us, with a face and tone of serious anxiety, that two of the principal Nejdean agents belonging to the Kôt had just come into the K'hāwah, under pretext of medical consultation, but in reality, said he, to identify the strangers. We put on our cloaks—a preliminary measure of decorum equivalent to face and hand-washing in Europe—and presented ourselves before our inquisitors with an air of conscious innocence and scientific solemnity. Conversation ensued; and we talked so learnedly about bilious and sanguine complexions, cephalic veins, and Indian drugs, with such apposite citations from the Coran, and such loyal phrases for Feysul, that Aboo-'Eysa was beside himself for joy; and the spies, after receiving some prescriptions of the bread-pill and aromatic-water formula, left the house no wiser than before. Our friends too, and they were now many, well guessing what we might really be, partly from our own appearance, and partly from the known character of our host (according to old Homer's true saying, *αἰεὶ τὸν ὅμοιον ἄγει θεὸς ἐς τὸν ὅμοιον*), did each and all their best to throw sand into Wahhabee eyes, and everything went on sociably and smoothly. A blessing on the medical profession! none other gives such excellent opportunities for securing everywhere confidence and friendship.

A custom unknown in Shomer and in Nejed, but very common in other parts of the East, fixes certain days of the week for holding public fairs in such and such localities, whither the inhabitants, and more particularly the villagers, of all the neighbourhood round repair, to sell or to buy, while auctions, games, recitations, races, and similar inventions of man's busy levity, keep up the animation. On the whole, it is an excellent practice, and one to which Europe herself is no stranger. In Arabia these fairs have been held from the remotest known antiquity, and lasted sometimes a fortnight together; witness the fair of 'Okād, where the seven Mo'allaķāt are said to have been first recited; the fair of Ṣanaa' in Yemen, and others alluded to by old chroniclers.

The same usage has prevailed from time immemorial in the province of Ḥasa. The weekly fair of Hofhoof is held on Thursday, that of the great village of Mebarraz to the north on Monday, and so on. Aboo-'Eysa, who was very desirous to impress us with a great idea of his adopted country, and to that end sought occasions to show us the most and the best of it, took care to let us know the whereabouts of the fair. We went thither, and passed several hours of much amusement among the booths erected on these occasions, chatting with townsmen and peasants amid a scene the animation of which might almost rival that of Epsom on the Derby-day, or Frankfort during a "Messwoche." The place of meeting was on the open ground beyond the northern gate, close under the outer walls of the Kôt. The vendors were mostly, if not entirely, villagers, and had brought with them wares recommendable by their cheapness rather than their elegance: heavy sandals, coarsely-woven cloaks, old muskets and daggers, second-hand brass utensils, besides camels, dromedaries, asses, and a few horses. Others, wandering pedlars by profession, and never absent in crowds like these, exposed in temporary booths glass bracelets, arm-rings, ankle-rings, copper seals, and beads destined for the necks of girls and (I am sorry to have thus to couple them) of asses, with an occasional European drinking-glass, imported through Koweyt or Baṣrah, and mirrors whose distorted reflection might have saved any fair woman the trouble of making mouths in them. The booths themselves were arranged almost symmetrically, and formed streets and squares; in these latter were great heaps of vegetables and dates piled up before male and female sellers, bags of meal and flour, heaps of charcoal, faggots of firewood, with bundles of sugar-cane for the sweet teeth of Hofhoof. Around, asses were tethered, foolish-looking camels stood neck in air, and half-a-dozen youngsters of the town made an immense dust by racing horses under pretence of trying them for purchase. Jokes and laughter were heard everywhere, and Arab gravity half forgot itself in this promiscuous out-of-doors assembly.

When Monday came we visited Mebarraz, performing the journey thither on donkeys equipped with side-saddles — a circumstance for which I must apologize to my fair readers, lest they should deem it an unjustifiable usurpation of their privilege; but side-saddles are the fashion of Ḥaṣa for all donkey-riders, men or women indifferently. Thus mounted we cantered off to the village, if indeed a population of nigh twenty thousand souls might not claim for Mebarraz the name of town. But it is unwalled, and the fort belonging to it stands on an isolated eminence at a little distance by the west. I could not but admire the position of the castle, equally adapted to discover and to repel an enemy advancing from any direction on the level plain around, or to repress the townsmen themselves should they prove unruly; the loopholes of the fort are within musket-shot of the houses below. The building is square, and resembles the Kôt of Hofhoof in every respect, size excepted, which is not above a fourth or fifth of the stronghold at the capital.

Near this fort the fair was held; its resemblance to that just described at Hofhoof renders description unnecessary. The principal object in the town itself is a large and not inelegant mosque, recently erected by the anxiety of Feysul for the spiritual welfare of his subjects. The building was raised at the monarch's own expense; but an extraordinary contribution exacted from the province in the following year may have more than compensated the treasury of Riaḍ for its pious outlay. The town is of very irregular appearance; it contains many handsome houses, intermixed with wretched hovels; the inhabitants of Mebarraz are in the main little different from those of Hofhoof, except that they represent more of the landed and less of the commercial interest. One of our party, 'Obeyd by name, owned a kinsman among the townsfolk, and availed himself of the circumstance to compass a dinner invitation, at which I saw honey for the first time since many months. The dwelling of our host was absolutely like a middle-class house at Ḥoms or Ḥamah, with small matted rooms, low windows, a little courtyard, a well, and with that peculiar air of seclusion and privacy, even in the midst of a street, which may have struck my readers if they have ever entered the abode of a friend (a native of course) in Syria, at Mosoul, or at Bagdad. Ḥaṣa in fact already approximates to the mixed districts, though the Arab element is yet predominant.

Almost the whole space between Hofhoof and Mebarraz, a distance of about three miles, is filled up with gardens, plantations, and rushing streams of tepid water. Here and for many leagues around grow the dates entitled "Khalāṣ,"—a word of which the literal and not inappropriate English translation is "quintessence,"—a species peculiar to Ḥasa, and the *facile princeps* of its kind. The fruit itself is rather smaller than the Ḳaseem date, of a rich amber colour, verging on ruddiness, and semitransparent. It would be absurd to attempt by description to give any idea of a taste; but I beg my Indian readers at least to believe that a "Massignum" mango is not more superior to a "Junglee," than is the Khalās fruit to that current in Syrian or Egyptian marts. In a word, it is the perfection of the date. The tree that bears it may by a moderately practised eye be recognised by its stem, slenderer than that of the ordinary palm, its less tufted foliage, and its smoother bark. Another species, also limited to this province, is the Reḳab; it would hold the first rank anywhere else. During my stay in Arabia I counted a dozen kinds of date, each perfectly distinct from the other; and I doubt not that a longer acquaintance might have enabled me to reckon a dozen more. As to the Khalās in particular, its cultivation is an important item among the rural occupations of Ḥasa; its harvest an abundant source of wealth; and its exportation, which reaches from Mosoul on the north-west to Bombay on the south-east, nay, I believe, to the African coast of Zanjibar, forms a large branch of the local commerce.

I return to our road: it is a raised causeway between deep irrigation on either side, with an occasional pool or small swamp; should any of my readers have journeyed in the neighbourhood of Vellore, Tanjore, or Negapatam, they may recall to mind the highways there, and from them form a tolerable idea of those in Ḥasa. Curious to see, in the midst of all this fertility, exists, not far from Mebarraz, a small lake whose waters are impregnated, or rather saturated, with salt, till the margin of the pool is covered with a thick crust, and the adjoining ground is for some acres wholly barren. Other similar salt patches occur here and there in a strangely arbitrary manner; the intervening soil is generally quite free and fertile. About a hundred yards beyond Mebarraz to the north, is a beautiful spring, forming a small but deep lake, to which its warmth has given the significative name of "Sakhneh,"—"heat." The water had no perceptible mineral flavour, but the temperature of the pool could not have been under 85 to 90 degrees Fahrenheit. Hither the townsmen of Mebarraz resort to bathe; we imitated their example, and after a good swim returned to dine in the carpeted house of 'Obeyd's relative—his uncle, I believe.

On another day Aboo-'Eysa proposed a trip to Omm-Sabaa' (literally, "the Mother of Seven"). My readers will naturally suppose a call on some respectable matron with a large family; but even in Ḥasa, where the fair sex are under much less restraint than in Nejed, a special visit to a lady would be looked on as an oddity. The "Mother of Seven" is in reality a large hot spring, gushing up from the depths of a natural basin, out of which seven streams, the daughters of this fruitful parent, flow in different directions and fertilize the land far and wide. The spot itself is about eight miles distant from Hofhoof, due north. When the moment came we assembled, a band of twelve in all; our companions were friends of some standing, and well inclined to be merry. The muster-roll ran as follows: Barakāt and myself, five gentlemen (they deserved the name) of Hofhoof, two mulattoes or half-castes, a negro, and a couple of lads. Aboo-'Eysa remained to keep house at home; his wife's care had provided us with boiled chickens, pastry, molasses, coffee, and other good things. We mounted our donkeys and cantered off, but took care not to pass through the town for fear of encountering some Nejdean observer. Instead of keeping the streets we made a circuit outside the city walls, amid tanks and fields, often at imminent risk of falling off the narrow causeway on the back of some buffalo weltering in the mud beneath, racing our beasts, and ascertaining by actual experience that Arabs on a pleasure party can rival all the freaks of Western schoolboys on an extra half-holiday. We left Mebarraz, its fort and spring, on one side, and then went three or four miles at full speed over a wide plain, where palm-trees bordered the right, and the Ḥasa mountain-range stretched arid and fantastic on our left, while all along were ranged from distance to distance watch-towers and isolated forts, now abandoned to decay. Next the road narrowed, and led us between two good-sized villages, then wound forward amid plantations and tanks, till at last the rush of waters and a broad grass-banked stream conducted us, as we followed its course, up to Omm-Sabaa'.

This fountain rises in a circular hollow, about fifty feet in diameter, and very deep, from whose centre well up waters so hot that no bather dares venture on a plunge without first inuring his feet and arms to the temperature by cautious degrees. The basin is brim-full from rim to rim, and from seven apertures in the stony margin run out the seven streams whence the fountain takes its name, broad and deep enough to turn as many water-mills, were such placed on their course. Some of the channels are natural, but the total number of seven has evidently been completed by art; whether with any planetary reference I do not venture to decide; but an analogous arrangement which we shall afterwards meet with in the cisterns of the Persian coast, and which is undoubtedly of a religious or rather a superstitious origin, would somewhat incline me to think no less of Omm-Sabaa'. The stonework that surrounds the pool is evidently ancient, but there is no inscription or record of date, an omission of which I have already remarked the universality in Central and Eastern Arabia. All around palm-trees and Nabaķ shade the grassy banks; deep masses of vegetation shut out the distant view, and veil from sight the little village of Zekkah, which stands at about a quarter of a mile distant to the east. The waters of Omm-Sabaa' flow the same, winter and summer. Fish, frogs, and other aquatic creatures cannot live within the heated basin, or even in the streams near their immediate origin, but they abound a little farther down the channels.

The sun now sat high and bright in his meridian tower; the breeze was delightful; we examined the fountain-head in all its bearings, then bathed, swam, wrestled, drank coffee, chatted, dined, smoked, slept, and bathed again. All went merry as a marriage-bell till we discovered that, by one of the omissions inseparable from a picnic, no coffee-cups had been brought, a circumstance which had remained unnoticed till the coffee itself was ready, and nothing remained for us but to drink it out of the sooty coffee-pot wherein it had been prepared. Luckily one of the party, cleverer than the rest, bethought him of trying the generosity of the Zekkah households, and rode over at a venture to the village, whence he soon returned with a donkey-load of cups. Trivial circumstances these: I recount them merely by way of counterpoise to the many stilted and padded descriptions of Eastern life, and of Arab in particular. Meanwhile the 'Aṣr came on; by common consent prayers were supposed to have been said, and we remounted our side-saddles and galloped homewards; some of our companions got thrown on the way, others stopped to pick them up; at last we all arrived safe at Hofhoof, rather late and tired, but in high spirits, and well contented with our excursion.

I have described with tolerable minuteness two of the Ḥaṣa hot fountains; there are three hundred such, according to Aboo-'Eysa's version, in the province. I would not warrant the numerical precision of this statement; but I can vouch for the great frequency of these sources, having met with more than a dozen within a very limited space; one in particular, at about three miles' ride eastward of Hofhoof, proved even more abundant in its supply than Omm-Sabaa' herself, though of a more supportable temperature. The heat, varying in degree, but never absent, is doubtless owing to subterranean causes; but the water must be derived from the uplands of the interior, and from Ṭoweyḳ in particular. The pools and torrents which form during the winter on its plateaus or furrow its valleys are soon reabsorbed in the marly or sandy soil, and seem lost for ever to their duty of fertilization and life. But it is not really so; they have only dived a space to reappear once more on the surface, and to compensate on the coast for what they have left undone in the inlands. Few travellers in the interior of Syria, especially towards the east and south, where, as I said on a former occasion, the territorial features of Arabia begin to show themselves, but must have been struck by the rapidity with which its torrents, streams, nay rivers, hide themselves underground in the fissured soil of the waste. But, it may be asked, why do not the waters of Ṭoweyḳ burst out at once near the mountain's foot, instead of pursuing a subterraneous course of full sixty or eighty miles to emerge in Ḥaṣa? To this question I may suggest a conjectural yet a not unfounded answer. The moisture percolating through the limestone strata of Ṭoweyḳ, follows them, I should suppose, to a considerable depth in their eastward curve, till on approaching the coast-formation it meets with a stratum of impermeable granite, itself warmed by igneous agency beneath. Here, unable to descend any farther, the water remounts, by the common law of fluid level, through the broken soil above, and regains the surface bearing with it in its heat the token of its hidden journey. My readers will doubtless remember that granite and basalt predominate in the coast-formations of Arabia, whereas limestone, chalk, and the like, are the almost exclusive features of the centre.

Before we leave Ḥaṣa I must add a few remarks to complete the sketch given of the province and of its inhabitants; want of a suitable opportunity for inserting them before, has thrown them together at this point of my narrative.

My fair readers will be pleased to learn that the veil and other restraints inflicted on the gentle sex by Islamitic rigorism, not to say worse, are much less universal and more easily dispensed with in Ḥaṣa; while in addition the ladies of the land enjoy a remarkable share of those natural gifts which no institutions, and even no cosmetics, can confer; namely, beauty of face and elegance of form. Might I venture on the delicate and somewhat invidious task of constructing "a beauty-scale" for Arabia, and for Arabia alone, the Bedouin women would on this kalometer be represented by zero, or at most 1°; a degree higher would represent the female sex of Nejed; above them rank the women of Shomer, who are in their turn surmounted by those of Djowf. The fifth or sixth degree symbolizes the fair ones of Ḥaṣa; the seventh those of Ḳaṭar; and lastly, by a sudden rise of ten degrees at least, the seventeenth or eighteenth would denote the pre-eminent beauties of 'Omān. With Ḳaṭar and 'Omān we have yet to make acquaintance. Arab poets occasionally languish after the charmers of Ḥejāz; I never saw any to charm me, but then I only skirted the province. All bear witness to the absence of female loveliness in Yemen; and I should much doubt whether the mulatto races and dusky complexions of Ḥadramaut have much to vaunt of. But in Ḥaṣa a decided improvement on this important point is agreeably evident to the traveller arriving from Nejed, and he will be yet further delighted on finding his Calypsos much more conversible, and having much more too in their conversation than those he left behind him in Sedeyr and 'Aareḍ.

In a district hardly less agricultural than commercial, I might be expected to say something about ploughs and harrows, spades and flails. But the great Niebuhr in his account of Arabia has so faithfully and so minutely described the instruments customary in Arab tillage, and their use, that nothing is left for me to add, Nor need I especially sketch the peasant, much the same all the world over; nor the peasant-houses, generally mere earth hovels or palm-leaf sheds; the latter perhaps the more numerous of the two in Ḥasa. But I should not pass over in silence the increasing number of kine, all hunchbacked, Brahminee-bull fashion; they are often put to the plough, though not exclusively, being at times replaced by asses; by horses, I need hardly say, never. Regarding the horse, I have only to notice that the breed here resembles that of Shomer, namely, a half-caste Nejdean. Dromedaries are many and cheap; they yield the palm of excellence to those of 'Omān alone.

In Ḥaṣa only, throughout the whole course of my long journey, did I meet with the genuine produce of an Arab mint. In Djowf and Shomer the currency is Turkish or European, identical in short with that of Syria, Egypt, and 'Irāḳ, from one or other of which three sources whatever coin circulates in the Djowf is derived. In Nejed proper, where Turkish money is no longer passable, nor have the French or German coinages, francs or florins, found acceptance, the Spanish rial and the English sovereign are privileged by retaining their monetary value. For small change the inhabitants of Sedeyr, 'Aareḍ, and Yemāmah avail themselves of what they call a "Djedeedah," or "new coin," doubtless so entitled on the principle of *lucus a non lucendo*, for it is in fact very old; a piece of debased silver about the size of a full-grown sixpence, and which, so far as the faint vestiges of inscription and superscription can with pain and labour be deciphered, though oftener not a vestige of them remains, seems to have issued from the Egyptian mint at a date far anterior to the Moḥammed-'Alee dynasty. Its value equals two ordinary Syrian "gorsh," and in consequence hovers between that of an English fourpence and fourpence halfpenny. The smallest currency in Nejed bears the name of Khorḍah; it consists of little irregular copper bits, now square, now round, sometimes triangular, often polygonal; these are the melancholy productions of the Baṣrah mint, at a date of two or three hundred years back. The inscription, which gives the names of the local governors who issued this coinage, is almost Cufic, so coarse and so angular are the letters. Thirty of these "bits," or Khorḍah, are considered equivalent to a Djedeedah; their single value is thus between one-third and one-fourth of a farthing. But Khorḍah or Djedeedah, all is foreign; the Wahhabee government has not nor ever had a mint of its own.

But in Ḥasa we find an entirely original and a perfectly local coinage, namely, the "Ṭoweelah," or "long bit," as it is very suitably called, from its form. It consists of a small copper bar, much like a stout tack, about an inch in length, and split at one end, with the fissure slightly opened; so that it looks altogether like a compressed Y. Along one of its flattened sides run a few Cufic characters, indicating the name of the Carmathian prince under whose auspices this choice production of Arab numismatics was achieved; nothing else is to be read on the Ṭoweelah, neither date nor motto. Three of these are worth a "gorsh," and accordingly every copper nail separately may equal about three farthings. This currency is available in Ḥasa, its native place, alone; and hence the proverb, "Zey' Ṭoweelat-il-Ḥasa," "like a Ḥasa long bit," is often applied to a person who can only make himself valuable at home. Silver and gold Ṭoweelahs were issued in the days of Carmathian glory; but they have been long since melted down. Besides the copper Ṭoweelah, this last monetary vestige of former independence, the Persian "Tomūn," gold or silver, and the Anglo-Indian rupee, anna, and pice, are prevalent in Ḥasa. Turkish or French coinage will not pass in the province, no more than the Nejdean Khorḍah and Djedeedah. Owing to the commercial character of the population, money is here much more plentiful, and consequently of less relative value, than in the interior. My readers may rightly conjecture that throughout Arabia barter is by far more frequent among the villagers, and even the poorer townsmen, than purchase;

though in Ḥaṣa even a peasant can not unfrequently count down silver Tomāns and brass Ṭoweelahs when occasion requires. But among Bedouins and even villagers in Nejed, computation in an artificial medium surpasses the ordinary range of human faculties.

During our stay at Hofhoof, Aboo-'Eysa left untried no arts of Arab rhetoric and persuasion to determine me to visit 'Omān, assuring me again and again that whatever we had yet seen, even in his favourite Ḥaṣa, was nothing compared to what remained to see in that more remote country. My companion, tired of our long journey, and thinking the long distance already laid between him and his Syrian home quite sufficient in itself without further leagues tucked on to it, was very little disposed for a supplementary expedition. Indeed, considering the strong attachment that the inhabitants of Central Syria, and above all the Christians, bear to their native land, and the difficulty that there is in inducing them to quit it for anything like a serious journey, I might rather wonder that Barakāt had come thus far, than that he was unwilling to go farther. Englishmen, on the contrary, are rovers by descent and habit; my own mind was now fully made up to visit 'Omān at all risks, whether Barakāt came with me or not. Meanwhile, we formed our plan for the next immediate stage of our route. My companion and I were to quit Hofhoof together, leaving Aboo-'Eysa behind us for a week or two at Ḥaṣa, whilst we journeyed northwards to Ḳaṭeef, and thence took ship for the town of Menāmah in Baḥreyn. In this latter place Aboo-'Eysa was to rejoin us, not however by the route of Ḳaṭeef, but by that of 'Ajeyr, a seaport much nearer than Ḳaṭeef to Hofhoof, and lying at only twenty-four hours' distance south-east by east on the shore of the Gulf. Our main reason for thus separating our movements in time and in direction, was to avoid the too glaring appearance of acting in concert while yet in a land under Wahhabee government and full of Wahhabee spies and reporters, especially after the suspicions thrown on us at Riaḍ. Ulterior arrangements about 'Omān were to be deferred till we should all meet again together at Menāmah. Aboo-'Eysa's quality of pilgrim conductor obliged him to visit Baḥreyn anyhow, in order there to arrange several affairs relative to the transport of his future companions. From Baḥreyn his way lay by sea to Aboo-Shahr, the customary rendezvous of Persian pilgrims, and their starting-point for Mecca. The ordinary allowance of time for a caravan from Aboo-Shahr to Mecca, *viâ* Nejed, is about two months, including the sea-passage from the Persian to the Arabian coast; hence the pilgrims must all be assembled and ready at Aboo-Shahr by the end of the first week in Show'wāl (the month succeeding Ramadhan) at latest.

Barakāt and myself prepared for our departure; we purchased a few objects of local curiosity, got in our dues of medical attendance, paid and received the customary P. P. C. visits, and even tendered our respects to the negro governor Belāl, where he sat at his palace door in the Kôt, holding a public audience, and looking much like any other well-dressed black. No passport was required for setting out on the road to Ḳaṭeef, which in the eyes of government forms only one and the same province with Ḥasa, though in many respects very different from it. The road is perfectly secure, plundering Bedouins or highway robbers are here out of the question. However we stood in need of companions, not for escort, but as guides. Aboo-'Eysa made enquiries in the town, and found three men who chanced to be just then setting out on their way for Ḳaṭeef. One of them was a half-Bedouin, of the class called in Syria "'Arab-ed-Deerah," or "Bedouins of the cultivated land," he belonged to Benoo-Hājar; the second was a genuine Ajmān; the third a townsman of Hofhoof. They readily consented to join band with us for the road. Our Abyssinian hostess supplied us with a whole sack of provisions, and our Hofhoof associates found us in camels. Thus equipped and mounted, we took an almost touching leave of Aboo-'Eysa's good-natured wife, kissed the baby, exchanged an *au revoir* with its father, and set out on the afternoon of December 19th, leaving behind us many pleasant acquaintances, from some of whom I received messages and letters while at Baḥreyn. So far as inhabitants are concerned, to no town in Arabia should I return with equal confidence of finding a hearty greeting and a welcome reception, than to Hofhoof and its amiable and intelligent merchants.

We quitted the town by the north-eastern gate of the Rifey-'eeyah, where the friends, who, according to Arab custom, had accompanied us thus far in a sort of procession, wished us a prosperous journey, took a last adieu, and returned home. Our own way plunged at once into a labyrinth of luxuriant and well-watered palm-groves, mostly Khalāṣ, where we wound in and out for a couple of hours amid rushing water-channels, and over narrow bridges, till near sunset we skirted a large reedy swamp, with just room left for a camel to foot between the clustered trees and the oozy marsh; at last emerging on a little sandy space, which separates the exclusive territory of Hofhoof from that of Kelābeeyah. This last is a good-sized village, situated about seven miles north-east of the capital. Here we bivouacked on a little hillock of clean sand, with Kelābeeyah on our right, and the dark line of the Hofhoof woods on our left, while at some distance in front a copious fountain poured out its rushing waters with a noise distinctly audible in the stillness of the night, and irrigated a garden worthy of Damascus or Antioch. The night air was temperate —neither cold like that of Nejed, nor stifling like that of Southern India; the sky clear and starry. From our commanding position on the hill I could distinguish Soheyl or Canopus, now setting; and following him, not far above the horizon, the three upper stars of the Southern Cross, an old Indian acquaintance; two months later in 'Omān I had the view of the entire constellation.

While enjoying the repose of the quiet hours, we were aroused from our half-sleep by the tread of approaching camels. They bore several travellers coming up from Ḳaṭeef. The new arrivers halted by our side and dismounted for half an hour's chat; for what Arab can pass another without interchange of news? From these men we learnt an incident of the day, curious because it illustrated the anti-Arab tendency of the Wahhabee government. An individual, native of Ḳaṭeef, had not long before detected in a young man of the same province the seducer of his young and unmarried sister. According to Arab ideas, such disgrace can only be washed out in the blood of the guilty parties; and the Ḳaṭeefee taking the law into his own hands, by a proceeding in full accordance with ancestral usage, which assigns to the nearest relative the task of avenging family ignominy, slew both his own sister and her paramour. Now the Wahhabees, following the prescriptions of the Coran, assign a much milder punishment to the faults of unmarried persons; and hence when the news of this affair reached Riaḍ, orders were given to arrest the jealous Ḳaṭeefee, and bring him to trial for wilful and unjustifiable murder. The execution of the mandate was entrusted to Belāl, governor of the entire province, who in his turn sub-delegated the disagreeable duty to Farḥāt, the special governor of Ḳaṭeef. Farḥāt sent his police to apprehend the culprit; but the whole neighbourhood was leagued together to screen the homicide and favour his escape. At last, after a search of some weeks, he was discovered in a peasant's house, taken prisoner, and sent to Hofhoof. This proceeding had excited great indignation throughout Ḳaṭeef, where public opinion justified the brother, and condemned the Wahhabee administration for opening a door to laxity in domestic morals.

We were yet engaged in hearing and commenting on these events when a second inhabitant of Hofhoof, well mounted and armed, came up from the south, and requested the favour of a place in our band, a proposition no sooner made than granted. Next morning our party, now increased from five to six, set off; we passed close under the hill on which stands Kelābeeyah. The name of this village implies it to be a colony of Benoo-Kelāb, a Nejdean tribe descended from Ḳēys, and settled here at a very early date. My readers will not confound Kelāb with Kelb, a very different clan of Ḳaḥṭānic origin, and the mortal enemies of Kelāb and of all the numerous progeny of Ḳēys-'Eylān. Long residence in Ḥaṣa has not obliterated national antipathy, and the inhabitants of Kelābeeyah are up to the present day ill-looked on by the surrounding population, proud of their Ḳaḥṭānic kindred through Modḥaj, Ḳoḍaa'h, and Kindah.

After leaving Kelābeeyah behind us, we traversed a large plain of light and sandy soil, intersected by occasional ridges of basalt and sandstone. Everywhere were indications of abundant moisture at a very slight depth below the surface; dwarf-palms, shrubs, nay, reeds and rushes, sprang up at short intervals, and now and then we passed a little pool in some sheltered hollow, fringed with overhanging bushes, while the ruins of two large villages, now deserted like Auburn, witnessed to the decline of the land under Nejdean rule. Hundreds and hundreds of the inhabitants have recently emigrated; a few families northward, the greater number to the islands adjacent to Baḥreyn, to the Persian coast, and the kindred dominions of 'Omān. Over those who remain behind misgovernment does its gradual but steady work of ruin, by the same process that has under Ottoman influence placed a desert between Bagdad and Mosoul, and reduced Syria to about one-eighth of its former population.

We journeyed on all day, meeting no Bedouins and few travellers. At evening we encamped in a shallow valley, near a cluster of brimming wells, some sweet, some brackish, where the traces of half-obliterated watercourses, and the vestiges of crumbling house-walls indicated the former existence of a village, now also deserted. We passed a comfortable night under the shelter of palms and high brushwood, mixed with gigantic aloes and yuccas; and rose next morning early to our way. About sunrise, while crossing a sandy eminence, we sighted at no great distance on our left the village of Hedeeyah, and here took our last view of the Ḥaṣa mountain-range, already much lower than at Hofhoof, but of the same fantastic outline. Our direction lay north-east. In the afternoon we caught our first glimpse of Djebel Mushahhar, a pyramidical peak some seven hundred feet high and about ten miles south of Ḳaṭeef. It belongs to a series of hills, among which this mountain, the "Mushahhar" or "Conspicuous" (a name reminding me of the Maltese "Conspicua") is the only one that attracts notice; this intervening range divides the territory of Ḳaṭeef from the province of Ḥaṣa, itself two or three hundred feet above the ocean-level.

The country over which lay this day's march was much like that which we had traversed the day before—sand-hills and plains, with now and then a rock, a cluster of palms, or a ruined village, to break the monotony, and everywhere a remarkable abundance of underground waters, oozing through the soil, and in general sweet and good, but now useless for want of hands to profit by the fertility they would confer. Were a better rule to take the place of the actual tyranny, we might easily see five hundred villages or towns instead of fifty, the round number at present assigned to those in Ḥaṣa. A peculiar feature of the vegetation hereabouts is a huge aloe, already alluded to; its thorny leaves and dense tufts attain not unfrequently a height sufficient to shelter travellers, camels and all; this plant is common in Ḥaṣa, but I never saw it in the interior or the uplands.

It would be impolite to dismiss our companions without a few words of description. Of all Bedouins that I have met with in the course of my wanderings, early or late, the Benoo-Hājar, Benoo-Khālid, and Ajmān, are at once the most spirited and the most courteous; the very licence of manner, inseparable from the nomade, becomes in them much less barbarous and repulsive than in others. This is in part a consequence of their frequent intercourse with the townsmen of Ḥaṣa, whose sociable and courteous ways they have also in their measure adopted. These clans are better armed and clad than the average of their desert brethren, though the principal items of wearing apparel are in make and form the same, differing only in the quality of the material, and the gayness of its colours. All are provided with muskets, and several, besides spear and sword, wear at their belts the crooked poniard of 'Omān.

Towards the latter part of the afternoon we gradually mounted the broad low range of the Ḳaṭeef hills, having Djebel Mushahhar at a considerable distance on our right. But the sea, though I looked towards it and for it with an eagerness somewhat resembling that of the Ten Thousand on their approach to the Euxine, remained shut out from view by a further continuation of the heights. Here we exchanged the sands of Ḥaṣa for a rocky and blackish ground; the air blew cold and sharp, nor was I sorry when at evening we halted near a cluster of trees, exactly at the boundary line of the Ḳaṭeef territory. The spot is further marked by the village of 'Azmiah, now half desolate; the houses yet inhabited were of so wretched and unpromising an appearance that we preferred to encamp leeward of a noble aloe hedge, and to make our supper off our own provisions. Our dromedaries (beautiful creatures to look at) were turned loose to graze, when lo! they took advantage of the dusk to sheer off, nor were they recaptured without much difficulty; thus giving us a proof of what I had often heard, and have mentioned in the first chapter of this work, that a camel when once his own master, never dreams of coming home, except under compulsion.

Next day we rose at dawn, and crossed the hills of Ḳaṭeef by a long winding path, till after some hours of labyrinthine track we came in sight of the dark plantation-line that girdles Ḳaṭeef itself landwards. The sea lies immediately beyond; this we knew, but we could not obtain a glimpse of its waters through the verdant curtain stretched between.

About midday we descended the last slope, a steep sandstone cliff, which looks as though it had been the sea-limit of a former period. We now stood on the coast itself. Its level is as nearly as possible that of the Gulf beyond; a few feet of a higher tide than usual would cover it up to the cliffs. Hence it is a decidedly unhealthy land, though fertile and even populous; but the inhabitants are mostly weak in frame and sallow in complexion. Our road, the highway of Ḳaṭeef, led straight for an hour or more across an extent of whitish soil, the dried-up bed of a shallow salt-marsh; but in front, on our right and on our left, stretched one continuous mass of palm-groves, where wound serpent-like the broken arches and channels of an old aqueduct, the work of the Carmathian dynasty. This served formerly to supply Ḳaṭeef with better water than that to be had in its immediate vicinity; the entire length of the construction must have been about five miles. Running streams, once conveyed over its masonry, now wandered at random about the level, or stagnated in pools. The atmosphere was thick and oppressive, the heat intense, and the vegetation hung rich and heavy around; my companions talked about suffocation, and I remembered once more the Indian coast. When arrived under the shade of the tall close-set trees, we had to keep a causeway, narrow like that of Bunyan's Valley of Desolation, but not equally straight, and where a "Christian" himself might have reasonably feared to slip into the quagmire of mud and water on either side. Luckily for us, instead of Apollyon and blasphemous fiends, we met at every turn harmless peasants and artisans coming and going, and still increasing as we approached the town. Another hour of afternoon march brought us to Ḳaṭeef itself, at its western portal; a high stone arch of elegant form, and flanked by walls and towers, but all dismantled and ruinous. Close by the two burial-grounds, one for the people of the land, the other for the Nejdean rulers and colony—divided even after death by mutual hatred and anathema. Folly, if you will, but folly not peculiar to the East.

The town itself is crowded, damp, and dirty, and has altogether a gloomy, what for want of a better epithet I would call a *mouldy*, look; much business was going on in the market and streets, but the ill-favoured and very un-Arab look of the shopkeepers and workmen confirms what history tells of the Persian colonization of this city. Indeed the inhabitants of the entire district, but more especially of the capital, are a mongrel race, in which Persian blood predominates, mixed with that of Baṣrah, Bagdad, and the 'Irāḳ. During the triumph of the Benoo-'Abbas, and their frequent persecutions of the Shiya'ees, these last took refuge by multitudes in Ḳaṭeef, under the shelter of its Carmathian princes; an immigration which contributed largely to the industry and activity of the capital town in particular, while it tended to corrupt its morals and to vitiate its pedigrees. Among the villagers of Ḳaṭeef, Arab descent may claim a larger share; yet even here the Persian type is clearly perceptible. Needs hardly say that all are Shiya'ees, or rather "Khowarij," "freethinkers," men who have passed through all gradations of Eastern misbelief, from Moḥammed to 'Alee; from 'Alee to the Imāms, Isma'eel, Moosa, or Aboo-Ḳāsim; from the Imāms to the Ḳā'im-ez-Zemān, and from the Ḳā'im to Pantheism, Materialism, or sheer and undisguised Pyrrhonism: a subject and a phase of the human intellect worthy of more serious research than has yet been bestowed on it. Meantime I would refer such of my readers as may desire a glimpse into this strange world of eastern light or darkness, to the preface of the late Baron Sylvester de Sacy, in his work on the Druses; it contains much information, equally interesting and valuable.

We urged our starting dromedaries across the open square in front of the market-place, traversed the town in its width, which is scarce a quarter of its length (like other coast towns), till we emerged from the opposite gate, and then looked out with greedy eyes for the sea, now scarce ten minutes distant. In vain as yet, so low lies the land, and so thick cluster the trees. But after a turn or two we came alongside of the outer walls, belonging to the huge fortress of Ḳarmooṭ, and immediately afterwards the valley opening out showed us almost at our feet the dead shallow flats of the bay. How different from the bright waters of the Mediterranean, all glitter and life, where we had bidden them farewell eight months before at Gaza! Like a leaden sheet, half ooze, half sedge, the muddy sea lay in view waveless, motionless; to our left the massive walls of the castle went down almost to the water's edge, and then turned to leave a narrow esplanade between its circuit and the Gulf. On this ledge were ranged a few rusty guns of large calibre, to show how the place was once guarded; and just in front of the main gate a crumbling outwork, which a single cannon-shot would level with the ground, displayed six pieces of honeycombed artillery, their mouths pointed seawards. The castle walls are high and strong, of mingled brick and stone; they might resist a first attack; the entrance is double-doored, and flanked with towers. Long stone benches without invited us to leave our camels crouching on the esplanade, while we seated ourselves and rested a little before requesting the governor to grant us a day's hospitality and permission to embark for Baḥreyn.

The castle of Ḳaṭeef stands on the innermost curve of a little bay, itself scolloped out in the base of a much larger one; its aspect is almost due east. To north and south run out two long promontories, like advancing horns, tipped, the one by the fortress of Dareem, the other by that of Dāman. In a straight line the distance between these two points is about twelve miles, but much more if one follows the semicircular curve of the bay. Within this hollow rot the shallow waters of the Gulf; when full tide creeps in they present the delusive appearance of calm depth, but at ebb reveal innumerable shoals, islets, tufts of sea-plants and banks of sand, with narrow winding channels between, full of mud and slime. The shore, except in a very few places, melts imperceptibly into the sea; sometimes it is bare and sandy, sometimes fringed with palm-trees and undergrowth down to its extreme verge. The first glance sufficiently explains to the spectator why the localities on this coast are so unhealthy, and how justly they merit their bad reputation for fever and other forms of disease.

In the lesser or inner bay before us rode at high water and stranded at ebb some twenty or thirty Arab barks, varying in size from a small schooner down to an open fishing boat, but all equipped with lateen sails, the only rig here known. One large hull not far from land attracted our notice, and we felt a suitable thrill of reverential awe on learning that it was Feyṣul's navy, with which, sometimes in line and sometimes in column (like the gallant soldier who singly formed square to receive the charge of the enemy), Nejed was to resist and conquer all the infidel fleets of Baḥreyn, 'Omān, and England united, should they madly venture an attack. This important vessel, squadron, or navy, was in size equal to an ordinary Newcastle collier, and about as well fitted for warlike manœuvres, judging by the exquisite clumsiness of her build. However "the natives" looked on her with great dread, and never mentioned her but in an undertone. She was now getting her masts in, and completing her other fittings. A little to one side of the coast battery mentioned above, and close by the filthy shore, stood the custom-house, a palm-leaf hut, long and narrow, entitled the "Ma'āsher," or "tithing-place," the decimal system of percentage being here applied to government dues on commerce no less than on agriculture. Farther on were dank palm-groves and patches of salt-water swamp; a dreary scene, and which might have furnished Shelley with another Maddalo, not at Venice, but at Ḳaṭeef. Only the bright sun did its best, though not very effectually, to clear the prospect.

Barakāt and I sat still to gaze, speculating on the difference between the two sides of Arabia. But our companions, like true Arabs, thought it high time for "refreshment," and accordingly began their enquiries at the castle gate where the governor might be, and whether he was to be spoken to. When, behold! the majesty of Feyṣul's vicegerent issuing in person from his palace to visit the new man-of-war. My abolitionist friends will be gratified to learn that this exalted dignitary is, no less than he of Hofhoof, a negro, brought up from a curly-headed imp to a woolly-headed black in Feyṣul's own palace, and now governor of the most important harbour owned by Nejed on the Persian Gulf, and of the town once capital of that fierce dynasty which levelled the Ca'abah with the dust, and filled Ḳaṭeef with the plunder of Yemen and Syria. Farḥāt, to give him his proper name, common among those of his complexion, was a fine tall negro of about fifty years old, good-natured, chatty, hospitable, and furnished with perhaps a trifle more than the average amount of negro intellect. He was dressed rather more handsomely than became a strict Wahhabee, but his quality of negro might go far to excuse this fault; besides, on out-stations even Wahhabees are apt to forget the restrictions of home-teaching. Around him were the sallow-complexioned Nejdeans of his train, their spleens all suffering from congestion consequent on frequent ague fits, and their faces yet sourer than when absorbing a discourse from 'Abd-el-Kereem or 'Abd-el-Laṭeef in Riaḍ on the backslidings of the time.

Aboo-'Eysa, who had friends and acquaintances everywhere, and whose kindly manner made him always a special favourite with negroes high or low, had furnished us with an introductory letter to Farḥāt, stating how graciously we had been received, and how honourably treated by Feyṣul at the capital, but prudently suppressing the untoward circumstances of our abrupt departure thence. Of our onward destination the letter said nothing; but our plan was to set our faces as though towards Koweyt and Baṣrah, whilst we should in reality look out for a passage to Menāmah; this was to avoid the rousing of any suspicion on the governor's part by a premature mention of Baḥreyn.

But as matters went there was little need of caution. The fortunate coincidence of a strong north wind, just then blowing down the Gulf, gave a satisfactory reason for not embarking on board of a Baṣrah cruiser, while it rendered a voyage to Baḥreyn, our real object, equally specious and easy. Nothing is indeed more common for seafarers who intend making for one of the various harbours on the Gulf coast, than to weather out a day or two of contrary gale in the conveniently situated ports of Menāmah or Moḥarreḳ. Besides Farḥāt himself, who was a good easy-going sort of man, had hardly opened Aboo-'Eysa's note, and got the first lines read to him by an attendant (for his own eyesight was not a little weakened by ophthalmia), than without more ado he bade us a hearty welcome, free from all suspicion or thought of guile, ordered our luggage to be brought within the castle precincts, and requested us to step in ourselves and take a cup of coffee, awaiting his return for further conversation after his daily visit of inspection to Feysul's abridged fleet.

We now stood within the palace, a building ascribed by tradition to Aboo-Sa'eed-el-Djenābee, or Ḳarmooṭ, himself, though I can hardly believe it to be in reality of so ancient a date, and should rather assign it to the sixth or seventh century of Islam. This appears from the style of architecture here employed, much lighter and more elegant than what few relics we possess of the third century after the Hejirah; and secondly, from the great extent and lavish ornament of the edifice, more accordant with the works of long-established power than with the first years of a new and revolutionary dynasty, which had yet everything to acquire and do. Perhaps part of the foundations and the lower storey may be due to the Djenābee, while his successors have completed the superstructure.

The outer enclosure is square, and surrounded by the high walls under which we had lately passed on the outside; with lofty corner towers, and a moat towards the land; the front is defended by the sea. At the south-western angle, the farthest from the entrance, stands the palace itself. In its present condition, partly thrown down and broken, partly clumsily patched up in later times, it were hard to make out the precise details of the original plan. First comes a large portico or arcade, in the so-called Moresco style, supported on ranges of light columns three arches in depth, and five, if I remember right, in length, crowned by cross-vaulting, and stuccoed over with arabesque ornament, now defaced. Hence admittance is given to what must have once been a long covered gallery, though it now shows only the side walls and pillars, with here and there an abutment jutting out for a broken arch across it. By this one enters an inner court, round which are many apartments in a tolerable state of preservation; and on one side is the reception hall, a long, large, and wide room, with handsome pillars in the midst, and windows in the Persian style, divided into compartments by little columns; at the further end of the hall is a raised dais, where once a monarch sat, and now a negro. Beyond and within is an inextricable labyrinth of chambers, galleries, closets, and passages, in a first, a second, and a third storey; here is a falling staircase, there a door opening on vacancy. The windows, where they yet remain entire, are filled with a beautiful stone trellis, never the same in pattern throughout the whole range of the palace, and marking much ingenuity and taste. Lastly, a few yards beyond the reception room or Ḳ'hāwah, and on the ground-level, is what seems to have been a court for public audience, with large round columns, and vestiges of decoration much resembling that yet common in Bagdad houses, where bas-relief takes the place of colours. This part of the building has been defaced into a Wahhabee mosque, and has been wofully cut about to form a Miḥrāb and the other arrangements of Mahometan devotion. And this is all that time and war have spared of the old royal Carmathian residence. "Those who built this must have been much more civilized than its present occupants," was the first remark of my companion. Alas! that it should be applicable not to Ḳaṭeef alone, but to an entire empire from the Danube to the Tigris.

It is worth remarking, that although the arch is known and is continually employed in Ḥasa, vaulting is not equally so, except in its most simple or barrel form: the same may be said of the covered passages yet existing in the castle of Djowf; they too exhibit only barrel-vaulting. The palace of Ḳarmooṭ was accordingly the first building which we had seen, since our departure from Gaza, in which cross or rib-vaulting appeared, a decided advance in architectural science, and henceforward to be met with repeatedly in Baḥreyn, on the Persian coast, and in 'Omān. In the two latter districts, a further progress in constructive skill is signalized by the frequency of the dome or cupola, formed by concentric ranges of brick or stone shaped to the double curve; all phenomena indicative of foreign art and influence. For the Arabs when left to themselves appear never to have been architects enough to put even a simple arch together, much less a vault or a dome; and their unassisted edifices in Shomer, Ḳaseem, and Nejed, whether ancient or modern, afford sufficient proof of this strange ignorance or neglect. But when once taught by the sight of

Greek or Persian building, they readily copied the superior models of Irān and Syria, till they became themselves tolerable, but never first-rate, constructors. The relics of Ḥimyarite labour in Ḥaḍramaut, at Naḳab-el-Ḥajjār for example, or elsewhere, belong to a different race, namely, the Abyssinian, a point which we will investigate more accurately in the next chapter.

Barakāt and I were soon introduced into the Ḳ'hāwah, and seated there, while a blazing fire of palm-wood dispelled the damp chill of these old ruins. The furniture was tolerably good, and the coffee excellent. Farḥāt now came back from his walk, and entered with us into animated discourse about Riaḍ, Feysul, 'Abd-Allah, the siege of 'Oneyzah, and so forth. We naturally gave the best accounts, and threw over everything that *couleur de rose* hue, so much recommended by the highest political and diplomatic authorities. In the room were present also some twenty or more Nejdeans, belonging to the fort garrison, which amounts in all to two hundred and fifty or sixty men; on the other side of the Ḳ'hāwah sat in silence a few of the town inhabitants, dressed in large turbans and clipped Persian vests; there was little love lost between them and the upland Arabs. Two or three "skippers," owners of the smacks in harbour, and with all the careless jolly way that such men have a professional right to when on shore, were also here, and talked much; black and white servants filled up the background.

A good supper was brought in, fish and flesh; and after it had been concluded in due form by coffee and fumigation, Farḥāt, with a delicacy of politeness which almost surprised us, said that our luggage had been already taken upstairs, into a room prepared for our reception, and that, as we were doubtless tired, we might perhaps wish to follow it. Nay, he took the very civilized precaution of having us lighted up the steps—a measure not in the least superfluous, considering the dilapidated state of the staircase; it was of stone, but ruinous and neglected.

My readers may, like ourselves, be somewhat amazed at such excess of courtesy from such a personage. But nothing happens on earth without a reason, and there was a sufficient one for this.

My old patient Djowhar, who, after regaining his health, had left Riaḍ on his official duties long before our own departure from 'Aareḍ, and just when the tide of court favour was running at its strongest in our advantage, had passed by Ḳaṭeef when on his way to Baḥreyn. Received with all the honour due to a lord-treasurer, he had during his stay in the castle indoctrinated his brother negro Farḥāt with so favourable an idea regarding us, that when we arrived ourselves, with the additional recommendation of Aboo-'Eysa in our pocket, we found every one in the best possible dispositions, and Farḥāt would have done anything to please. Indeed, he proceeded this very first evening to render us the greatest service in his power, by having diligent enquiries made whether any vessel or boat was shortly to sail for Baḥreyn, promising us the first departure should be ours; "though," added he, "were I to consult merely my own inclinations, you should not go hence till after giving me at least eight days of your company." We thanked him, and followed the lamp up the winding stairs, where we found ourselves quartered in a room once perhaps honoured by royal repose, with mats and carpets duly spread on the floor; two windows looked on an inner court, the empty side spaces, formerly occupied by cupboards, seemed to indicate that the chamber had in old times belonged to the Ḥarem. Love, or they are sadly belied, was much in fashion among the Carmathian princes. We closed the doors carefully, lighted our pipes, had a good smoke (to keep the mosquitoes out), and went to sleep.

The next day passed, partly in Farḥāt's Ḳ'hāwah, partly in strolling about the castle, town, gardens, and beach, making meanwhile random enquiries after boats and boatmen. Ḳaṭeef offers what might almost be called a violent contrast to the general features of Arabia. The rank luxuriance of its garden vegetation surpasses by much the best-watered spots about Hofhoof, and the heavy foliage drooping in the heavy air aroused in me remembrances of a rainy season in the Concan, and sensations which had been sleeping for many a year. The water that nourishes the palms is brackish, for the land-level rises so little above the sea, that the tide runs far back through the plantations and mingles its brine with the copious fountains descending from the hills to the west. It is curious that the date-palm, like the cocoa-nut, instead of taking injury from salt-water, seems to thrive the more for it. The date-groves of Ḳaṭeef extend for several leagues in a broad belt along the coast, and their produce, if not equal in quality to that of Ḥasa, exceeds it in quantity. Lemons and citrons grow here, besides vegetables of all kinds; corn too, though the main food of the inhabitants seems to be fish and rice. This latter article is cheap, thanks to the Indian trade, through Baḥreyn.

The town itself, damp and dingy as it is, offers little to invite visitors, nor much to instruct them. I noticed a strip of paved road, and close by an arch evidently belonging to more thriving days, when Ḳaṭeef was a capital. The townsmen, taking us for Nejdeans by our dress, scowled silent ill-will as we passed; they are a busy but not an amiable race. I cannot think the situation of Ḳaṭeef well chosen. Its great unhealthiness and its want of ready communication with the interior, are hardly compensated for by a harbour half choked with mud, and capable of receiving none but the smallest sea-craft, and even those at high tide only. Besides, sand-banks running out on every side render the entrance of the port difficult and even unsafe. On the other hand the bay is well sheltered by its northern and southern promontories, with the islands of Ṭāroot and Soweyḳ, and is conveniently situated for trade with Baḥreyn, Aboo-Shahr, &c. Were it cleared out and kept in order, it might become a haven worthy of the name; but under Wahhabee administration such improvements are scarcely to be hoped.

It was noon when we fell in with a ship-captain ready to sail that very night, wind and tide permitting. Farḥāt's men had spoken with him, and he readily offered to take us on board. We then paid a visit to the custom-house officer to settle the embarkation dues for men and goods. This foreman of the Ma'āsher, whether in accordance with orders from Farḥāt, or of his own free will and inclination, I know not, proved wonderfully gracious, and declared that to take a farthing of duty from such useful servants of the public as doctors, would be "sheyn w' khaṭā'," "shame and sin." Alas, that European custom-house officials should be far removed from such generous and patriotic sentiments! Lastly, of his own accord he furnished us with men to carry our baggage through knee-deep water and thigh-deep mud to the little cutter, where she lay some fifty yards from shore. Evening now came on, and Farḥāt sent for us, to congratulate us, but with a polite regret, on having found so speedy conveyance for our voyage. Meanwhile he let us understand how he was himself invited for the evening to supper with a rich merchant of the town, and that we were expected to join the party; nor need that make us anxious about our passage, since our ship-captain was also invited, nor could the vessel possibly sail before the full tide at midnight.

Accordingly, after sunset we all went in great state, the governor at our head, to the house of our evening's entertainer. It was a fine three-storeyed dwelling, where the furniture and domestic arrangements, the small rooms, the profusion of carpets, with little knick-knacks of childish ornament, bespoke a Persian much more than an Arab taste. Nargheelahs stood ready in a side-closet for whoever might require them; and while Farḥāt, his principal retainers, and ourselves were seated on the cushioned divan, we were drenched all round, "thrice and once," with rose-water, and regaled with tea in pretty china cups presented by well-dressed serving-lads with the grace of Shirāz and Ispahan. The conversation was however dull—principally on bales of cloth and sacks of rice; the townsmen, who composed two-thirds of the assembly, having little interest in the affairs of Riaḍ and 'Oneyzah, except precisely what it was better to conceal than to display, while Farḥāt and his men observed the gravity befitting true believers when in the presence of free-thinkers and infidels. The supper was long in going by; it mustered four or five courses, with small Persian side-dishes of sweet but unknown materials; an endless circulation of tea-cups complicated the business, and we did not rise till near midnight. Farḥāt then wished us a prosperous journey, and insisted on receiving a letter from Baṣrah to assure him of our safe arrival there. This letter I never sent, for the simple reason that, more shame for me, I never once recalled to mind his courteous request till this very moment, (July 20, 1864) when, seated on the shore of a German lake amid pines and beeches, I am conjuring up to memory the muddy coast and dense palm-groves of Ḳaṭeef. "Tempora mutantur," and I may well add, "et nos mutamur in illis." Be it so; the outer shell may vary, but the kernel of human life is everywhere much the same.

Before leaving Ḳaṭeef I will add a word on the life of its Nejdean garrison. It is a very dull existence, hardly less so than that of our own troops and officers at 'Aden. Shut up by the antipathy of all around, and somewhat by their own apprehensions, within the walls they guard, in an uncongenial climate, and restricted to a bill of fare unlike the produce of their own land, while an irrational austerity denies them even the pastimes of games and tobacco, I have seldom or never seen Arabs so profoundly under the tyranny of "spleen," "ennui," or whatever else may denote "the awful yawn that sleep cannot abate." Many are out of health; all out of spirits. Their general term of residence is from two to three years, but some remain longer. They never intermarry with the females of the town, nor can often partake of the solace afforded by social intercourse. Hence they are a prey to intense "Heimweh," and no wonder. I shall not soon forget the sadness of a poor 'Aareḍ youth, worn down by fever and home-sickness, stretched on his death-bed in the castle of Ḳaṭeef. His only regret was for his native mountains, and he declared that could he but see them again, life or death were all one to him; but the thought of dying in this hated land was intolerable misery. In fact an Englishman at Hong Kong is hardly so far from home as a man of Nejed at Ḳaṭeef. I sat an hour or so by the lad's side, and tried to console him with whatever cheerful news I could muster from Riaḍ; nor was it easy for me to put aside his entreaties to remain by him and talk about Nejed a little longer.

From our town supper we returned by torchlight to the castle; our baggage, no great burden, had been already taken down to the sea gate, where stood two of the captain's men waiting for us. In their company we descended to the beach, and then with garments tucked up to the waist waded to the vessel, not without difficulty, for the tide was rapidly coming in, and we had almost to swim for it. At last we reached the ship, and scrambled up her side; most heartily glad was I to find myself at sea once more on the other side of Arabia.

CHAPTER XIV

Baḥreyn and Ḳaṭar

When the night is left behind
In the deep West, dim and blind,
And the blue noon is over us,
And the multitudinous
Billows murmur at our feet,
Where the Earth and Ocean meet;
And all things seem only one
In the universal sun.—*Shelley*

A BAḤREYN CREW—ARAB SAILORS—HARBOUR OF ḲAṬEEF—CHRISTMAS-DAY AT SEA—NOBLE PASSENGERS—SKETCH OF THE KHALEEFAH FAMILY—A WELL-EDUCATED NEGRO—ISLANDS OF BAḤREYN—MOḤARREḲ AND MENĀMAH—THEIR APPEARANCE—LANDING AT MENĀMAH—OUR FIRST DAY THERE—WE TAKE LODGINGS—A BAḤREYN DWELLING—MENĀMAH—ITS INTERIOR—ITS HARBOUR—CASTLE ISLAND—BAḤREYN—ITS POPULATION—TOWNSFOLK OF MENĀMAH—STRANGERS—STATE OF THE ISLAND—LATE CHANGES—THE PEARL FISHERY—OTHER TRADES—LIVE STOCK—PRESENT CONDITION OF THE GOVERNMENT—REMARKS ON TOLERATION—A WINTER STORM—ABOO-'EYSA ARRIVES—SCHEME FOR VISITING 'OMĀN—YOOSEF-EBN-KHAMEES—A SEPARATION—PASSAGE TO MOḤARREḲ—ITS CASTLE—INTERIOR OF THE TOWN—A KHALEEFAH CHIEF—MOOHEETH THE ḲĀDEREE—TENETS OF THE ḲĀDEREES—SPECIMEN OF THEIR POETRY—A MIDNIGHT STORM—WE EMBARK FOR ḲAṬAR—FRESH WATER OUT AT SEA—COASTS OF BAḤREYN AND ḲAṬAR—RĀS REKAN—BEDAA'—DESCRIPTION OF ḲAṬAR—ITS FISHERIES—GOVERNMENT—MENĀṢEER BEDOUINS—WATCH-TOWERS—BENOO-YASS—AĀL-MORRAH—MOḤAMMED-EBN-THĀNEE—HIS RESIDENCE AND CHARACTER—LIFE AT ḲAṬAR—INTERIOR OF BEDAA'—MOSQUES—VISIT TO DOWḤAH—TO WOKRAH—AN ARAB HAWKING-PARTY—TWO BEDOUIN "LIONS"—THE DAHNĀ—ITS EXTENT AND NATURE—THE ḤIMYARITES—THEIR HISTORY—DEPARTURE FROM ḲAṬAR—A SHIP AND CREW OF BARR-FĀRIS—SEA HOSPITALITY—DESCRIPTION OF BARR-FĀRIS AND ITS INHABITANTS—ROCKS OF HALOOL—A GALE—LANDING AT CHARAK—CUSTOMS OF THIS COAST—A VISIT TO THE CHIEF—LATEST NEWS FROM 'ONEYZAH—SUBSEQUENT FATE OF THAT TOWN AND OF TĀMIL—A WALK ABOUT CHARAK—WE EMBARK FOR LINJA—LUMINOUS APPEARANCE OF THE SEA—WAHHABEE EXPLANATION—INTRODUCTION TO THE HISTORY OF 'OMĀN.

Our crew were six in all, the captain and five men. Natives of the island of Moḥarreḳ, whither we were now bound, they had all the features characteristic of its inhabitants. Rather undersized, slim but well-made, dark-complexioned, with regular and pleasing faces, almost beardless, and smooth-skinned as Hindoos, they were very tolerable specimens of their strange race—Nabathæans, if local tradition say true, but crossed with Persian, Arab, and 'Omānee blood till they have assumed a peculiar type of their own, with something of each, yet properly belonging to none. Good sailors, good men of business, and, what is important for a traveller, nowise over-exacting, polite, civil, cheerful, often merry, they might in a social though perhaps not in a nautical point of view bear an advantageous comparison with the crew of many a European schooner. Their dress is very peculiar; it consists of a large coloured cloth round the waist, tightly girded up between the legs when work is to be done, else let down over the knees, a rough overall, a handkerchief knotted round the head, or a turban for fair weather when at rest and lounging on the deck; last, they throw over their shoulders a large reddish-brown cloak, and by it complete their seafaring equipment, lighter and more expeditious than that of Van Tromp's crew with their seven inexpressibles and six dreadnought jackets. When on shore they are hardly to be distinguished from the land population. These men are thoroughly versed in all the ins and outs, the shoals and channels, of the shallow Bahreyn sea, and very rash would be the stranger ship that should venture on its inextricable labyrinths without native help on board.

We shall see in the remainder of this work that Arab sailors are numerous; but they hardly form a distinctive class of society, nor is any line drawn deep and broad between them and the inhabitants of terra firma. The son of Neptune does not here regard the votaries of Ceres or Mercury as objects of ridicule or antipathy, however slight; nor does the "land lubber" laugh or look askance at the Arab tar; all are much the same in feelings and habits. This absence of "caste" demarcation springs in great measure from the 'long-shore character and short duration of navigation on this Gulf; circumstances which render the navigator less a sailor than a beach-man, or hardly even that. Had the Arab to plough the Atlantic, or to thread the Pacific Archipelago, he might soon come to resemble our own "Jacks" both aboard and on shore. But, as matters stand, a marked license of manners is perhaps the main moral feature common to both.

Our captain, Moleyk, welcomed us on board his craft, and made up a round of coffee without delay. We inhaled our pipes in the delightful assurance of being at last out of Wahhabee territory, and beyond the reach of all "no smoking allowed" regulations, and then, in nautical phrase, "turned in" under the shelter of a large deck-cabin near the stern, where we soon fell sound asleep; undisturbed, at least for my part, by all the running, trampling, and shouting of the sailors getting our ship under weigh.

Next morning, the 24th of December, we found ourselves some miles out at sea, and enjoying a full view of the coast, of its flat shores, its palm-groves, its "glaring sands and inlets white," of the little islands scattered here and there, of the advanced forts of Dāman and Dareem, and far behind the pyramidical outline of Djebel Mushahhar, the only high land in sight. Ḳaṭeef itself lay at the bottom of the Gulf, and so low as to be hardly visible. But the fortress-lines on Rās Ṭannoorah had a picturesque effect, and recalled to the mind days of Portuguese and Dutch exploits on these coasts, now abandoned to their own inadequate resources. Our ship was clear beyond the horns of the bay, and Barakāt and I expected to sail merrily on for the Baḥreyn channel, when to our great disappointment our skipper informed us that he expected passengers from the village of Soweyḳ, whose white outline we could just discern on the Dareem promontory, and that we must near land to take in this new freight before continuing our farther course. A captain on board his craft is the most absolute of monarchs, nor has constitutional opposition a place in any naval code, European or Oriental. We submitted in silence, and near noon furled our sails opposite Soweyḳ, about two hundred yards from what is shore at high-water, but separated from us at low tide by a sheet of mud and sand. Here we awaited our promised acquaintances, who being great personages kept up their dignity by making us expect them twenty-four hours before giving us the honour of their company.

Thus Christmas-day dawned on us warm and still where we lay, "idle as a painted ship upon a painted ocean," hourly looking out for the arrival of our fellow-passengers, who seemed to have entirely forgotten their previous engagements. At last the skipper himself lost patience, girded up his loins, and waded ashore, whence he returned after noon with his additional freight, and our deck was variegated by gayer dresses than it had before displayed.

The first of the band was a young chief of the El-Khaleefah family, an only son, and the heir of a large fortune; along with him came his grave and respectable uncle, next a well-dressed and well-informed negro attendant; two distant relations of the chief's, and a dusky lady into whose domestic position we were too polite to enquire, made up the number of six. But before entering on further details, it may be well to introduce my reader in a general way to the aristocratic clan of Khaleefah, a name known far and wide in these regions, but perhaps less generally familiar to European ears.

The family of El-Khaleefah, themselves natives of Ḥaṣa, though not of Hofhoof itself, had for at least two centuries (and, I rather believe, more, but I could obtain no accurate statement of earlier date), enjoyed the vicarious supremacy of the islands of Baḥreyn, sometimes in the name of the Carmathian rulers of Ḳaṭeef, sometimes supported by the authority of Persia, and sometimes tributary to 'Omān. But whatever was their nominal subordination, they reigned with an authority next to absolute in Baḥreyn itself, yet not renouncing for this their fair lands and heritage in Ḥaṣa and on the coast of Ḳaṭeef. About ten years since the harmony of the Khaleefahs was disturbed by a family quarrel, in which a younger branch of the clan, headed by Moḥammed-el-Khaleefah (now governor of Baḥreyn), drove from the island their kinsmen, who had been awhile in the possession of the viceregency, and compelled them to retire to the mainland, there to become subjects of Feyṣul in common with the other inhabitants of Ḥaṣa. War ensued, and was complicated by Persian, 'Omānite, and Nejdean interference, besides an occasional message from the Turkish government at Bagdad, till the matter was patched up by a reconciliation which put Moḥammed at the rudder of the Baḥreyn administration, in quality of vassal to the Sultan Thoweynee, ruler of 'Omān, and under the obligation of an annual tribute to be paid to Nejed for peace and quiet's sake. His vanquished cousins obtained certain local privileges from the Wahhabee government, their supporter in the preceding broil, but had to content themselves henceforth with the family property about Dareem and Soweyḳ, renouncing all claim to the waters and to Baḥreyn. This war was signalized by a great sea-combat, already alluded to, when the Wahhabees, turning sailors for the occasion, assailed Baḥreyn in ships; and it was the defeat of this expedition, destined to replace on the throne the banished branch of Ebn-Khaleefah, joined with the prudent use made by Moḥammed of his victory, which brought about the above treaty.

The Khaleefah family, if we except certain dissipated habits, accounted for, though hardly excused, by wealth and power, are a very tolerable set of men, and remarkably free from the sanguinary propensities of Nejdean and Wahhabee chiefs. Accordingly, no sooner was the first heat of war over than they made good friends again with each other, and no attempt to disturb the new arrangement has since ensued. The young nobleman now on board our schooner was the head of the conquered party, and on a visit to his victorious uncle Moḥammed; this latter resides in the town of Moḥarreḳ, at no great distance from Menāmah, though separated from it by a narrow arm of the sea.

With such important characters in the ship, we, who were at best only quiet professional men, yielded to nobility the only above-deck cabin, and took our place amidships. But 'Aroos, our handsome friend, would not allow himself to be vanquished in the contest of courtesy, and invited us to a share of his shelter and table, an invitation which we gladly accepted, the more so since his accommodations and cookery were decidedly better than ours. Much small-talk followed, and much mirth; but local jests lose their point when related at four or five thousand miles' distance and after two years' interval.

With the negro in attendance, Ḍahel by name, we had a more interesting and a more "profitable" conversation. The man was remarkably intelligent, and a good though quiet talker; well acquainted too with all the topics in dispute, whether theoretical or practical, between the Wahhabees and their neighbours. Like most "of his skin," that is, negroes, he was decidedly adverse to fatalist and to rigorist dogmas, nor did he disguise his partiality for Moseylemah, whom he averred to have been a very "pretty" man, generous, brave, and so forth; nor his dislike to the later tenets of Riad. By his account, Moseylemah's teaching corresponded in all essential points with that of Karmooț-el-Djenābee; and the known fact that those of the "lying Prophet's" adherents who, after escaping the sword of Khālid, preferred exile to Islam, retired mainly to Ḥasa and Kaṭeef, renders it very probable that the subsequent outbreak of Karmooț in that very region was a continuation, though somewhat modified by time and its changes, of the movement commenced by Moseylemah. Hence we have another key to the bitter hatred of the Carmathians against all who bore the title of Islam, and the ruthless vengeance which accompanied their ravages in the Mahometan territory, above all wherever they fell in with the descendants of Tameem, apostates in their eyes from the old patriotic cause of Nejed.

Meanwhile the sluggish tide flowed in, and we floated out to sea once more. But the north wind, our best friend for the way from Kaṭeef to Menāmah, had fallen, and was succeeded by chopping gales, that kept us twenty-four hours on up-and-down tacks, making little progress. At last on the following afternoon we came in sight of Baḥreyn, and by evening were close under the two islands which bear that name. The southern island is much the larger, and is therefore often called Baḥreyn to the exclusion of its northern companion, which more commonly bears the name of Moḥarreķ, from the capital situated on it. Between the islands runs a narrow sea-arm, scarce a mile in breadth, and very shallow. I have seen horsemen, and footmen too (though with the water in some places up to their breast), cross it at ebb-tide. Both Baḥreyn and Moḥarreķ are low as low can be; indeed the latter is a mere shoal just raised above the sea-level; however, its soil is light and sandy, and hence it is dryer and healthier than its neighbour, whose western side is equally low, but composed of a dark and tenacious mould, steeped in moisture like a very sponge. Towards the east Baḥreyn rises, and even pretends to what courtesy calls "Djehāl," or "mountains,"—hills, in fact, lower than the Grampian range, but set off to advantage by the surrounding flats.

Before landing, I may add that in the whole salt-water space between Ḳaṭeef and Baḥreyn the soundings are shallow, in no place above three fathoms, while in countless spots low tide leaves the bottom bare. No dread here of breakers and the violence of the waves, but much of running aground, to which one is exposed every moment. Hence the general practice of anchoring at night, and sailing only by day,—a weary precaution to the impatient traveller.

The town of Moḥarreḳ, situated on the southern side of the islet to which it gives its name, lies like a long white strip on the shore of the channel that separates it from the town of Menāmah, whose buildings occupy a corresponding position on the northerly marge of the larger island. Thus these two sea-ports look each other in the face, somewhat like Dover and Calais, though fortunately for them with friendlier feelings, since in case of war no Boulogne fleet would be required to cross the Baḥreyn channel. Moḥarreḳ is far the prettier of the two to the eye; its white houses, set off by darker palm-huts (for the extreme mildness of the climate renders this mode of habitation very common, and almost desirable), the large low palaces of the Khaleefah family, much resembling the better sort of "bungalows" at Malabar Point or Breach-Candy (I give this illustration for the benefit of my Bombay readers, should I be honoured by such), two or three imposing forts close to the sea-shore, a long coast-battery, good for show at a certain distance; all these form an *ensemble* worthy of a sketch, if not of a picture. I much regretted that evening my want of drawing implements, though had they been by me I could ill have used them in presence of 'Aroos-el-Khaleefah and his companions.

Along the low sand-line that completes the island rise many small detached groups of palm-huts, with an occasional white plastered residence, amid tall date-trees; the whole has a quiet and peaceful air. Three weeks hence we shall set foot on the island of Moḥarreḳ, and to that visit I defer its fuller description.

Menāmah, though larger in extent than Moḥarreḳ, has a less showy appearance; it is a centre of commerce, as its *vis-à-vis* is of government; and hence has fewer palaces to present, and less

display of defensive architecture. However, near its western
extremity, a large square mass of white building, with a few
cannon arranged battery-like in front, announces the residence
of 'Alee, brother of Moḥammed, vice-governor of Menāmah,
and wiser than his kinsman, if report be true. Little is to be
seen of the town itself on a sea approach; the first range of
dwellings and warehouses shuts out the rest from view; and,
except the palace of 'Alee, no other edifice of importance stands
near the water's edge. Indeed the first aspect of Menāmah is
positively dingy; for the beach-quarter is three-fourths occupied
by sailors and fishermen, whose cabins have no pretence to
beauty. The beach, too, is of dirty shingle. Around, especially
to the west and south of the town, dense groves, and the green
vegetation of a fertile soil, take off the glistering look peculiar
to Moḥarreḳ, while the many masts of fishing-smacks and small
craft in front form a kind of brown palisade, adding to the
duskiness of the sea-view.

Wearing slowly up with a side wind, we anchored before Moḥarreḳ, a little after sunset. Soon a boat came off from the
shore, and conveyed our fellow-passengers to the residence of
their kinsman the viceroy; while we, having no immediate object in landing, remained to pass the night on board-ship. Early
next morning we hailed one of the numerous light fishing-boats
that ply in the shallow waters of the Baḥreyn channel, and were
soon dancing before the breeze on our way to Menāmah. At
about an hour after sunrise we landed on the low beach opposite
the custom-house or Ma'āsher.

The arrival of strangers, many or few, from north or south, is
an every-hour occurrence here; and a passing look, or a chance
" good morrow," was all the notice taken of us by the many who
thronged the landing-place. We on our side were not without
hopes that Aboo-'Eysa might have preceded us hither, and be
waiting for us in some quarter of the town. Accordingly we
placed our slender baggage under the care of the officers in
the custom-house—a mere shed, filled with merchants, sea-
captains, and the like (all hard at work with their pipes, till
the smoke darkened the narrow precincts, and went curling up
through the palm-leaf thatch)—and passing through a low gate,
we made for the nearest and largest coffee-house, where, as in

barbers' shops of old, news and new comers are of right to be sought and found. It was now eight good months since we had last sat in a public coffee-house, and that in the suburbs of Ghazzah (or Gaza), of Palestine; the rest of our journey having been through lands too backward in civilization or too forward in bigotry, or both one and the other, to admit of such establishments. But Baḥreyn is beyond the Wahhabee circle, and breathes the atmosphere, so to speak, of Baṣrah and Persia. We gladly took our seats on the high matted benches, amid turbaned townsmen and gaily-dressed shopkeepers, to enquire about the latest arrivals from the port of 'Ajeyr, whence Abuo-'Eysa was to embark, according to our parting agreement. Meanwhile the white-vested waiter prepared and presented our coffee, after filling the huge Nargheelahs here in use with the strong 'Omān tobacco, the bugbear of Riaḍ; but here *nous avons changé tout cela.*

No news was however to be learnt touching the individual in question; the strong north winds then prevailing, which had favoured our voyage from Ḳaṭeef, were directly in the teeth of any one desirous of a passage to Menāmah from 'Ajeyr. We left the coffee-house, and went through streets and lanes searching up and down, and addressing ourselves to every person who might seem to afford the faintest prospect of the desired information, till we got thoroughly ashamed of our own enquiries, and gave up our April-fool's errand; the more that we had now to think how and where to find a berth for passing the time of our sojourn, till our friend should arrive from Ḥasa.

Nor was this an easy quest. Baḥreyn, like most eastern localities, has no inns properly speaking; and the Khāns, which here as elsewhere apologize for that deficiency, had too unpromising and insecure a look to allow the fixing our residence in any one of them. For many hours we sought in vain where to establish ourselves, and much regretted the good English custom of a placard with "lodgings to let," not introduced here in the front windows. At last we entered a pretty coffee-house, much like a "Sailors' Home" in situation near the beach, in size and style of customers. Its owner, a very civil man, took our cause in hand, ordered his head man to supply his place awhile, and went in quest of quarters for us, taking Barakāt along with him, while I remained behind to chat with sailors and gaze at the sea through a disorganized telescope fixed in the look-out. About sunset the two returned, having found what might seem sufficient for a short stay, nor did we purpose more. Now followed a hard knot to untie at the custom-house, where an arbitrary duty of five silver tomāns had been put on our baggage, according to the true seaport "do the strangers" principle; though much less was really due. My readers may observe from this circumstance, that the Persian currency here takes the place of the Arab; an advantageous change, since the monetary scale of the Shah is much easier to reckon by than the complicated and ever-changing valuations of rials and "Gorsh." A second remark might be, that foreigners are held fair game all over the world. But we were now strong in our new alliance with the coffee-house proprietor, and were moreover backed up by a young sailor, who happened to be next-door neighbour of our intended host in the lodgings just agreed on. Hence he felt himself in duty bound to take up the cudgels in our defence, and we resolutely refused to pay an item above the legal duty; till at last we succeeded in making the unjust publicans accept it, and got under weigh for our domicile about nightfall. We set our baggage on a donkey, and crossed the market-place, accompanied by the coffee-house master and the lad above-mentioned, till a few lanes, all the more intricate because yet unfamiliar, brought us to the desired spot. Here we entered by a narrow door, and found ourselves in a large open enclosure of palm-branches about eight feet high, set in the ground side by side and closely interwoven; within the enclosure, and divided from each other by a little space, stood two long palm-leaf huts; one for us, the other was the abode of our sailor and his family. Our dwelling was about thirty feet in length by ten in breadth, with as much to the top of the sloping thatch-roof; a hurdle-like screen divided the interior into two unequal compartments; the lesser served for a store-room, the greater for habitation. The floor was strewn, the general custom here, with a thick layer of very small shells, almost all of the Helix tribe, and each barely the eighth of an inch in length; these the boys bring in basketfuls from the shore, to form a clean and dry indoors footing; over this a large reed mat had been spread. We made our preliminary arrangements for beautifying and fitting up the apartment, and were soon honoured by the presence of the proprietor himself, who from his pretty brick and plaster house close by came to see us installed, while his servants brought according to custom the introductory supper of rice, fish, shrimps, and vegetables for the new guests. Of course we invited our good-natured friends, to whose diligence we owed this shelter, to partake of our meal; and we all passed together a very pleasant evening, with a feeling of security and calm such as we had hardly known since our first departure from Jaffa.

Next morning we renewed our search after Aboo-'Eysa, but to no purpose. Not a single arrival from 'Ajeyr for many days past, and the north wind still prevailed, and precluded all chance so long as it should last. It was now the 28th December 1862, and we were destined to wait in daily hope and daily disappointment till the 8th January following, in the year of grace 1863. Meanwhile, with little to do (for at Bahreyn I gave myself a holiday from my medical functions, and became a gentleman at large), we acquired that knowledge of the town, the island, the inhabitants, and their ways, which I will now briefly record, though I can hardly imagine this island to be altogether a novel topic of description to my readers, after the many Europeans, and our own countrymen in particular, who have visited its shores. Yet many visit who never describe, at least never pourtray. For us, wandering up and down in street and market, gossiping here and lounging there, now with a friend on our hands, and now a quarrel, we ended by becoming hardly less intimate with Menāmah and its little world than if we had been born and bred within its precincts.

Like most sea-port towns, the length of Menāmah beachways is much greater than its depth, though it is fairly broad also. The entire range towards the sea is above a mile and a quarter, while the houses reach inland for about a third of a mile. The average level of the ground on which it stands is about twelve feet, or even less, above high-water mark; the coast, after a slight rise at the beach itself, slopes down again inland, till the brackish water oozing through here and there to the surface, suggests that in some spots it must be, like Holland, even lower than the surrounding sea. The greater number of dwellings are mere palm-leaf cottages, each with its enclosure; the description just given of our own may serve for a general sample. These cabins vary in size, and are mostly arranged in streets and rows with some faint attention to the laws of geometry. Half of them at least are tenanted by the sons of Eastern Neptune—fishermen, boatmen, sea-captains, and the like; hence at almost every gable or corner flutters a long rag, tied pennon-wise at the end of a pole, to indicate which way the wind blows, and enable the inhabitants to regulate their avocations accordingly. Mixed with these meaner abodes, or separate from them, and forming distinct quarters of the town, are large houses of brick and stone, constructed in what, to save circumlocution, I shall call the Persian style of architecture; they are often alike elegant and spacious, with ogival arches, balconies, terraces, porticoes, and latticed windows; here dwell the nobler and wealthier inhabitants, merchants, proprietors, and men of the government. But half these edifices are falling into decay, and only present desolate intricacies of vaults and rubbish, sad tokens of a decadence the causes of which I will presently relate. Not far from the sea, and occupying almost a central position in the length of the city, is the market-place, a labyrinth of narrow shop-lanes, some vaulted, some sheltered from the heat by over-roofing thatch; at their midmost point of meeting is a small covered square, where is situated the principal coffee-house of the town; there are besides at least a score of others, generally near the beach. In different quarters of Menāmah are several mosques, a few for Sonnee, the most for Shiya'ee devotion.

At the south-western extremity of the town, and hard on the shore, rises the lofty and somewhat imposing residence of 'Alee-ebn-Khaleefah, the immediate governor of Menāmah. Round the houses are a few thinly-planted gardens, for the soil on which the town is built is unpropitious to cultivation; but a quarter or half a mile beyond, dense palm-groves hem in the view. In front spreads out the saucer-like bay, now just bathed in rippling waters, now a damp sand-flat, now covered with waves of considerable depth, and exhibiting a daily difference between high and low tide, rivalling that of the Wash or of the Kelpie's Flow in the "Bride of Lammermoor." Countless ships, varying from the largest to the smallest Arab build, cutters, smacks, fishing-boats, and all kinds of sea-craft, figure here, some drawn up on the beach, others half-stranded on the wet sands, others farther out in deep water. Over all a mild climate and a generally cloudless sky; cold is here unknown, and a relaxing warmth the prevailing rule, though this in summer alternates with days of great and oppressive heat.

Behind the town stretches a wide plain of level saltish soil, utterly barren and often swampy. At its further verge stands a large square fortress, the style of whose walls and buttresses might remind a Yarmouth boy of the Roman Borough Castle, except that the Baḥreyn edifice is somewhat loftier. It evidently served in old times as a stronghold and defence to the town of Menāmah; now it is dismantled and breached everywhere. Connected with this castle I heard several extravagant legends undeserving of record; the only certain tradition is that which ascribes its erection to the Carmathian princes during their days of equivocal prosperity. Many paths cross the plain in various directions, leading to little villages beyond; mere clusters they of thatched cottages, but densely inhabited, and much resembling the "Ganws" of Ceylon and Jafnapatam. Far off looms the solitary mountain which alone rescues Baḥreyn from the title of a low sea-girt shoal.

The island itself is about fifty miles in length, and thirty at its greatest breadth. Except the port of Menāmah, it is little visited by strangers, nor indeed does it offer many attractions to such. Nejed has better pastures, Ḥaṣa better plantations, and both a better climate. Nor do the fifty or sixty hamlets that lie scattered in its interior keep up much communication with the thriving emporium on the north-west, and hence their inhabitants bear an almost savage look, indicative of an uncultivated mind, the result of isolation. These country folks are all, or almost all, Shiya'ees, and animated by the intensest hatred for Sonnees and Wahhabees; a Nejdean seldom ventures among them. Tillage supplies enough for themselves, and a surplus to carry to the Menāmah market, but nothing for more distant exportation. The coast-dwellers are of course fishermen; a few about the roots of the mountain above-mentioned live by hunting, a miserable resource, I was told. The total population of the island is reckoned at seventy thousand or thereabouts; but it is now on the decrease.

The town inhabitants, of whom I mainly have to speak, whatever may be the' truth of their origin, Nabathæan or otherwise, are at present a very hybrid race, yet fused into a general and distinctive type. Were I to say half way between Arab and Guzeratee, with a rather fishy look, not unnatural to such maritime beings, in the smooth placidity of their rounded off features, I should perhaps come the nearest possible to a description. They are neither tall in stature nor strong in limb, neither exactly white nor exactly brown, neither particularly well-favoured nor remarkably ill; yet they have a quick and intelligent look, a litheness of frame, an ease of manner, and a certain good-humoured expression that bespeak what one may for compendium's sake call a "handy race," like to thrive, better suited for peace than for war, for trade than for agriculture, and perhaps for sea rather than for land. It is a curious fact, nor wholly easy to decipher, that the Sonnees of Menāmah, a sixth of its population or thereabouts, are neither Ḥanbelees, as their vicinity to Arabia might lead one to expect, nor Ḥaneefees, like their Belooch and Affghan neighbours across the Gulf; nor Shāfi'ees, like the main body of orthodox Mahometans towards Baṣrah and Bagdad; but Mālekees, the Islamitic school predominant, as is well known, in Egypt and Northern Africa. Yet there is certainly no community of blood or emigration between Tunis and Baḥreyn. The remaining five-sixths are Shiya'ees of the Persian fashion.

Mixed with the indigenous population are numerous strangers and settlers, some of whom have been established here for many generations back, attracted from other lands either by the profits of commerce or of the pearl fishery, and still retaining more or less of the physiognomy and garb of their native countries. Thus the gay-coloured close-cut dress of the southern Persian, the saffron-stained vest of 'Omān, the white robe of Nejed, and the striped gown of Bagdad, are often to be seen mingling with the light garments of Baḥreyn, its blue and red turban, its white silk-fringed cloth worn Banian fashion round the waist, and its frock-like overall; while a small but unmistakable colony of Indians, merchants by profession, and mainly from Guzerat, Cutch, and their vicinity, keep up here all their peculiarities of costume and manner, and live among the motley crowd, "among them, but not of them."

After the decline of the Carmathbian dynasty in Ḳaṭeef, Baḥreyn became a dependency of Persia, and for a considerable period acknowledged no other rule or even interference. At the beginning of the last century 'Omān, having shaken off the Persian yoke, began to rise in importance, and claimed over the island a right of tribute and protection enough to counterbalance the authority of the Shirāz governor. Meanwhile the Khaleefah family had for many generations been gaining strength, and at last acquired the supremacy of Baḥreyn, though held in fief first from the Shah, and subsequently from the Sultan of 'Omān. We have already seen that 'Abd-el-'Azeez-ebn-Sa'ood added in his turn Baḥreyn to the Wahhabee land possessions; and needs not say that the Nejdeans enforced with all the intolerance customary but not peculiar to that sect, their religious code and observances. This rendered them extremely odious to a people among whom toleration, the ordinary result of free trade and open intercourse, had always been the order of the day, and who, though excellent men of business, have a marked turn for amusement, games, and social enjoyment of every description. When the Wahhabee chain was broken in the midst by the fall of Ḍerey'eeyah, Baḥreyn reverted to the hereditary authority of the El-Khaleefahs and the vassalage of Persia. But not long after Sa'eed, known by the emphatic title of "Es-Sultan," or "*the* Sultan" of 'Omān, now in the full course of other important encroachments on the maritime possessions of Persia, laid a claim, perhaps only that of the strongest, to Baḥreyn, and rendered the island tributary to his sceptre. After some years the reviving Wahhabee vulture, having again outspread its wings over Ḥasa, made a clutch at Baḥreyn. Much amused was I at the accounts given me by eye-witnesses of the naval contests which ensued between the Nejdean invader and the islanders; the battle of Actium would have been less anomalous in the judgment of a Trafalgar seaman. The advantage of superior courage was certainly on the side of the Nejdeans, but number and seamanship turned the scale in favour of the Baḥreyn fleet. After a sharp engagement off Dareem, in which some of the Nejdean boats were burnt and others disabled, a detachment of Feyṣul's troops succeeded in eluding the vigilance of the enemy, and effected a descent on an unguarded point of the island. Once landed, they marched straight on Menāmah, but on arriving there found themselves surrounded, as in a net, by the skilful combinations of 'Alee-el-Khaleefah, and cut off from the possibility of a return to their ships, of which the islanders took quiet possession. 'Alee used his prisoners well, and in concert with his brother Moḥammed sent them back to Ḥaṣa not only uninjured, but loaded with propitiatory presents, and accompanied by fair offers of peace. On this occasion the Khaleefah family disputes, which had supplied Feyṣul with a pretext for the invasion of Baḥreyn, were finally settled in the manner recorded a few pages back. But Moḥammed was henceforth obliged to forward an annual tribute to Riaḍ, as price of alliance and support, though when occasion requires he does not hesitate to lay claim now to Persian, now to 'Omānee, and at times even to Turkish protection, when hope or fear incline. British interference has of late years somewhat influenced the political position of the island, but without as yet occasioning any advantage to the inhabitants; nay rather, though indirectly, the reverse.

At Baḥreyn, strictly speaking, begins the pearl-coast and fishery; from hence it extends round the east of the island and the promontory of Ḳaṭar down the great southern bay of the Persian Gulf to the frontiers of Sharjah in 'Omān. Pearl oysters are indeed to be found north of Baḥreyn along the shores of Ḳaṭeef and the adjacent islands, and a fishery there exists, but its product is scanty, nor any way comparable to that of Baḥreyn and the easterly Gulf coast. Round Baḥreyn itself the fishery is abundantly copious, and furnishes occupation to at least half the inhabitants of the island. Moḥammed-el-Khaleefah here holds the pearl monopoly, and exacts a rated tax on every boat that puts to sea in this quest, beside a percentage on the product, while any one who ventures to take up an oyster without government licence may be prosecuted or persecuted according to law; that is, according to the noble governor's pleasure. On a rough calculation the number of fishing-boats which ply the coasts of Baḥreyn in search of pearls, cannot be less than from two thousand to two thousand and five hundred, yet no complaint is made that the labourers outrun the harvest. The diving season is from April to October inclusive; negroes are especially employed in this submarine portion of the work. They are excellent plungers, and can remain under water about two minutes; but I never heard any one boast of being able to hold his breath for a longer period. I had omitted to say that these dusky gentlemen are very numerous in Baḥreyn, where, free from Wahhabee coercion, they "play upon the banjo, play upon the fiddle," and signalize themselves by childish freaks of al kinds and qualities; a liberty dearer to the true negro heart than any civic freedom soever.

While the poorer classes employ themselves in the labours of fishery, the richer sort one and all follow merchandize and commerce, either within the limits of the island, by trafficking with strangers who resort thither, or themselves voyaging to the surrounding sea-coast, from Baṣrah to Bombay, and from Kurrachee to Zanjibar. However, the "Baḥārinah" (to give the inhabitants of Baḥreyn their collective Arab name, as "Zaḥālinah" stands for those of Zaḥleh, and "Karākinah" for the men of Karak) are as a general rule inferior in book-keeping and the methodical work of business to the 'Omānees and Indians settled among them. But in handicraft they have few equals throughout the East—weavers, workers in metal, wood, and leather, tailors, dyers, in short, artisans of all kinds, abound in Menāmah, and excel, taking the standard of Oriental excellence (in what respects art and taste, too often beyond European), in their several professions. Medicine, however, and other learned or studious pursuits, are deplorably behindhand. Within the land, agriculture is not wholly neglected; but the inherent poverty of the soil is a positive drawback; and except enormous citrons (I never saw them of such a size elsewhere), the vegetable produce of Baḥreyn, though varied by labour, is mostly below mediocrity. Moisture encourages growth; but its quality is not equal to its quantity; thus palms are numerous throughout the island, but the dates are wretched.

To add a word touching live stock: camels have been imported hither from the Arabian coast; but "the poor things look unhappy," the moist soil and climate being ill adapted to their arid constitutions. Oxen and kine are not rare, though meagre, and affording miserable beef, as we found on trial; sheep few; asses fare better, which indeed is often the case elsewhere. But fish of all kinds, scaly, smooth, and shelly, load the market stalls: I doubt if any spot of the entire globe can boast an equal abundance. Hence the principal nutriment of the "Baḥārinah" is fish; and Lent, at least the Lent described in "Beppo," runs all the year round in the island. Barakāt and I found, on exact computation, the average price of fish in the market of Menāmah to be only one-twentieth part, and no more, of what it is on the Mediterranean coast of Syria, for instance at Beyrouth, Ṣeyda, and the neighbouring ports. This is an additional reason for the comparative neglect of cattle and sheep breeding. In short, Baḥreyn is a daughter of the sea, and the sea is, and always will be, her best nursing mother; the lean and the fat lions of St. Mark's at Venice are the proper type and measure for the prosperity of this island and its resources.

The actual government of Baḥreyn deserves slender praise. Before the first Wahhabee invasion Baḥreyn enjoyed a higher degree of prosperity than has ever been since her lot, if we may trust local tradition (for of documentary history there is little to guide us), confirmed by the mute testimony of ruined houses and fallen Khāns. The foolish restrictions and unaccommodating policy of the Nejdean sectarians tended immediately to break up commerce, and to drive the merchants elsewhere. When the island was at last in 1818-19 freed from foreign pressure, and drawn into the progressive movement of 'Omān, a kindred empire, it resumed somewhat of its old activity, till family dissensions between its rulers, and Persian or latterly Wahhabee intermeddling, again checked its advance. The personal character of the present viceroy, Moḥammed, has added considerably to the evils of its position. This governor is a perfect Sybarite, marrying on trial, so to say, every fortnight; while every fortnight sees a new divorce, followed by a new marriage, and all this accompanied by great display, expense, and lavish waste in pensioning off the old love and purchasing the new; not to mention the scandalous publicity of these transactions, and a *nec nisi legitimè vult nubere* enough to put Rome and Messalina to the blush. Nor does Moḥammed ever, it would seem, bestow a single thought on the well-being of his subjects; a very Charles II, alike improvident and impolitic, he has done his best by submissions abroad, and exactions, taxes, duties, fines at home, all directed to supply his own private, or rather public, debauchery, to ruin his land, and to drive his subjects to unwilling emigration. Wahhabee influence, powerless for morality and good, all powerful for bigotry and decay, and now strongly felt at Baḥreyn (thanks to the weakness of Moḥammed), especially in the capital and about the palace, has concurred with the desolating process; the "chosen people" seeing with orthodox indignation the abominations of Shiya'ee or Indian polytheism and infidelity openly tolerated so near their sanctified land. A small colony of Jews, men whose presence in a town may often be regarded as the thermometer of its well-doing, has thus been harassed, till the unfortunate Israelites have been recently obliged to quit Menāmah, and seek elsewhere less theology and more good sense. The Hindoo Banians have been also more than once brought to the verge of a similar resolution. Meanwhile the native inhabitants, or Baḥārinah, have emigrated, and are daily emigrating, by scores and hundreds, to the great advantage of the seaports where they finally settle, and the corresponding detriment of their own island. From Baṣrah to Mascat, either shore of the Persian Gulf (Barr-Fāris, where the Wahhabee system prevails, excepted) is literally peopled by men of Baḥreyn, merchants, shopkeepers, artisans, fishermen, day labourers, and what not; while a colony of two or three hundred Baḥārinah have within the last few years rendered the little island of Ge's, uninhabited before, one of the most important trading points of these seas. But it is especially under the tolerant rule of 'Omān, the wisest, perhaps, at least in this respect, of the East, that the exiles of Baḥreyn have sought and found shelter and even encouragement.

By the conduct just described, Moḥammed-ebn-Khaleefah has earned from his subjects one degree of hatred, and the Wahhabees two. But peaceful and yielding as are the natives of

Baḥreyn, their dissatisfaction vents itself in complaints or expatriation alone; popular revolutions after the European fashion are, perhaps unfortunately, little in accordance with Asiatic sentiment or weakness. But of all misquotations, as applied to the East, the worst would be the well-known couplet of the "Traveller"—

> How small, of all that human hearts endure,
> That part which laws or kings can cause or cure.

Probably the poet was thinking of Europe, perhaps of England, when he wrote these epigrammatic lines, hardly true even in the Western world. But, putting Europe aside, my reader may easily judge whether or not kings and governments have power both to "cause," and to "cure" also, if they will, in the East.

Much talk goes on in Menāmah, no less than in Ḥasa, about what our diplomatists would call "annexation" to some more liberal government. However, neither Ṭeheran nor Constantinople offer the desired prospect; 'Omān, though in other respects well fitted, is not at the present moment powerful enough to help; perhaps—but conjectures or hints would alike be here out of place. For one remark only I beg my reader's leave. Whoever becomes ruler in the East, and thereby finds himself in presence of Sonnees, Shiya'ees, pagans, and Heaven knows what, would do well to make "absolute toleration" his maxim and the device of his banner in whatever regards national customs, religions, and even prejudices; and these three words are very commonly identical, in Asia at any rate. I mean not that a foreign ruler needs decorate Somnauth, or honour a Juggernath procession with his official presence, no, nor offer candles and flowers (I have seen it done) to a pot-bellied statue of Goneshwa; nor would he deem it wise to imitate those who apply state finances to building mosques in Algiers, and who head European proclamations with the formulas of Islam. I mean that toleration which consists in letting alone, not interfering, not taking notice; in short, considering the philosophy and the religion of subjects as matters not amenable to government cognizance, and beyond its pale. Such conduct is alike reasonable and safe. Mental and religious progress will best find their own way when freed from unseasonable auxiliaries no less than from disgraceful opposition. Truth, like virtue, in Dryden's verse, "needs no foil, but shines by her own proper light;" while, conversely, to borrow Lord Macaulay's scarce less brilliant phrase, "Falsehood, though no match for truth alone, has often been found more than a match for truth and power together." Forbearance has a healing tendency; and a government that steadily keeps to it will not only attain its first and primal object, namely, order, tranquillity, and social well-being, but will also at no distant period have within reach its secondary and incideutal aim; I mean moral, intellectual, and religious advancement. But they who make the essential of the incidental, and would enforce what they should at most indirectly encourage, will assuredly forfeit both one and the other, no less than the rulers who run into an opposite extreme, and hold it a point of policy to maintain ignorance and error. The history of European colonies in East and West abounds with proofs of this double proposition. The line of conduct to be kept is no doubt narrow, narrower than the pass between Scylla and Charybdis; but he who runs his ship on the rocks, or steers too close on the vortex of the whirlpool, shows himself in either case a bad pilot, and is to blame for the wreck that follows.

During the twelve days that we awaited the arrival of Aboo-'Eysa, we passed most of our time in the various coffee-houses, and especially in that called a few pages back the "Sailor's Home," whose owner had so obligingly aided us at our first arrival. Here we often met Persian merchants, come for their morning coffee, skippers from all ports, 'Omānees, Beloochees, Indians, and others, while each consumed a good ounce of tobacco in his large reed-tubed Nargheelah, and our hours went by less tediously than they often do with strangers in a foreign land. From the maritime and in a manner central position of Baḥreyn, my readers may of themselves conjecture that the profound ignorance of Nejed regarding Europeans and their various classifications is here exchanged for a partial aquaintance with those topics; thus, "English" and "French," disfigured into the local "Ingleez" and "Fransees," are familiar words in Menāmah, though Germans and Italians, whose vessels seldom or never visit these seas, have as yet no place in the

Baḥreyn vocabulary; while Dutch and Portuguese seem to have fallen into total oblivion. But Russians, or "Moscôp" (that is, Muscovites), are alike well known and well feared, thanks to Persian intercourse. Besides, the policy of Constantinople and Ṭeheran are freely and at times sensibly discussed in these coffee-houses, no less than the stormy diplomacy of Nejed and her dangerous encroachments; ship news, commerce, business, tales of foreign lands, and occasionally literature, supply the rest of the conversation. Of religious controversy I never heard one word. In short, instead of Zelators and fanatics, camel-drivers and Bedouins, we have at Baḥreyn something like "men of the world, who know the world like men," a great relief to the mind; certainly it was so to mine.

I should add to our catalogue of occupations a little medical practice into which I was beguiled by flattering requests, friendly visits, and now and then a stroll about the plain and to the little hamlets beyond, in one of which we witnessed a weekly recurring fair, like in most respects to those of Hofhoof and Mebarraz, described in a former chapter.

The most remarkable incident, if it may be called one, of these days, was a tremendous northerly gale, accompanied by pouring rain, thunder, and hail, while the sea did its best to reach what fury so shallow a puddle could attain. Trees were blown down and palm huts unroofed, despite of their strong lacings and withies, while news came of ships cast away and of boats swamped, till we got extremely fearful that Aboo-'Eysa and his companions might be five fathoms deep somewhere between 'Ajeyr and Menāmah, and undergoing the "sea-change" sung of by Ariel. Our friend and his train had, in truth, just before the storm, ridden down to the sea-coast at 'Ajeyr, and were on the point of embarking, when the hurricane surprised them; and after passing half a day wet to the skin among the sand-hills, in the vain hope of seeing the storm blow over, they had returned to a village some way inland, there to await better weather. All this we learnt from themselves a few days later.

Of the local governor and the men of state we saw little; indeed we avoided them as much as possible, and even declined a chance invitation from 'Alee to his palace; thinking it enough knowledge of the Baḥreyn El-Khaleefahs to hear "their evil report;" nor do I imagine that a nearer acquaintance with them would have brought us to a more favourable opinion.

At last, on the 6th of January, 1863, the wind veered to the south, and on the 9th of the month our long-expected Aboo-'Eysa arrived; with him was an entire squadron of retainers, three white, two black, beside a coffee-coloured mulatto lad, all gaily dressed in silk, and silver-hilted swords; while Aboo-'Eysa, in a grand embroidered cloak, looked like a bridegroom on his way to church. We could not help laughing at this ostentatious display of men and finery, but it was not without its reason. For Aboo-'Eysa purposed going on next to Aboo-Shahr, in quality of head man to the Perso-Arab caravan; and thus a good appearance of wealth and high standing was indispensable to carry through his business with success, especially among Persians, and in a land where display is everything. Indeed without this, all the patents of Feyṣul and credentials of Maḥboob would have been thrown away on his Shiya'ee flock. From a curious love of contraband achievements, which made part of his character, he had chosen to land his men and goods (the latter were of considerable amount), not at Menāmah, but behind a small promontory at some distance from the harbour, thus escaping duties and tolls, though not without running a narrow risk of detection from Moḥammed-el-Khaleefah's coast-guard. Once ashore, he took up lodgings for himself and his retainers in a large house towards the farther end of the town, at almost half a mile distant from our own abode, and there he lived in great state, keeping open parlour for all comers, and forming a temporary centre for all the coffee-drinkers and news-mongers of the neighbourhood. At quieter hours we arranged our personal projects for the remainder of the journey.

Schemes were formed and discussed, rejected or revised, till at last we agreed on adopting a plan sketched out by our friend while with us in his Hofhoof retirement, and in furtherance of which a large part of the wares he now brought with him had been purchased. This plan was not a bad one, though circumstances beyond the reach of ordinary calculation concurred to render its success less complete than it might otherwise have been.

Aboo-'Eysa had procured above twenty loads of the best Hasa dates, the genuine Khalās, well packed in oblong rush-cases, and at the same time he had given order for four handsome mantles of Hofhoof manufacture, woven and embroidered by the most skilful hands. Three very elegant ones were adapted to the wardrobe of subordinate chiefs; the fourth, of extraordinary richness and beauty, seemed to disdain any shoulders but those of a king. All these articles of luxury and show were to be put in charge of one of his retainers, and presented in Aboo-'Eysa's name, three of the robes to an equal number of chiefs whose domains lay between Bahreyn and Mascat, and with each robe was to be associated a suitable number of date-chests, to give additional sweetness to the present. The fourth and costliest garment, along with a third of the fruits of the land, was to find its destination in the Sultan of 'Omān himself, in acknowledgment of patronage afforded our friend on a former occasion. My readers perhaps know that to offer presents, though without any special or immediate object, but merely by way of a reminder or rekindler of good will, is a common proceeding in the East. They have besides the very general result of a return given on the spot by the receiver to the bearer, besides an assurance of future support and countenance when required. The expected fees were, so calculated Aboo-'Eysa, sufficient to requite his retainer for the difficulty and dangers of the journey. Meantime I was to accompany the gifts and their bearer under the scientific character of a deep-read physician, on the look-out for I know not what herbs and drugs, which I was to suppose discoverable in the south-eastern regions; and when under covert of the introduction thus obtained, and the good will likely to ensue, I had succeeded in sufficiently examining the land and the people, I was to return with my bear-leader to Aboo-Shahr, where I should find Barakāt arrived long before with Aboo-'Eysa. For this latter had about three months to pass at the above-mentioned town, while getting his pilgrims together, and preparing for their journey across Arabia to Mecca.

Barakāt, so said Aboo-'Eysa, could not safely accompany me; much less could he take my place. The scheme was certainly clever, and may perhaps have a suggestive value for investigators, whenever their circumstances permit the like proceedings; but it was an adventurous project, requiring mature forethought and careful arrangement. Nor did my Syrian companion and myself like the idea of a severance which, though expected to last barely two months, might (and so in fact it did) prove much longer; indeed it had nearly been perpetual, at least for this stage of existence. But I was to appear a casual and unimportant associate to Aboo-'Eysa's messenger; and accordingly the companionship of a third would hardly have admitted of a plausible explanation, and might have engendered suspicion. It seemed also unadvisable and rash to expose both at once to a real danger of shipwreck; the season was unfavourable; part, indeed half the way, must be made by sea, and the Persian Gulf offers a somewhat dangerous navigation even for European sailing ships in the winter and early spring; much more for Arab sea craft. However Barakāt and I encouraged each other to hope the best in all ways, and I could not think of losing so good an opportunity for at least scraping an acquaintance, if I may be allowed the phrase, with 'Omān, though I knew that it could be only superficial this time; yet it might serve to open the way to a more thorough and lasting intimacy.

Yoosef-ebn-Khamees, for that was the name of my destined associate, was a very curious individual, and not unlike some of Shakespeare's supplementary characters. He was a native of Ḥaṣa, half a jester and half a knave; witty, reckless, harebrained to the last degree, full of jocose or pathetic stories, of poetry, traditions, and fun of every description, whether coarse or delicate. But he had one sterling quality, which in an affair like the present more than counterbalanced whatever weighed in the opposite scale, namely, a boundless attachment, a real devotion to Aboo-'Eysa, not inferior to that of Evan Maccombich to Fergus, or of Caleb to Ravenswood. The origin of this feeling was not however in kith and kin; it was due simply to Aboo-'Eysa's singular kindheartedness and liberality, which had rescued Yoosef from utter poverty, and had maintained him for a considerable time past in a decent and even honourable position. How their acquaintance first came about were long to tell; enough that for the five or six years during which

Aboo-'Eysa had inhabited Hofhoof, he had been constantly to Ebn-Khamees that best of friends, a friend in need; nor had all the careless prodigality of his *protégé*, who threw away whatever was bestowed on him faster than he received it, ever checked the munificence of Aboo-'Eysa in his favour.

Yoosef when a mere lad had borne arms, at least a lance, in the contest which gave Feyṣul the ascendency over Ebn-Theney'yān. He had also been art and part in the great naval expedition already mentioned against Baḥreyn, when the Nejdeans made their unsuccessful attempt at sea empire; and Ebn-Khamees, after imitating the poltroonery of Horace at Actium, had no more shame than that poet to recount his own ridiculous cowardice. For though adventurous enough in other respects, he had a horror of bloodshed which would have done honour to the Peace Society itself; nay, he could not even stand by to see a sheep killed for dinner. Yoosef was now about thirty-six years of age, tall, and (notwithstanding a slightly comical turn of features) handsome, with a little black beard where some prematurely grey hairs, the result of horror on seeing an unlucky comrade killed by his side in the Baḥreyn battle, contrasted oddly with his youthful appearance, and gave occasion to many a jest of others against him, and of him against himself. For Yoosef, like Falstaff of old, was "not only witty in himself, but the cause that wit was in other men;" although in physical conformation he was the very reverse of our own jovial knight, being remarkably slim and slender in form.

We had already become acquainted with each other at Hofhoof, where Yoosef was Aboo-'Eysa's constant guest, or rather satellite, and were on excellent terms. I had therefore no difficulty in accepting him for my guide, nor he any objection to my society, though he knew nothing about the real object of my coming.

Matters having been arranged on this footing, we awaited a favourable occasion for putting to sea. But the wind was adverse, and day by day dragged on till the 23rd of January, when a southerly breeze and a good ship combined to carry off Aboo-'Eysa and his retainers, with Barakāt, to Aboo-Shahr, while Yoosef and I were to cross the channel next day for Moḥarreḳ, and there embark for the port of Bedaa' on the coast of Ḳaṭar, where resided Moḥammed-ebn-Thānee, the first and nearest of the chiefs to whom our visit and our presents were addressed.

One of those presentiments which are not so uniformly explicable as frequently experienced by human creatures, regarding the shipwreck which in fact lay before me, led me to entrust Barakāt with the keeping of all my papers, notes, and whatever I had of any value, except a small stock of money to meet the emergencies of the journey. A fortunate precaution, and without which the present work would have perished in embryo, with much else, off the Sowādah islands.

It was a fair and sunshiny afternoon when, after many good wishes for a speedy meeting, and mutual recommendations, as wont among parting friends, we separated—Aboo-'Eysa, accompanied by his retainers and Barakāt, going on board their schooner for Aboo-Shahr, while Yoosef-ebn-Khamees and myself remained to keep house, and passed the evening in comparative loneliness and silence. During the fortnight that Aboo-'Eysa had been master of the dwelling, his hospitable and even showy habits had kept it continually full of talk and diversion, of visitors and coffee; a strange contrast to its present stillness, always more ungenial in a large house than elsewhere. We supped together as best we might, and held little conversation for the rest of that evening. I felt uncommonly lonely; but the hope of an interesting and well-occupied journey, followed by a prompt and successful return, went far to console me. Yoosef too, though as melancholy as a gib-cat or a lugged bear at the departure of his patron, beguiled his fancy by prognosticating a prosperous voyage for Aboo-'Eysa, without sea-sickness or danger. Hope deceived us both, as events will show.

Next morning we took a small boat, and unannoyed this time by the custom-house officers, whose whole business lies with imports, we crossed over to Moḥarreḳ. There we found on enquiry that the Ḳaṭar-bound vessel with which Aboo-'Eysa had made a previous arrangement for our freightage, was lying off the castle at the eastern extremity of the town. To reach it we had to walk about a quarter of a mile across wet sands and over a little dyke-like promontory, just broad enough to allow of a causeway between the ooze on either side, till we reached the large square fort, strongly built and provided with artillery, though not precisely after the model of Woolwich; it stands on the extreme headland, and is surrounded by a thick outer wall of considerable extent. Here were once the quarters of a Baḥreyn garrison; but now the building only serves as a stable for the handsome stud of Moḥammed-el-Khaleefah. Two dromedaries were grazing close under the walls; they had been sent a few days before as a present from the Sultan of 'Omān, in acknowledgment of some customary remittance of tribute. These animals were excellent specimens of the thorough-bred 'Omānee dromedary; the giraffe-like elegance of their form, the brightness and even something like intelligence of their eye, their smooth mouse-brown skin, and their airy step and gait, fully sufficed to distinguish them from those of any other race, and justified the high reputation of the breed.

Just off the Castle-point lay our bark, ill-built, ill-rigged, and ill-manned; but these defects mattered little, as we did not intend to take her farther than Ḳaṭar, a short sail; besides, any ship however slight, if but guided by a knowing pilot, may venture almost fearlessly on the quiet waters of this bay, to which the Arabs have given the name of "Baḥr-ul-Benāt," or "the Girls' Sea;" whether from visions of mermaids—here, no less than the "Cacquets" of Brest, the object of popular credulity; or perhaps from the gentle, peaceful, and smiling character of the bay itself, which thus represents (in all but in its shallowness, I would trust), the likeness of an amiable young lady. We put our goods and chattels on board, recommended them to the care of the captain, an "old old man, with beard," which should have been "as white as snow" had it but been better washed and combed; and after receiving his assurance that all would be ready for sailing next morning at sunrise, we returned to the town.

As a whole, Moḥarreḳ is curious and worth the seeing, though it contains no particular building of notable importance. Curious, I say, from its Perso-Arabic appearance, its small snug houses, its paved market-place, and its high-raised benches everywhere along the walls, announcing an out-of-doors life; besides, it owns a degree of close packing and agglomeration, different from the straggling style of most Arab cities, where ground value seems the last consideration, elbow-room the first. In point of commerce this capital is inferior to Menāmah, and the market-place less crowded and less extensive; on the other hand, it is decidedly the neater of the two; possibly in accordance with the well-known proverb that "where no oxen are, the crib is clean." Many spacious but low palaces are jotted about, where reside different members of the El-Khaleefah family. Yoosef, relying on some acquaintance of old date, formed under the wing of his master Aboo-'Eysa, took me to visit one of the chiefs, Ḥāmid by name, uncle of the present governor. Ḥāmid received us with much politeness; the introductory ceremonies differed in nothing from what I have often described. When conversation warmed into familiarity, I had some difficulty in framing decent pretexts for non-acceptance of kindly offers of patronage, would I but consent to remain at Moḥarrek, and set up as doctor to the royal family; a proposal too honourable and too advantageous for rejection, had I really been what I seemed. After a while we rose and went to take up our lodgings for the evening at the small house of a certain Mogheeth, a friend of Yoosef's and native of Ḥasa. He was a quiet literary man, gaining his livelihood partly as scribe and partly as schoolmaster. These two professions are often united in the East; and in the absence of printing-presses and publishers, copyists often make good profit, and are never wholly without work. Moreover Mogheeth was a mystic, belonging to the Ḳāderee sect, whose strange tenets and suspected orthodoxy would require other pages than these to explain them as they merit. Suffice to say that 'Abd-el-Ḳādir-el-Gheelānee, founder of the Ḳāderees, if he did not (as is more than probable) lay direct claim to divine honours, at least assumed to himself a much higher position than Mahomet among his followers; and left the Ḳāderees for heritage a whole scheme of semi-pantheistic Persianism, thinly veiled by Islamitic nomenclature.

The members of this curious association (at least all whom I have had the good fortune to become acquainted with) distinguish themselves by remarkable urbanity and kindliness to strangers; in the present instance our Ḳāderee host was a model in this respect. Mogheeth soon embarked on religious conversation; indeed hardly any other was to be heard under his roof; and I was pleased to find my new friend alike sensible in his ideas, and sincere in his convictions, which rested in the main on the broad basis of a spirituality adapted to every land and every age, because founded on a reasonable appreciation of what the Deity is, and what man. Nor were his moral conclusions inferior to his theoretical axioms; for either I must refer the Orientalist to the well-known "Tey'eeyat-el-Kubra" of the great Ḳāderee poet 'Omar-ebn-el-Fāriḍ.

However, as I have on former occasions attempted to give a few specimens of Arab poetry in love or war, my readers may not be undesirous to see what flight the Eastern Muse can wing in a more heavenward direction. I will accordingly here insert a short poem dictated to me by Mogheeth, during a conversation of which the topic was "that undiscovered country from whose bourne no traveller returns;" though my friend took a more cheerful, if not a distincter, view of the matter than Isabella's brother Claudio, or even Hamlet, appear to have done. Meanwhile the verses themselves are highly illustrative of a vein of thought common among the Ḳāderees, though by no means peculiar to them alone.

Mogheeth related, on the authority of Ḳāderee tradition, how the famous Aḥmed-el-Ghazālee, native of Ṭoos in Persia (my learned friends will recognise the author of "Lobāb-el-Aḥya," who flourished about the year 1180 A.D.), said one day to his disciples, "Go and bring me new and white garments, for the king has summoned me to his presence." They went; and on returning with the objects required, found their master dead; by his side was a paper on which were written the following stanzas:—

Tell my friends, who behold me dead,
Weeping and mourning my loss awhile,
Think not this corpse before you myself:
That corpse is mine, but it is not I.
I am an undying life, and this is but my body,
Many years my house and my garment of change;
I am the bird, and this body was my cage,
I have wing'd my flight elsewhere, and left it for a token.
I am the pearl, and this my shell,
Broken open and abandon'd to worthlessness;
I am the treasure, and this was a spell
Thrown over me, till the treasure was released in truth.

Thanks be to God, who has deliver'd me,
And has assign'd me a lasting abode in the highest.
There am I now the day conversing with the happy,
And beholding face to face unveiled Deity;
Contemplating the Mirror wherein I see and read
Past and present, and whatever remains to be.
Food and drink too are mine, yet both are one;
Mystery known to him who is worthy to know.
It is not "wine sweet of taste" that I drink;
No, nor "water," but the pure milk of a mother.
Understand my meaning aright, for the secret
Is signified by words of symbol and figure.—
I have journey'd on, and left you behind;
How could I make an abode of your halting-stage?
Ruin then my house, and break my cage in pieces,
And let the shell go perish with kindred illusions;
Tear my garment, the veil once thrown over me;
Then bury all these, and leave them alike forgotten.
Deem not death death, for it is in truth
Life of Lives, the goal of all our longings.
Think lovingly of a God whose Name is Love,
Who joys in rewarding, and come on secure of fear.
Whence I am, I behold you undying spirits like myself,
And see that our lot is one, and you as I.

I should notice that the "water" and "wine" denied in these verses are among the pleasures of a future state most emphatically promised in the Coran; nor is the rejection of that bodily resurrection, so strenuously asserted by Mahomet, less remarkable in the stanzas of Ghazālee, the whole current of whose ideas, as here expressed, is indeed eminently anti-Islamitic. While reciting this poem, Mogheeth, in true Oriental guise, fell into a sort of extasy, burst into tears, and had much difficulty in completing his dictation. Meantime Yoosef, like the host in the "Two Gentlemen of Verona" during the songs of Thurio and the discourses of Sylvia, was "fast asleep." At a late hour Mogheeth and I followed his example.

After midnight we were all awakened by loud peals of thunder, which ushered in a tremendous storm of wind and rain; and when morning dawned, not only was our chance of sailing that day at an end, but it was even impossible to put a foot out of doors, so fiercely raged the tempest. It blew from the north. Yoosef and I exchanged doubtful hopes that Aboo-'Eysa and his crew might somehow have reached Aboo-Shahr before the coming on of the hurricane. But the fact was, as we learnt nigh three months later, that the gale caught them before doubling Rās Ḥaleelah, on the Gulf, and drove them back almost to Baḥreyn, not without some danger and more alarm. Nor did they work their way up again to Aboo-Shahr till after many days of tossing and discomfort.

For us, like sensible men, we remained under shelter, till at last, after twenty-four hours, the storm spent its rage, the sun reappeared, and we summoned our sea-captain and proposed sailing. But the old man averred that the sea was yet too rough for a vessel like his (an assertion in which he was perhaps right), and put us off to the following day. Nothing remained for the moment but to roam up and down the streets, to sit in coffee-houses, to walk along the sandy beach, and to visit a little suburban village, where the meagre soil ill enabled some "Amphion" of Moḥarreḳ "to raise a small plantation," till we returned home and held deep discourse with our ascetic and philosophical host. Mogheeth hated the Wahhabees from the bottom of his heart; indeed, their arrival at Ḥaṣa had been the cause of his leaving it; they held him for a heretic, and he regarded them as intolerant bigots; accusations which in all lands generally presuppose one another.

At last, on the morning of the 26th, our venerable Palæmon reappeared and invited us to his bark, where she lay rocking off the Castle promontory. Mogheeth and three or four more of his way of thinking, accompanied us through the town and down to the beach. I expressed a hope of meeting again on my return from 'Omān; "Let us pledge our meeting in another world," answered Mogheeth; "there it will be more lasting." Saying this, he pressed my hand and we parted.

A light boat took us on board the ship. Close by we witnessed that curious though not unique phenomenon, a spring of fresh water gushing up in the midst of the salt sea. The source in question is situated at a distance of about sixty yards from shore at low-water mark, and we watched well amused the Undines of Moḥarreḳ wade out with their pitchers on their heads, till they reached a little rock, the landmark (or seamark, if you will) of the spring, which pours up from below with force enough to drive back the brackish waves on every side, leaving a large circle of potable water, within which the Naiads plunged their crockery, and returned laden with what an uninformed bystander might have supposed a cargo of brine for some saline baths inland. Our ship, in size equal to a small brig, was full of live stock; passengers of all ages and sexes, but of low condition, bound for Ḳaṭar, six or eight sailors, and some scores of sheep to keep us company. (N.B. no cabin.) Yoosef and I took possession of the highest and most dignified post, that on deck near the stern, and a little before noon we got under weigh. The sea was still roughish, and my companion sea-sick—Nelson was so occasionally, I believe; for myself, I enjoyed an immunity from that annoyance, purchased by many voyages and much rough weather on the ocean.

"On we swept," and passed many a shoal and reef, just perceptible by a change of colour upon the face of the water or a long treacherous ripple; to our right was the coast of Baḥreyn, its sandy monotony broken here and there by some small and dingy village. Near nightfall we sighted the western corner of Ḳaṭar, called in many maps Baḥran, but on what authority I hardly know; certainly no one here ever gives it that name. Now "Baḥran" is simply the nominative of which "Baḥreyn" is the genitive or objective case; and hence I suspect that our geographers may have been led astray by some grammatical misapprehension of a phrase. The coast of Ḳaṭar before us looked rocky, but not high; it is very desolate-seeming; at intervals rise small watch-towers, much like those seen on different points of the Syrian shore, and ascribed by popular tradition to the Empress Helena, wife of Constantine the Great.

During the night we were startled from slumber by the grinding of our keel upon a reef, an event followed by so much confusion, shouting, and awkward unseamanship, that our getting off was more the work of lucky chance than of the crew. Next day we had to endure foul wind and drizzling rain with nothing to shelter us, while we slowly worked our way up under Rās Rekan, the northernmost cape of the Ḳaṭar promontory; a somewhat bold headland girt with cliffs thirty or forty feet high; we were long in getting round it. I noticed a good-sized fort on the heights; it belongs to a village situated in a gorge close by, but I have forgotten the name.

By the morning of the 28th we had fairly rounded Rekan, and drove southwards before the gale for Bedaa'. The line of coast was all along steep, but of inconsiderable height; five or six villages, the abodes of fishermen, intervene between the cape and Bedaa', opposite which we arrived towards evening. Ebn-Khamees went on shore to pay his compliments to the chief and prepare a lodging; but the hour was late, and I preferred remaining on board the night. Next morning my companion returned to fetch me, and we waded together across a wide sandy reach till we entered Bedaa', the principal town of Ḳaṭar at the present day.

It is the miserable capital of a miserable province. To have an idea of Ḳaṭar, my readers must figure to themselves miles on miles of low barren hills, bleak and sun-scorched, with hardly a single tree to vary their dry monotonous outline: below these a muddy beach extends for a quarter of a mile seawards in slimy quicksands, bordered by a rim of sludge and seaweed. If we look landwards beyond the hills, we see what by extreme courtesy may be called pasture land, dreary downs with twenty pebbles for every blade of grass; and over this melancholy ground scene, but few and far between, little clusters of wretched, most wretched, earth cottages and palm-leaf huts, narrow, ugly, and low; these are the villages, or rather the "towns" (for so the inhabitants style them), of Ḳaṭar. Yet poor and naked as is the land, it has evidently something still poorer and nakeder behind it, something in short even more devoid of resources than the coast itself, and the inhabitants of which seek here by violence what they cannot find at home. For the villages of Ḳaṭar are each and all carefully walled in, while the downs beyond are lined with towers, and here and there a castle "huge and square" makes with its little windows and narrow portals a display of strength hardly less, so it might seem, superfluous than the Tower of London in the nineteenth century. But these castles are in reality by no means superfluous, for Ḳaṭar has wealth in plenty, and there are robbers against whom that wealth must be guarded.

Whence comes this wealth amid so much apparent poverty, and in what does it consist? What I have just described is, so to speak, nothing but the heaps of rubbish and the rubbishy miners' huts about the shaft's mouth; close by is the mine itself, a rich and never-failing store. This mine is no other than the sea, no less kindly a neighbour to the inhabitants of Ḳaṭar than their dry land is a niggard host. In this bay are the best, the most copious pearl-fisheries of the Persian Gulf, and in addition an abundance almost beyond belief of whatever other gifts the sea can offer or bring. It is from the sea accordingly, not from the land, that the natives of Ḳaṭar subsist, and it is also mainly on the sea that they dwell, passing amid its waters the one half of the year in search of pearls, the other half in fishery or trade. Hence their real homes are the countless boats which stud the placid pool, or stand drawn up in long black lines on the shore; while little care is taken to ornament their land houses, the abodes of their wives and children at most, and the unsightly strong-boxes of their gathered treasures. "We are all from the highest to the lowest slaves of one master, Pearl," said to me one evening Moḥammed-ebn-Thānee, chief of Bedaa'; nor was the expression out of place. All thought, all conversation, all employment, turns on that one subject; everything else is mere by-game, and below even secondary consideration.

I mentioned robbers and the danger of pillage. From each other, indeed, the men of Ḳaṭar have, it seems, little to fear. Too busy to be warlike, they live in a passive harmony which almost dispenses with the ordinary machinery of government itself. Ebn-Thānee, the governor of Bedaa', is indeed generally acknowledged for head of the entire province, which is itself dependant on the Sultan of 'Omān; yet the Bedaa' resident has in matter of fact very little authority over the other villages, where everyone settles his affairs with his own local chief, and Ebn-Thānee is for those around only a sort of collector-in-chief, or general revenue-gatherer, whose occupation is to look after and to bring in the annual tribute on the pearl fishery. Moḥammed-el-Khaleefah has also a sort of control or presidential authority in Ḳaṭar, but its only exercise in the hands of this worthy seems to be that of choosing now and then a pretty girl (for the female beauty of 'Omān extends itself, though in an inferior degree, to Ḳaṭar), on whom to bestow the brief honours of matrimony for a fortnight or a month at furthest, with a retiring pension afterwards. While I was myself at Bedaa' the uxorious Khaleefah paid a visit to the neighbouring town of Dowḥah, and there lightly espoused a fair sea-nymph of the place, to be no less lightly divorced long before my return from 'Omān. No solemnity was spared on the occasion; jurists were consulted, the dowry paid, public rejoicings were ordered, and public laughter came unbidden; while Moḥammed wasted the hard-gained wealth of Menāmah and Moḥarreḳ in the pomp of open vice.

Zabarah, the largest of the island towns, indeed the only one of any territorial importance, is the residence of one of the El-Khaleefahs; but it does not therefore claim any particular pre-eminence over the remaining localities of the province.

But if the people of Ḳaṭar have peace within, they are exposed on the land side to continual marauding inroads from their Bedouin neighbours, the Menāṣeer and Aāl-Morrah. The former of these tribes is numerous and warlike, and their favourite range of rapine or pasture extends from the frontiers of Ḥaṣa to those of 'Omān proper near Sharjah. Few nomade clans give more annoyance to the inhabited districts, and few, if accounts be correct, have amassed a greater amount of ill-gotten opulence from plunder and bloodshed. These marauders possess large droves of camels and flocks of sheep, acquired and augmented at the expense of the villagers; and from the barren desert hard by, their retreat when pressed by danger, they bring their animals to pasture on the narrow strip of upland that lies between the coast-hills and the Dahnā. Hence the necessity for the towers of refuge which line the uplands: they are small circular buildings from twenty-five to thirty feet in height, each with a door about half-way up the side and a rope hanging out; by this compendious ladder the Ḳaṭar shepherds, when scared by a sudden attack, clamber up for safety into the interior of the tower, and once there draw in the rope after them, thus securing their own lives and persons at any rate, whatever may become of their cattle. For to scale a wall fifteen feet high is an exploit beyond the ingenuity of the most skilful Bedouin. At times the Menāṣeer, emboldened by impunity (for the people of Ḳaṭar have no great pretensions to warlike valour), attack the main villages, and carry off more valuable booty than kine and sheep. Hence the origin of the strongholds or keeps within the towns themselves, and of the walls which surround them.

Further down the coast towards the east begin the settlements of Benoo-Yass, an ill-famed clan, half Bedouins, half villagers, and all pirates; the very same whose cruisers have in former times given to this district the ominous name of "Pirate coast." The head point or main centre of Benoo-Yass is Ṣoor; it is, so I was informed, a mere aggregation of huts, clustered under some old and ruined fortresses, dens of the robbers. The Benoo-Yass belong to the original inhabitants of 'Omān, and though devoid of its civilization, partake in its political and national feelings; hence they are not only haters of all Muslims and Wahhabees, but even fierce enemies and aggressors whenever occasion permits. When plunder is the order of the day, they readily join hands with the Menāṣeer, though widely different from them in origin and in appearance. For the Menāṣeer, judging by tradition, physical outline, and dialect, are a branch of the great 'Abs family, of whom was the famous 'Antarah-ebn-Sheddād, and are, accordingly, by race Nejdeans from Ḳeys-'Eylān, while Benoo-Yass trace their origin to the Ḳaḥṭānee family of Moḍhej, and travelled hither northwards from Ḥaḍramaut, so runs their tale. Profit, however, like misery, may unite strange bedfellows. Both the Menāṣeer and Benoo-Yass have been much repressed of late by the activity of Aḥmed-es-Sedeyree, the Nejdean resident at Bereymah (the same whose brother 'Abd-el-Maḥsin-es-Sedeyree entertained us at Mejmaa'); while at sea the red 'Omānee pennon of the pirates has grown pale before the redder cross of St. George; and none but pearl-oysters and fishes have any violence to fear in this bight of the Persian Gulf at the present day.

Of the third great clan hereabouts, namely, Āal-Morrah, the tenants of the Dahnā itself, and still more numerous and widespread, though luckily less pugnacious, than the Menāṣeer, I have already made mention. The Bedouins of this tribe, who visit Ḳaṭar and 'Omān, now for trade and now for plunder, do not acknowledge Wahhabee sovereignty, but are, after their irregular fashion, some of them tributaries to the Sultan of 'Omān, while some remain at the bidding and buying of subordinate land-chiefs.

The climate of Ḳaṭar is remarkably dry; under the arid breath of the encroaching desert, the sea-air only a few miles inland seems to lose all trace of humidity. The soil is poor, gravel and marl mixed with sand; occasional springs of water supply wells laboriously pierced through the encrusted upper strata. The gardens are small and unproductive, nor did I see any corn-fields or date-groves worthy of the name. The air too is said to be unhealthy; perhaps the rotting pools of stagnant sea-water that border all the coast, are the cause of this.

Such is the general outline of Ḳaṭar. On landing at Bedaa' we went right to the castle, a donjon-keep, with outhouses at its foot, offering more accommodation for goods than for men. Under a mat-spread and mat-hung shed within the court sat the chief, Moḥammed-ebn-Thānee, a shrewd wary old man, slightly corpulent, and renowned for prudence and good-humoured easiness of demeanour, but close-fisted and a hard customer at a bargain; altogether, he had much more the air of a business-like avaricious pearl-merchant (and such he really is), than of an Arab ruler. Round him were placed many sallow-featured individuals, their skins soddened by frequent sea-diving, and their faces wrinkled into computations and accounts. However, Ebn-Thānee, though eminently a "practical" man, had thus far put his sedentary habits to intellectual profit, that by dint of study he had rendered himself a tolerable proficient in literary and poetical knowledge, and took great pleasure in discussing topics of this nature. Nay, he even pretended to have some medical skill, and did I think really possess about the same amount of it that many an old woman may boast of in a country village of Lancashire or Essex. Besides, he liked a joke, and could give and take one with a good grace.

He enquired about my journey. I replied that I had no special business on hand for Ḳaṭar, and that I was merely on my way to Mascat in search of herbs and drugs. Ebn-Khamees, who was now an important character, thanks to the presents in his charge, sat close by the chief in all the grandeur of a new black mantle and a silken head-dress, furnished by Aboo-'Eysa. Moḥammed-ebn-Thānee himself wore a Bengalee turban, of the date of Suraj-Dowlah, to judge by its dingy appearance; his robe was an overdress which a Damascene grocer would have been ashamed to display out of doors.

He apologized for want of room to lodge us suitably in the palace itself. I cast a look round its narrow precincts and loop-holed stone walls, and fully accepted the excuse. Ebn-Thānee had by anticipation caused a warehouse close by to be emptied of the dates it held, and fitted up in Ḳaṭar style for our reception; that is, mats were spread, and nothing more. We of course expressed due thanks for hospitality here regarded as munificent, drank coffee, talked awhile, and retired.

Ebn-Khamees had soon shot his bolt, that is, offered his presents. But their receiver, the old pearl-monger, could not with equal speed make up his mind about the amount to be tendered in requital, and no less than eight days passed before a suitable retribution had been proposed and accepted. This delay, especially in bad lodgings and with much before us better worth seeing, was annoying enough, the more so that four days were fully sufficient for knowing all worth the knowing in so monotonous a country. However, the time did not go by wholly without profit, for it gave me leisure to make some excursions into the vicinity.

The town of Bedaa' itself was soon explored. It owns a long narrow and dirty market-place, where some Baḥreyn shopkeepers and artisans ply their business on a small scale; for the rest, Bedaa' consists of a mass of little narrow dingy houses, separated by irregular lanes. The total amount of its inhabitants when on land, which is not often the case, reaches about six thousand; a few colonists from Ḥasa come hither to try their fortune and grumble at the country. Everywhere one meets fishermen's wives, and their brats, more dirty and more clamorous than any in Crabbe's "Borough," and ill-dressed men, too careworn to be sociable. If we go down to the beach, we find there line on line of huge black boats, whose grooved edges show where the divers' cords have been let down, for a rope is always tied round the waist of the plunger, while the other end is held by his companions, and by this they draw him up when required. And now my reader may fairly appreciate Bedaa', and the attractions it presents to eyes, ears, and, like most seaport towns, to nostrils also. Still the people are not by nature ungracious or inhospitable, but they are over-engrossed by their occupations; and lastly, long-continued diving, accompanied by all the privations and hardships inseparable from weeks and months at sea in open boats, give to the males the appearance of men totally knocked-up.

Till within quite recently Bedaa' owned neither mosque nor any other recognized place for public worship, and we must hope that every one satisfied his devotional obligations in private. But since the late Nejdean invasion, and the establishment of Aḥmed-es-Sedeyree at Bereymah, a "revival" in favour of Islam has taken place in some parts of Ḳaṭar, and two mosques now adorn the town of Bedaa'. One of these edifices is large, but plain and unornamental, in the approved Wahhabee taste; it stands to the north of the castle. The other, situated at the opposite extremity of the village, is smaller, but much handsomer, with an open arched portico in semi-Persian style. Moḥammed-ebn-Thānee, whether from political motives or from sincere conviction, I know not, perhaps from a mixture of both, is very devout, and often performs in person the duties of Imām in the larger mosque, for want of a more appropriate personage in this town, where few sacrifice to Minerva. The smaller "Mesjid" is destined for the use of his eldest son and heir Ḳāsim, a more dashing character than his father, but equally close-fisted. His castle or residence, a white square building with little battlements and pointed windows, almost like imitation Gothic, stands near the southern extremity of Bedaa': beyond it low rocks shut in the bay.

We were soon tired of drinking bad coffee, for the berry of Yemen here gives place to the inferior produce of India, unpalatable stuff to those accustomed to real Mokha; tired too of hearing or spinning long yarns in Ebn-Thānee's divan, and of snuffing up the bad air of a dirty coast and muddy beach. So we resolved to diversify our Ḳaṭar existence by a few trips to the localities around. My first visit was to Dowḥah, a village to the north of Bedaa', and of about half its size; it is situated, as its name of "inlet" or "creek" imports, in a small deep bay, where the cliffs behind, sixty or eighty feet high, give it a somewhat picturesque appearance. But the houses of Dowḥah are even lower and meaner than at Bedaa', and the market-place is narrower and dirtier. Two castles overtop the place: one stands on the neighbouring cliff, the other within the town itself;

the chief is a small sub-collector to Ebn-Thānee. Hither, three days before my departure from Ḳaṭar, arrived the wife-hunting governor of Baḥreyn in pacific quest of a temporary Helen, as above described.

My next excursion was to Wokrah, a town equalling Bedaa' in extent, but situated higher up on the shore, and of a more cheerful character. Its young chief, also a Moḥammed by name, but not of the Ebn-Thānee family, proved intelligent and polite, besides being much more hospitable than his namesake at Bedaa'. In government and police Wokrah is independent of any other town. Under the patronage of its chief, several small traders and artisans from Baḥreyn have established themselves here; and Wokrah has on the whole a thriving look. The road leading to it from Bedaa' is bleak and barren, close along the coast; the distance is within ten miles. I made the journey on a hired donkey, these animals being the ordinary conveyance in Ḳaṭar for short distances; my beast was equipped with a side-saddle, which made me look if not like a gentleman, at least in one respect like a lady, while my long Arab shirt might represent a riding-habit. Nor did I take with me any companion, so secure are the coast-roads, and so many the comers and goers in this land where business supersedes or suspends mischief.

But my associate Ebn-Khamees, more in search of profit than of pleasure, imagined that a few packages of dates might be acceptable to Ḳāsim, the old chief's son, and would needs try his luck with that nobleman, in spite of all I could say to the contrary. Ḳāsim was at the time absent from Bedaa' on a hawking-party some twelve or fourteen miles off to the south-west. We procured dromedaries, mounted, and rode on our way, over desert uplands and pebbly tracts. We passed bands of women in quest of water from the distant wells; and flocks of sheep, or rather of goats, for the breed is of ambiguous appearance, well guarded by numerous shepherds; occasionally we met some traveller with his lance over his shoulder against the perils of a Bedouin frontier. No trees, little herbage, and a cold keen wind from the north.

At last we reached the desired spot, a tolerably grassy valley amid undulations and hillocks on the marge of the "waste and howling wilderness." Here in tents, bivouac guise, was the young chief with his retainers, on the look-out for partridges and quails, of which he had hitherto caught few; with an eye too on hares, or I had better said on those equivocal animals, half hare, half rabbit, which abound on the Arab mainland. Ḳāsim had with him about twenty horsemen, falconers, and half a dozen lovely hawks, besides two brace of greyhounds ("Selāḳee" they call them here); a thorough hunting-party, except that there was not a single fowling-piece among them. We remained half a day in his highness's society, and enjoyed a sort of Arab pic-nic, enlivened by hawking. For a minute description of this sport in the East, I may refer my readers to that well-known and accurate work, Layard's "Nineveh."

Here I met with two Bedouins, one a Menāṣeer, the other a Morrah; men remarkable for having traversed the Great Desert from this side of Arabia to the Yemen, and who were in consequence regarded as "lions" even by their own countrymen. According to their account, the achievement which they had executed was wholly undesigned on their part; they had gone on a visit to the "Aḳḥāf," a low chain of limestone hills and grassy valleys, which occupy the position marked "Wadi Djebrin" in some maps, to the south of Yemāmah, where they had some business of clan or camels to settle. But having misdirected their course too far to the south, they lost the "Aḳḥāf," and wandered on from sand-ridge to sand-ridge, and from valley to valley, lucky to fall in every now and then with a brackish well whence to fill their water-skins, or a few dwarf-palms to supply them with something not "wholly uneatable," till after about two months' roving, according to their computation of time, and keeping their faces steadily to the south-west, they reached Maa'reb on the frontiers of Yemen.

In returning they took a safer but a more circuitous road, following the comparatively inhabited lands of Ḥaḍramaut, and thence the sea-coast up to 'Omān. To my enquiries, freely made and freely answered (for neither suspicion nor ill-will had room here), respecting that long line of shore often denominated "Mahra," and its inhabitants, they answered that the greater part was destitute of towns and even of villages, and offered nothing but mud-huts and palm-leaf cottages, where dwelt men belonging to certain dusky tribes whose language was, said they,

Abyssinian. These are, I believe, the Ḥimyarites, the same about whom much learned inquiry has been made, and who seem in fact to have been an Abyssinian colony of ancient date, long prior to the famous invasion of Elisbaan the Najāshee, in the sixth century; but who have preserved to the present day the archaic form of their mother tongue, just as the old Turkish settlement between Bagdad and Kerkook yet speak the proto-Turkish dialect, elsewhere softened down and blended with stranger elements—in Anatolia for instance, and at Constantinople. Much should I have desired to visit the Ḥimyarite district, but was unable for many reasons, nor did I meet with any of its genuine inhabitants. Subsequent hearsay information, however, picked up in 'Omān, tended to confirm in every respect the statements of my Bedouin friends. Arabs of this class, though bad deductive reasoners, are excellent superficial observers of men and customs, nor do I see any cause for doubting their word in a matter like this where mere outside facts are concerned.

Tradition (I will not call it history) does indeed make Ḥimyar, the supposed founder of this race, a great-grandson of Ḳaḥṭān, and a younger brother of Saba, the famed Yemanee monarch. But where so manifest a difference obtrudes itself both in complexion and in language, we may be excused for suspecting a degree of inaccuracy in the genealogical tree, though intermarriages may, and probably did, somewhat supply the want of primal consanguinity. To such affinity, and to the influence which the comparatively organizing spirit of the Abyssinians would give them over the unstable Arabs, we may perhaps ascribe the great spread of the Ḥimyarite name and language in the south, and even its partial introduction into the Northern and Syrian desert under the Yemanee dynasty of Ghassān. It is to be remarked, that up to the present day with none do Arabs so readily contract marriage as with Abyssinians: the two races have much in kind.

Arab annalists, supported in this respect by the results of modern research, assign to the Ḥimyarite dynasty an important part in the story of Southern Arabia; and the investigations of Welsted and of others in Ḥaḍramaut leave no doubt regarding the Ḥimyarite character of that province. That a fictitious lineage should have attempted to blend the origin of the conquerors, at least of their chiefs, with that of the conquered race, is no wonder; we have already seen an example of this in the attempt to derive the Northern Arab stock, typified by Ismael, from the blood of Ḳaḥṭān: and thus Yemanee vanity may have sought to console itself for submission to a foreign rule, by an imaginary amalgamation of its rulers with their subjects. Besides, the Arabs of the south, or Yemen, were themselves, it is highly probable, of African origin, though referable to a still more ancient date; and family alliances may, indeed must, have subsequently led to a partial affinity, the groundwork of that universal identity which Mahometan chroniclers above all would fain introduce. Thus Ḥimyar—did such a person ever exist—may, the better to consolidate his rule, have taken to wife the daughter of some Yemanee "Ḳeyl" or king; or if not he, at least one of his descendants. Superior in the art of government and the science of established power, no less than in architecture and some at least of its accompanying arts, to the Arabs around, the Ḥimyarites became ultimately masters of a large portion of the Peninsula, and founded a kingdom remarkable for its extent and comparative durability. We find an analogous attempt at South Arabian conquest made by the more recent Ethiopians of the sixth century, under Abrahah, and followed by complete success; nor could the Ḳaḥṭānee chief, Seyf-Yezen, shake off the foreign yoke till aided by the arms and treasures of Persia. That Arab chroniclers should have delighted to claim the victor for a kinsman, and thus obviate the disgrace of acknowledging foreigners to be stronger or more civilized than themselves, is perfectly natural. So even in our own times Persians would fain persuade themselves that Alexander the Great was no other than a son of the very Darius whom he overthrew at Arbela; the Macedonian conqueror, having been when a child "put to nurse, was by a beggar woman stolen away" from his Iranian palace, like Jack Cade from the house of Mortimer, and returned in arms but to claim his right;—all lest Persians should seem to have yielded to others than Persians. Nor are more westerly historians always exempt from similar weaknesses.

Enough of the Ḥimyarites, or "Reds," be they who they may.

They are not, however, the only tenants of the south-eastern coast, which is also (so says report) extensively colonized by thorough-going blacks, natives of Zanjibar and its vicinity, especially near the island of Massora and Rās-el-Ḥaḍḍ. By what process these negroes got there, and what part they play in the general drama of the land, I will afterwards explain. On the present occasion I was much pleased with my Menāṣeer informant, who, grown daring by a first adventure, ended by proposing to me a second trip in his society through the Great Desert, and a visit hand in hand to the limits of Ḍofār and Ḥaḍramaut. But enough, not of water but of sand, had been mine already in the weary days of the "Dahnā" and "Nefood," and the projected expedition was deferred to an indefinite future. The enterprise would certainly be laborious, and not wholly without danger; but its execution is not impossible, and might lead to interesting discoveries.

Yoosef-ebn-Khamees delivered his presents and received fair words, but little else. Ḳāsim appeared to me even less amiable than his father; narrow-minded and less well informed than the old man, while at the same time he was more pretentious and haughty. He affects the Nejdean in dress and manner, but has far more devotion at heart for the *diva pecunia* than for the precepts of the Coran. His men, like those of Justice Shallow, had a "semblable coherence with their master's spirits," which rendered their society dry and unprofitable.

Next morning we took leave of Ḳāsim, and returned by the way we came, to eat fish and drink bad coffee with Ebn-Thānee. We waited yet a couple of days, hoping for a favourable wind to convey us straight across the Gulf to 'Omān. The land journey by the coast would have required at least a fortnight, perhaps more; and the reports current in Ḳaṭar touching the rapacity of the Benoo-Yass, their treachery and other ill qualities, did not encourage us to try their hospitality, especially with Yoosef's presents and retributions in our keeping. Besides, all affirmed the road to be even more desolate and monotonous than that of Ḳaṭar itself, and that it could offer nothing to repay our labour in traversing it. The sands of the Dahnā reach the very margin of the sea: a glance at the map will enable my reader to understand this district.

Accordingly we proposed following the diameter of the semicircle over-sea, in preference to its sandy circumference, and thus make direct for Sharjah, the first considerable town situated within the territory of 'Omān proper. For this a worthy young sea-captain, native of Charak on the opposite Persian coast, offered us his ship and services. But here again the future had for us more roundabouts in store than had entered into our original calculation. "The traveller can reckon his setting out, not his return," says a trite Arab proverb, true in some degree everywhere, but most so in the East.

Our captain was soon ready for sailing, and his crew on board. We made our parting arrangements, and on February 6, while a lovely evening promised a fair morrow, and a light west wind seemed to ensure us a good and speedy passage to Sharjah, we took our leave of Moḥammed-ebn-Thānee, who had now become very intimate in his way, said adieu to three or four other friends acquired at Bedaa', and entrusted ourselves to a little boat, wherein Fāris, to give our captain his proper name, with his younger brother Aḥmed and two of the crew, had come to fetch us off to the ship. We now crossed by rowing the same space that I had footed over the sand some days before; but then it had been ebb, whereas now the full tide was running in ten or twelve feet deep. The flux and reflux of the waters is here only once in twenty-three hours, that is, at every alternate period; at Baḥreyn and on the coasts of Persia and 'Omān it is once in eleven. The peculiar position of Ḳaṭar and of the Benoo-Yass region at the bottom of a deep gulf, will explain this meteorological phenomenon to my scientific readers; the Arabs content themselves with noticing and wondering at it. After a quarter of an hour's pull we reached the schooner. She was large and well built, provided with an elegant captain's cabin, a fore-cabin, and other nautical arrangements; in fine, she was infinitely superior to the miserable craft in which we had left Baḥreyn. She was built for quick sailing, with two masts, large lateen sails, and a jib; her stern and prow were prettily carved; indeed the latter surmounted the waves with a sea-nymph figurehead; a token of non-compliance with the Islamitic prohibition, which excludes the representation of whatever has life from the sphere of ornamental art.

When we got on board, the crew, all of them cousins to each other seventh remove, and relations of the captain himself, received us very heartily. It is the custom on most Gulf ships that passengers, of high or low degree, no matter, are looked upon as the captain's own guests for the voyage, and as such have a right to his table and fare, free of extra charge. My readers will have remarked long before this, that in the East the relative position of travellers, whether by land or sea, and of those who conduct them, has a very intimate, nay almost a family character; all are considered as forming one moving household during the journey or voyage. Nor are the links thus united wholly broken by separation at the journey's end; the title of a special friendship and fellowship remains for years, and may be claimed afresh by either party whenever need or good will suggests, nor can such claim be decently rejected. The reasons of this are too obvious for explanation; railways and other wholesale means of communication do away with these feelings, by removing the causes which produce them in uncivilized countries.

Yoosef and myself, thinking it beneath our dignity to receive without return, had laid in at Baḥreyn a stock of the best coffee to be had for love or money, and with this we repaid in some degree the rice, fish, and vermicelli (a common dish here), of our naval hosts. But before introducing my readers to Barr-Fāris and its inhabitants, of whom were the crew, I must attempt to give a general idea of that land and its people.

From Rās Nahend westward to Rās Bostanah on the east (both localities are on the northern side of the Persian Gulf), extends a not unfertile strip of coast, hemmed in between high mountains and the sea. Arab enterprise and courage have for many generations past detached this strip of land from the feeble rule of Ṭeheran and its Shirāz representative. Here a colony of Arab chieftains, with their retainers, mostly natives of Eastern Nejed, has established itself, and, partly by the sword, partly by intermarriage, has subdued or incorporated with itself the original village population. From these united elements has sprung up a species of confederacy, mutually allied against the claims of the Shirāz governor, whose authority (that is, on the Persian muster-rolls) extends over Barr-Fāris and the villages which it contains. But besides their continual antagonism with Persia, the inhabitants are but too often disunited from each other by alternate depredation and international strife, in which Persian cruelty, acquired from the neighbourhood, and, as it were, imbibed from the atmosphere of this continent, gives a darker character than elsewhere to Arab brigandage. At the rise of the first Wahhabee empire, the chiefs of Barr-Fāris, mindful of their origin, hailed the dawn of Nejdean supremacy, in which they trusted to find a powerful ally against Shiya'ee aggression; and the more to ensure Wahhabee cooperation they adopted the peculiar tenets of the new or regenerated Islam, with all its bigotry and savage intolerance. Up to the present day they maintain many of the genuine Wahhabee dogmas and feelings, as a rallying point against their Persian enemies, though the taming hand of time has somewhat softened down the excess of their fanaticism.

The chiefs of Barr-Fāris claim direct descent from the great clan of Meṭeyr, our old acquaintances in Upper Nejed; two or three trace their lineage to Benoo-Khālid, the fallen masters of Ḥasa. If the spirit of subdivision, of jealousy, of plunder, and of revenge, be an authentic guarantee of Bedouin origin, they are well provided with credentials. Nor is the fickleness proper to the nomade wanting here, even after many years of fixed habitation; theirs is still that curse of instability which has hindered, and ever will hinder Bedouins, however numerous and favoured by circumstances, from enjoying the benefits of peace, or profiting by the successes of war.

Such are the chiefs: the subjects of Barr-Fāris present every imaginable gradation between the Persian and the Arab, very hybrid in form and feature, till the eye of the beholder is often puzzled to distinguish between Nejdean and Shirazee. Their dress is, however, almost entirely Persian, and so in most respects are their domestic manners. The open and unembarrassed hospitality of Arabia is on this coast exchanged for a cooler and a more guarded style; conversation with the stranger guest is often limited by formalities; and a feeling of loneliness unknown to the inmate of an Arab village, whencesoever he be, may readily creep over the sojourner under the roofs of Barr-Fāris. The general state of the land is far from thriving.

Frequent attacks from Persia on the land side, and bitter intestine dissensions, joined with the pernicious narrowmindedness of religious bigotry, have gone far to ruin commerce, the only profitable resource of this coast. Pearl-oysters are absent from the deep waters that bathe the shore, and even fish are much less abundant than on the southern or Arab side; while agriculture in a somewhat poor and rocky soil, with little water at hand, hardly suffices for existence, much less for wealth. Thus the whole energy of Barr-Fāris, turned in former times to commerce, for which the excellent harbours of the coast, and its important communications by land and sea, rendered it eminently suited; its population were pre-eminent in sea-craft and traffic, nor were any ships or sailors from Boṣra to Mascat more adventurous or more highly esteemed than theirs. They still maintain somewhat of their old nautical reputation and activity; but I have already noticed that Mahometanism is, like all despotism, adverse to the freer element, and the number of the vessels no less than the daring of the sailors is much diminished nowadays. In no more unsuitable place could Wahhabeeism have found a rooting, and nowhere are its baleful effects more evident. But it is time to return to our voyage.

We were now under full sail, but the morning breeze veered to the south, and kept us somewhat out of our intended course, while the sultry heat of the day portended a storm. The afternoon sky was already overcast, and the breeze rose in fitful gusts, when we sighted and before sunset came right under the island of Ḥalool, a mass of rocks apparently of volcanic origin, and starting abruptly from the sea; they contain among their recesses a good spring, but only one, of fresh water; and to this Ḥalool owes frequent visits paid it by the fishermen of Ḳaṭar during the pearl season. Very little grass, however, finds root on its black ledges, and it has no fixed population. Ḥalool, as my readers will learn from the map, is one of the numerous islets that stud this bay; I have heard their number reckoned at thirty-six by a sea-captain who professed to have touched at each and all. But most of them are mere reefs, devoid alike of water and of vegetation; five or six alone deserve the name of islands, and furnish, however scantily, the necessaries of a miserable existence to the boats' crews on the pearl fishery, when they cast anchor by them in quest of water, or to fetch off a lean goat from the pastures.

The sun now went down amid large masses of vapour, and a violent south-easter blew all night; we drove before it, and when morning dawned over the tossing waves we were far away from the direction of Sharjah, and had entered on the deep waters known by the name of "Ghubbat-Fāris," or the "Persian depth," beyond the prospect of returning to Ḳaṭar, or of reaching 'Omān, and on the contrary rapidly approaching the northern coast. Our captain attempted many nautical manœuvres to bring the ship about, but in vain, and he was at last obliged to give up the trial, and to make straight for Barr-Fāris. About noon a white glimmer on our left indicated the low and sandy island of Ge's, where Baḥreyn enterprise has established a settlement, flourishing because free. Meanwhile the huge rounded outline of Djebel Atranjah, or "the Citron mountain," which overtops the bay of Charak itself, rose before us, and soon we had the whole line of the Persian coast in view.

It contrasts strongly with the Arabian. Its mountains are lofty, often two thousand feet in height, rough in outline, yet less barren than the Arab coast-range. In some places the crags come right down to the sea; in others a shore strip, ploughed up by violent winter torrents, but with no perennial stream to water it, extends two or three miles back towards the interior, till it is lost within the mountain gorges. One wide and romantic-looking pass, a little to the east, behind Charak, leads to Shirāz; and by this road the invading armies of Persia have often descended on Barr-Fāris. The mountain sides are thinly sprinkled with fig-trees, orange-trees, and other wood vegetation; here and there is a streak of scanty tillage; in the plain below are palm-groves, but meagre and unproductive, with just enough of other cultivation to keep the inhabitants from famine.

Charak itself was once a good-sized town, to judge by the great extent of its ruined walls, but it is now reduced to a hamlet of two thousand souls or thereabouts. It is situated at the base of a well-sheltered semicircular bay, fenced in by jutting promontories; this bay is in turn an indentation belonging to a much larger scoop, the western horn of which is at

Chiro, while its eastern extremity constitutes Rās Bostanah; its general aspect is between south and south-east. The town, for so its inhabitants persist in calling it, is composed of small but neat white plastered houses; the pretty little mosque is constructed in Persian style; it belongs to the date of the first Wahhabee dynasty. At some distance inland rises a strong keep or tower, situated on a small isolated hill; here in better days was stationed a Belooch garrison. The Belooches are the Swiss of these regions; but of them more anon.

With sails spread to the southerly gale we entered the harbour about two hours before sunset, and landed without difficulty on the clean shelving beach. Our captain, whose house and household were in the town, invited us to become his guests on shore as at sea. But the usages of Charak, where the traditions of Arab hospitality are tempered by Persian niggardliness blended with Wahhabee stiffness, do not permit of introducing strangers directly under the family roof-tree. Accordingly Fāris caused a small side chamber adjoining the mosque, and destined to the reception of travellers like ourselves, to be swept out and matted; he then brought cushions and coffee, and finally sent us, by the hands of his younger brothers, a good supper prepared after the variety of Persian cookery. Smoking is strictly prohibited in Barr-Fāris no less than in Nejed, and we were compelled to seek out stealthy nooks and corners wherein to enjoy our pipe. No one of the townsmen came to visit us; but while we sat at the mosque gate "eyes looked" curiosity, if not "love, to eyes that spoke again;" and Barakāt and I made at our leisure many reflections on the difference between lands and lands, people and people.

Next morning the wind proved still unfavourable, and precluded sailing. To pass the time, Fāris took us in his company to pay a visit of politeness to the local chief, 'Abd-el-'Azeez-el-Meteyree. We traversed a part of the town till our way opened into a grassy plot, where some high trees, of what peculiar species I do not know (their growth resembled that of the beech, but the foliage was different), gave an agreeable shade to visitors waiting for an audience. Here stands the castle of 'Abd-el-'Azeez, a small but strong building, with a courtyard in form of a quadrangle, and a high Gothic-looking portal.

At the gate we found several pointed felt bonnets and genuine inland Persian dresses; the wearers were a deputation from Shirāz sent down a day or two before to extract some hardly-obtained tribute or homage of dubious allegiance in behalf of the governor of the province, and the Shah his master. They met, as I subsequently learned, with little success, for 'Abd-el-'Azeez, who is a strenuous Wahhabee, and as insubordinate as ever Nejdean could be to Persian, steadily refused to allow the "enemies of God" any share of the goods of the land. We asked and obtained admittance. In a divan near the portal, where swords, spears, and guns made a martial display, we found our chief, a young and remarkably handsome man, dressed after the etiquette of Riaḍ; he claims untainted lineal descent from Benoo-Tameem and Ṭābikhah, "though," so whispered me Ebn-Khamees in a prudent aside, "he has no more title to it than you or I." But whoever were his progenitors, 'Abd-el-'Azeez was redhot with warlike zeal, and highly excited by good news fresh come from 'Oneyzah. For the first time since our departure from Riaḍ, we now got hold of important tidings respecting that fated town. I will here relate what 'Abd-el-'Azeez told us, and then take occasion to add a brief recital of the events which followed soon after; events melancholy in themselves, and precursors of much mischief.

When the Ḥaṣa contingent arrived at Riaḍ, bringing the artillery with them, 'Abd-Allah, son of Feyṣul, prepared to put himself at their head without delay, and march on 'Oneyzah. But the old and wary fox, his father, compelled the impetuous prince to await the arrival of 'Obeyd from Djebel Shomer. Ṭelāl had indeed been called on to come in person, and to take his place among the Nejdean commanders; but he declined compliance, not over liking a business of which, had he been a classical scholar, he might have well said, but to himself in private, *tua res agitur paries cum proximus ardet.* Not thus 'Obeyd: delighted at having so good an opportunity for butchering his fellow-creatures in the name of their Creator, he lost no time in getting together men and ammunition, and came down on Ḳaṣeem about the middle of December. Feyṣul then gave the signal, and 'Abd-Allah set out, leading with him the entire force of Ḥaṣa, besides the troops of 'Aareḍ, and whatever else remained behind from the central and southern provinces; thus mustering a body of fifteen thousand men or near it; a force which, when added to the besieging army already in the field, must have amounted to twenty-three or twenty-four thousand regular troops at least, besides four or five thousand Bedouins, who after long wavering which side to take, now prudently determined to join the certain winner. 'Oneyzah was thus left to her own unaided resources, which might come up to four thousand fighting men at the utmost.

After much skirmishing, a decisive battle was fought in January. Zāmil and El-Khey'yāt are said to have performed prodigies of valour, and 'Abd-Allah was near being surrounded and killed, as it is much to be regretted that he was not in good earnest. But where the combatants are in the respective proportions of five to one, a drawn battle is for the less numerous party hardly better than a defeat; and the men of 'Oneyzah, now fully aware of the overwhelming superiority of the enemy, and that they themselves could in consequence but ill afford the loss of a single man, shut themselves up within their walls, and were blockaded in form.

So stood affairs when 'Abd-el-'Azeez gave us what was then the latest information. The rest I learnt in April, when on the point of leaving the confines of Arabia for Bagdad. After more than a month of close siege, the outer walls first, and then the inner, gave way before the Wahhabee artillery, and the town was taken by assault. The inhabitants fought to the last; when all hope was over, Zāmil and Khey'yāt cut their way through the assailants, and escaped to a southern refuge in Wadi Nejrān, where they are believed to be yet concealed from the vengeance of the conqueror. But seven hundred from among the principal citizens of 'Oneyzah were slaughtered on the spot, besides a promiscuous massacre of the common people; and the fated town was plundered and utterly ruined, not to rise again so long as the Wahhabee should be master of the land. No barrier now remained between the Wahhabee armies and Mecca; and preparations were made for realizing the great dream of Nejdean ambition, the sovereignty of the holy city. This long-cherished design, the glory and the ruin of the first 'Abd-Allah, may, it seems likely enough, be carried out by the second. The Ottoman has neglected his best chance for checking the fanatics of Nejed by the timely succour of 'Oneyzah, and the Shereef has little now before him but, in common phrase, to shut the stable door after that the horse has been stolen, unless indeed Egypt, or some other more vigorous power, intervenes to rescue the Arabian peninsula from the Wahhabee blight, now overhanging alike the shores of the Red Sea and of the Persian Gulf. This has yet to be seen; for myself and my readers we will now return to Charak, where we left 'Abd-el-'Azeez and his retainers rejoicing in the vengeance of God on the infidels of Kaseem, and recounting the glories of the favoured and orthodox sect of 'Abd-el-Wahhāb.

We drank coffee and left the audience. Fāris, with much politeness and a certain feeling of good taste not common in the East, proposed to take me a walk about the town, and to show me whatever in it was worth the seeing. This was not much; however, my cicerone pointed out to me the broken traces of the old outer walls, and indicated their course amid fields and trees, with all the interest of the Antiquary at the Prætorium of Kaimprunes. Hence he led me to the foot of the small marly cone on whose summit frowns the dismantled round tower mentioned a few pages back, a rival of our own Norfolk Caistor Castle in form and size. It is situated just beyond the old fortifications, which form a semicircle of about a mile and a half in circumference, with the shore for base: a torrent-bed where winter rains run down from the Persian mountains, passes through the centre of this space, like an arrow across a stretched bow. Fig-trees, oranges, lemons, and other orchard trees, grow between the town-wall and the houses; without are thinly-planted palm-groves, like men opening out for sword exercise; beyond, a few fields strewn with fragments of rock up to the mountain-base. Scattered cottages are to be seen here and there, but the country is poorly peopled, and the only villages of any size are those situated on the shore itself. Wells are not wanting at Charak,—better off in this respect than most localities of Barr-Fāris, but the water is brackish. Fāris led us about for a walk of two or three hours, and we then returned home.

The rest of the day passed in making enquiries about the means of continuing our journey. Little traffic exists between

Barr-Fāris and Sharjah, whither we now desired to direct our course, and we were in consequence advised to take passage on board a ship of Chiro, then lying in the Charak harbour, and about to sail for the port of Linja, or Linya, to call it as they do here, softening the hard Arab "j" or "jeem" into a "y"; a local mispronunciation, whence "Mesjid" becomes "Mesyid," "'Ajman" "'Ayman," and so forth. Linja is situated some twenty miles east on the same coast as Charak, and once there we should have no difficulty in crossing over to Sharjah. The captain of the Chiro vessel, a ruddy-featured seaman, visited us in our apartments at the mosque the same evening, and we made our bargain with him for a passage the following day.

Early next morning, the 10th February, I went to bathe in the clear sea waters, for off the muddy shores of Kaṭar I had not ventured on a swim. But on this occasion I was near meeting with an untoward accident from the dart of a large sting-ray, which I saw close by me just in time to avoid it. Polypi, sea-nettles, molluscæ, and other marine monsters, swarm in this Gulf; sharks too are very common; so that a swimmer off shore at Barr-Fāris would do well to look before he plunges.

About noon we went on board, and soon the vessel unfurled her sails for Linja. We had in our company several silent gentlemen of Charak, well dressed, and apparently richer in purse than in words. I should remark that the natives of this coast are in general grave even to dullness, say little, and have little to say. We cleared the harbour, and by sunset were off Cape Bostanah, a fine headland, with two or three villages near the point; while the dim and dreamy outline of the island Faroor, a volcanic reef not unlike Ḥalool, broke the southern sea-rim far away. At nightfall we doubled Cape Bostanah. The sea was brilliantly phosphoric; every ripple flashed in light; and large glowing masses, molluscæ of some shining species, floated like globes of hot iron at a small depth below the surface. I maliciously enquired of our Wahhabee friends on board what could be the cause of this fiery appearance, and was told with all possible seriousness that it was due to the reflected glare of hell, supposed to be situated immediately under the Gulf. With corresponding seriousness I enquired whether the vault of the infernal regions was transparent? possibly of stone glass?

and suggested that without some such medium interposed the water above might put out the fire. But my informants replied that Divine omnipotence fully sufficed to obviate any such inconvenience, and that God's will was quite answer enough to dispense with further search. A second remark of mine on the very slight degree of heat developed by the eternal conflagration, which did not seem to have any effect whatever in warming the superjacent sea, was silenced by the same compendious answer; and I was told that this phenomenon was also a pure result of God's will, not of any want of caloric in hell-fire itself. Whereon I thought it prudent to leave the matter alone. But I could wish that those who take pleasure in exalting the sublime theological and spiritual conceptions of Mahometans, might pass a few months among the Wahhabees of Barr-Fāris or of Nejed: intimacy would go far to modify such views.

About midnight we were in the bay of Linja or Linya, where countless lights gleaming from the shore cheered the darkness, and made me long for the discoveries of dawn. Day came at last, and showed us anchored at some two hundred yards from land; between it and us lay a mass of shipping, large and small; a theatre of white houses amid trees and gardens lined the coast far away on either side of the harbour.

Linja belongs at present to the 'Omānee government—a fortunate circumstance, and the source of its remarkable prosperity. To the same rule pertains the entire Persian coast from Rās Bostanah to the frontiers of Djask. How this was brought about, under what circumstances, and with what result, can only be understood by those who have at least a general idea of the history of 'Omān and its dynasty. That history I will now accordingly give, or rather sketch, by way of prelude to this last phase of my narrative. The subject is an interesting one, and requires a new and distinct chapter.

CHAPTER XV

'OMÂN

I do at length descry the happy shore
In which I hope erelong for to arrive;
Fair soil it seems from far, and fraught with store
Of all that dear and dainty is alive.—*Spenser*

OROGRAPHICAL LIMITS OF 'OMÂN—GENERAL CHARACTER—EARLY HISTORY AND SOURCES OF POPULATION—LATER COLONIES—SABEANS ACCORDING TO ARAB AUTHORITIES—SABEANS OF 'OMÂN—MAHOMETANISM IN 'OMÂN—ITS DEFECTION DURING THE FIRST CENTURY—CARMATHIAN IMPULSE—LATER PHASE OF MIND IN 'OMÂN—THE BIAḌEEYAH—ORIGIN OF THE NAME—THE POLE-STAR—ANNUAL FAST—SOCIAL CONDITION AND WOMEN-DISGUISEMENT PRACTISED—NIEBUHR AT MASCAT—HOW FAR MISINFORMED—GENERAL CHARACTER OF THE INHABITANTS—TOLERATION—'OMÂN WITCHES AND SORCERERS—STORY OF A WIZARD OF BAHILAH—NEGROES IN 'OMÂN—THEIR NUMBER, CONDITION, AND INFLUENCE—HISTORY OF THE LAST THREE CENTURIES IN 'OMÂN—THE PORTUGUESE—THE DUTCH—THE PERSIANS—'OMÂN RECOVERS HER INDEPENDENCE—DYNASTY OF EBN-SA'EED—ACCESSION OF ES-SULṬAN SA'EED—HIS EARLY SUCCESS AND POLICY—WAHHABEE INVASION—SUPPRESSION OF PIRATES—LATER CONQUESTS AND GOVERNMENT OF SULṬAN-SA'EED—HIS VISIT TO MECCA—HIS DEATH—TRIPLE DIVISION OF THE KINGDOM—WAR BETWEEN THOWEYNEE AND MÂJID—WAR BETWEEN THOWEYNEE AND AMJED—ENGLISH INTERFERENCE—POPULAR REVOLT—THOWEYNEE INVITES THE NEJDEANS—EXPEDITION OF 'ABD-ALLAH-EBN-SA'OOD—KHÂLID-EBN-ṢAḲAR—HIS HISTORY—HIS RAVAGES IN THE BÂṬINAH—'ABD-ALLAH REACHES BEREYMAH—EXPEDITION AGAINST DJEBEL-AKHDAR COMMANDED BY ZÂMIL-EL-'AṬEEYAH—PROGRESS—RESULT—GENERAL PACIFICATION—CONDITIONS IMPOSED—LATER CONDUCT OF THOWEYNEE—"IMAM OF MASCAT"—HOW FAR ERRONEOUS—ADMINISTRATION OF THE KINGDOM—CONDUCT OF AḤMED-ES-SEDEYREE AND OTHER NEJDEANS—PERSIAN COAST—LANDING AT LINJA—THE TOWN—ITS HARBOUR, COMMERCE, AND INHABITANTS—REFLECTIONS—'OMÂNEE ADMINISTRATION—DO'EYJ AND HIS HOUSE—INTERIOR AND MARKET OF LINJA—PERSIAN DEPUTATION—DEPARTURE FOR SHARJAH—A GALE—TWO DAYS ON ABOO-MOOSA—ARRIVAL OFF SHARJAH.

'AAMÂN in an Arab mouth, or 'Omān according to our customary European misnomer, now too widely established by usage to be abandoned without a species of affectation, is the name applied on most maps to the sea-coast district comprised between Rās

Mesandum, and Rās-el-Haḍḍ, the extreme eastern shoulder of the Peninsula. Arabs give to 'Omān, however, a much wider range, extending it from Aboo-Ḍebee, a village on the easterly limit of the territory now occupied by Benoo-Yass, to the neighbourhood of Ḍofār itself, far down the southern coast, with whatever lands lie between these points. 'Omān thus taken comprises the province of Mahrah, to cite our own geographers, the promontory of Rās-el-Haḍḍ, and the entire district thence reaching to the "Pirate coast," with whatever belongs to Rās Mesandum on either side. The 'Omān of Arabia touches accordingly Ḥaḍramaut on the south, and Ḳaṭar, or at least its immediate vicinity, on the north, and forms a huge crescent, having the sea in front, and the vast desert of Southern Arabia for background. But in a political sense of frequent occurrence, 'Omān has a yet wider acceptation, since it then includes, besides the above-named territory, that also of Benoo-Yass, Ḳaṭar, the Akḥāf, all the islands of the Persian Gulf from Baḥreyn eastward, namely, Djishm, Ormuz (or Hormooz, as the natives call it), Larej, and many others of lesser note, besides the entire coast on the Persian side from Rās Bostanah to Djask. Lastly, the same rule extends over a long strip of the African shore opposite to Zanjibar, while the island that bears that name, Socotra too, and whatever adjoins them, are subject to the 'Omānee sceptre.

A first glance at the map will convince my readers that 'Omān is essentially a maritime kingdom, namely, one in which commerce and sea-trade must play an important, perhaps the most important part. Yet the land possessions are by no means wanting in intrinsic value. 'Omān proper, as we may not unsuitably call the province which has given its name to the entire empire, is, it would seem, the richest portion of the Arabian peninsula, both in agricultural produce and in mineral treasures, while its extent inland is sufficient to afford ample field for industrial labour of every description. The African possessions are said to be also very fertile, at least in part; but for these I must refer my readers to other authorities than myself, having never crossed the line to the south. But whatever may be the land wealth of 'Omān, it is principally the immense extent of sea-coast, and the important position of that coast itself, comprising the keys of the Persian Gulf, added to the excellent harbours which everywhere indent its shore, that give to the people and government a definite and peculiar character.

At a very early period this part of Arabia received its first known colonists from Yemen. These belonged, it would appear, not to Ḥimyar but to the Ḳaḥṭanee tribes, previous to their admixture with any foreign element of descent. The principal family whose chiefs headed the original settlement was, according to 'Omānee tradition, that of the Ya'aribah, and their descendants maintained the uninterrupted though by no means the unlimited sovereignty of 'Omān till the beginning of the eighteenth century, when the last of these rulers, Seyf-ebn-Sultan by name, was dethroned by Aḥmed-ebn-Sa'eed. This latter, himself of the Ghafaree family, but allied by marriage with the Ya'aribah whom he supplanted, having by his skilful valour delivered his country from the Persian yoke, imposed on it by Taḳee-ed-Deen, was in return proclaimed king by his grateful fellow-citizens assembled at Mascat. A brief contest ensued with the partisans of the old dynasty; Ebn-Sa'eed prevailed, and ultimately obtained the mastery of the entire kingdom; while the Ya'aribah had henceforth to content themselves with a local authority over their family domains, situated in Djebel-Akhdar, where they still enjoy unmolested feudal rights analogous to those of the Campbells in the Western Islands, powerful chiefs of a clan.

The Ghafaree no less than the Ya'aribah, claim direct genealogical descent from Ḳaḥṭān himself, the Odin of Arabia; and the authentic population of 'Omān boasts a cognate though not equally royal origin. Djelandee, Tho'al, 'Aḍra, Yeshḥar, and other tribes of the great Ḳaḥṭānee family, seem to have resorted hither at a very early date; from the Djelandee sprung the Benoo-Ryām, who inhabit the heights above Nezwah. But over and above these first tenants of the soil other tribes of northerly or Ismaelitic lineage have in process of time incorporated themselves with the Ḳaḥṭānee stock. The numerous clan of Fezārah, driven from Nejed by the unceasing hostilities of Kelāb and Tameem, have taken up here their principal abode, and from them comes no inconsiderable part of the sea-coast population.

Kenānah and Ḥedāl, both of Nejdean origin, have followed the same track, till among the Arab inhabitants of 'Omān, one fourth or thereabouts appear to be of non-Ḳaḥṭānee descent ; a conjecture further warranted by a slight difference in dialect and in feature, with an occasional variety in religious tenets, enough in short to establish a distinction for which oral tradition alone might else seem an insufficient guarantee. Negro and Abyssinian blood predominates to the south-east.

On the north-western flank of Rās Mesandum, from the village of Ajmān to Sha'am, exists a singular colony of unmixed Nejdean descent, and of comparatively recent establishment, the Djowāsimah. Like the inhabitants of Barr-Fāris they trace their ancestral stem to Meṭeyr; their settlement seems to have taken place within the last two hundred years. The Djowāsimah are Wahhabees of the Wahhabees, and consequently bitter enemies of all around them; innate fierceness of character heightened by fanaticism, and the protection ensured them partly by the inaccessible ramparts of their craggy nest, and partly by Nejdean alliance and patronage, enables them to maintain their ground against all assailants by land or sea.

With this local exception, and a few others of less importance to be noticed in the course of our narrative, the tenets of Ebn-'Abd-el-Wahhāb, and even of Mahomet himself, meet with slender countenance in 'Omān, where, even more than in Ḥasa, religious belief, blended with the civil and moral existence of the people, has a very ambiguous and multiform stamp; the natural result of new creeds half adopted and engrafted on old ones but half laid aside. Something analogous may be observed in other nations; and few indeed, if any, are they who have not more or less sewn a new piece on an old garment. But nowhere is the patchwork more evident than in the eastern angle of Arabia, from Aboo-Ḍebee to Rās-el-Ḥadd, and even farther down to Ḥaḍramaut itself.

The old religion of 'Omān was Sabæan, and apparently of the fashion once predominant not only in Chaldæa but in Persia also, before that the dualistic theory had corrupted the simplicity of the older system. I need hardly remark that this solar and astral worship, sometimes symbolized on earth by fire, and excluding all art-made forms, was very different from the

Assyrian *cultus*, or from the curious and complicated dreamery of the Mendæan Sabba', or "Christians of St. John;" though many European authors, in common with the Arab historian Shems-ed-Deen-ed-Dimishkee, apply indifferently the term "Sabæan" to all these, and to others besides. The Sabæism of which I have here to speak was older in origin and simpler in form.

Of these Sabæans, as they existed in part of Yemen, in 'Omân, and in some other portions of Arabia, if, indeed, they did not claim almost the entire Peninsula in its first antiquity, Arab writers give us the following, but scanty, information. That they worshipped the seven planets, and pre-eminently the sun; that they observed a fast of thirty days, set apart in the early spring, before the vernal equinox; that their chief annual feast coincided with the entrance of the sun in the sign of Aries (a fact which supposes a solar, not a lunar, computation of the months); that they had a special veneration for the two great pyramids of Egypt, believed by them to be the sepulchres of Seth and Idrees; that their stated prayers recurred seven times a day (though some authors say five—a divergence of statement which may admit of easy explanation), and that during their devotions they turned their faces to the north; lastly, that they possessed a book, or code of laws, ascribed to Seth himself (in what language, unhappily, is not said), and believed to contain the dogmas and institutions of that primæval patriarch. Other points of less importance, and it may be less authenticity, are added by Muslim authors; for instance, that the Sabæans venerated the Meccan Ca'abah, and that they even had an anticipatory belief in Mahomet: readers familiar with the dreams of those who would fain discover a proleptic Christianity in the sculptures of Yucatan and the hieroglyphics of Luxor, may easily imagine how such ideas might find their way into a Mahometan mind, regarding those of a different and a more ancient religion. "He that is giddy thinks the world turns round" has a very wide application.

Two points, negative indeed, but of great importance, seem to have distinguished the ancient form of Sabæism: one, the absence of image-idols and idolatry; the other, the equal absence of any hierarchy or priestly caste. Presidence in worship was, it seems, the privilege merely of greater age or of family headship, and involved no special and inherent distinction between the functionary and those around him. Fire-worship, at least in the fashion now practised by the Parsees of India or elsewhere, with a regular priesthood and sacred rites, appears to be a comparatively recent invention or introduction; our records of the primitive Sabæans do not allude to the existence of any such practices among them.

Lastly, Arab tradition unanimously assigns to the Sabæans the east of the Peninsula for their principal abode and stronghold, at a time when the West, and in some degree the Centre also, had adopted a more complicated and idolatrous, or semi-idolatrous worship. Subsequently the complete and lasting conquest achieved by Islam in Yemen, with the latter condition of that province, must have extirpated thence every trace of Sabæism, at least in its older phase. How far 'Omān underwent or eluded the same process, and how much it has preserved of its archaic customs, the following recital may help to elucidate.

During the lifetime of Mahomet 'Omān acquiesced in the new religion of the Prophet, though Arab historians while recording the fact say next to nothing about the means by which it was effected, or the colouring which it took. Separated as that portion of Arabia is from the rest of the continent by the intervening desert, and consequently of difficult access except by sea, a path little followed by the earlier warriors of Islam, the inhabitants of 'Omān would better than their brethren elsewhere escape the annoyances of military molestation and of a too accurate inquest into their orthodoxy, by a timely submission to "the powers that be," and tribute paid when asked for; a compromise advantageous for either party. Events which are recorded under the reign of 'Omar, imply that during the life of that Caliph the Mahometan religion continued to prevail, however superficially, in 'Omān. Soon after broke out the great strife between 'Othmān and 'Alee, and the entire Peninsula, with whatever stranger lands had by this time been fused into the Mahometan empire, separated into two factions of mortal hostility, thus beginning a long and bloody strife, to which twelve centuries have not wholly put an end. Eastern Arabia sided with 'Alee; the West was mostly for 'Othmān. Meanwhile the people of 'Omān, quiet in their desert-bounded nook, troubled neither their heads nor their hands about the matter, and sent not a single combatant to swell the ranks of this or that party. Hereon 'Othmān and 'Alee each despatched messengers to the chiefs of Djebel-Akhdar, and the Bāṭinah, requesting to know on which side they meant to declare themselves, and which of the contending factions might hope for the support of their numerous troops. Here I must, in parenthesis, remind my readers that I am not pretending to give a history of critical exactness, namely, one founded on authentic records and the certain testimony of documents; I simply relate what exists in local tradition by word of mouth and in writings of comparatively late compilation; telling the tale as I had it from the inhabitants of the country, and consequently with no higher claim on circumstantial belief than my narrators themselves. Were I indeed asked my own private opinion, it would be that the main outline of facts is probably correct, whatever ornamental superstructure Arab imagination may have added to the original and narrower ground-plan. Why we may, without wronging our own discernment, attribute a somewhat higher value to local and popular tradition here than elsewhere, I have already stated in a corresponding remark prefixed to the history of the Wahhabee dynasty.

To proceed, the respective messengers of the rival caliphs, who had come together on their long journey in peaceful fellowship, with a courtesy worthy of Astolpho and Bradamante themselves, were presented at the same time before the great national congress at Bahilah, the ancient capital of the land. There they delivered their summons, and received from the nobles of 'Omān the most sensible of all answers, namely, a curse on both the factions with their leaders inclusively, and a declaration that 'Omān had nothing to do either with them or their quarrels.

Such a reply, however just and expedient, could hardly meet with the merited applause from 'Alee and 'Othmān. The latter, however, and with him his lieutenants and successors in the cause, Ma'owiah, and his kin, was too far separated from 'Omān by distance of space and by other more pressing occupations, to be able to take much practical notice of the affront. But 'Alee, whose centre of strength and military action lay much nearer to the backsliding province, found leisure for an expedition to its frontiers, and if he did not succeed in enforcing by the sword full obedience to his right, divine or prophetic, he at least inflicted evils enough to acquire for himself a double dose of hatred not yet forgotten in 'Omān, where the name of 'Alee has the preference of detestation above that of his competitor up to the present day.

However, the victories of Benoo-Ommeyyah, and the establishment of a Damascene caliphate far off from these lands of the extreme East, freed the Ya'aribah and their dependants from 'Alee and his molestations. A period of great silence follows in the annals of the country. It has been said, and with some degree of truth, that nations, like families, are then the happiest when fewest events break the even current of their history. Should this general rule hold good for 'Omān, we must say that hardly any part of the world from lat. 1° to lat. 360°, has enjoyed a longer period of happiness. For eight centuries neither war nor revolution, neither invasion repelled nor aggression attempted, gilds or stains the pages of 'Omān, and the land had rest, not forty but twenty times forty years. Renouncing all further intercourse with the troublous Mahometan world, abolishing alike the pilgrimage of Mecca and the law of the Coran, they remained apart, at liberty to follow what form of government and of religion pleased them best without disturbance from foreign intervention or compulsory creeds.

One event alone, a memorable epoch in the history of Islam, one storm that lashed all around them into fury, rippled the still surface of 'Omān and diversified its annals. The inhabitants of Djebel-Akhdar and the Bāṭinah were not wholly estranged from the neighbouring regions of Ḥasa, and the outbreak of the Baṭineeyah or secret sects so widely diffused through the latter province, had its origin mainly in 'Omān, a land long before schooled by the teaching of the Ḳaṭaree and his fellows. Hence when the Carmathian movement convulsed Arabia, 'Omān was not wholly exempt from the vicissitudes which deluged the Peninsula with blood, and her mountains supplied a large contingent to the troops of the Djenābee and Aboo-Ṭāhir. When the Carmathians were in their turn subdued, 'Omān had all to fear from the vengeance of the victorious party, a vengeance that they only escaped through the strength of their territorial position. An expedition was directed against them by one of the Abbaside caliphs (which, I could not learn), and laid waste the villages of Ḳaṭar and the province of Sharjah up to Djebel-'Oḳdah, beyond which the invaders were unable to penetrate.

These new hostilities on the part of Islam suggested to the sectarian 'Omânees the expediency of new measures, and above all of a distinctive badge which might serve as a rallying signal in war and danger. To this end, like the kindred tribe of the Druses in the far-off West, the men of 'Omân assumed the white turban for their especial token, and from it acquired the name of "Abâḍeeyah" or "Biaḍeeyah," that is, "White Boys," to give the word a corresponding Irish translation, in contradistinction to the green of the Faṭimites and the black of the Abbasides. The title of Biaḍeeyah, first peculiar to the Carmathians alone, soon became common to the entire population of 'Omân, and has remained theirs up to the present day. Maḳreezee, it is true, would assign to the name another origin, and supposes it a corruption of "Beydaneeyah," or followers of Beydan, a Persian heretic of the third century after the Hejirah. But to waive other considerations, such as the total absence of all historical evidence that this same Beydan ever visited Arabia, or attained even in his own native Persia sufficient celebrity to give his name to an entire sect, the laws of Arab derivation cannot permit our adopting the explanation given by the learned Tâj-ed-Deen Maḳreezee. The "dal" or "d" of "Beydan" has nothing in common but dissimilarity with the "dad" or "ḍ" of "Biaḍeeyah," nor would the final "n" of "Beydan" or "Beydaneeyah' have been so easily elided. Arab attempts at etymological research in their own language are generally no less unfortunate than those of the Latin writers in theirs, or even more so; for never was ancient Europe so uncritical as the East in all times, the present included.

With the relics of Sabæan practice, and a groundwork of Carmathian free-thinking, the Biaḍeeyah, like the Druses, Ismaileeyah, Ansęyreeyah, and other similar sects, mix certain modifications derived from Mahometan law, and sufficient for a disguise when necessary, or at least for a species of apology in presence of Muslims. Their "Mezârs," or buildings set apart for religious veneration, supply the deficiency of "Mesjids," or regular mosques, but they very rarely assemble for any stated form of worship; their prayers are muttered in a low and inaudible voice, accompanied by inflexions and prostrations different from those employed in Mahometan devotion. Many on these occasions turn to the north, others in other directions, perfectly regardless of Ḳiblah or Ca'abah. Whether the name of "Yāḥ" or "Yūḥee" (for I heard now one occur and now the other), which is by them, and by them alone, it would seem, applied to the polar star, has any connection with credence or worship, I am unable to say. Nor could I discover the etymology or special signification of the word; it is used throughout 'Omān, and on all the coasts of the Persian Gulf frequented by 'Omānee sailors. Among Arabs elsewhere the Pole-star enjoys the less mystical title of "Djedee," "the Goat," or of "Mismār," "the Nail," from its "true fixed and resting quality," of which "there is no fellow in the firmament." Venus, or "Zahra'," to give her the customary Arab name, here becomes "Farḳad," a term elsewhere applied to Arcturus in Boötes. "Semāk" is sometimes the name of the bright star in Capella, sometimes of Arcturus; "Semākān," its dual form, often belongs to Gemini, or to two stars of the first magnitude in Cygnus. These latter names are anything but constant; Arabs seem to care as little about precision in their astronomical nomenclature as in everything else.

The annual fast of the Biaḍeeyah lasts a month; it is of even greater strictness than the Mahometan; abstinence is enjoined till the appearance of the stars (in this the Biaḍeeyah resemble the Jews), and only one meal is taken in the twenty-four hours. Its period is regulated, so said my informants, by the will of the sovereign, here the supreme religious authority, whence perhaps his customary European misnomer of Imān. Three towns alone in the whole kingdom have right to the public celebration of official prayers; they are the three capitals, Ṣoḥār, Nezwah, and Bahilah; Mascat, whose importance is of comparatively recent date, does not stand on the list.

Polygamy, though not unfrequent, wears a different form from that assumed in Mahometan countries; one alone of the fair sex being admitted to the legal title and honours of spouse;

the rest, many or few, are only concubines. The laws of inheritance are also different from those laid down in the Coran; the share of the female being here equal to that of the male, not one half only. In the general bearings of society, too, women are much more on a footing of equality with their masculine fellow-species in 'Omān than elsewhere, nor are their faces subjected to the Islamitic veil. This is a real advantage, since the feminine beauty of 'Oman is unrivalled in Arabia, perhaps in Asia; at least I have never seen among other races of the East such graceful forms, or such lovely and regular features. Certainly the fervent adorers of large dark eyes, arched eyebrows, flowing hair, classic outline, slender waists, and stately demeanour, may find here a greater number of suitable idols for their devotion, than in Nejed, in Syria, in Egypt, or, I verily believe, in Persia either. The men too, though slender and dusky complexioned, are generally handsome, their look is intelligent, and their gait sprightly. I should add that wine is freely and avowedly drunk, especially towards the interior; the vineyards that produce it are cultivated in Djebel-Akhdar.

Had I been at the time acquainted with some notices of Mahometan writers already alluded to, but with which I became conversant only after my return, I should have been less surprised than I was at the frequent enquiries made of me in 'Omān regarding the Pyramids of Egypt, a memory still prevalent here, and derived from old Sabæan times. And had I been able to make a longer stay, and to follow up the intimacy which in a passing way I contracted here and there with the men of the country, I might have perhaps learned something worth knowing about the books of Seth, or other documents of religious and legal import. But events hurried on the course of my way, and circumscribed my means of information; while the caution inherent to all dissidents from the Mahometan religion in this part of the East, renders the inhabitants of 'Omān very unwilling to let a stranger into much of their real belief and practices; still less would they hasten to put into his hands written evidence of a code and creed at variance with the Coran. This feeling is less prominent among Bedouins of the wilds, or those whom their central and inland position guards against too frequent and inquisitive visits; but it is fully developed here where the sea-coast and constant commerce brings to 'Omān daily and hourly crews of Sonnees and Shiya'ees, of Wahhabees and natives of the Yemen and of Mecca. Owing to this, a semblance of Mahometan ways and speaking is often assumed; and the Biaḍeeyah, a compound of Sabæans, Bāṭineeyah, and Carmathians, inheritors of Moḳannaa' and Aboo-Ṭahir, will at times pass themselves off on a stranger for tolerably orthodox Mahometans. But closer acquaintance has marked them out for infidels, and the worst of infidels in the opinion of all their neighbours, Wahhabee, Sonnee, and even Shiya'ee; and up to Baṣrah no Mahometan speaks of a Biaḍee or 'Omānee otherwise than as of a "Khārijee" or "one without the pale," the opprobrious title of utter defection from the faith and the Prophet of Islam.

Niebuhr, who when coasting 'Omān visited Mascat only, but whose sound and honest narrative contains many interesting and accurate hearsay details regarding this kingdom, which was then at a moment of great depression, has been led into a curious mistake regarding the customs and character of the Biaḍeeyah. Having, it would seem from his narrative, formed acquaintance with some Nejdeans resident at the port of Mascat—for this port always musters a good number of merchants and small traders come from the inland part of Ebn-Sa'ood's dominions, or from the Mahometan coast provinces—he fell into the error, not unnatural in so short a stay, of attributing the severity of Wahhabee manners, their abstinence from tobacco, their regular attendance at prayer, their simplicity of apparel, in a word all the distinctive features of their sect, to the native population of the land, and pronounces the Biaḍeeyah not only orthodox Muslims, but almost fervent ascetics. Now the truth is, that as regards tobacco, no people perhaps in the world, the Turks of Stamboul not excepted, make a more frantic consumption of that article than do the good folks of 'Omān; and well they may, since tobacco is a staple produce of their country, both for use and exportation, besides being remarkably good and cheap. The market-places of Mascat and of the other towns are full of tobacco-shops, and the mouths full of pipes. Then for prayers: Mascat possesses indeed three or four mosques set apart for Mahometan worship, and to which the Muslim colony resorts: there prayers are no doubt regularly performed and attended, especially by Nejdeans.

But it would be very hard to find a single Biaḍee in those or in any other mosques, and the Biaḍeeyah are the real men of Mascat, not the foreigners of five prayers a day. Lastly, in simplicity of dress, and aversion to ornamental display, I fear that 'Omânees have no better claim to Niebuhr's commendation than the inhabitants of Vienna or of Paris; my reader shall judge for himself a few pages further on.

I should add that Niebuhr and his companions had, it appears from his account, assumed Turkish costume, and announced themselves as come from Constantinople. This conduct would suffice to ensure a traveller the finding Mahometanism everywhere, even among those most averse from it in reality. At the present day a Turk, or one known for an agent of the Turkish government, will often meet with a seeming satisfactory profession of Islam in districts where none but Druses, Ismaileeyah, and their like, really inhabit, nay, even among the Christian populations of the interior. This was still more the case in the middle of the last century, the epoch of Niebuhr's voyage, when the Turkish name exerted a greater influence than it does now. Dissimulation is the inevitable consequence of bigotry in government, and it remains habitually engrafted in the subject races, even when its original and special causes have passed away. But to return to Niebuhr: he must at Mascat have fallen in with a genuine Nejdean colony, perhaps of the Wahhabee sect, which was then in its first rise; these very Nejdeans, whom in his passing visit, the great German traveller took for a sample of a people with whom they have nothing in common but local residence and mutual hatred. To say this is no disparagement of Niebuhr; circumstances did not permit him to detect a very plausible error, into which many others besides himself have fallen.

A confidential and intimate connection, a wide-spread ramification of intercourse, is kept up between the Bâṭineeyah (my readers are already acquainted with the term) of Ḥasa and 'Omân; the former are indeed, properly speaking, an offshoot of the latter. The tendencies of this underhand organization and of those who maintain it, their bitter hatred and resolute opposition to Islam, especially in its Wahhabee form, may in part be gathered from what we have already stated.

In valour and tenacity of purpose the people of 'Omān are inferior to none of the Arab race; the inhabitants of Djebel-Akhdar and Djailān are especially famed for military courage. But commerce and agriculture afford them too solid attractions to permit their energy turning habitually, like that of the Nejdeans, to war and plunder. In disposition they are decidedly, so far as my experience goes, the best-tempered, the most hospitable, in a word the most amiable of all the Arab race. Toleration to a degree not often attained even in Europe, exists here for all races, religions, and customs; Jews, Christians, Mahometans, Hindoos, all may freely worship God after their own several fashions, dress as they think best, marry and inherit without restriction, bury or burn their dead as fancy takes them; no one asks a question, no one molests, no one hinders. And if Wahhabees are at times excepted from this comprehensive forbearance, looked on with real and effective dislike, thwarted in their doings, and even insulted and killed when occasion permits, they must ascribe such treatment to their own encroaching spirit, and insolent and domineering ways. They are avowed enemies of the state, and if treated accordingly have no right to complain.

'Omān is pre-eminently a land of amusement, of diversion, of dance and song, of show and good-living. All this has, however, its darker side in a laxity of morals, to which the beauty of the women and the good humour of the men certainly contribute. Severity on what regards maiden virtue or marriage vow is not a distinctive feature of 'Omān. Another stain is thrown on the land by the prevalence, real or pretended, of the black art, and a superstitious belief in sorcery, mere juggling we may suppose, but openly avowed and continually practised. This is a bad symptom. To such practices 'Omān owes the ill-sounding name of "Belād-es-Soḥārah," or "the land of Enchanters," a title very commonly given it by foreigners; though some explain it by the frequency of a milder enchantment employed by the Circes of the country against the Ulysses, though never so steady and so wise, who visit their shores. Be that as it may, many a Nejdean is deterred from adventuring in 'Omān by fear least the eyes of some young woman, or the witch-rod of some old one, should transform him into a loving sheep or a sheepish lover. Tales of men thus "translated" by the process which, if Falstaff say true, "in some respects make a beast a man; in some other a man a beast," besides appalling narratives of invisible sorcerers, of magic transmutations, and of philtres surpassing all in the "Arabian Nights" or "Grimm's Stories," are rife throughout these regions; and Ovid, were he alive, might add twelve more good-sized books to his bulky "Metamorphoses," from the chronicles of 'Omān alone.

But powers even more terrible than those which clothe a man in sheep's wool, or make him an ass in body as well as in mind, are ascribed not only to the elderly ladies of 'Omān, but to male conjurors and magicians of the most dangerous caste. Many were the stories regarding such which I heard recited in the undertone of fearful conviction; but my readers might, I fear, consider them better adapted to a place in Croker's "Fairy Legends" than in a serious voyage of the nineteenth century. These tales are, however, strongly illustrative of the belief and tendencies of the habits and manners of the nations which give them "a local habitation and a name." I will therefore here insert by way of episode a narrative strange enough both in itself and the circumstances which accompanied it, and which seem to give it a kind of authenticity not always to be obtained in similar matters. My informants had been, or professed to have been, themselves present at the legal examination of which mention will be made in the course of the tale itself.

The scene was fixed by the narrators at about fourteen years back, during the reign of the Sultan Sa'eed, monarch of 'Omān, and remarkable for his great success in arms and skill in government. At that date a young merchant, native of the town of Mascat, and recently married to a beauty in the same city, embarked on commercial business in a ship bound for the coast of Zanjibar. After a prosperous navigation he arrived at the market for his traffic, and there remained as wont is three or four months, selling his wares, and laying in a new and appropriate cargo for his return.

One evening, while resident in a village situated on the main coast of Africa opposite the island of Zanjibar, he was sitting on the roof of his lodgings, and by his side was also seated an acquaintance, picked up in the country, an 'Omānee like himself, but a native of Bahilah, and for some time past resident in the Sowâḥil, as the Arabs denominate this part of the African shore. Chance had thrown them together, and community of race in a foreign land had naturally induced a certain degree of intimacy. The sun had just set, and the friends side by side on the terrace were smoking their pipes in placid enjoyment, when the merchant remarked a strange and serious expression come over his companion's face, and enquired the cause. "Did you see what I am at the moment seeing," answered the wizard, for such he was, "you would look even graver than I do." Of course this reply led to further enquiry, on which the seer of Bahilah, after a suitable show of reluctance to communicate disagreeable news, at last said, "I have just beheld such a one," naming a young debauchee of Mascat, "enter your house at this very hour, and precisely when there is no one at home but your wife, who has greeted his visit with a hearty welcome."

It was now the turn of the married man to look grave indeed. With not more vehemence did Othello demand of Iago, his hand at his throat, that "ocular proof" which was to assure him his own dishonour, than the merchant exacted of the wizard a minute relation of all that should pass between his guilty wife and her paramour. The magician paused awhile, then, gazing into distance, said "They are now seated hand in hand in loving talk;" and lastly proceeded to describe a scene such as Dante wisely leaves to the imagination of his readers, when in the person of Francesca of Rimini he recounts the progress of unlawful love. "'Tis an old tale and often told."

The indignation of the injured husband rose to its highest pitch. "Are there no means to forestall, or at least avenge, the crime?" he exclaimed. To the latter clause of the question the seer replied that he was indeed possessed of the most effectual means for that end, and would willingly exert them. "Do so then," eagerly rejoined the merchant. "Not so fast," answered the magician; "we must first preclude the possibility of ill-consequences to ourselves." Here he then directed the husband to draw up on the spot a document, empowering his friend, the magician of Bahilah, to take vengeance on the adulterous woman and on her paramour. The paper was soon written, dated, signed, and sealed. "Now call up the entire family to whom this house belongs, and let them all sign and seal as authentic witnesses, after which I myself will countersign." The wizard's orders were fulfilled; by this it was night, and the whole party sat round in silence on the roof under the starry southern hemisphere; the writ of death lay in the midst. "Now give me your dagger," said the man of Bahilah to him of Mascat. The latter drew from his belt the crooked silver-handled dirk worn by every freeman of 'Omānee descent, and handed it to his friend. He took it, turned to the north, and after a few muttered words twice stabbed the air. "Now go and sleep in peace; your vengeance is complete, and the criminals are both dead," said he to the gazing husband.

Not long after our merchant quitted Zanzibar, and returned to Mascat. On his first landing he was told that his only brother had been cast into prison, and was still there, on suspicion of murder. "Your wife," so said the townsman, "and with her such and such a one" (naming the very individual already denounced by the seer at Zanjibar), "were found one morning dead within a chamber of your house; a dagger had pierced them twice through and through. No trace could be obtained of the murderer or of his weapon; but as your brother seemed the person most likely to have done the deed, he was arrested and questioned before the judges. Nothing was discovered that showed him any way guilty; however, Government willed his remaining in custody till your arrival, that a fresh examination of the matter might then take place."

The merchant repaired without delay to the civic authorities, and told them his tale. The case seemed too strange not to be well sifted; it was referred from tribunal to tribunal, till the Sultan Sa'eed declared that he reserved its cognizance and judgment to himself in person.

The monarch accordingly caused the merchant and his brother to be brought to Nezwah, his customary residence, and there detained them under good treatment, but without permission to quit the town. Next he sent his orders to Zanjibar, that all who had signed the document or been any way witnesses of the scene on the housetop, should be sent over to 'Omān without delay. In due time all parties were assembled at Nezwah—the African householder, his family, his neighbours, and the magician. The king then publicly held a court of justice in the open air;

the document was produced; all present recognised and authenticated their respective signatures, and cross-examination only confirmed the correctness of the merchant's statement. Whereon Sultan Sa'eed declared himself incompetent to decide guilt or to award punishment in such a case, and dismissed alike the men of Mascat and of Zanjibar, after granting them a handsome recompense for loss of time, and trouble incurred. But he strongly advised the magician to be henceforth more discreet in the exercise of his preternatural powers, a recommendation shortly after extended by royal proclamation to all the wizards and conjurors of 'Omān. And if Sa'eed did no more, popular rumour assigns a very special reason for his forbearance; namely, that his own wife, the mother of the present monarch, was the very Hecate of Arab witches, and worthy to preside at any weird meeting of black cats, broomsticks, he-goats, and magic cauldrons.

Enough of 'Omānee sorcerers and their doings. But the source whence this extraordinary proficiency in the occult sciences has been derived deserves mention, not so much from any intrinsic importance in the subject itself as on account of its coincidence with a number of parallel circumstances, almost enough to warrant a generalization. That source is the slave population, hither imported from Africa near and far. I have already made some mention of the slave-trade carried on between the eastern coasts of Africa and the ports of 'Omān. Nor need I here enter into the details of the traffic itself, and of the means adopted to keep it up, nor describe an 'Omān slave-ship and her cargo; though in truth (this I say for the consolation of my anti-slavery readers—that is, I trust, of all) slavery, from the first to the last, after the manner in which it is practised here, from time immemorial, has little but the name in common with the system hell-branded by those atrocities of the Western hemisphere, the end of which, under God's blessing, appears now imminent. My present topic is the black population as it exists when fairly settled in 'Omān, and the influence it exerts on this part of Arabia, an influence hardly to be understood by our own unamalgamating Anglo-Saxons, but deeply felt and widely extended among the more impressible Kaḥṭānee population. I say Kaḥṭānee, not Arab, in contradistinction to the Northern and Central races, both of which, but especially the former, have a large admixture of that iron fibre which renders the European, and above all the Saxon, machine (to borrow Hamlet's phrase) so remarkably independent of impressions from without. Hence among the Arabs of Shomer, and even of Nejed, negroes, whatever their number, hardly weigh for more in the scale of national habits and feelings than they would in Norfolk or in Yorkshire. But in 'Omān the case is very different.

Should we say that every year a thousand negroes, men, women, and children, are imported into 'Omān, we should be considerably below the cipher commonly given in the country itself. Now of all the Nigritians thus "forced from home and all its pleasures,"—or perhaps we might instead say, taken from an existence befitting only the boars and tigers of a jungle, to lead henceforth a life somewhat more resembling that of reasonable bipeds—about half, some say two-thirds, remain for the rest of their days fixed within the limits of 'Omān and the adjacent provinces. Most of these, indeed all who do not die in early youth (an event comparatively rare in so healthy a climate and with masters more like to kill by over-kindness than the reverse), sooner or later obtain their liberty, and thus a new element is added to and freely mixed up with the original or white population. But although a negro while living to execute his master's orders and under his direction, may often display many valuable qualities, and attain a certain degree of importance, the same negro, when free and his own lord and master, seldom adapts himself to any position in society except the lowest and the least intellectual. Hence the emancipated blacks remain mostly servants, water-carriers, gardeners, ploughmen, common sailors, divers, and the like; and although their number is immense, reaching a good fourth of the entire population, they confer but little or nothing to the cause of social culture and advance. In two points alone they maintain a decided superiority, but a superiority of evil bearing; the one point is superstition, the other immorality. Fetichists on their own land, negroes remain so no less on the Arab soil; and with fetichism they bring all its Libyan accompaniments of jugglery, magic spells, poisoning and the like, till these discreditable practices have passed to a certain extent into the white society, and the dusky tutors are equalled or even outdone by their fair-skinned disciples. In a word, the great prevalence of local and degrading superstitions, the dangerous tampering with malignant cosmical influences, be they what they may—the fetichism of trees, animals, reptiles, and heaven knows what—in brief, devilry of every kind and shape, is by the popular voice of 'Omān (nor, it would seem, unreasonably) ascribed in the main to the influx and contagion of the negro population. Yet the allusions of some old Mahometan writers might lead us to imagine that somewhat of this perversion is really the indigenous growth of the Eastern Arab Peninsula, and that it existed prior to and independent of African importation, though certainly increased and deepened by the latter.

The second point, namely, immorality, will not surprise any-one who considers the tendency of a slave population to en-courage the grossest vices among their masters themselves, and the strong sensual passions of the African race. The low moral standard hitherto notorious in the Southern States of the Ame-rican Union is an example of this fact within easy reach of European observation, and may save me from entering further into the details of a very disagreeable subject.

Much remains to say regarding the physical features of the land itself and its productions, a wide topic and full of inter-esting variety; this will be sufficiently illustrated in the course of our narrative. But before resuming the course of its long-interrupted thread, I must draw yet a little more on the stock of my reader's patience, while I set before him a compendious sketch of the later political history and condition of this king-dom: to omit this would render much that follows neither intelligible nor profitable. Mere travelling, whether on the reality of horses and camels, or in the easier conveyance of a book by the fireside, avails very little where the history and government of the land traversed is unknown. So sailors seeing all the world see nothing, and, to borrow the simile of an in-genious writer, resemble men gazing on the wrong side of an embroidery—all stitches, blotches, and confusion of tints, with-out meaning or idea.

After a long period of nigh eight hundred years, during which some movements among the Bedouin tribes connected with

'Omān, a few unimportant incidents of individual rather than of a national character, and a certain complicity already recorded with the Carmathian outbreak of Ḥaṣa, are all that history records of 'Omān; Portuguese enterprise, the exploits of Albuquerque, the conquest of Ormuz, and subsequently of Mascat, first bring this kingdom on the scene of general history. During the preceding interval it does not appear that 'Omān had acquired any of those foreign possessions which now give it half or more than half its importance; Persia still kept her coast and gulf, the Carmathian rule of Ḳaṭeef yet reached Rās Mesandum; while Africa, Zanjibar, and Socotra in the sixteenth century of our era, knew 'Omānees only as simple traders, perhaps slave-dealers. Within, the government appears to have retained its original form, that of an aggregate confederation rather than an absolute monarchy, in which the Ya'aribah then held the first place and the title of royalty, much as the family of Sa'eed do now.

But by the Portuguese invasion all this was changed. It was the signal for wide-extended conquests and wars by sea and by land, in which Portugal, Holland, and Persia all took part, and each in turn obtained transitory advantages, while none of the three reaped the abiding profit. 'Omān, with its islands and coasts, was at first the passive scene of foreign conflict, till roused by the excess of her own ruin she became also a combatant, discovered her own strength, and made of her very losses a great and lasting gain.

In the sixteenth and seventeenth centuries she seemed utterly lost. The Portuguese held Mascat, with other important points on the coast. Ormuz too was theirs, with her sister islands; and their fleet, master of the sea, destroyed the commerce and cut off the communications of Eastern Arabia. Next the Dutch appeared, enemies indeed to the Portuguese, but no less enemies to the native powers, and added a new rival, while they thwarted the old. Lastly, the Persians, profiting by intra-European jealousy, regained their footing in Ormuz, and thence descended on 'Omān, whose inhabitants they regarded as subjects, and tyrannized over as foreigners.

The principal events of this protracted struggle are well known. The Portuguese, after about a century and a half of disputed possession, were at last driven utterly and for ever from the shores of 'Omān and the Persian Gulf; the Dutch won forts, stations, and islands, then lost them all; while the valour and skill of Sa'eed, governor of Ṣoḥār, chased the Persians from the mainland, and placed the kingly crown on his own head. All this has been recorded by different historians of the East, and embodied in chronicles and narratives. One of the clearest and best, though somewhat over-concise, is that of Niebuhr; the French writers whom I have been able to consult are too inexact, and the Portuguese too ignorant, for unqualified commendation.

Aḥmed-ebn-Sa'eed was proclaimed Sultan of 'Omān in 1759, and held the throne till about 1780. His reign, after a few preliminary contests with the competitors of his inauguration, contests said to have been attended by little bloodshed, was peaceful and even prosperous. During this period the limits of the kingdom were pushed westward up to Ḥaṣa and Baḥreyn, and the authority of Aḥmed reached Ḍofār on the southern coast. His memory is still popular, though eclipsed by that of his grandson, *the* Sultan Sa'eed, as he is often emphatically called.

Aḥmed on dying left his crown to his son, whose name I have not learnt. Nor was his sovereignty marked by any events of note; a peaceful and progressive though not a glorious time, if glory be indeed synonymous with conquest. 'Omān was, however, steadily rising in commerce and importance; a period of tranquillity enabled her to develope at leisure her great resources. This Ebn-Sa'eed, to give him the family patronymic, died at a comparatively early age, during the first decade of the present century, and was succeeded by his son Sa'eed, the greatest of the name.

Sa'eed, though young in years when he ascended the throne, was old in counsel. From the first he perceived that the strength of his kingdom lay rather by sea than by land, and accordingly at once commenced the formation of a navy strong enough to assure him the mastery of the Persian Gulf. Before long he had mustered and equipped about thirty frigates, constructed, after European model, in the western seaports of India, and well fitted up with cannon; the red pennon of 'Omān, derived from Yemen, fluttered overhead. With this fleet

Sa'eed took possession of the island and coast of Zanjibar, of the Ṣowâḥil, of Socotra, and ultimately, by a long-continued sea blockade, compelled the Persian government to surrender that important strip of their coast which now belongs to 'Omân, besides the islands of Ormuz, Djishm, Larej, and ultimately Baḥreyn. All these localities Sa'eed visited in person, encouraged and regulated their commerce, opened new communications of traffic, and rendered his kingdom the most wealthy and prosperous, if not in all Asia at least in Arabia.

The Wahhabee empire was now in its first bloom of strength, nor could the report of so great riches accumulated by their less warlike and infidel neighbours but provoke the cupidity of the orthodox Ebn-Sa'oods. Followed 'Abd-Allah's great invasion, and the capture of Mascat, after which 'Omân remained for a few years tributary to Nejed. Somewhat later took place those local skirmishes in the neighbourhood of Râs-el-Ḥaḍḍ and the coast opposite Massora, when the Anglo-Indian troops were brought into collision with the natives of those regions; an event speedily followed by the entire putting down of the pirates who, though not precisely under the orders of Sa'eed, yet not also without some connivance on his part, rendered the navigation of the Persian Gulf difficult and even dangerous to European craft.

The overthrow of the Wahhabees by Ibraheem Basha restored Sa'eed to independence; and during the rest of his reign, which from first to last occupied nearly fifty years, 'Omân recovered all her former prosperity, and even augmented it. She now became an emporium for the commerce of Africa, Persia, and India; while numerous colonies of merchants, especially from the latter country, were encouraged by the liberal policy of Sa'eed to take up their residence in Ṣoḥâr, Barka, Mascat, and the other sea-ports, bringing with them a skill and persevering industry seldom to be found among the Arabs themselves.

While subject to the Wahhabees, 'Omân had yearly paid a considerable sum under title of tribute to the governor of Mecca, an office then held, or rather usurped, by 'Abd-Allah-ebn-Sa'ood. It was natural enough that Sa'eed, when once freed from the Nejdean yoke, thought it superfluous to continue his forced contributions to the maintenance of the sacred city. However, the Shereef of Mecca was of a contrary opinion, and threatened to stir up serious hostilities in case the Sultan of 'Omān should persist in non-payment of this Arab Peter's-pence. Messages were exchanged; till the resources of epistolary diplomacy proving insufficient, Sa'eed, who seems to have been a great lover of movement, and very desirous of seeing the wonders of the world abroad, resolved to pay in person a visit to the Shereef, and thus settle the matter.

With a large and sumptuous train the sultan set out on his sea-voyage to Djiddah, and reached Mecca, where his splendour, so saith the 'Omānee historian, excited universal admiration. The Shereef proved courteous, and all was progressing favourably; nothing now remained but to fix a moderate quittance of the Mecca claims, when Sa'eed begged of the Shereef to do him the favour of conducting him to the sacred house or Ca'abah, that he might himself see the temple, the wealth of which he was henceforth to increase. The Shereef consented, and they entered the sacred precincts together. Sa'eed enquired where the faithful of the different orthodox sects made their prayer, and was duly shown the stations of Shāfi'ees, Ḥanbelees, and the rest. "And where is the station of the Biaḍeeyah?" enquired the prince. A question more easily asked than answered; in fine, the Shereef admitted that there was none. Hereon Sa'eed rejoined that he could not see any reason for contributing to a worship in which he had no share, and forthwith left Mecca; nor was there any more talk of tribute during his reign. We shall see further on how the claim was renewed in the days of his son Thoweynee.

Sa'eed on his deathbed divided his ample possessions between his three sons. To Thoweynee, the eldest, he allotted 'Omān from Barka eastwards, with Djebel-Akhdar and the adjoining provinces, besides the dependencies in the Gulf. Mājid, the second in age, obtained the African possessions, while the younger, Amjed, had for his share the westerly mainland of 'Omān from Barka to Ḳaṭar, with Ṣoḥār for capital. This impolitic measure, attributed to the influence of the queen-mother, and her calculating hatred to her own children, prepared long wars and many disasters, if not total downfall, for the empire of 'Omān.

No great foresight was indeed required to predict the consequences of this triple arrangement, nor were they long in coming. The first dissension broke out between Thoweynee and Mājid; the former claimed tribute and allegiance, the latter refused both. A naval war between the brothers ensued, and lasted two or three years, till English interference, and perhaps the distance of the localities themselves, put an end to it. A yearly tribute was fixed, by the payment of which Mājid purchased absolute and independent sovereignty over Zanjibar and the Ṣowāḥil, for government, trade, and policy.

The next contest, resulting also from the fatal partition made by the old king, was much more pernicious both in itself and in its results. Thoweynee, whom his father's will had rendered lord of two-thirds of the mainland of 'Omān, with its most important centres of government and traffic, master besides of the great sea-ports on either side of the Gulf, with two-thirds of the national commerce at his disposal, was no longer content with a divided rule, and sought to deprive his younger brother Amjed of his share of the inheritance, that he might rule alone, sole and absolute master in 'Omān. But Amjed, though the weaker of the two in material resources, possessed a powerful auxiliary to his cause in the sympathy of almost all the native population from Sharjah to Rās-el-Ḥadd; a sympathy acquired by his amiable conduct, and by his good administration within his own immediate territory. Accordingly, when the dispute between the two brothers ripened into war, Thoweynee found the task before him more difficult than he had anticipated, for the entire Bāṭinah, the largest and most populous province of the kingdom, sided against him with Amjed; Nezwah, Bahilah, and Djebel-Akhdar, followed the example; and Thoweynee's superiority by sea could avail him little against an enemy who held far the greater part of the mainland with its three capitals, and now threatened in his turn to besiege his assailant in Mascat.

Once more English intervention made itself felt; pity that it was in favour of the more unworthy party, namely, Thoweynee. Amjed, who still held the open country, was invited by his elder brother to a conference in Mascat, and there, in spite of solemn engagements and promises, was treacherously detained prisoner; immured in a fortress of the city, he remains a captive to the present day. Thoweynee was now sole sovereign by land and sea; but this perfidy towards his too-confiding brother, joined to his own negligent and dissipated conduct, so irritated his subjects, that they continued in arms even after the loss of their leader Amjed, nor was the sultan able to compel them to subjection. After some ineffectual attempts at putting down the rebellion, Thoweynee, in an evil hour for 'Omān, called for aid on the Wahhabee.

Feyşul cared very little which of the brothers wore the crown, nor had one infidel more claim on his patronage than the other. But Thoweynee's appeal furnished a long-desired pretext for an interference the end of which must be to give the keys of the richest portion of Arabia into the hands of the Nejdean mountaineer. Besides, the revolt in 'Omān itself bore a peculiarly national character. It was a Biaḍee movement, headed by Amjed, himself a thorough-going Biaḍee, and its aim had been less the enthronement of a particular man than of a popular principle, and the confirmation of old Carmathian and anti-Mahometan usages. Hence it could not but be especially odious to Feyşul, whose elevation both within his own kingdom and on its frontiers mainly depended on the depression of the national element. Hence no time was lost in complying with the ill-advised proposal thus made; a large army was without delay collected at Riaḍ, the entire Nejed from Ḳaseem to Ḥasa sent in its levies, volunteers from Shomer joined the force, and the supreme command was given to 'Abd-Allah.

The Wahhabee army advanced by the coast-road of Ḳaṭar till it reached Sharjah, where a congenial ally was already awaiting them. This was Khālid-ebn-Şaḳr, by birth a Nejdean of the Djowāsimah, a clan of which I have before made mention, and settled on the north-western side of Cape Mesandum. Khālid, by dint of long and bloody contests with his own brother and uncle, had become master of the town and of the entire province of Sharjah, which he now ruled in fief from the Sultan of 'Omān. My readers may form an idea of this chief from a fact which signalized the domestic war between Khālid and his relations. While yet a mere youth he had by force turned his uncle out of Sharjah, and occupied the palace in his own name. But in a few weeks the lawful possessor returned with troops sufficient to make good his claim, and Khālid foresaw that he could not stand the chances of a siege. He retired; but first to have anyhow his revenge on his elder kinsman, he set fire to the town and burnt down a full third of it, determined to ruin what he could not keep.

Hating the 'Omānee government and the Biaḍeeyah with the hatred of an orthodox Wahhabee, for such he was in theory, though his unbridled licentiousness and personal vices rendered him a very heathen in the carnal and practical part, Khālid had long since formed the project of detaching his province from the main body of the kingdom, and thus making himself independent not in fact only—for that he had been during the years of anarchy which followed the death of the Sultan Sa'eed—but in title also. For the execution of this design he could reckon with certainty on the support of all his ferocious kinsmen on the Djowāsimah coast, perfect Wahhabee brigands; but they were not enough. The want was now supplied by the arrival of 'Abd-Allah, his natural ally by blood, by character, and religion. The plan of the 'Omān campaign was discussed and settled between this *par nobile fratrum*. 'Abd-Allah entrusted Khālid with the subjugation of the Bāṭinah and Ṣoḥār, while he himself, with the main body of his troops, was to march simultaneously on Djebel-Akhdar, and master the mountain district: all this in the name of Thoweynee, who, like the horse in the fable, seeking an ally had found a tyrant.

A few days later Khālid, accompanied by his own savage soldiery, and reinforced with Nejdean troops, descended on the Bāṭinah, where he put all who opposed him to the sword, burnt the villages, plundered the towns, and massacred everywhere in the name of God to his heart's content. Fājirah, Shināz, Ṣoḥam, and other coast-towns of lesser note, were sacked and ruined; and Khālid still advanced bearing all before him, till near Soweyḳ he gave the native inhabitants, collected in battle array to bar his progress, so terrible a defeat that the entire Bāṭinah lay at his mercy, or rather at the disposal of his rapacious cruelty.

Meanwhile 'Abd-Allah, with a numerous army, had reached Bereymah, four days' march from Sharjah, at the foot of Djebel-'Oḳdah, where rises the first great peak of the mountain chain of Ḍāhirah; its course is from north-west to south-east, parallel with the range of Djebel-Akhdar, but further inland. The heir of Feysul now stood at the entrance of the strongholds of 'Omân, but thought it hardly prudent to adventure his own sacred person amid the mountain defiles: accordingly he remained at Bereymah, while he sent forward a large exploratory force under the command of Zâmil, the same whose later history at 'Oneyzah has been already told, but who was at that time in apparent favour with the Nejdean government.

The expedition, like all others of Wahhabee organization, bore a religious name, that of "Ghazoo," and was of course directed against the enemies of God. A pretty fragment of Nabțee verse, composed on the occasion by some poetic warrior, and in which the orthodoxy of Nejed is everywhere contrasted with the infidelity of 'Omân, was recited before me in Ḥasa; Mahomet himself would not have exhorted the Ṣaḥḥâbah in another key. But the choice of Zâmil-el-'Âțeeyah for field-marshal in 'Abd-Allah's absence, damped the holy flame, and turned the edge of the sword of Islam. This choice was necessitated by the young chieftain's superior military qualities, no less than by his great popularity, not only in Ḳaseem, but even in Nejed proper, and among all not absolutely zelators or fanatics. But Zâmil was at heart alike adverse to Wahhabee dogma and Wahhabee rule, and looked with more sympathy on those he was to conquer than on those who had equipped him to the conquest. Hence he desired nothing more than to bring matters to a peaceable issue, which might prevent a considerable accession of strength to 'Aareḍ, while it secured to 'Omân immunity from plunder and slaughter. Meanwhile his own personal conduct disavowed any bigoted or even religious feeling; his spacious war-tent was from morning to night filled with officers and chiefs of the highest rank, to whom, after military council and discussion, Zâmil openly set the example, not of Coranic lectures and long prayers, but of a gaiety bordering on dissipation, of mirth and laughter, nay sometimes of dance and intoxication. Under a head so inclined, the body naturally took a similar direction. All began to look on the inhabitants of the land through which they advanced, in a friendly, because a congenial manner, and Zâmil had no difficulty in obtaining what he desired, namely, a march unstained by blood, and ending in timely peace. But although 'Abd-Allah felt and understood the stratagem whereby his lieutenant frustrated the policy of Riad, he was unable to counteract or punish it at a time when nine-tenths of the army would have been ready to turn their arms against him in defence of Zāmil, had need required it. However, Zāmil's head was already in the Wahhabee court beheld in anticipation on a spear, and Feyṣul, well informed of whatever took place in 'Omān, only waited a convenient season to wreak his wrath on the whole family of 'Âṭeeyah. These particulars I learnt from my companion Yoosef-ebn-Khamees and others, who had themselves borne arms under Zāmil in the campaign.

With very slight opposition the invaders threaded the valley of 'Obree, and reached Mokhanneth, a large village situated immediately behind the chain of Akhdar, whence the road divides to Nezwah on the left, and to Bahilah on the right. Beyond Mokhanneth lie the passes of Akhdar, difficult of access, especially for invaders, and now occupied by mountaineers resolute in their defence. Zāmil had throughout proceeded in a manner very different from that of Khālid in the Bāṭinah; everywhere on his route he guaranteed to the inhabitants peace and security, on the sole condition of acknowledging the sultanship of Thoweynee; and in pursuance of this system he treated the villagers as friends, while he restrained his own followers from all plunder and outrage. Arrived at Mokhanneth, the 'Omānees, well knowing with whom they had to deal, gave him and his army a perfectly hospitable reception; the chiefs of the Ya'aribah and others of the mountain came forward to meet him. In the congress which followed, the 'Omānee leaders assured Zāmil that they were all willing to submit themselves to Thoweynee on fair conditions, and that there was accordingly no further need of hostile demonstrations on either side; only they protested withal against foreign interference, and gave Zāmil with his officers to understand, that should they venture within the passes of Bahilah, few of them would ever return to tell the tale.

While Mars was thus on the decline, Venus took the ascendant. The large eyes and slender waists, the engaging manners and courteous address of the fair women of 'Omān, did no less, alack the day! to subdue the warlike propensities of the Nejdeans, than the covered menaces of the brave men and their more diplomatic negotiations. Zâmil himself, unless much belied by fame, fell a willing conquest to a patriotic beauty of the land, whose noble *amor patriæ* had placed her above all considerations of secondary virtue; while on many of his most fire-eating warriors a similar charm worked so strongly that the frail noose of Cupid strengthened into the more lasting bonds of Hymen; and more than one gallant captain remained to play the peaceable good-man in the quiet villages of Djebel-Akhdar.

In short, the expedition ended, like the majority of novels, in match-making and settlements, till matters went so far that Zâmil had considerable difficulty in tearing himself away from the Cleopatras of Mokhanneth, and leading back to Bereymah those followers whom persuasion or main force could induce to follow his retrograde movement.

The singular manœuvre of pardonable seduction above related, had been organized by order of Thoweynee, who was by this time fully awake to the danger which his inconsiderate ambition had brought on himself and on his kingdom, and strove to avert it, or at least diminish, ere it should be too late. When negotiation had, in the manner just described, rendered abortive the main attack directed against the heart of his kingdom, he hastened to put a stop to the growing ravages of Khâlid in the Bâṭinah. But Khâlid and his troops were animated by a spirit very different from that of Zâmil and his men; plunder and bloodshed were their aim, not pacification and allegiance, nor had Thoweynee at his disposal military force sufficient to oppose to the movements of the invaders whom he had himself invited. The only resource left was to procure the intervention of 'Abd-Allah. Thoweynee calculated, nor was his calculation wrong, that gold might finish with the Wahhabee prince what beauty and fair words had begun with his lieutenant; so taking with him a suitable quantity of the "universal solvent," he advanced in person to Bereymah, where 'Abd-Allah had remained in head-quarters.

By liberal presents down in hand, and still more liberal offers for the future, Thoweynee convinced the heir of Nejed that 'Omân had now satisfactorily returned to the allegiance of her lawful sovereign, and that war and violence were no longer necessary. On this ground he demanded the immediate recall of Khâlid. The son of "Ṣakar," or "Vulture" (an appropriate name), abandoned his half-devoured prey, and came, but most unwillingly, to Bereymah, highly indignant at the check thus put on his success. But 'Abd-Allah's orders were positive, and, moreover, an argument of the same nature which had already prevailed on the Prince of Riaḍ, helped to convince his Djowāsimah ally of the expediency of peace. Meanwhile the inhabitants of 'Omān, from one end of the kingdom to the other, had forgotten their civil quarrels, and were now rapidly uniting into a formidable army of defence; and 'Abd-Allah, however ferocious and fanatical, had yet enough of his father's prudence in him to recoil before a desperate struggle so far from his own territory. Peace was accordingly concluded, on condition that the Wahhabee army should be withdrawn from the land, that Khālid should recall his troops from the Bāṭinah, and content himself with the provinces of Sharjah, Ḳalhaṭ, and the mountains of the Cape, under payment of an annual tribute to Thoweynee, now undisputed sovereign over the whole of his father's dominions in Arabia. On his side the 'Omānee monarch promised to forward a yearly present to Riaḍ, under title of contribution to the Shereef of Mecca; to permit the establishment of a permanent Nejdean garrison in Bereymah, for the avowed purpose of keeping down the Menāṣeer and Āāl-Morrah, grown insolent during the late disturbances—this garrison was to be in the pay and under the immediate orders of Thoweynee; lastly, the king agreed to admit a certain number of Nejdeans (about three hundred, I believe), into his own personal service and guard. On these terms the treaty was ratified by either party, and 'Abd-Allah with his troops finally evacuated the land, leaving behind them an accumulated debt of hatred which generations cannot pay. All this took place about ten years ago.

Since that time no further civil contests have agitated 'Omān. Thoweynee, a Sybarite in private life, and in public a very negligent though by no means unintelligent prince, holds his own more by leaving the subordinate chiefs of the country in full possession of their old hereditary authority, and thus ruling through them, than by his own immediate action. His own special attention and administration turns principally on the seaports and commerce; but the society of Abyssinian concubines, of licensed jesters and boon companions, pageants of horsemanship and parties of pleasure, are the real business of his life.

It will not be amiss to remark here that the title of "Imām of Mascat" is unused in 'Omān itself, and belongs to European, not to Arab nomenclature. Thowcynee is not an Imām in the proper and Mahometan sense of the term, and Mascat is not his capital. The word "Imām" does indeed in a general way denote anyone who takes the precedence, especially in war or prayer, sometimes also in science and literature. In Nejed Feyṣul is sometimes, but very rarely, denominated Imām by his subjects, and I have heard the same word applied twice or thrice to his heir 'Abd-Allah. But even in Nejed, "Sultan" is in far more common use; while in 'Omān, Thoweynee invariably enjoys that distinguished title. Hence his correct address is "Sultānō-'Aamān," i. e. "Sultan of 'Omān." For official capital he has his choice between Bahilah, Ṣoḥār, and Nezwah; the latter is the most usual.

A second remark on the peculiar character of this government may seem almost superfluous. My readers will have already perceived that it is in fact a limited monarchy, limited not indeed by charters and acts, but by the coexistence of a powerful aristocracy, by hereditary privileges and the prescription of popular rights. 'Omān is less a kingdom than an aggregation of municipalities; each town, each village has its separate existence and corporation; while towns and villages are again in their turn subject to one or other of the ancestral chiefs, who rule the provinces with an authority limited on one side by the traditional immunities of their vassals, and on the other by the prerogatives of the crown. These prerogatives consist in the right of nomination and deposition (on complaint), where local governors are concerned, though the office remains always within the same family; in fixing and levying port and custom-house dues; in the exclusive management of the navy; in the keeping up a small standing army, about six or seven hundred men; lastly, in the transacting of all foreign affairs for alliance or treaty, peace or war. The administration of justice and the decision of criminal cases does not here, as in Nejed and Shomer, come under cognizance; these matters are reserved to the Ḳaḍees or local royal judges; in short, the whole course of law is considered to be entirely independent of the sovereign, except in very extraordinary circumstances. Again, the taxes levied on land or goods (sea-port commerce excepted) are fixed and immutable, save by local or municipal authority; the sultan enjoys, but cannot change them. From all this it follows that the main support of the Sultan of 'Omān lies in the good-will of his people and in the prosperity of the sea-trade; while, on the other hand, should he be, like Thoweynee at this day, a negligent ruler, the evils that follow are rather indirect than immediate, while the nation at large goes on much the same, whoever may be at its head; one might almost say, it governs itself. Thus 'Omān approaches nearer to what we call a mixed or constitutional government than any other in Arabia, perhaps in the entire East.

A word only remains regarding the position now occupied by the Wahhabees in 'Omān. My readers may well suppose that a hostile invasion, and more especially the conduct of Khālid-ebn-Ṣakar, and no less of his subordinate the Meṭeyree, a desperate brigand worthy of his master, has not done much to conciliate the Biaḍeeyah with the dogmas and institutions of Ebn-Sa'ood. Alva was scarce more hated in the Netherlands, or Cortez in Mexico. The Wahhabee influence, maintained by the Djowāsimah on the west, by the Bereymah garrison, and the other adherents or soldiers of the cause scattered throughout the principal towns of the Bāṭinah, at Ṣoḥār and Barka for instance, or incorporated with the body-guard of Thoweynee, has however much diminished, and at the time of my visit I found the Wahhabee party wholly insignificant. To this many causes have contributed.

Thus Aḥmed-es-Sedeyree, whom Feyṣul appointed governor of Bereymah, and fixed him there in order to separate him from the rest of his family, has by degrees dismissed almost all his Nejdean retainers one after the other, and now lives more like an 'Omānee than a Wahhabee ruler; surrounded by natives of the country whose good-will Aḥmed has conciliated at the expense of his master's policy, principles, and tribute; neglecting the first, disavowing the second, and pocketing or squandering the third, instead of sending it to the Riaḍ treasury. During my stay at the capital of 'Aareḍ, I heard from the men of court more than one severe nor wholly unmerited censure passed on the backsliding Sedeyree; but distance, and the danger of breaking with a powerful subject (for Aḥmed is the head of his family, one of the chief in Nejed), besides the probability of open disobedience, have hitherto prevented Feyṣul from ordering his recall.

The other Nejdeans in 'Omān have also afforded many deplorable instances of the Arab proverb, "Forty days' company make the man like his fellows." Some of these quondam orthodox have openly thrown aside the Wahhabee man, outer and inner; dress gaily, smoke like volcanoes, and talk no less freely, and with total omission of stereotyped religious phraseology, than any Biaḍee of Akhdar; while others have put an additional barrier between their old and their new selves by an "infidel" alliance with some fair but honourable syren of the land. However, the Mahometan merchants settled in Mascat and the larger sea-ports maintain tolerable decorum, partly owing to their frequent connection with their native lands, and partly from self-respect inspired by collective number. The Sonnees too of old Nejdean families, here established for generations back and thinly scattered through the Bāṭinah, with the Djowāsimah of Rās Mesandum, hold fast to their peculiar tenets with all the pertinacity of antagonistic bigotry. But these are anomalies, and 'Omān in general has no disposition to adopt any form of orthodox Islamism, least of all the Wahhabee.

On the opposite side of the Persian Gulf where we are now about to land, the Shiya'ee sect prevails. Here, as elsewhere, the 'Omānee government leaves entire liberty to its subjects in these respects, at least so long as no particular trouble or danger is to be apprehended; the Persian forms of prayer, of Khoṭbah, and the rest, are observed in public without comment or interference. Other peculiarities of this coast will be noticed during the stay—fortunately for my readers not a long one—which we are about to make at Linja.

On the morning of the 11th February we came ashore in the ship's boat. Close alongside of the middle quay is a small dock, partly dry, partly with just enough water to float vessels of Arab calibre, and capable of containing from sixty to eighty such; it is protected in front by a high sea wall of not unskilful construction, and by a breakwater on either side. What shipping cannot here find place anchors out at sea in the wide sandy bay; I counted about a hundred sail within the port at the time of our arrival. The entire harbour is sheltered to the west by Cape Bostanah; to the east by a corresponding promontory and the island of Djishm; on the north stretches the mainland and mountains of Persia; a southerly gale is the only one which has access to trouble the waters of Linja.

The town itself lies close along the water's edge, with a narrow intervening beach of dry white sand. From this the ground rises twenty or thirty feet, so that the houses are for the most tolerably secure from damp, and enjoy a free circulation of air from the broad and open plain behind. The old town, so to call it—namely, that which existed before the local rule was transferred from Shirāz to 'Omān—is small and compact, and might admit of between four and five thousand inhabitants; nearly half of it consists in market-places, narrow but fairly neat—coffee-houses and similar establishments, besides a large mosque by the sea-side. The houses in the old town are solidly built, partly stone, partly brick, and whitewashed; their appearance is snug and even ornamental, at least in the judgment of one fresh arrived from Ḳaṭar. The carved work, when it occurs about the doors, the windows and balconies, the pointed and often double arch, the close lattices, and the little freaks of ornament about the parapets and angles, bespeak a Persian taste. Low walls surround this quarter of Linja, or rather once did so, for in many parts the frail bulwark has now totally disappeared.

Since the epoch when Sultan Sa'eed made this place his own, and rendered it a free port, exempt from all custom-house exactions, a slight harbour-duty alone excepted, Linja has rapidly risen in importance, and has of late years attained five times the size of its former self under Persian misgovernment and extortion. Another source of its actual prosperity is the wise toleration which, in accordance with the principles of 'Omānee administration, has replaced Shiya'ee narrow-mindedness, and attracted numerous residents not only from Baḥreyn, Ḳaṭeef, Ḥasa, and Baṣrah, but even from Beloochistan, Loodianah, and India itself. In consequence, new houses, indicating by their lighter construction recent well-being, run far east and west along the bay, or reach back towards the mainland, till it requires an hour or more to walk at an even pace from one end of their range to the other. Opposite the dock rises a jutting rock, almost the only one hereabouts; it is crowned by an old castle and tower of mediæval look, now ungarrisoned; for Thoweynee sensibly trusts rather to wooden than to stone walls for the defence of his sea-ports. The palace of the 'Omānee governor, a lad of twenty or thereabouts, by name Seyf, and native of the Bāṭinah, stands further east; it forms a large square, four storeys high, with ogive windows and much Persian ornament; its general effect reminded me of some old town-halls on the Continent, particularly in Belgium and Flanders. Farther on are several shipwright yards, where many vessels are in active progress of construction; some of them were of large size, and, so far as I could reduce the computations of this country to English measure, of about a hundred and fifty to two hundred tons burden. The shipwrights themselves are often Indians from the Bombay side. On either side and behind the town are gardens, many and green, but more for show than produce, the soil being poor, calcareous, and sandy, while want of water renders irrigation difficult. Indeed, Linja cannot boast a single spring, or even a tolerable well; the main supply of water is here from the huge cisterns which collect the overflow of the winter torrents as they furrow the plain from the distant mountains of the north down to the seashore, and store it up to last throughout the year. These cisterns are generally circular, from thirty to sixty feet in diameter, and from twelve to twenty in depth, sometimes more; they are surrounded by high stone walls, and surmounted by a vaulted dome, to preserve their contents from the drying action of sun and wind. Round the inner margin runs a wide stone ledge, though this is sometimes wanting, so that the water comes right up to the wall of the cupola, and is only accessible by the door or doors, and by steps thence leading down to the bottom, like the covered wells in Guzerat, and, indeed, in India and the East at large. Each cupola has five doors, in memory of the five personages dear to Shiya'ees—'Alee, Moḥammed (not the famous Prophet of that name, if report say true, but a son of 'Alee's), Faṭimah, Ḥasan, and Ḥoseyn—and by these doors enter those who come to draw water; no one is excluded, no toll is taken, the benefit is public in the fullest sense of the word. Some few cisterns are of an oblong form and are surmounted by a cylindrical vault; these have only one door. The water is better than I should have expected; the calcareous lining of the pits below may have something to do with its purity.

Meanwhile Linja is a very busy town both by sea and land: ships casting anchor, ships weighing anchor, schooners, cutters, luggers, boats, merchant-vessels, fishing craft; seafaring men from all coasts, dissimilar in dress and feature, similar in their unmistakeable sailor-caste, like copper, silver, and gold pieces all stamped with the same queen's head. Merchandise, too, from Shirāz and Ispahan, merchandise from Khorassān and Herat, merchandise from Sinde and Bombay, merchandise from 'Omān and Zanjibar. Persians, Tartars, Indians, Beloochees, Arabs, 'Omānees (for these last are in the common parlance of the land invariably contradistinguished from Arabs, and their country from Arabia: thus the term "Arab" implies in 'Omān a stranger, and men speak of going to Arabia much as an Englishman might of going to Denmark or to Ireland), negroes in plenty, now and then a Syrian, an Armenian, an Egyptian, besides a colony of Jews, better thriving here than in Baḥreyn, and a multitude of the Baḥārinah themselves, who find Thoweynee's immediate rule preferable to that of El-Khaleefah. It is a good specimen of a commercial town in the East, and an excellent place for studying the men and the manners of half Asia.

Yoosef went to look out for a lodging for both of us, and I remained awhile seated at the foot of the old ruined tower already mentioned to contemplate the first scene of unmixed prosperity that I had beheld for many years, reflecting too on the advantages of a government which contents itself with simply ensuring the security of its subjects without meddling in their social or individual affairs. The mania of doing too much—of regulations, monopoly, centralization, of government religion, government education, government control and patronage; in a word, the "protective" system—goes far in many lands, east and west, to paralyse the vitality of nations, to check their advancement, to blight their true prosperity, and ultimately to compromise their existence itself. Of this we have seen a remarkable instance, on an Arab scale, in Nejed, and something analogous may be observed in the history past and present of more than one nation of higher name and pretensions than the Arab. There, in place of unshackled energy and self-developing Freedom, with all the cornucopia of blessings she bears in hand, we find the large standing army and the heavily-taxed populace, a gorgeous capital and impoverished provinces, much of trappings and display with a nation of slaves, or rapidly becoming such, and at last a decreasing and demoralized population ending in unpitied downfall. Over the grave of many a government, no less than of many a valetudinarian, might well be inscribed the motto, *Stava bene; volera star meglio; sto qui.* It is natural enough for theorists to talk about the paternal duties, the divine rights, the τὸ πᾶν of governments, and compare them to fathers, tutors, gods-on-earth, and what not. Might we not more simply say that the first, often the only office of governments, is that of magistrates; their capital affair to assure their subjects the quiet enjoyment of what Arabs not inaptly call the "three precious things," namely, their life, their household honour, and their property? For these they are responsible to those they govern; for the rest, let individuals, corporations, villages, towns, shires, and provinces, arrange their own matters as they see best. "The fool knows more in his own house than the wise man does in his neighbour's," says a true Spanish proverb; and men very commonly get on all the better for not being meddled with. Kings, emperors, parliaments, states, whatever be the name or form under which the Avatar of rule appears, should have the wisdom to know themselves for what they are—first magistrates of the land, and that alone; let furtherance, not interference—order, not creation—be their watchword, and all parties will be gainers, and great gainers.

Such, at any rate, has been (I thought), except in a very few and transient instances, the uniform course of the 'Omânee administration, and it has met with its deserved results. With a territory containing in square miles scarce half the extent ruled by the Wahhabee, they have full twice as numerous a population, and twenty times the revenue and wealth.

And if their pages present fewer exploits of military prowess, less men killed before their time on the field of glory, and less brilliant or bloody events than what signalize the history of power concentrated in one individual hand, they can offer in requital centuries of quiet well-doing, thriving towns, a thickly-peopled land, princes loved by their subjects, and subjects rendered prosperous by their princes—facts which we shall see more fully confirmed as we continue, or rather conclude, this waning narrative; for in the brief recapitulation of 'Omânee history in this chapter, I have needs-must imitated the book of Judges, where "the land had rest forty years," takes up but a line hardly noticed between the periods, briefer in fact, though much longer in recounting, where we read in detail the contest of Jephtha and Ephraim, or the invasions of Sisera and Midian.

Another and a somewhat analogous line of thought suggested itself at the view of the old tower, once the stronghold of armed garrisons, and now abandoned to decay. Extensive preparations for military defence are a tolerable thermometer to mark the proportional weakness of those who make them; and fortifications betray the real and intrinsic debility of governments, just as crutches prove weak legs. Where energy and national feeling are wanting, material means of stone-work and brick-work must take their place; the stipend of the soldier is often a proof of the apathy of the citizen, and a sign that the government itself is either not national, or else that it has outgrown and smothered the nation. Not that such means can reasonably be altogether neglected; not that when kept within limits of due proportion they are to be called a superfluity, still less an evil. But a staff, to pursue the former metaphor (though but to describe, not prove, as Prior has it), is a very different thing from a wooden leg; a traveller may do well to have a brace of loaded pistols at his waistband; but what should we think of a land where every one must needs wear them by his own fireside?

But we are both of us desirous—my reader to be at the end of these generalizations, and I myself to see Yoosef return with tidings of a lodging and a breakfast. And here he fortunately returns, but not alone; with him is a pug-nosed, thickset, good-natured young fellow, whose grimed hands and soot-stained dress announce him for a blacksmith. Do'eyj, for such is his name (identical by the way with the Doeg of David's time, so little does the East change), is a native of Ḥasa, but long since established here in his honest and profitable calling. He purposes to have us both to board and lodging, and now comes to present his compliments in person, and invite me to accompany him to his Vulcanian abode. The house was a tolerably good one, our friend's position in life considered; it contained several apartments, arranged round an open courtyard; near the principal entrance stood the forge and its accessories, for the ship constructions carried on in the docks close by gave it plenty of occupation.

Here lived with the master of the house his two brothers; the dwelling was moreover a frequent resort of Baḥārinah, 'Omānees, and so forth, but not of Persians, who seldom mix with the Arab population. And here we passed three days, waiting for a change of wind to bear us to Sharjah. There was neither necessity nor thought of calling on the governor Seyf; Linja is a commercial town, a sea-port, part and parcel of the great world where every one comes and goes for himself, and no one seeks acquaintance with others, except for some special reason and purport. In the enchanted circle of Arabia, where all dance on since four thousand years at least in the same magic ring, never overstepping its limits, nor enlarging it to admit a foreign measure, chiefs, sultans, governors, and the other "dons" of the land, are not to be passed by without receiving the honour of a salutation, and without conferring in return the ostentatious tokens of their greatness in the form of hospitality; a very "patriarchal" but nowise business-like proceeding. Once without that magic circle, we, like the rest, followed the world's tide, which carries every one forward on his own line, straight be it or crooked, but unblended with the track of those around, except where the eddy of pleasure or profit whirls them for the hour together. In fact, for a voyager to call on the governor of Linja without a reason of weight of special cause, would be much like calling on the Lord Mayor of London because one happened to have taken a three days' lodging in Fleet Street.

It is a pretty place this Linja, with its white houses along the open shore, or overhung by palms not the less graceful for being almost barren—its crowded markets—the large glittering cupolas of its reservoirs, with rows of pitcher-bearing forms coming and going—its palm-leaf workshops—its docks sounding with the hammer, and steaming with the vapours of pitch and tar—its boats that line the gleaming beach—its clear air and bright sun. For us, we passed our time in roaming about the town, conversing with shipwrights and merchants, and in visiting the villages or rather the suburbs of that neighbourhood, for the plain is well peopled, considering the want of springs and of permanent streams—a want which I can hardly account for, since the high mountains of Persia are at only half a day's distance to the interior, and the season rains are here abundant. Perhaps the great lightness of the soil absorbs whatever is poured down upon it from the uplands. From the sea-shore we could see, across the waves to the south-east, the heights of Djishm above Basido', and farther off the rugged outline of Cape Mesandum, a cheering view which announced our approach to the mouth of the Gulf. Another and a favourite occupation of ours was to walk up and down the market-place and examine the wares exposed for sale: Persian carpets of every possible size, shape, and colour, cheap and plenty; woven cloaks and dresses from Khorassān; weapons too in abundance from the same province; glassware, crockery, and the like from Europe or America, through India; above all, English cloth and linen, mixed with the manufactures of Tanna, near Bombay; articles of Arab dress from 'Omān and Ḥasa; copper work from Bagdad, and girdles from Ṭerabolous; rice, indigo, spices, coffee, adulterated drugs, dried fruit, &c. &c.; much to tempt the buyer and profit the seller. In proportion is the Babel-like throng, and the swarming of this human bee-hive. However, order and security reign in town and country; the Persians of the coast, if let alone, are a quietly-disposed race; and the government, though foreign, is deservedly popular.

While we were yet at Linja, arrived a deputation from Shirāz to negotiate for the establishment of Persian custom-house duties at the port. The immediate occasion of this unwelcome embassy was curious enough. About six months before, the governor of Shirâz had sent in a claim to certain tributary dues, withheld, so said he, by the 'Omânee authorities. Seyf denied alike the claim and the money, and sent the messengers back empty-handed. Followed terrible denunciations of Achæmenian vengeance from Shirâz. While matters stood thus, two wealthy merchants of Linja, who had been present in Seyf's Mejlis or council-hall, gave notice to their fellow-tradesmen in the town and on the coast, warning them of impending danger. Hereon the principal inhabitants of Linja held an assembly, and agreed to furnish the sum required out of their own private purses, on condition of the withdrawal of official exaction. Each man had his quota assigned him, the list was made out, the money collected, and the merchants sent word beforehand to their friends at Shirâz, begging them to inform the Persian governor of the city that his claims should be satisfied, so he would leave them in peace and quiet. But when Seyf heard of this arrangement, he summoned the townsmen before him, and declared that he could not permit a similar transaction, and that the sum, if paid at all, should be paid out of the government treasure, not out of private purses; and with this he countermanded the transmission of the money. The Persians waited awhile to see whether anything was forthcoming either from Seyf or from his subjects, but in vain; it was the old proverb of two stools and their unlucky consequences. They were, however, determined not to give up the game so lightly; and, in order to face the garment of extortion with some new colour, let the tribute go by, and demanded in its place the re-establishment of the old custom-house system, for the benefit of the Shirâz treasury. But this again Seyf and his councillors were nowise disposed to permit; much altercation took place, but I know not how the affair ended, as we left Linja before its conclusion. I should remark, that although this strip of coast has been annexed to 'Omân and under its rule for nearly thirty years, the Persian court still asserts a sort of general authority over the land which it was unable to defend; while the kingdom of 'Omân for its part has too much interest in keeping up a good understanding with Teheran to permit an absolute rejection of its proposals or occasional interference. Hence compromise is often resorted to on these occasions, and even observed—that is, so long as the Persian envoys remain in presence.

Events like this, together with much talk about India and Khorassân trade, import and export, shipping and sea adventures, made up the staple of the conversation heard or shared in Linja. In the East, where overland communications are regulated by the slow pace of camels, and sea news by the caprice of winds, ten miles equal a hundred of Europe in the separation of localities, and a hundred are tantamount to a thousand and more. Hence my readers must not wonder if I say that on this coast we heard no more of Nejed and Shomer than if we had been in Gloucestershire—nay, perhaps less. For in Gloucestershire newspapers exist at any rate; not so in Linja. Besides, present business, buying, selling, and trafficking occupy all thoughts, and leave no room for foreign curiosity. Nor did the mosque, though large and handsome in its way, nor the other buildings of the town, present much worthy of particular consideration. The scenery too in the neighbourhood of the town is mostly tame, though the mountain ranges in the distance offer a fine blue outline, but of arid semblance. Nor was I at all sorry when after three days of south wind a northerly gale sprung up, and a sea-captain introduced himself at our door with the offer of a passage on his ship bound for Sharjah, and ready to sail.

Among the main articles of traffic at Linja are sheep, which are carried over in great quantities from Persia to 'Omân, where pasture land is comparatively scarce, and what exists is principally destined to the rearing of dromedaries. A sheep-merchant of Sharjah, 'Abbas by name, whom some seventh degree of cousinship connected with Ḥasa, had just embarked a cargo of about two hundred head; and this was the business of the voyage. Along with 'Abbas were several friends, also from Sharjah; he himself was a jovial open-hearted fellow, a perfect 'Omânee; indeed, we had much ado to prevent his paying the fare on our account to the master of the ship.

On the 16th of the month we made sail a little after noon, in company with some islanders of Djishm, silent uncommunicative men, wrapped up in thick Persian overalls; the crew were mostly negroes; among the Sharjah passengers was the butcher, with his knife all ready for the sheep. The wind was high, and we soon cleared the shipping and the bay. During the night the gale veered to the east, and the sea became so rough, that of the sheep, too closely stowed in the hold, about twenty died and had to be thrown overboard. At dawn we were off the rocky island of Aboo-Moosa (mutilated into Bomosa in many maps—a fair example of what Arab words become in the mouths of English sea-captains), and here our skipper resolved to anchor, for the waves ran high, and to continue our voyage would have compromised the lives of the fleecy survivors. We sought out a little creek, and there anchored to await calmer weather; the sheep were swum on shore, to enjoy the blessings of temporary liberty and the pasture which the island affords.

A high conical peak five or six hundred feet in elevation and of volcanic appearance, some ridges of basaltic rock, and the rest of the island composed of ups and downs covered with grass and brushwood—such is Aboo-Moosa; its total length being about five miles, and its breadth between two and three. At its south-western corner are found a few brackish wells; thus provided, Aboo-Moosa is not an unfrequent shelter and temporary abode for crews in sea-chances like our own, though the only regular inhabitants of the island are wild-fowl and conies. It is also in the winter season a supplementary pasture-ground for horses and camels belonging to Khālid-ebn-Ṣaḳar, the governor of Sharjah, who often sends hither part of his live stock to pass two or three months of grass-cropping. At the time of our arrival some twenty good steeds, Khālid's property, gambolled about the plain at the mountain foot, while several dromedaries belonging to the same owner were sauntering here and there in the full privilege of their innate listlessness. With these animals, and in quality of their guardians, were half-a-dozen or more herdsmen and horse-keepers; lastly, a small 'Omānee fishing smack, driven hither as we had been by a sea too high for her to weather, lay in another creek some way off. The eastern side of the island, on which we had cast anchor, presents many similar points of retreat; the western is ironbound, and the waves now broke on it in white foam. Far off over the sea to the south-west we could just distinguish a dim dream of rocks belonging to Ṣeer, an island in the Pearl Bay.

The comparative solitude of the place produced a great effect on the imaginative mind of my companion Yoosef, unaccustomed to such loneliness; and he observed, with a melancholy laugh, "Were all our friends ashore to guess where we are at this moment, would any one of them hit on Aboo-Moosa?" This he said while standing on the shore; for, finding that our stay might be a long one, we had after consultation agreed to swim to land; inasmuch as our craft was moored at some distance from the beach, and had not the advantage of a jolly-boat, or "Djāliboot," as Arabs call it, with a slight modification of the English name. So a jib-sail is here a "Djeeb," a main-mast "Meyānah," a brig "Breek," &c. We carried each on his head, one a carpet, one the coffee-pots, another the cooking utensils, and so forth, till we had enough to establish a complete land encampment high up on the beach opposite the ships. We:—that is ourselves, the negroes, and the 'Omānees, who are mostly excellent swimmers and relished the fun; as for the sulky fellows of Djishm who could not or would not swim, we left them to guard the ship against Tritons and mermen.

Two days we made Aboo-Moosa our abode, awaiting a lull in the gale, now favourable, but too strong. To kill the time, we clambered up crags, made friends with the herdsmen and the fishermen, who were no less desirous than ourselves to find some one to talk to, and explored the island from one end to another; while Yoosef, unaware that all that glitters is not gold, collected large bits of spar, here in great plenty, conceiving them to be something very precious. Nay, though it was now mid-February, the mildness of the atmosphere encouraged us to repeated feats of swimming, though we little expected that within a few weeks we should have occasion to bring it to a more serious trial.

"How happily the days of Thalaba went by" in such amicable society, and amid such varied amusements! I at any rate had here no business on hand, medical or other, and felt lazily glad when I heard the roar of the breakers announcing from hour to hour the impossibility of leaving our Arab Patmos. However, everything on earth or sea must have an end, and on the evening of the 16th, the sea had calmed into a ripple, under the drooping westerly breeze; sheep and men swam on board again, and before sunset Aboo-Moosa was fading, perhaps for ever, from our retrospective view. And here, readers and all, we will turn in for a few hours of pause and quiet sleep before entering on new scenes and new regions.

CHAPTER XVI

The Coasts of 'Omān

Yes, I remember well
  The land of many hues,
Whose charms what praise can tell,
  Whose praise what heart refuse?
Sublime, but neither bleak nor bare,
Nor misty are the mountains there;
Softly sublime, profusely fair,
Up to their summits clothed in green,
And fruitful as the vales between,
    They lightly rise
    And scale the skies,
And groves and gardens still abound;
    For where no shoot
    Could else take root,
The peaks are shelved and terraced round.—*H. Taylor*

ARRIVAL AT SHARJAH—ITS KHOWR OR HARBOUR—GENERAL VIEW OF THE COAST AND TOWN—YAḲOOB THE ENGLISH ANTI-SLAVERY AGENT—REFLECTIONS—TOWN OF SHARJAH—'OMÂNEE USAGES—MOSQUE—DISPOSITIONS OF THE PEOPLE—COMMERCE OF SHARJAH—METALS IN 'OMÂN—HOSPITALITY—KHÂLID-EBN-ṢAḲAR AND HIS COURT—THE ḲEYSAREEYAH AND SOOḲ—REST OF THE TOWN—CASTLE AND TOWER—A TRIP TO THE INTERIOR—VIEW TOWARDS DJEBEL-'OḲDAH—ḌOBEY'—A SEA-STORY AND A STRANGE ESCAPE—EMBARKMENT ON A SHIP OF SOWEYḲ FOR ṢOḤÂR—CREW AND PASSENGERS—COAST AND ITS VILLAGES—RÂS-EL-KHEYMAH—THE MOUNTAIN COAST AND RO'OS-EL-DJEBAL—'OMÂNEE BOAT-SONG—VISITS AT SHA'AM AND KHABB—CHARACTER OF THE INHABITANTS—A SEY'YID—METOOṬ—CAPE MESANDUM AND THE ROCKS OF SALÎMAH—A STORM—LAREJ—WE ARRIVE AT ORMUZ—THE ISLAND—THE PORTUGUESE FORT—PHAROS-TOWER—CAUSES OF THE PROSPERITY AND DECLINE OF ORMUZ—FURTHER DETAILS REGARDING THE ISLAND—SHARKS—MEANING OF "AWWÂL"—MIXED LANGUAGE SPOKEN—PASSING CAPE MESANDUM—ROOBAH—LEYMAH—A SQUALL—HARBOUR OF LEYMAH—SCENERY AND VILLAGE—APPREHENSIONS OF THE INHABITANTS—A TEMPLE—GULF OF ḌEBEE—ḲALḤAṬ—ḲAṬAA'-L-LOḤA—THE BÂṬINAH—ITS CHARACTER AND PRODUCE—FÂJIRAH—SHINÂZ—EFFECTS OF WAR—FARḲṢAH—LANDING AT ṢOḤÂR—ITS GOVERNOR FAKHAR—OUR HOST 'EYSA—HIS HOUSE—DOMESTIC ARCHITECTURE IN 'OMÂN—ACTUAL CONDITION OF THE BÂṬINAH—POLICE—CASTLE OF ṢOḤÂR—BELOOCH GARRISON—THE ḲEYSAREEYAH AND

MARKET—POPULATION—GARDENS—DOMESTIC USAGES AND HOSPITALITY—GENERAL DISPOSITIONS OF THE PEOPLE—MA'WAH—HARBOUR AND FISHERY OF SOḤÂR—WE EMBARK FOR MASCAT.

ON the morning of the 16th February, 1863, we sighted the 'Omânee coast between Aboo-Ḍebee and Ḍobey', long—low, and sandy, but well lined with palm-groves and villages ranged along the glistering shore. Far in the distance like a cloud rose the heights of Bereymah or Djebel-'Oḳdah; and to the north, another blue day-vision indicated the peaks of Ro'os-el-Djebal, and Cape Mesandum. Our course lay for Sharjah; and, after some tacking and veering, we worked up to the entrance of its harbour or Khowr, a narrow creek, opening out at right angles into the sea, and then, after some forty yards, turning sharp to run inland, parallel with its parent ocean, for a league and more, much like the line followed by the Yare from Gorleston to Yarmouth—but here the resemblance stops. At the harbour entrance is a bar, to cross which requires skill and experience; beyond the water is perfectly calm, and not very deep; enough indeed for fishing boats and 'long-shore cruisers, but a large ship would not find wherewithal to float her.

Sharjah (that is, "Sharḳah," or "the Easterly;" but the "j," a mispronunciation of the "ḳ," has established so firm a right of prescription in this name, that I shall not interfere with it in my orthography, contenting myself with having noticed the error once for all) lies close behind the Khowr. The town is walled in, but not strongly, on the land side; towards the sea, or rather the creek, it is absolutely open. Nearly opposite the bar stands a small compact castle, where Khâlid makes his residence; the old or central town consists mainly of brick or stone houses; while endless rows of cottages, half wood, half palm-leaf, and chiefly tenanted by fishermen, sailors, and their like, extend along the beach, especially to the north, and make up with the town itself a total about one-third larger than Linja. The entire population appears to range between twenty and thirty thousand souls.

We "shot o'er the seething harbour bar," entered the Khowr, and soon landed with the help of a boat, brought up for our service by some of 'Abbas's acquaintances, whom we had seen and hailed from the ship. Just at this moment an English-built yacht skimmed by, and danced over the breakers at the harbour-mouth to the north. On her deck sat a stout elderly man, dressed Bagdad fashion, and in whose face, as the cutter passed close under our bows, I recognized the well-known Armenian type. To my enquiries regarding the personality of an individual so unlike all around him, I received answer that this was Yaḳoob, British agent at Sharjah for the suppression of the slave trade, and that he was now probably on his way to visit some one of his many wives at the coast village of Mefraz, a few miles off; for Yaḳoob enjoyed a large and varied stock of household happiness, one Mrs. Yaḳoob being at Sharjah, another at Mefraz, and a choice elsewhere.

"Really my countrymen might find a better use for their money than in lining this gentleman's pockets," thought I; very glad meanwhile at the good luck which conveyed him away from Sharjah at the exact instant of my entering it. For an eye so well practised as Yaḳoob's could hardly have failed recognizing me within a day or two at farthest; and I, on the contrary, desired to keep up the full liberty of my incognito. Not that to be known for what I was would in 'Omān have exposed me to any serious risk; only it would have deprived me of that freedom of intercourse and movement which I now possessed. As to Yaḳoob himself, I heard a great deal about him, though fortunately his domestic trammels detained him at Mefraz till after my departure from Sharjah. His name, face, and entire manner convinced me beyond doubt that he must be of Armenian, and consequently of Christian origin, though here he passes for a Mahometan, and certainly proves himself one in point of polygamy; his native town is, I understood, Basrah. His official occupation is to prevent the import and sale of slaves. But Yaḳoob, while pocketing the English coin bestowed on him for philanthropic ends, thinks it wisest, for many reasons, to remain good friends with all parties; and accordingly gives the slave-dealers to know—not in ambiguous phrases, but in the plainest Arabic—that should they indeed buy or sell slaves in the public market-place, he must necessarily interfere with them, or else his employers might interfere with him. But should they pursue their traffic anywhere else—in private houses for instance, or other out-of-the-way localities, where he was not obliged to be on the watch—they might reckon on his knowing nothing about it, and need fear no notice on his part. This obliging conduct is of course requited with suitable gratuities, to make assurance doubly sure; and thus Yaķoob compasses a double gain, and the merchants continue their business as steadily and profitably as ever, in spite of the equivocal representative of Great Britain at Sharjah.

Might I add that for England's own sake I could wish that either she would let the matter altogether alone, or else would employ means better adapted to her ends? Distance and other circumstances will, I trust, prevent the publication of these lines from having any injurious effect on Yaķoob's position; but he is only a specimen of an entire class—one of five hundred, or five thousand, who in the far East gather round the union jack to pick up its golden fruit, and make a mock of the tree that bears it. Perhaps it can hardly be otherwise; Horace assures us that "Exilis domus est ubi non et multa supersunt, Et dominum fallunt et prosunt furibus," and ours is a large house to keep by land and ocean. I must, however, remark, that while England has acquired for herself in these regions great honour and respect, due not to fear only, but to gratitude also, in putting down the pirate pest once so rife in this Gulf, she has also drawn on herself a considerable share of odium and (I regret to say it) of ridicule, by her opposition to the existing slave trade; and, still more, by her way of going to work about it. I am no advocate, Heaven forbid! of slavery and slaves; though my readers may have observed from the statements contained in the last chapter, that the masters themselves are ultimately far more sufferers than the slaves, in 'Omān at least, perhaps elsewhere too. Whether interference be in itself wise or not, is a second and a complicated question. But if we must interfere, I may suggest that half a dozen tight cruisers would be more to the purpose than sixty Yaķoobs, and shot would be better bestowed than sovereigns.

While I made these or similar reflections, Yaķoob cleared out of the Khowr, and we landed. Here for the first time we were in what is properly called 'Omān, just as on crossing the limits of Ḳaseem one enters the strict territory of Nejed. Putting foot on shore I was strongly reminded of India, and that in more than one particular. A mild mellowness of climate, very different from the brisk air of Ṭoweyḳ or Shomer, no less than from the heavier atmosphere of Ḥasa and Ḳaṭeef; a style of house-building not unlike that of Baroda and Cambay; the dress of the inhabitants, a broad white or fringed cloth wrapped round their loins and reaching down to the knees, a light turban or a coloured Indian handkerchief knotted round the head; their dusky complexion, slim forms, and easy gait, less stately but lither and more graceful than that of Benoo-Ṭā'i or Benoo-Tameem—all this and other peculiarities of nature and art too minute for description, suggested the idea of Guzerat or Cutch rather than of Arabia, and contributed to explain and justify the distinction drawn by the 'Omānees between their country and the rest of the Peninsula. 'Abbas, the sheep-merchant, had constituted himself our host; his house lay amid a labyrinth of lanes and byways, and though within the city walls was constructed of wood and thatch only. But the inside was well furnished and cheerful, and if any deficiencies existed, they were covered by an almost lavish hospitality. Certainly, had Niebuhr been there entertained along with us, he would hardly have stigmatized the Biaḍeeyah with an over-ascetic rejection of tobacco and coffee, both of which were in constant requisition and rapid circulation during our three days' residence in Sharjah. Wahhabee terminology is here unknown, or at least unused; the pious "Semm'," or "say in the name of God," which accompanies the offer of the Nejdean coffee-cup, is here exchanged for the more trivial "Dook," or "Duk," a familiar abbreviation of "Doonek," or "at your service;" while a knock at the door is answered by "Ḥod," a word equivalent to "come in," but from what etymology I am wholly ignorant.

However, as the present ruler, Khālid-ebn-Ṣaḳar, professes the orthodox faith, a large and loosely-built mosque has been constructed near the market-place; and to this edifice I can bear witness that it is admirably adapted to religious meditation by the stillness of its lonely precincts, hardly ever disturbed by anyone in or out of prayer-time. More than once I entered it at the Mu'eḍḍin's call to see whom I should find there; and had to make a speedy exit for fear of becoming charged with the double responsibility of Imām and congregation. The reason is obvious: Khālid and the whole tribe of Djowāsimah kith and kin are bitterly detested at Sharjah by the 'Omānee population, that is, by more than nine-tenths of the town, already alienated body and soul from Islam, its edifices, and its votaries.

This town is for Western 'Omān precisely what Linja has of late years become for the opposite Persian coast—a centre of export and import, a point whither converge the many lines of land and sea trade, and thence diverge again in all directions. From Bedaa' to Rās Mesandum, and even beyond that cape down to Dobey', there is no other seaport locality of any great importance, no other general market-place and emporium for commerce. Hither is brought whatever manufacture Western 'Omān supplies, in wool, in cotton, or in metal; here is the main sale of dromedaries and asses; here too is the principal slave-market of the inner Persian Gulf. Besides, it is through Sharjah chiefly that the neighbouring lands receive the goods of Persia and India, here disembarked and hence distributed over a very wide circle. This constant current of trade gives to Sharjah an air of activity and of wealth not to be found in any other Arab port of the southern side, and attracts to it strangers of many countries and of motley races, enough to form almost a population by themselves; though the 'Omānee character has a general and decided pre-eminence. Were the harbour suitably cleared out, and the government in other hands than those of Khālid, Sharjah would considerably rise in importance; as matters stand, it has rather fallen off during late years.

The natives of Sharjah are in general an honest, good-natured, hospitable, and thriving race; the dagger, which here and throughout 'Omān even to Rās-el-Ḥadd is worn at the belt of every free man, is more for show than use. In Sharjah I saw for the first time good specimens of that peculiarly beautiful gold and silver filigree with which in 'Omān these weapons, besides the more pacific utensils, such as belts, cups, and pipes, are often adorned; it is of a perfection rarely now to be met with in the workmanship of any other land. This branch of handicraft supports numberless families in the larger towns. The gold thus employed is mainly, if not entirely, brought from India, or rather by way of India; though that precious metal is said to exist in the interior of 'Omān itself, namely, in the continuation of Djebel-Akhdar behind Bahilah; but no one could, or perhaps would, state its whereabouts and its quantity with the precision which I should have desired. Copper mines occur in 'Omān, and are regularly worked; lead too is procured in the neighbourhood of Rās-el-Ḥadd; I have myself observed traces of iron in many localities; of other metals I heard and saw nothing. But salt-mines are very common, and are much worked, both for home consumption and for exportation; lastly, the sea throws up amber in such abundance as to render it a staple article of the royal revenue. This substance, with pearls, salt, and gold—if indeed the latter really exists, for which point I must rely on my informants—are the only government monopolies in 'Omān, where the old Roman policy has made little progress, nor needs, perhaps, be regretted.

But to return to Sharjah, from which we are too widely digressing. Our hours went by here in a peculiarly friendly manner, in visits, dinners, and suppers; for the natives of Sharjah seemed anxious to make us experience the truth of what I had often heard elsewhere regarding their sociable disposition. The guest in this town finds a much greater variety in the fare set before him than in Arabia Proper and among Arabs: fish, flesh, prawns, eggs, vermicelli, rice, sweetmeats of all kinds, honey, butter, dates, good leavened bread, and other eatables are placed before him—not piled up in one huge platter after Nejdean fashion, but each placed in its separate dish; while the repeated invitations to vigorous trencher-work might seem excessive in number and urgency even to a starving man. Moreover at Sharjah and throughout 'Omān no special introduction is required; open house is the order of the day; it is the *Viel Gäste wünsch' ich heut'* of Goethe; and the slenderest pretext, a look, a good morrow, an enquiry about the way hither or thither, suffices for an invitation, followed by a display of hospitality proportioned to the time of day. This among the 'Omānees; for my Djowāsimah friendships were few and superficial, and with Khālid-ebn-Ṣaḳar himself I made no acquaintance, beyond a passing salutation given and returned where he sat holding his morning audiences by his castle-door.

His dusky face and thickset limbs gave him a very Dirk Hatteraick appearance, fully borne out by the tenor of his public and private life. I have already recorded a sample of his conduct in my account of his expedition against the Bāṭinah, but it is only a sample. Khālid is said to take a special pleasure in the Gessler-like amusement of placing a lemon on the head or in the extended hand of some one of his followers as a mark for his own personal musket-practice; and his capricious cruelty renders him no less dangerous to his friends than to his enemies. However, in quality of vassal to the Sultan Thoweynee, he is in many points under a certain restraint, and can change nothing in the general order of commerce, duties, customs, or privileges of the province. Many attempts have been made to remove him from office; but his Nejdean alliances have enabled him to keep his post, in defiance of an almost universal hatred.

Towards the southerly end of the town is situated the large market-place, divided into separate Sooḳs or quarters, according to the received Eastern custom. Near its centre stands the Ḳeysareeyah, a long and lofty vaulted building, strongly constructed, and furnished with iron-bound gates, duly closed at nightfall to guard the riches it contains. In a thick stone tower within the precincts of the Ḳeysareeyah is kept the government treasure. The shops around are neat and well-built, and the whole has an air of solidity and wealth. Instead of Arab warehouses, in which goods and owner are alike on the ground-level, or even a little below it, we find here regular shops, with raised seats, counters, and shelves, much like the arrangements ordinary in Bombay or Madras, with the frequent addition of a strongbox, denoting cash, and account-books of businesslike size and shape. Merchants, chiefly Hindoos or Loothians (natives of Loodianah), make great display of Cachemire shawls, Bengal manufactures, Persian arms, and jewellery of various kinds, much beyond whatever I could have anticipated in Arabia; customers too are not wanting. The slave-traffic is unceasing, and few of the town merchants but have a share in it; it is carried on within-doors, in compliance with the prudent recommendation given by Yaḳoob.

The northern quarter of the town owns a large number of weavers' establishments, wherein are made the light red cloaks common in 'Omān; long cotton robes, somewhat different in fashion from the Nejdean smock; carpets too, and curtains for domestic use. In lands guiltless of factories and steam-engines, this business is a lucrative one, and employs many hands. Goldsmiths and silversmiths ply their patient labour; blacksmiths are to be met with at all corners. The streets are clean, but with no idea of symmetry; where palm-leaf dwellings are in the majority, the lanes are narrow and tortuous. Of course the narrow space left for quay between the houses and the creek or Khowr is full of small ships and boats; some of the latter, even here, have their sides furrowed by the traces of divers' ropes, and accordingly belong to the pearl-fishery. This is in fact the extreme eastern limit of the pearl coast, and it is much less productive between Aboo-Ḍebee and Sharjah than farther back in the Bay.

Just within the town walls on the land side rises an octangular stone tower, with a castle adjoining; and from this tower is, I suppose, derived the custom of putting down "Sharjah Tower" on many maps, instead of simply giving the name of the town. This edifice is, unless I confound it in my memory with what I saw in Ormuz a little farther on, of elegant form, ornamented with herring-bone patterns, and pierced with loopholes here and there; its height about seventy feet. The castle alongside is irregular, more resembling a barrack than a stronghold, but also of stone; it appears much more recent than the tower. No one could tell me anything regarding the history of either, or who had reared them. But both now serve for a depôt or arsenal, and the doors are kept carefully locked, a circumstance which prevented me from visiting the interior.

The outer walls of Sharjah are of stone—not granite or limestone, but of a reddish-yellow sandstone found in the neighbourhood. These walls are broken and ruined everywhere, their yellow bastions filled with sand, and their curtain pierced with holes, through which vagabond boys leap in and out in all directions.

Beyond the walls stretches a large extent of sand, gradually rising in height for about half a mile. The slope is studded with palm-trees, and here and there a hedge of cactus or thorn shuts in some isolated garden or well, but the soil is too light for much produce. Occasionally tangled shrubs of Indian jungle-growth form knolls of verdure; the climate is tropical, and had I been possessed of a thermometer, it would, I am sure, have stood at 80° Fahrenheit in the shade, even on this 17th of February. Some Bedouin tents belonging to 'Aamir, a quiet peaceful district, diversify the scene.

Asses are here in plenty for hire, and good conveyances they prove for a short distance. On a couple of these beasts—inferior perhaps to the Egyptian breed, but of remarkable wiriness and endurance—Yoosef and I took an excursional ride, the better to occupy the third day of our sojourn at Sharjah. We had for companion of our trip a young townsman in his gay yellow overdress, and a purple Bengal handkerchief round his head; a silver-hilted dagger adorned his girdle. We followed the road of the interior leading to Bereymah, in a south-easterly direction, amid groves of wild dwarf palm, interspersed with fenced gardens and clusters of peasants' huts, till we attained a rising ground, surmounted by a small watchtower, like those described before in Ḳaṭar, and had in view the wide inland plain. There at some distance on the east stood a village, Ḥowṭah by name, and southward lay open pasture-lands, whence a far-off encampment of Menaṣeer Bedouins sent up columns of thin blue smoke against the glittering sky. Beyond extended a series of low hills, containing, so our companion asserted, numerous hamlets, and belonging to a territory entitled Sha'āb, or "gorges;" in the distance gleamed a higher range, the first mountains of 'Oḳdah, in the centre of which lies Bereymah.

I had almost made up my mind to follow this road in good earnest, and thus traverse 'Omān by the interior. But to do this would have required a longer period of time than my present circumstances allowed; indeed a month's land journey would hardly have brought me to Mascat, much less to Rās-el-Ḥaḍḍ. So we deferred this project to a future occasion, perhaps reserved to others than Yoosef and myself, contenting ourselves with our distant survey of the Sharjah district, after which, as noon was now past, we turned our donkeys' heads seawards, till we came back to the coast near Ḍobey' a little before sunset.

Like Sharjah, Ḍobey' has its Khowr, a very large one, resembling an inland lake, and separated from the sea by a broad belt of white sand. The village itself is populous, but unfortified, and built in a very straggling way, well provided with gardens and wells, besides maintaining a whole navy of boats, destined not so much for the meagre pearl-fishery of this coast, as to work in the south-westerly bay beyond Aboo-Ḍebee. We alighted under a cluster of palms that overshadowed some houses near the entrance of the village, and rested awhile to breathe beasts and riders, while the neighbours entertained us with many stories touching Benoo-Yass and their doings. We had already met two or three bands of these same Benoo-Yass—handsome dark-featured men, of a very piratical look, armed to the teeth, as the saying has it, with guns, short spears, and daggers. Their long black hair, dishevelled on their shoulders, gave them a romantically savage appearance. Among all the enemies of Islam these men are said to be the bitterest; and their cruising exploits on the Gulf were no less often prompted by motives of sheer hatred against Nejdean captains and ships, than by the desire of prize and profit. I give an instance of their proceedings.

Six Nejdeans, who had come down to the Ḳaṭar coast on trading business, were desirous of a passage to Râs-el-Kheymah, not far from Cape Mesandum. A sloop, manned by sailors of Benoo-Yass, offered to convey them. The Nejdeans had nothing of value about them, and were tolerably well armed; they embarked, and the vessel spread sail for the eastern side of the Gulf. But the crew had taken them on board merely to have an opportunity of gratifying their animosity to the Muslims, and watched their moment. One noon, when some of the passengers lay sleeping on the deck, and the rest were off their guard, a rush was made, and they were mastered. Five of the Wahhabees were full grown men; the sixth a boy. The Benoo-Yass bound the five hand and foot, and flung them thus into the sea, where of course they soon perished; as to the boy, whether thinking him unable to swim, or perhaps out of a half feeling of compassion for his tender years, and wishing to give him yet a chance for life, they threw him into the water unbound. Lastly, they collected whatever had belonged to the Nejdeans, arms, goods, and clothes, and having cast all overboard, that nothing might remain to witness against them, returned to their native town of Ṣoor.

The boy continued to swim so long as his strength bore him up, though more from instinct than hope, since neither land nor ship was in view, except the pirate vessel herself, fast receding from sight. At last he could hold up no longer, ceased his efforts, and sank. But children are light of weight, and he soon rose again, though almost unconscious, to the surface, where he continued to float all that evening and night, and next day also till the afternoon; for the sea was quiet, and the warm temperature rendered so long a stay in the water much more bearable than would be imagined in Europe. At last a ship of Sharjah happened to pass that way; the crew saw the lad, and contrived to pick him up, but he was long before recovering the free use of his mind and of his tongue. They brought him to Sharjah, where he told his tale; some wealthy citizens took him under their protection, and he remained an inhabitant of the town. By a curious chance I fell in with him in the street the very day that I had heard the recital of his adventures; he is now a well-looking young man of three or four-and-twenty; when the event just related took place he was about twelve years old. He told me that from the first moment of his sinking to that when he was picked up, he was conscious only of one feeling—namely, that of dread lest the sea should roughen, and that for all the rest he had neither thought nor knowledge; unconscious at the time how he had got into so precarious a position, and with no distinct hope or idea how he was to get out of it.

After a short rest under the shed where we had halted, we resumed our way and reached Sharjah after nightfall. There a sea-captain, belonging to the town of Soweyḳ in the Bāṭinah, was seated in our room, conversing with 'Abbas our host. He intended sailing next day, and we agreed with him to embark in his vessel—I had almost said his boat, for she was no bigger than a middle-sized yacht—and take our chance of fair gales to round Mesandum and reach the Bāṭinah.

Next morning our captain led us down to the harbour's mouth, where the ship lay. She was manned by five 'Omānee sailors; and had on board four passengers, besides ourselves, a young chief of Fezârah descent; his family, though Nejdeans in origin, have by long sojourn in 'Omān transformed themselves into Biaḍeeyah like those around them, and rule the little coast town of Ṣoḥâm. Zeyd, to give him his proper name—or Zoweyd, in familiar designation—added to good birth and wealth (for he was well-to-do in the world) the advantages of literature and learning, such as 'Omān affords. Gifted with a most retentive memory, a quality not uncommon where books are scarce, he would recite by heart hundreds of the verses ascribed to 'Amroo-l-Keys, and to other ante- and anti-Islamitic poets, and amongst them a curious rhyming parody of the "Soorat," known as "Es-Sâ'ah" or the "Hour," and of another entitled "Hal 'ata" or "Has there come,"—ludicrous pieces, but containing poetry of great merit, and a union of imaginative and burlésque fancy not unlike some authors of the Italian school. Besides, Zeyd had many a story to tell of the land and its rulers; and it was from him that I collected much of the information, whatever be its value, which I have already given touching the usages and the chronicles of 'Omān, or which I am yet to give. The young chief was very conversable, and politely willing to answer any discreet questions. Along with him were two attendants or retainers; to complete the party, we numbered also on board a red-hot Wahhabee from Râs-el-Kheymah, a village till within late years infamous for the piratical doings of its inhabitants—men who now only await a good opportunity to make the present equal the past, did the Union Jack permit. This worthy lost no possible occasion for theological discussions, much reminding me of Gifted Gilfillan's outpourings in "Waverley." Had it not been for fear of Khâlid and the Djowâsimah he would have been certainly thrown into the sea, to cool at leisure, as has been the luck of more than one of his sect when in the hands of Biaḍeeyah sailors.

We took a friendly farewell of 'Abbas and others who had accompanied us down to the water's edge, and embarked. The hours of sailing here depend on the tide; for at low water it is impossible to bring even Arab small craft over the bar at the mouth of the Khowr. It was now near noon, the 20th of February, the flood was in; "a light wind blew from the gates of the South," and out we danced into the green sea. We coasted pretty close along the land, for the water is here deep within a few yards of shore, and while sailing past could clearly distinguish all the comers and goers on the beach-road. Soon we came off Mefraz, a good-sized village, three or four miles north of Sharjah, where a handsome square palace shelters some members of the Ebn-Ṣaḳar family; the plantations around are superior in extent and fertility to those of Sharjah. In the afternoon the wind slackened, and towards evening we anchored off Ajmān, often called and written Aymān; it is a small Djowāsimah town. Here our Wahhabee went ashore for the night, but no one else thought fit to follow his example, since the population of this region are well known as uncompromising fanatics. Next day the breeze slacked, and we slowly worked up to the north, passing Ḥomeyreeyah, Ommel-Ghoweyn (I suspect a popular mispronunciation for Ommel-Akhoweyn, or "the Mother of the two Brothers"), Ḥowārah (a word implying whiteness, as Ḥomeyreeyah does redness), and half-a-dozen small hamlets planted on the beach; many of them have the advantage of a Khowr or port, others are mere roadsteads. The country between and behind is not absolutely sterile like Ḳaṭar, nor yet exactly fertile; the inhabitants, now that sea-robbery is forbidden them, live principally by fishing. Here and there an old fort or tower occupies some rising ground, or stands perched on an isolated rock. Meanwhile the mountain-chain, known by the name of Ro'os-el-Djebal, which forms the backbone of the promontory, gradually approaches the shore in all its rugged grandeur, throwing out granite cliffs and masses of basalt, till at last the Djowāsimah villages have scarce room to nestle between mountain and sea. On the second morning, that of the 22nd, we anchored off Rās-el-Kheymah, the largest and worst-famed, but fortunately the last of the Wahhabee colonies on this coast. Situated in a sheltered bay, somewhat resembling that of Messina in its almost circular form, it offers to the eye a mass of palm-leaf huts, without order or beauty; on the adjoining crags are some faint attempts at fortification; the population is said to be five thousand or thereabouts, but they make up for their scantiness of number by a valour exaggerated into real ferocity.

Here our Wahhabee preacher went ashore for good, to the great satisfaction of the captain and his crew, who sent after him curses enough to have sunk a man-of-war. Freed from his disagreeable company we sailed cheerily on; the weather was delightful, the sky cloudless, the gale gentle but favourable, and the coast extremely grand, nothing inferior to that of Calabria and the Abruzzi. Now the granite wall went sheer down into the blue ocean; now it spread out into clefts down which winter torrents ran, and where little villages niched themselves like eagles' nests; close by them patches of green sprinkled on the mountain-ledges indicated one means of subsistence for the tenants of these eyries, while numerous boats and log-canoes presenting the catamaran construction of the Malabar Coast, all busily engaged in fishing, made known the other. This same afternoon we reached Sha'am, a largeish village, lining the shingly beach close under the cliffs that wall it in from the land side. Here we lowered our boat and went on shore, the sailor-gang singing in merry chorus, and the water calm as a lake. We had a long pull before reaching land; and now for the first time I heard what in the rest of our coast-voyage was of every-day occurrence, an Arab "tarantella," or extemporary satirical song, like those of the Italian improvisatori, and the Trasteverini in particular. Our sailors showed themselves rivals of the western rhymesters in fancy and wit; the metre was adapted to the stroke of the oars, and every alternate line repeated a chorus "Ya Ṣabāḥ-al-Kheyri dā'im," or "O abiding morn of good fortune." The opening stanzas contained nothing but general expressions of mirth and rowers' encouragement; then followed a good-humoured caricature of all on board, beginning with the captain, who took the joke in excellent part, and followed by a humorous review of crew and passengers. When my turn came I was honoured with a couple of stanzas, while the singing rascal grinned as he looked towards me, and the sailor on the bench by my side pushed me to arouse my special attention, adding, however, "No offence is meant, and none should be taken; you see we all come in for a share." Subsequently I heard like recitations from men of Ṣoḥār and other towns of the Bāṭinah; indeed, they are common throughout 'Omān. But they are also peculiar to it; at least I was never thus entertained in Nejed or Shomer.

The inhabitants of Sha'am and of Ro'os-el-Djebal in general are a strange set. Kaḥṭānees and Yemanees by descent, they have for ages past dwelt in these mountains, and on this rocky coast, which they seldom or never leave to visit other lands. Their language is indeed a dialect of Arabic, but isolation has rendered it so barbarous, that a stranger from 'Omān itself, not to mention Nejed or Ḥaṣa, can hardly get on without an interpreter in Ro'os-el-Djebal. "Lisan-oṭ-ṭey'yoor," "bird's speech," Yoosef called it, and declared that he hardly understood one word in ten. All here are staunch Biaḍeeyah, nor have they much to fear from their dangerous neighbours, the Wahhabee Djowāsimah; such is the strength of their mountain fastnesses; their poverty is another nor, perhaps, less effectual protection. This part of Cape Mesandum, from one side to the other, forms the province of Ro'os-el-Djebal, and is the wildest and barrennest of 'Omān; the people are looked upon as half savages, yet they are not really such in character; they furnish good sailors to the central government, and have often rendered valuable service in naval war. Each village has its chief, nor does any one appear to claim a predominant authority over the rest; indeed, the want of ready communication amid these precipitous mountains is alone enough to prevent any effective organisation. After some hours at Sha'am, we returned to pass the night on board, for the worthy fishermen of the village had nothing at home to offer us, except what was inferior even to our own ship provisions—wretched fare that too. Next morning we sailed on, rounding headlands and skirting cliffs, now gliding over green depths, under the dark shade of high rocky walls, now dashing into bright sunshine and sparkling waters; while far and near light fisher-boats skimmed the sea, or lay-to while taking up or casting their nets; sometimes farther out large sails spread in the direction of Linja or Baḥreyn; and overhead on our right frowned the giant crags that sever the Persian Gulf and the Indian Sea. Before noon we entered a lovely bay, deep retired amid lofty rocks on every side, with one narrow entrance alone left to the broad waters within, through whose glassy clearness we could see, far below, the stony bed of the creek; neither storm nor wave could here find access. At the farther end of the bay was a small plain, watered by mountain streams, where palms and gardens announced the diligence of the villagers of Khabb, such being the inharmonious name of this fairily-placed hamlet. Here we landed and passed a couple of hours on shore; the village itself had little to show but small thatched cabins and half-dressed or half-naked fishermen. It were almost superfluous to say that mosques—things never absent from the smallest Wahhabee locality—are not to be found in any village of Ro'os-el-Djebal. But very often, instead of the Mesjid, a small cupola, carefully fenced in, and planted around with a little grove, forms an object of local devotion; this the inhabitants style a "Mezār," or "place of visit," sometimes "Sey'yid" or "Lord," while the indignant Nejdeans call it "Ṣanam" or "idol." These edifices, like the corresponding "Mezārs" of the Metāwelah and Anṣeyreeyah in Ṣyria, are often to honour the burying-place, or at least the memory, of some apocryphal patron, unknown to Mahometan tradition. Such was the case with the "Sey'yid" or "Ṣanam" of Khabb, a pretty little dome, crowning a square construction; the name of its tenant, real or imaginary, was 'Abbas; and regarding him a long story was told me, of which I could not make out head or tail, only it seemed to be of Persian origin.

All along the coast is carried on a considerable fishery; its special object consists in certain small fishes entitled Meṭooṭ, very much like whitebait or diminutive anchovies in size and shape, but not so delicate in flavour. They are eaten uncooked, after having been simply salted and dried in the sun, without any further preparation. Our captain was very desirous to take in a cargo of Meṭooṭ for Soweyḳ, where they are in great requisition; but after considerable altercation, he and the villagers could not agree on the price; and a little after noon we re-embarked without the proposed freight, and sailed off in hopes of rounding Cape Mesandum that very evening. But destiny had in store for us the visit of other localities by the way. The afternoon was already far advanced when we reached the headland, and saw before us the narrow sea-pass which runs between the farthest rocks of Mesandum and the mainland of the Cape. This strait is called the "Bab" or "gate:" it presents an imposing spectacle, with lofty precipices on either side, and the water flowing deep and black below; the cliffs are utterly bare, and extremely well adapted for shivering whatever vessels have the ill-luck to come upon them. Hence, and from the ceaseless dash of the dark waves, the name of "Mesandum," or "anvil," a term seldom better applied. But this is not all, for some way out at sea rises a huge square mass of basalt, of a hundred feet and more in height, sheer above the water; it bears the name of "Salāmah," or "safety," a euphemism of good augury for "danger," like the "Eumenides" of Greek mythology. This rock has been witness and cause of many a shipwreck—so many, indeed, that Arab sailors generally aver that it was placed there on purpose by the devil himself, and that, like the Inchcape rock, it is still haunted by invisible demon-wreckers. Several small jagged peaks, just projecting above the surface, cluster in its neighbourhood; these bear the endearing name of "Benāt-Salāmah," or "Daughters of Salāmah." In fine, what between the rocks of the cape itself, the terrible cliffs of Mesandum, the ominous Salāmah and her treacherous family, worthy in every way of such a mother, besides the craggy islands of Larej and Ormuz at no great distance, the passage is far from open or safe, especially for Arab navigators. Moreover the powerful and capricious currents that sweep through the narrow inlet, and the frequent storms that brood and burst over the mountains of Ro'os-el-Djebal and 'Omān, or rush down from the high Persian range behind Bander-'Abbas on the opposite side of the strait, render the spot doubly perilous.

This it was now our turn to learn, not by chart, but by personal experience. A little before sunset, and just as we approached the "Bāb" above mentioned, the wind fell; a dead calm succeeded, and lasted about an hour, during which the current carried us far back to the west; then suddenly followed a violent south-wester; the sea, very deep here even close in-shore, rose in billows, and we drove right for Salāmah, where we only missed by a few yards a most undesirable acquaintance with the Mother and her Daughters. The captain and his crew were at their wits' end; Yoosef cried like a child; Seyf looked grave; for my own part, I jammed myself between the timbers to avoid rolling over and over, and then, like Jonah in one respect at least, went to sleep for want of better occupation. All night we drove hither and thither as the storm willed, under a moonless and starless sky, while the great waves gleamed fire-tipped as they curled and broke around. Morning dawned through clouds, mist, and gale; we now found ourselves close under Larej, a dreary-looking island, rock-girt and scantily inhabited. Neither landing-place nor safe anchorage was here to be had, so the crew managed to get the ship round Larej, and we now ran before the wind for Ormuz; the sailors showed more skill in managing the little canvas we could bear than I had given them credit for.

I was not at all sorry to have an opportunity for visiting an island once so renowned for its commerce, and of which its Portuguese occupants used to say, that were the world a golden ring, Ormuz would be the diamond signet. The general appearance of Ormuz indicates an extinguished volcano, and such I believe it really is; the circumference consists of a wide oval wall formed by steep crags, fireworn and ragged; these enclose a central basin, where grow shrubs and grass; the basaltic slopes of the outer barrier run in many places clean down into the sea, amid splinter-like pinnacles and fantastic crags of many colours, like those which lava often assumes on cooling. Between west and north a long triangular promontory, low and level, advances to a considerable distance, and narrows into a neck of land which is terminated by a few rocks and a strong fortress, the work of Portuguese builders, but worthy of taking rank amid Roman ruins—so solid are the walls, so compact the masonry and well-cemented brickwork, against which three long centuries of sea-storm have broken themselves in vain. The greater part of the promontory itself is covered with ruins; here stood the once thriving town, now a confused extent of desolate heaps, amid which the vestiges of several fine dwellings, of baths, and of a large church may yet be clearly made out. A solitary Pharos-tower of octangular form, like that of Sharjah, but of more graceful construction, rises at about a hundred yards from the land's end; it is built of brick and stone arranged in herring-bone patterns; within, a winding staircase leads up to the top; but the steps are broken away at twelve or fourteen feet from the ground, thus precluding all possibility of reaching the upper part without a ladder, an article hardly to be hoped for in the Ormuz of our day. From what I have seen of analogous constructions elsewhere, and particularly between Bagdad and Kerkook, I should think this tower was originally the minaret of a Persian mosque, and that it was subsequently applied by the Portuguese to the purposes of a lighthouse. Close by the fort cluster a hundred or more wretched earth-hovels, the abode of fishermen or shepherds, whose flocks pasture within the crater; one single shed, where dried dates, raisins, and tobacco are exposed for sale, is all that now remains of the trade of Ormuz. *Sic transit gloria* was the trite but unavoidable reflection I made on witnessing this dreary decay. I have seen the abasement of Tyre, the decline of Surat, the degradation of Goa; but in none of those fallen seaports is aught resembling the utter desolation of Ormuz.

The reason of its downfall is self-evident. The commerce of Ormuz depended partly on its Indian trade, and partly on the temporary importance given it as a Portuguese station, at a time when the Portuguese reckoned among the first navigators and merchants of the world. Subsequently the route opened by the Red Sea and Egypt gave the Indian trade another direction, while the decline of Portuguese enterprise and power has completed the decay of what commerce was here carried on in the sixteenth century. The importance of Ormuz depended much more on European activity, modified by the necessity of European stations in the East, than on invariable and therefore permanent causes. Strong on the sea, but unable by land to cope to any great extent with the native governments, the Portuguese unavoidably preferred an insular to a continental post, as better ensuring the security of themselves and their wares; and hence the harbour, itself a very tolerable one, afforded by Ormuz suited them better than the coast-ports of Linja, Bander-'Abbas, Ṣoḥār, and the rest, whither the tide of trade now flows; nay, even than Mascat, where their existence was at best precarious, and their action considerably shackled in many ways. In a military and political view also, this island, placed so near the entrance of the Gulf, and capably of easy fortification against assault, had an especial value. But at the present day, when either shore, Persian or Arabian, belongs to the same native government—while Mascat, Ṣoḥār, Linja, and twenty other harbours present each and all advantages equal or superior to those of Ormuz for shipping and commerce, with the land-trade into the bargain—the island has naturally sunk into comparative insignificance; and were it not for the salt-mines on its north-eastern side, whence every comer and goer has free leave to cut and carry away at will on condition of a trifling sum paid for the benefit of the 'Omān treasury, Ormuz would be almost or wholly desert. A petty 'Omānee governor with a few attendants now resides in the fort, to keep it up as it were; and ships storm-driven, like our own, seek shelter from bad weather; a few fishing-boats also hang about the coast.

There are no perennial springs in the island, but the heavy winter rains supply the vaulted cisterns, here constructed after the same patterns as those at Linja, with water enough to serve the scanty population with what they require all the year round. A deep trench surrounds the fort on the land side; the gates still retain their iron-plated doors of Portuguese date; the walls are in tolerably good repair, the vaultings little damaged, and the interior not much changed from what it was in old times. The actual Ḳ'hāwah or reception-room of the governor seems to have been once the domestic chapel of the garrison; it is capable of containing about three hundred men. The greater part of the castle is now uninhabited, and the present governor with all his train occupies only a corner, so to speak, within its large precincts; the rest—rooms, galleries, store-chambers, and ammunition vaults—are left, in Moore's phrase, to stand or fall as Heaven pleases.

The harbour itself consists of two bays, each a half-moon—one to the west, the other to the east of the promontory. The anchorage is fairly sure; and when the one side happens to be exposed to a gale, the other remains sheltered; besides, over this corner of the strait, sunk in a manner within the embrace of the Persian coast, ordinary gales have less power than somewhat farther out. Opposite the north-western harbour rises the high mountain, and under it the town of Bander-'Abbas. The sea-distance from Ormuz to the mainland is scarce ten miles; to the west the island of Djishm, to the south that of Larej, are in full view; Cape Mesandum and the range of Ro'os-el-Djebal close in the horizon.

The storm that had driven us on Ormuz lasted three days, during which period it was impossible to put to sea. Yoosef and I passed most of our time on shore; but as nine-tenths of the inhabitants spoke nothing but Persian, I could not hold much conversation with them. The governor was very polite, but by no means talkative; he offered us what hospitality the poverty of the island could afford; and a dish of mutton at his table seemed quite a luxury after the shark's flesh off which we were accustomed to make our meals on board. Sharks are very common throughout the Gulf, and nobody thinks himself above eating them; though the Hamlet-imagined process by which a king may go a progress through I know not where, may possibly be thus abridged by one stage at least. They are a nutritive, but at best an unsavoury food; their name here is "Awwāl," the Indian for "shark;" the genuine Arab denomination is "Kelb-ol-Baḥr," or "sea-dog." I was much amused on finding that Niebuhr himself, with other travellers, through want perhaps of sufficient conversance with local technicalities, have taken the word "Awwāl" for the name of a place, and have in consequence christened the island of Baḥreyn by the fish in question—common, it is true, off those shores, but not precisely identical with them. Hence Baḥreyn has in some maps and books become "Awwāl," or "shark," much as though a foreigner should, after a visit to our own eastern coast, set down England in his notes by "Herring" or "Mackerel." No island, in fact, large or small, within the Gulf bears the name of "Awwāl."

It is a matter almost too self-evident to need remark, yet it may be well not to pass it over in absolute silence, that the dialect, or rather the lingo, of sea-captains and sailors about 'Omān and Barr-Fāris, is an amalgam of Arabic, Persian, Hindoostanee, and occasionally of African or negro, along with a certain amount of queen's English, sadly clipped and mutilated, to complete the vocabulary. The life of these men passes in voyages now to the shores where Persian is spoken, now to Kurrachee, Bombay, Mangulore, Cannanore, and other Indian ports, now to Zanjibar and the Ṣowāḥil; the crews themselves are also in general a very mixed set, and bring with them on board other languages than Arabic. For what regards English words, my readers can readily understand how the wide-spread "oath of British commerce and the accent of Cockaigne" can find its way even hither. Hence a traveller who is not fully on his guard, and does not know enough of these several languages to distinguish sufficiently the one from the other, and to appreciate the distorted applications of this bastard nomenclature, lies open to many mistakes and misconceptions both in hearing and in rendering what he hears.

Along the northern and eastern coast of Ormuz are the ruins of small forts, raised by the Portuguese in their day; to the south such precautions would be superfluous, nature having there played the part of Vauban better than the engineer himself. I walked about the island, examined the dilapidated constructions, scrambled up the walls of the crater, looked at the salt-diggings, tried (with little success) to make Persians understand me, tried to make the governor chatty, and could not; he seemed to have taken "Ask me no questions, and I'll tell you no lies" for his motto; and sighed after fair weather and a northerly breeze to clear us out of the roads.

At last the breeze came, and on the morning of the 27th we were once more at sea, and running due south, till we repassed Salāmah and her daughters—but this time without fear, and on the eastern side—and came down opposite to the outer entrance of the Bāb or Gate of Mesandum, through which we had now no longer need to pass. We wore slowly on under the pillar-like rocks (I bethought me of prints seen long since of Fingal's Cave and the Giant's Causeway), and early next morning we put in for an hour or so into a sheltered recess, an inland lake were it not for the very narrow ribbon of water connecting it with the sea. At its further extremity stood the village of Roobah; it belongs to the wild province of Ro'os-el-Djebal, or "Mountain tops,"—a very appropriate name.

The object of our visit was still the same, namely, a cargo of Meṭooṭ; but none were to be had, so we cleared out of the little harbour, and sailed on for that of Leymah not far off down the coast. Leymah gives its name to a fine bay, and the village itself is the most populous and the most important amid all the hamlets of Ro'os-el-Djebal; it is also the nearest on the eastern side to the frontiers of the province. Beyond it commences the district of Ḳalhaṭ, or more often Ḳalhooṭ, a name in most maps and voyages placed to the south-east of Mascat, near Rās-el-Ḥadd. To this latter region my personal explorations did not extend; so I suppose that there must be thereabouts some town or village bearing that designation; but the only Ḳalhaṭ of which I heard mention when in 'Omān, was the province whose northerly limits are at the cape of Leymah, and its southern the Bāṭinah.

We entered the bay; but night was now closing in, and it was too late to go ashore for any useful purpose. Accordingly we anchored close under a horn of the coast, formed by jutting rocks that overhung the water, and resolved here to await the morning. But a little before midnight a sudden and violent blast, such as are much too common on this coast, rushed down from the mountains and broke on us with such violence that our vessel dragged upon her anchor, and drove on the rocks before that the crew, starting from their over-secure sleep, could put in execution the manœuvres necessary to get her round. While all as yet was hurrying and shouting, our bowsprit struck the crag and shivered; a moment more and prow and keel would have followed the example. However, by dint of extraordinary and not unskilful exertions, the sailors brought the ship about, after which we profited by the moonlight to run into the inner bay, where the anchorage was better, and the situation more sheltered.

Next morning dawned for us on a very pretty scene. It was a low shingly beach, behind which a wooded valley stretched far back between the mountains, and ended in deep gorges, also clothed with trees, though the rough granite crags peeped out here and there; on our right the village of Leymah, house above house, and row above row, clomb up the hill-side, like many a hamlet seen by me in the happy days of boyhood within the Swiss canton of Ticino, or—but in later and less rosy times—on the slopes of Lebanon. The cottages of Leymah were stone-built, with terraces and garden walls beside—they looked neat and comfortable; judging by the number of domiciles, the sum-total of the inhabitants may equal about two thousand. Further up were herds of goats clinging to the mountain ledges, and shepherds loitering among them; below in the valley, bands of blue-dressed peasant women moved in quest of water from the wells; on the beach were boats large and small, drawn up, or ready for the chances of fishery; and lastly—a joyous sight for our captain and his crew—whole piles of fresh Meṭooṭ lay glittering on the shingles, while others, spread out on the rocks, were drying in the sun.

We all landed; our captain and his men fell at once a bargaining for the Oriental anchovies, while Zeyd, Yoosef, and myself strolled for a couple of hours up the valley, where an abundant vegetation of mixed character—oaks, palms, lotos-trees, acacias, and particularly a glossy-leafed tree, belonging to the species here called Moḳsah, and laden with round berries which afford a sort of slime much used by bird-catchers, contrasted pleasantly with the past barrenness of Rās-el-Kheymah and Ormuz. The inhabitants whom we met, mostly shepherds or fishermen, were friendly enough: I drew some of them into conversation about the English, whose ships and steamers they may spy afar from their mountain nest. But questioners, like listeners, too often hear no good of themselves, and such was here the case. All the advantages, however real, of commerce, of civilization, of protection, and whatever else, can ill outweigh national antipathy, deepened by a fear of territorial encroachment—a fear justified to a certain extent, it may be, by too-neighbouring Indian conquests, Burmese acquisitions, Punjab invasions, Chinese wars, and many other world-famed examples of what invariably takes place sooner or later when iron comes in collision with clay—Europe with Asia. The events just alluded to were not done in a corner, and are no secret in 'Omān; they have gone far to instil a wholesome dread, but have also done little to conciliate love. Hence I fear that our countrymen, at least of the present generation, must content themselves at Leymah with the "*oderint dum metuant*" of Tacitus—words which sum up the position pretty exactly. My fisher friends seemed much alarmed lest Englishmen, should they ever become acquainted with the excellence of Ro'os-el-Djebal, and Leymah in particular, would leave their own sea-girt isle, and come over in a body—king, queen, and all (this a man of the place said to me me very seriously)—to colonize Cape Mesandum. I did not think myself bound to contradict such just apprehensions; besides, a fair complexion and the condition of a stranger might have rendered me rather a suspected defender of the British cause. So I sighed in sympathetic anxiety; and up to the present day the hearts of the men of Leymah doubtless palpitate at the idea of seeing Buckingham Palace and Westminster Hall suddenly transferred to Ro'os-el-Djebal.

On returning from our walk we visited the village. But in vain we searched its alleys and knocked at its doors in hopes of noontide hospitality; not a man was to be found; all were "not at home"—not in polite fiction, but in hard-working reality—fishing, sheep pasturing, drying or selling Meṭooṭ, and the like. A good woman left indoors invited us to partake of some indifferent bread, with water to wash it down, and that was all the entertainment Leymah could boast; coffee was out of the question. Near the picturesque torrent-course below the village stood a little cupola, the object of much veneration; and thereby hung a tale, and a long one too, which was narrated to me by an old man, in such uncommonly bad bird-twittering Arabic, that I understood nothing of the story, except that a sacred fire had once burnt here, but had gone out for some time since. On hearing this I lighted my pipe, and begged my aged friend to make use of it in compensation for the extinguished fire of the "Kubbah;" whereat he laughed very much, and accepted the invitation.

In the afternoon we went on board again, and for the rest of the evening skirted the coast of Ḳalhaṭ or Ḳalhooṭ; rocky, yet less so than that of Ro'os-el-Djebal. Next morning we were off the Gulf of Ḍebee, a magnificent bay, scarcely inferior in beauty to that of Naples; many small villages are jotted on its shores, and behind it circles a panorama of mountains worthy of Sicily. I much desired to stop and go on shore; but the captain was fully saṭisfied with his Leymah cargo of Meṭooṭ, and neither he nor the crew saw any sufficient reason for casting anchor at Ḍebee. So we skimmed on rapidly hour after hour by the coast, here fertile and thickly wooded, while the mountains recede more and more towards the interior, to unite with the great chain of Djebel-Akhdar behind the Bāṭinah. Since the late war all this territory belongs in a certain measure to Khālid-ebn-Ṣaḳar, who collects the revenues, but has no farther administrative authority; the inhabitants are without exception Biaḍeeyah. The main bulk of the population lies along the sea-coast, where the level lands allow easier cultivation, and the sea invites to fishing and to trade, pursuits the most congenial to the men of 'Omān. Ḍebee is the principal town of Ḳalhaṭ, and here resides the local governor; the inland limits of the province are determined by the mountain-chain which separates it from that of Sharjah. About noon we passed Zabarah, a small town, but surrounded by fruitful gardens; other lesser hamlets form a chain along the shore, for Ḳalhaṭ is much more densely peopled than Ro'os-el-Djebal, and the inhabitants are of a more civilized type.

Before evening we came opposite to a high precipitous peak, situated at a distance of ten to twelve miles from the coast; it forms the southern abutment of the Ro'os-el-Djebal range, and is entitled "Ḳaṭaa-l-Loḥa," or "the cutting off of beards," though whence the name I could not learn; below it passes the valley of Ḥamm, and here a road leads direct across the promontory to Sharjah, exactly opposite this point on the other side. From Ḳaṭaa'-l-Loḥa southwards, begins the Bāṭinah, following the coast as far as Barḳa, and reaching inland to the slope of Djebel-Akhdar.

The Bāṭinah is by much the richest though not exactly the most important province of 'Omān. Placed with the sea on one side and the high range of Djebel-Akhdar or "the green mountain" on the other, it is better watered than any other district soever of Arabia; the soil, moist with springs and drenched in the winter months by heavy rains, is besides intersected in every direction by mountain torrents, though none of these last deserve by their size or permanence to bear the name of rivers, or to find place as such on the map. This region is a great plain, of near a hundred and fifty miles in length by thirty or forty in breadth; inland it rises gradually into slopes and green hills, while seawards it is enough above the ocean level to ensure it against the unhealthiness of Ḳaṭeef and similar low coasts. The vegetation of the Bâṭinah may compete in luxuriance with that of the Indian Concan; nor is it dissimilar to it in character. Mango-trees, the cocoa-nut, the betel-palm, with several other sylvan productions better known to me by their Indian than by their Arab nomenclature: the wide-spreading smooth-barked Aâley', the Kathol or Jack-fruit; the Jamblu, here decorated with the borrowed name of Khowkh; the Papay, so frequent about Bombay; not to mention many lesser shrubs and undergrowth of the tropical Flora, are here mingled with the date-palms and Ithel which yet remain, as though to witness to the identity of the Arab soil. The agricultural produce is no less varied. Cotton, white, and red—indeed the latter is here the more common, and in great requisition for use; coffee, though more resembling the Indian in quality than that of Yemen; indigo, sugarcane, sweet potatoes or yams, corn, maize, millet, leguminous plants of many kinds, besides apricot-trees, peaches (Khowkh Fârisee), nuts, and, I believe, apples—though I am not quite sure whether these last are not imported from Persia; at least they bear here the Persian name of "Seeb," instead of the Arab "Ṭuffâḥ." Fertile vineyards clothe the sides of Djebel-Akhdar, and afford excellent grapes and wine; the inhabitants are fortunate in being Carmathian, not Mahometan, or the best gift of nature were thrown away on them. Lastly, oaks, plane-trees, and Nabaḳ, here of lofty growth, furnish timber for ships and house building; teak is brought from India.

The number of towns and villages in the Bâṭinah is said to surpass a hundred; from what I saw, I can readily believe it. At least the coast is one continuous line of gardens and habitations, from Cape Ḳornah, where the province commences, down to Barḳa, where it ends; far as the eye can reach nothing appears but cultivation and houses, with a deep background of green and foliage. Ṣoḥâr is the capital; Barḳa is the second town in importance; Low'wa, Soweyḳ, Fâjirah, Ṣoḥâm, and Meṣnaa' are considerable centres of population. Let us now pursue our voyage, and take each special object as it comes, in order and succession.

At night the breeze dropped, and we lay-to close on shore. With the bright glitter of Venus, welcomed by our sailors under the oft-questioned name of Farḳad, the land wind blew, and on we glided smoothly, steadily, by the coast, while the captain and Zeyd pointed out to me village after village, and town after town. Fājirah, one of the bloodiest scenes of Khālid's devastations; Shināz, where also great slaughter had been made, were especially noticed, not without comment: from their sea aspect they still looked large and thriving. War, like pestilence, rarely leaves lasting traces on the living world; no Mephistopheles can hinder the "new fresh blood" from circulating even brisker; and if returning spring cannot bring with her "work of gladness" exactly those whom autumn reaped, she soon replaces them by others, no less numerous, nor less reckless, than those who went before. The conflict of the Roses did not unstock the England of a few years later, nor the wars of the Empire, France: a generation hence, and the Northern States of America will number a denser population than they did ere Lincoln was president. Systematic ill government can do more to unpeople a land than Attila or the Black Death, and in almost as short a time. Shināz presented to our view one of those pretty buildings, half castle half château, peculiar to 'Omān, with a symmetrical white frontal, flanked by turrets and crowned with battlements, a high central gate, and behind a round tower, the whole bearing a southern Gothic stamp, and evidently constructed full as much in view of ornament as of defence. Indeed, an air of "ancient peace" and security passed into habit, is a prominent feature of 'Omān. Hence Zeyd and his countrymen spoke of the late Wahhabee invasion with those terms of mingled horror, amazement, and indignation, which men use when describing something to which they are wholly unaccustomed: war is no less abnormal in 'Omān than it is normal in Nejed and in Western Arabia. At evening we anchored off Farḳsah, close under a long range of houses, amid heavy clustering groves down to the very beach—a very Arab watering-place, not wholly unlike some of our own southern coast, but prettier; an hour after sunset we heard the evening gun of Soḥār booming across the waters.

Early next morning before sunrise we had reached the roadstead of Ṣoḥār, where Yoosef and I determined to land for good, and to pursue the rest of our way by land; a pity that we did not subsequently keep to our resolution—why, my readers will soon see. But *l'homme s'agite et Dieu le mène*; and on the backgammon board of life, chance and circumstance decide no less than forethought and skill. We now bade adieu, an unwilling adieu, to Zeyd and his companions, after many invitations on their part, and promises on ours, to call on them at Ṣoḥam; and went ashore in the ship's boat, ycleped "jāliboot" by 'Omānees. The captain came with us, and by a word in season persuaded the custom-house officers to let our baggage pass free. I should remark that we had yet with us the greater part of our presents; whatever in fact was destined for Thoweynee and for the Governor of Ṣoor.

Our first enquiries were after the chief, Fakhar by name, and a man of great importance. But he was unluckily absent, with most of his family, on a visit to the Sultan, and there was no one in his place to receive us. We waited for a moment undecided whether to go, when a young man observing our dilemma, came up, and asked where we meant to lodge. 'Ebn-Khamees recalled to mind an old 'Omānee acquaintance of his, whose guest he had been many years before, while on a commercial journey hereabouts with Aboo-'Eysa, and enquired after him. The lad replied that he knew the man in question, and offered to lead us to his house, which lay some way within the town.

Thither accordingly we went all three. It was still early, and 'Eysa, for so was he styled, was yet in the prolonged enjoyment of a morning nap; his riding-horse, a pretty little creature, stood tethered near his gate, and whinnied to us as we came up and knocked at the outer door. A neighbour next appeared; and all together we roused up the master of the house, who received us cordially, apologized for his slumbers, and straightway set about preparing breakfast, after very justly observing that, as we came from sea, we must no doubt have unusually good appetites.

'Eysa's house was itself of brickwork, but provided with wooden and thatched out-rooms, a pleasant arrangement for passing the hotter hours of the day, and common in 'Omān, where even at this time of year the weather is very warm: indeed, all in all, the climate is that of Bombay; and though the latitude is some degrees to the north, the temperature, from local causes, is not a whit less. Building in the Bātinah is solid, but great attention is paid to secure a free circulation of air; hence the doors are in general large, the windows many, though latticed, and the rooms lofty. Whitewashing takes the place of the Nejdean brown tint, the floors are sometimes of beaten earth, sometimes strewn with fine sand. A peculiar feature of 'Omānee domestic architecture, and one which has its significance, is the absence of any attempt at privacy, I mean the privacy of the ḥarem. In Nejed, and even in Ḥasa, Shomer, and the Djowf, we have seen that a distinction is aimed at between the men's and the women's apartments—not indeed so rigorously as in Syria and Egypt, yet enough to indicate a degree of jealousy, at least an unwillingness to admit a guest into the family life, or to allow him a glimpse into its private mysteries. Arabs are naturally jealous; and Mahometanism has given to this bad feeling the sanction of a religious duty. But in 'Omān the mutual footing of the sexes is almost European, and the ḥarem is scarcely less open to visitors than the rest of the house; while in daily life the women of the family come freely forward, show themselves, and talk, like reasonable beings, very different from the silent and muffled statues of Nejed and Riaḍ. Hence it follows that the ground-plan of an 'Omānee dwelling differs very materially from that of a Mahometan and even of an ordinary Arab abode, the apartments being often all on a line, and communicating together, not shut off into separate courts; while the Ḳ'hāwah or sitting-room, instead of settling near the gate, takes up its post towards the interior, or even in the heart of the habitation.

Our host 'Eysa, more endearingly 'Oweysa, was by profession a merchant, but held over and above a post in the chief's service; hence he was well able to entertain us with all the small talk of a local government. The ruling family to which Fakhar belongs is by his account an old one, and of genuine 'Omānee origin, descended from the Ya'aribah of Djebel-Akhdar. However the present chief was far from popular; many complaints against him had been forwarded to Thoweynee by the town Mejlis or aldermen of Ṣoḥār; in short, he had been obliged to undertake the journey on which he now was, in order to make his disculpation in presence of his

Sultan. To his retainers Fakhar was said to be liberal enough, but at the expense of the townsmen and the merchants; in short, 'Eysa's opinion was that it would go hard with him at Thoweynee's audience, unless indeed bribes could carry him through, an event of which there was yet a chance. This last circumstance gave occasion to sundry complaints regarding the negligence of the Sultan in redressing the grievances of the land; while the system of Sa'eed and his prosperous days and energetic government were a fertile subject of conversation and regret.

But though a certain falling off has taken place in the general administration, the police, established from old times throughout 'Omān, seems to be still very good. Unlike the "Zelators" of Nejed, these "Ḥurrās" to give them their Arab name, equivalent to our "guardsmen," confine their action simply to the maintenance of public order, the preventing squabbles, arresting delinquents, and the like; no spy system, official or non-official, has place here, and no offence is taken cognizance of, unless it interferes with the public peace. During the daytime the "Ḥurrās" may be met with, principally about the market-place; and their dress, of a somewhat more military cut than that of the ordinary townsmen, with the rich ornamentation of their daggers, sometimes a gun too, distinguishes them from amid the crowd. At night they walk up and down the streets, and challenge all who seem other than "true men" in the Sultan's name. Robbery, housebreaking, or murder are rare occurrences in the Bāṭinah, and the frequency of single and unarmed travellers throughout the country marks a population at once dense and orderly. No Bedouin tribes exist between Djebel-Akhdar and the sea; the comparatively few nomades who belong to 'Omān are to be found on the southern side of the mountain in the district entitled Ḍāhirah, and towards the eastern extremity of the range in the province of Djailān. This latter province furnishes the choicest dromedaries of 'Omān, and consequently of the entire Arabian Peninsula; in the Bāṭinah asses are very commonly employed for burden, or even for riding; horses, though smaller, and in other ways inferior to the Nejdean breed, are used by the richer classes.

After breakfast and the chat consequent on a first arrival, 'Eysa, together with some townsmen who had dropped in, and were already on a friendly footing with Yoosef and myself, proposed to show us the town, which is, as my readers know, one of the most important in 'Omān. The offer was gladly accepted, and we began by paying a visit to the chief's palace, a noble castle, with a triple circuit of walls, much ornamented after a style familiar to those of my readers who may have seen the great Kassab mosque at Bombay—a style of which pointed arches, round and slender columns, cross vaulting, and projecting balconies and turrets, are the main features; whilst a charge or overcharge of plaster decoration completes the minute detail. The castle of Ṣoḥār occupies a small rising ground within the city; its entrance is by a bridge, passing over a moat, and leading to a large inner gate; on the walls of the keep are placed a few small pieces of artillery, culverins in antiquated phrase, and four full-grown cannon stand ranged before the entrance. The guard here, and in other great towns of 'Omān, but especially at Mascat, are Beloochees; men renowned for their fidelity to their masters, while their Sonnee religion, which hinders them from mixing over-freely with the Biaḍeeyah of the country, besides their other diversities in language and customs, furnishes an additional safeguard against tampering and collusion. Nor is there fear of their fraternizing on the other hand with the Wahhabees, though Sonnees also in their way; an intense national antipathy divides the Beloochee and the genuine North Arab or Nejdean. During the first Wahhabee invasion Ṣoḥār was besieged and taken; but after the town had been lost, the castle, with the Belooch garrison, held bravely out, till all the provisions within were exhausted, and the 'Omānee chief, with a few retainers, sought and found means of escape over the castle walls by night. Next morning the Belooch garrison, despairing alike of help and resistance, threw the fortress doors wide open, and sallied out sword in hand to die, but not till their own death had been avenged by a frightful slaughter among the besiegers. The actual governor is wealthy, and the inner keep, into which we could not be admitted in his absence, is said to contain much treasure.

Like what I mentioned in Nejed and Ḥaṣa, no inscription here crowns the gateway or varies the walls, to commemorate builder, date, or event. Nor does this omission come from want of suitable material or of workmen, for a light yellow stone, easily carved, enters largely into the construction, and the ornaments of the building show no want of sculptural skill. This may be taken by way of additional proof that the Ḥimyarites, who seem to have had a mania for inscriptions, never occupied this precise part of Arabia; perhaps in the rear of Djebel-Akhdar and in the Djailān something might be found.

In front of the castle is an open place planted with trees and reaching down to the walls seawards; the town bulwarks are in good preservation, and furnished on this side with a few pieces of artillery; were not the circuit too large for efficient defence, Ṣoḥār might stand an Arab siege. From the castle we went to the market-place. It is a very large one, and much more regular than that of Sharjah; the shops and their contents resemble on the whole those at Linja, but the number of travellers who visit Ṣoḥār from land and sea gives the vegetable and the meat markets an unusual importance. The Ḳeysareeyah, vaulted as usual, and with huge folding doors, is spacious and long, and in size and construction fully equal to any Ṣooḳ at Bagdad; but many of its shops were empty. This, I was told, had been the case ever since Khālid-ebn-Ṣaḳar's occupation of the country, which, although brief in duration, had done much injury to commerce, and frightened away several pacific Banians. To make amends, the Wahhabees constructed a mosque, not far from the castle; it is now absolutely deserted, and stands in lonely ugliness. The rest of the Ṣooḳ or market-place is crowded with artisans and shopkeepers; the passages between the booths are protected by thatch against the heat of the sun.

Weavers, and smiths in silver, gold, iron, and copper, are here the staple workmen, and in industry and skill the artisans of 'Omān surpass those of Ḥaṣa no less than the artisans of Ḥaṣa outdo those of Nejed. Amid the crowds in the streets I noticed some dusky, strong-set fellows, dressed in a sort of kilt, and wearing a white head-dress: they carried short javelins in their hands, and each one had a knife at his belt in addition to the ordinary dagger. On enquiry I found these strangers to be men of Akhdar from the neighbourhood of 'Obree, and belonging to the Ya'aribah nobles of the mountain. Passing behind the Ḳeysareeyah, we entered a square courtyard surrounded by high houses, and planted with two or three trees; here stood a couple of Brahminee bulls, belonging to some Banians of the market. No Jews that I could learn of reside in Ṣoḥār; I heard of Parsees, but did not meet any.

From the market-place we continued our walk between two- or three-storeyed houses, and under several arches thrown at intervals across the main street, till we reached the northern gateway of the town; thence traversing a little sandy space left open around the walls, we entered the gardens, where we sat and rested awhile under shady trees and beside running waters. Everything here was tropical—sun, trees, shrubs, flowers, and men; the very wells and watercourses, neatly arranged with "Chunām," to borrow once more the Indian word, seemed transported from Guzerat; only a certain briskness in the air, and rather a more sinewy build and a livelier look of the gardening peasants, gave to me to know that I was not in the Hindoostanee vapour-bath, but on Arab soil. From the gardens we returned to the town, and skirted its walls by a road following the outside of the trench, for about a quarter of a mile; then passed a narrow bridge, re-entered the city by the eastern gate, and returned home. The entire circuit of the town may be about two miles; its fortifications enclose it all round, but the moat ceases towards the sea side.

Yoosef and I intended setting off that same evening, or at furthest next morning, on our land journey for Mascat; we should thus have had eight or ten days of road before us. But, to our great good fortune as we imagined, and to our great ill-luck in reality, at the very moment that we were discussing our route and dinner with 'Eysa, a sea captain, bound for Mascat, came in, and promised to take us in his ship, saying that a two days' voyage would land us in the desired port, that the wind was favourable, and that all promised a pleasant and speedy passage. We had already lost so much time in cruising about Mesandum and Ormuz, that we had now no more to lose, and we accordingly thought the opportunity too good to be neglected; the more so that the coast tract from Ṣoḥār to Mascat promised no very special interest, and I hoped for more liberty to visit Djebel-Akhdar, the main object of my desires, after an interview with Thoweynee, then reported to be at Mascat. 'Eysa was of the same opinion, and we ended by accepting the captain's offer.

We remained yet two days longer in Ṣoḥār. During this time we called on several of the good folks of the town, and passed cheerful hours in their society, amid entertainments much more varied and elegant in style than any yet witnessed by me even at Sharjah or Baḥreyn. The Nargheelah here wholly supersedes the pipe; and at evening parties, cakes and pistachio nuts are handed round from time to time, much like the after-dinner usage of English drawing-rooms. My readers may remember that in Shomer and Nejed the removal of the dinner or supper tray is a signal for the guests to withdraw also; a practical way of saying that they only came to eat, and now that eating is over, they may, in Corporal Nym's phrase, "shog off." In 'Omān the contrary is the rule, eating comes first, and then conversation is prolonged to midnight or even to the small hours, for it is no easy matter to get away from these sociable hosts. The pleasures of intercourse are further enhanced by song, seldom absent from an 'Omān party; the voices are in general good, though not of large compass; and the Nabṭee metre, here absolutely predominant, admits of many light airs, not unlike those of Persian music, but inadmissible in the recitation of Arab poems. The inhabitants of Ṣoḥār pride themselves on their sweetmeat manufacture, and are very profuse of them on these occasions, keeping these delicacies in perpetual circulation, as if alarmed lest the gratifications of the ear should be insufficient.

Conversation turned much on the state of the country, and I was struck by two things: one the great attachment, amounting to a real hearty loyalty, of this people for the reigning family, and for their nobles in general; the other their extreme hatred of Wahhabees, and, somewhat strange to say, of Turks; of these last they have not much personal experience, but what they have is enough to make them conceive an intense aversion against Ottomans, whether as rulers or as individuals. Many of the Ṣoḥār merchants had visited India, and were not wholly unacquainted with English affairs. I was much amused by hearing one Ṣoḥāree say, in a moment of familiarity, "If matters came so far that either the Muslims or the English must be masters of our country, we should decidedly prefer the latter, or even the devil in person, to rule over us, rather than the Muslims." The juxtaposition in this latter clause was not over flattering, but it expresses a feeling widely spread throughout 'Omān. Meanwhile all the negligence of Thoweynee has not impaired national allegiance to the family of Sa'eed, though nine out of ten would certainly prefer to have Amjed for their sultan.

Without the town, gardens and cultivation reach uninterruptedly to the villages beyond. I entered two of them: one by name Ma'wah at a couple of miles inland; the other—I have forgotten how called—lay more to the south. Ma'wah contains five or six thousand inhabitants, but most of its dwellings are mere sheds—sufficient for the mildness of the climate. The chief alone, and a few other wealthy individuals, enjoy habitations of brick. The common people, wherever I met them, were civil and *prévenant*; a stranger finds himself no stranger here. The dialect spoken is pure unmixed Arabic, but of the Ḳaḥṭānee variety before described; the pronunciation is less guttural and less emphatic than that of Nejed, but more correct in respect to that much vexed consonant Ḳaf, here endowed with its genuine value of Ḳ, not G, or Dj – a great comfort to the hearer. Beyond Ma'wah the whole land up to Djebel-Akhdar is alike cultivated and inhabited; there is neither waste nor desert. The mountain chain hems in the distant view, in form, character, and height not unlike the Apennines of Central Italy. A wide road leads from Ṣoḥār to Bereymah and the Ḍāhirah; another follows the coast to Mascat; a third conducts northward to Ḍebee.

Before quitting Ṣoḥār I ought to add that the actual number of its inhabitants does not, I think, exceed twenty-four thousand, several houses stand empty, and others have remained in ruins since the late war. Commerce too, that mainspring of sea-coast populousness, has been in great measure transferred to the vicinity of Mascat, and the temporary prosperity conferred on

Ṣoḥâr by the viceregal residence of Amjed has passed away with him, so that the town is now but half its former self. Still it numbers many opulent traders, and may at a future epoch easily regain what recent misfortune has taken away. The want of a Khowr or sheltered harbour is certainly a drawback, but the roadstead and anchorage are good, and pretty well sheltered to north and west by the promontory of Farkṣah, to the south by that of Sowârah. During my stay at Ṣoḥâr, I never saw less than twenty good-sized ships in the roads, sometimes more. The fishery off shore is excellent; the beach is covered with boats, and the stocked and crowded fish-market might rival Billingsgate—*minus* its abuse. The low sandy beach, the sailor children at play, the boats drawn up above tide-mark, the fishermen sauntering on shore, or shouting while they run their craft down to the water for a new trip, others wading breast-deep through the waves to bring their cockle-shell on shore, all recalled to mind some spots on our own eastern coast—yet how different in climate and people.

On the third day our captain, who had from the first engagement carried off our baggage on board (a measure which effectually prevented our breaking with him, as we had more than once thought of doing), came to 'Eysa's house and announced sailing time. It was the 6th of March, and we embarked. A vague presentiment of ill, though there seemed as then no special reason for it, made me "sad as night" on quitting our Ṣoḥâr friends who had accompanied us down to the beach; the same feeling was, curiously enough, shared by our host 'Eysa, and he showed it by repeated and pressing requests that we should not fail to write to him on our safe arrival at Mascat and give him good news. Yet no cause appeared for fear, the wind was favourable, the sea quiet, the ship a large one—so large indeed that she had been obliged to anchor a long way out, and we had nearly half an hour's pull in the boat before reaching her.

CHAPTER XVII

A Shipwreck—Mascat

Then out spoke the captain of our gallant ship,
And a well-spoken man was he:
"For want of a long-boat we all shall be drowned,
And go to the bottom of the sea."—*Old Ballad*

COAST OF THE BĀṬINAH—CREW AND PASSENGERS—DETAILS REGARDING THE ḌĀHIRAH, DJEBEL-AKHDAR, AND THEIR INHABITANTS—BARḲA—ITS CASTLE—SOWĀDAH ISLANDS—A SUDDEN STORM—DRIVING BEFORE THE WIND—THE SHIP FOUNDERS—SOME ESCAPE IN THE BOAT AND ON A PLANK—FURTHER INCIDENTS OF THE NIGHT—SEVERAL MORE ARE DROWNED—A DESPERATE RESOLUTION AVERTED—WE MAKE FOR SHORE—LOSS OF THE BOAT—A HARD SWIM—NINE COME TO LAND—THEIR CONDUCT—OUR WHEREABOUTS—A DREARY MORNING—WE SET OUT FOR THE SULTAN'S PALACE AT BAṬḤAT—FARZAH—REFLECTIONS—PALACE OF THE BAṬḤAH—THOWEYNEE AND HIS COURT—RECEPTION—GOOD TREATMENT—AN EVENING WALK—THE MEṬEYREF—OUR BOAT—ALMS RECEIVED—MEETING WITH TWO ALBANIANS—THEIR STORY—DETAILS REGARDING THOWEYMEE—OUR OWN POSITION—DEPARTURE FROM THE BAṬḤAH—VALLEY OF FARZAH—KHABR—RI'ĀN—'OMĀNEE IRRIGATION—PORTUGUESE FORTIFICATIONS—SUBURBS OF MAṬRAḤ—A NIGHT'S LODGING—MAṬRAḤ—ITS HARBOUR, MARKET, TRADE, AND POPULATION—AN 'OMĀNEE CANOE—ARRIVAL AT MASCAT—OUR HOST—A FRIEND IN NEED—GENERAL DESCRIPTION OF MASCAT AND ITS INHABITANTS—RELIGION—ENGLISH CONSUL—CLIMATE—RESEMBLANCE BETWEEN MASCAT AND 'ADEN—POLICE—CHANGES OF FORTUNE—HINDOOS—DISCOURSE BETWEEN A NEJDEAN AND A BANIAN—FAIR OUTSIDE THE TOWN—A WALK SOUTHWARDS—MEETING WITH MEN OF ZAḲEB—A TRIP—COUNTRY SOUTH-EAST OF MASCAT—CHAIN OF AKHDAR—POTTERIES—VILLAGE OF BENHEYR—RECEPTION—AN EVENING WITH THE CHIEF—VILLAGE ADMINISTRATION—A DANCE—RETURN BY KAMLEE—HEAT—A SHOWER-BATH—FURTHER DETAILS REGARDING THE KINGDOM OF 'OMĀN—ITS PROVINCES, POPULATION, AND MILITARY STRENGTH—REVENUES—THEIR SOURCES AND AMOUNT—PRESENT GOVERNMENT—A KOWEYT SHIP—KOWEYT—DEPARTURE FROM MASCAT—CONSTELLATIONS—RETURN UP THE PERSIAN GULF—BANDER-'ABBAS—CHIRO—A TYPHOID FEVER—ARRIVAL AT ABOO-SHAHR—AT BAṢRAH—KIND RECEPTION ON AN ENGLISH STEAMER—ARRIVAL AT BAGDAD—MEETING WITH BARAKAT—RETURN TO SYRIA—CONCLUSION.

Our course now lay along the remaining coast of the Bāṭinah, from Ṣoḥār to Barḳa. I was glad to find that our pilot, like most Asiatic navigators, kept the vessel close along shore, so that the fact of our being at sea made us lose but little of anything worth observing on the coast itself; indeed, the beach road, with men, asses, horse-riders, dromedary-riders, and foot travellers of all kinds and descriptions, was generally full in view, except where the palm-trees, by coming right down to the sea-edge, hid it awhile from sight, or some village interposed its white houses and leafy sheds between us and the highway. The crew was very interesting. The captain, his nephew, and his men, amounting to nine in all, were partly natives of Soweyḳ on the coast, partly from neighbouring villages — Biaḍeeyah of course. Besides these we had on board ten other fellow-passengers: two from Djebel-'Oḳdah, Sonnees but not Wahhabees; they belonged to one of those old Nejdean clans which I have already mentioned as scattered through different parts of 'Omān, and most numerous in the Ḍāhirah. Both were of amiable manners and well-read in Arab lore; very ready too to make friends with all around them; the ultimate destination of their journey was Mecca, which they proposed reaching by the sea and Djiddah, thus circumnavigating about two-thirds of the Peninsula. Fate had in store for one of them a much shorter cruise.

A third passenger was a Nejdean, born at Manfooḥah (my readers will remember the town close to Riaḍ) in 'Aareḍ; he was an ill-conditioned youth, who having, by his own account, quarrelled with his papa, had fled from the paternal roof, and was now, like some refractory lads elsewhere, seeking his fortune in the wide world. The seven remaining seafarers were natives of the Bāṭinah, all men of the lower classes, but cheerful and talkative like most of their countrymen. The Nejdean alone was ill-tempered and ugly; I should hardly think that his family shed many tears over his absence. In less than an hour we were "Hail fellow, well met!" with all; the ship was large and roomy, a two-master; plenty of provisions and Nargheelahs at disposal were on board; we hoped for a pleasant and an expeditious voyage.

I now learnt from the men of 'Oḳdah many particulars regarding Bereymah and the Ḍāhirah, which may here find place. Of Bereymah itself they said that the town was strongly nestled amid the passes of Djebel-'Oḳdah, and surrounded by several villages where lived a population partly Sonnee, portly Biadee; they added that Aḥmed-es-Sedeyree, the Nejdean governor, had long since adopted in every respect the ways and fashions of the country, and was by no means inclined to leave it, whatever summons might come from Riaḍ. That Djebel-'Oḳdah itself was a lofty mountain, equalling in height the range of Ro'os-el-Djebel, that the soil around was light, and the vegetation less luxuriant than in the Bāṭinah. That beyond Djebel-'Oḳdah extended east and south a long series of hills parallel to Djebel-Akhdah; between these two chains, said they, lies the Ḍāhirah, a tract more abounding in pasture than in arable land, but well peopled. They added that the inhabitants of the Ḍāhirah are less attached than any others to the government of 'Omān; half of them at least are Sonnees, others are Bedouins, and the religious tendencies of the former, no less than the predatory habits of the latter, inclined them to sympathise with Nejed rather than with the Biaḍeeyah and their rulers. Hence during the Wahhabee foray, many clans of the Ḍāhirah sided with the invaders, and bore arms against their own countrymen of the plains. The dromedaries of the Ḍāhirah are fleet and enduring; the sheep of the province rival the Nejdean breed.

From Mokhanneth eastward begins a labyrinth of rocky and thickly wooded gorges, amid which are situated the towns of Nezwah and Bahilah; this latter they described as a strongly fortified place, with a double range of walls, high gates, and houses of two and three storeys high. If the account given by the natives be true, Bahilah must considerably surpass in size both Riaḍ and Hofhoof, and be well worth the visiting.

They told us too many tales regarding the Morrah Bedouins, who frequent the Ḍāhirah; tales also regarding Burghash, the present chief of Bahilah, and not a few legends of sorcerers and witches. The Biaḍeeyah sailors on their part had much to say; some of them had taken part in the naval expeditions of Sa'eed, and had been present at the Hogues and Cape St. Vincents of those seas. Nowhere is the 'Omānee government more loved or better served than in the navy; and in spite of all the terror inspired by English frigates and guns, I should doubt whether the seamen of Ḍebee and Barḳa would be inclined to surrender their maritime supremacy off these coasts without a struggle. In the fatal year when Khālid wasted the Bāṭinah, the first to oppose him were the natives of Ḳalḥaṭ and of Ro'os-el-Djebal, sailors by profession, but then land soldiers in the cause of their country; and, though insufficient to bar the fury of the Wahhabee onset, they held it awhile in check, and boast of having slain a large number of the invaders.

With such conversation we beguiled the time, while our vessel glided on, passing Ṣoḥām, Soweyḳ, and Meṣnaa', till on the 8th of the month we were close off Barḳa. Thus far the coast had been uniform and level, fringed with palm and cocoa-nut trees, and glistering with whitewashed villages, amid which the pretty castles of the local chiefs shone out to the sun. But near Barḳa a range of barren iron-red rocks, at first low, but soon rising in height, appeared lining the shore, and extending eastward all the way to Mascat. Barḳa seemed from its sea view a good-sized town, not much inferior to Ṣoḥār; it possesses a castle of unusually large proportions aud, judging from a distance, of considerable strength. A lovelier coast I have seldom beheld: in front, the fresh green produce of the early spring, and behind, the bold mountains of Akhdar, six thousand feet above the ocean level, and on which, according to Captain Welsted's account, snow sometimes falls; but no trace of it was visible now. From Akhdar a transverse chain of hills here comes down to the coast, and puts an end to the Bāṭinah, while it begins what at the present day is called the province of Mascat, a less fruitful land, but very thickly inhabited. In the castle of Barḳa I was told resided a half-brother of Thoweynee's, the offspring of Sultan Sa'eed by an Abyssinian slave; he died not long since. A land breeze arose this day, and took us out to sea, till in the afternoon we got among the Sowādah islands—low barren reefs, about three leagues from land; and there we remained for a few hours, in a dead calm of ominous import.

Towards evening a light south-westerly breeze sprung up, and we spread our sails, hoping by their aid, though the wind was not precisely from the right quarter, to find our way, after some tacking and wearing, into Mascat harbour. But the breeze rapidly grew till it became a strong gale, and in half an hour's time it was a downright storm, baffling all nautical manœuvres. One of our sails was blown to rags, the others were with difficulty got in, and when night closed we were driving under bare poles before a fierce south-wester over a raging sea, while the sky, though unclouded, was veiled from view by a general haze, such as often accompanies a high storm. The passengers were frightened, but the sailors and I rather enjoyed the adventure, knowing that we were by this time far off the coast, clear of all rocks, and in short anticipating nothing worse than a day or two extra at sea before getting round to Mascat. The moon rose, she was in her third quarter, and showed us a weltering waste of waters, where we were scudding entirely alone; some other vessels which had been in sight at sunset had now totally disappeared. The passengers, and Yoosef-ebn-Khamees among the number, dismayed by the mad roll of the ship, no longer steadied by a stitch of canvas, by the dashing of the waves, and all the confusion of a storm, sat huddled below in the aft-cabin, while the helmsman, the captain, and myself, held on to the ropes of the quarter-deck, and so kept our places as best we might; the two Sonnees with the Nejdean recited verses out of the Coran; the 'Omânee sailors laughed, or tried to laugh, for some of them too began to think the matter serious; no one however anticipated the sudden catastrophe near at hand.

It may have been, to judge by the height of the moon above the horizon, about ten of the night or a little earlier, when we remarked that the ship, instead of bounding and tossing over the waves as before, began to drive low in the water, with a heavy lurch of a peculiar character. One of the sailors approached the captain and whispered in his ear; in reply the captain directed them to sound the hold. Two men went to work and found the lower part of the vessel full of water. Hastily they removed some side boardings, and saw a large stream pouring into the hold from sternwards: a plank had started.

The captain rose in despair full length, and called out "Irmoo," "throw overboard," hoping that lightening the ship of her cargo might yet save her. In a moment the hatchways midships were removed, and all hands busy to execute the last and desperate duty. But no more than three bales had been cast into the deep when a ripple of blue phosphoric light crossed the main deck; the sea was already above board. No chance remained. "Ikhamoo," "plunge for it," shouted the captain, and set the example by leaping himself amid the waves. All this passed in less than a minute; there was no time for deliberation or attempt to save anything.

How to get clear of the whirl which must follow the ship's going down was my first thought. I clambered at once on the quarter-deck, which was yet some feet raised above the triumph of the lashing waves, invoked Him who can save by sea as well as by land, and dived head foremost as far as I could. After a few vigorous strokes out, I turned my face back towards the ship, whence a wail of despair had been the last sound I had heard. There I saw amid the raging waters the top of the mizen-mast just before it disappeared below with a spiral movement while I was yet looking at it. Six men—five passengers and one sailor—had gone down with the vessel. A minute later, and boards, mats, and spars were floating here and there amid the breakers, while the heads of the surviving swimmers now showed themselves, now disappeared, in the moongleam and shadow.

So rapidly had all this taken place that I had not a moment for so much as to throw off a single article of dress; though the buffeting of the waves soon eased me of turban and girdle. Nor had I even leisure for a thought of deliberate fear; though I confess that an indescribable thrill of horror which had come over me when the blue glimmer of the water first rippled over the deck, though scarce noticed at the time, haunted me for months after. But at the actual moment the struggle for life left no freedom for backward-looking considerations, and I was already making for a piece of timber that floated not far off, when on looking around more carefully I descried at some distance the ship's boat; she had been dragged after us thus far at a long tow, Arab fashion, though who had cut her rope before the ship foundered was what no one of us could ever discover. She had now drifted some sixty yards off, and was dancing like an empty nutshell on the ocean.

Being, like the Spanish sailors in "Don Juan," "well aware That a tight boat will live in a rough sea, Unless with breakers close beneath her lee," I gave up the plank, and struck out for the new hope of safety. By the time I reached her, three of the crew had already established themselves there before me; they lent me a hand to clamber in; others now came up, and before long nine men, besides the lad, nephew of the captain, were in her, closely packed. So soon as I found myself in this ark of respite, though not of safety, I bethought me of Yoosef, whom I had not seen since the moment of our wreck. He was not along with us; but while, scarce hoping, I shouted out his name over the waters to give him a chance of a signal, "Here I am master, God be praised!" answered the dripping head; and we hauled him in to take his fortune with the rest.

We were now twelve—namely, the captain, his nephew, the pilot, and four of the crew; the remaining five consisted of one of the passengers from 'Oḳdah—for the other had gone down in the ship, the runaway scapegrace of Maufooḥah, and a native of Soweyḳ, besides Yoosef and myself. Three others at this moment came swimming up, and wished to enter. But the boat, calculated to contain eight or nine at most, was already over-loaded, especially for so mad a sea, and to admit a new burden was out of the question. However the poor fellows got hold of a spare yard-arm which had floated up from the sunken vessel; this we made fast to the boat's stern by a rope, and thus took the three in tow clinging to it, two passengers and a sailor.

Four oars were stowed in the boat, and her rudder, unshipped, lay in the bottom, along with a small iron anchor and an extra plank or two. The anchor was without delay heaved overboard by the pilot and myself as a superfluous weight, and so were the planks. Meanwhile some of the sailors proposed to do as much for the passengers; observing, not without a certain show of reason on their side, that with so many on board there could be remarkably little hope of ever reaching shore, that the boat was after all the sailors' right, and the rest might manage on the beam astern as best they could. Fortunately during the voyage I had become a particular friend of the captain and pilot, besides earning the especial good will of a merry sturdy young seaman now in the boat. So I addressed myself to them first, and then to all the crew, and declared the expulsory proposition to be utterly unjust, wicked, and not fit for discussion, particularly in a moment when we all stood so exceedingly in want of God's help and favour; and then, to cut short reply, I proceeded, aided by the pilot, who seconded me manfully throughout, to distribute the oars among the sailors; as indeed it was high time to do in order to steady the boat, over which every wave now broke, threatening to send us to the bottom after her old companion. The captain took post at the rudder, while the pilot and myself set to baling out the water, partly with a leathern bucket which one of the crew had kept the presence of mind to bring with him from the ship (holding the handle between his teeth no less cleverly than Cæsar did his sword off the Alexandrian Pharos), and partly with a large scoop belonging to the boat; both implements were in constant requisition, since every bucketful or scoopful of water thrown out was by the next wave repaid with usury, so fiercely did the storm rage around.

The Sonnee of Djebel-'Oḳdah sat up in the boat, repeating verses of the Coran, and now uttering an ejaculation to invoke Divine help, now reciting the customary call of prayer or Adhān, to which Mahometans ascribe an almost magical virtue. The captain's nephew showed extraordinary spirit for a boy of his age; the sailors managed their oars with much skill and courage, keeping us carefully athwart the roll of the sea; the rest, and I am sorry to say Yoosef-ebn-Khamees for one, were so terribly frightened, that they had completely lost their wits, and lay like dead men amid the water in the boat's bottom, neither raising a head nor saying a word.

Indeed our position, though not wholly without a gleam of hope, seemed very nearly desperate. We were in an open overloaded boat, her movements yet further embarrassed by the beam in tow, far out at sea, so far as to be quite beyond view of coast, though the high shore hereabouts can be seen at a long distance even by moonlight, with a howling wind, every moment on the increase, and tearing waves like huge monsters coming on as though with purpose to swallow us up—what reasonable chance had we of ever reaching land? All depended on the steerage, and on the balance and support afforded by the oars; and even more still on the providence of Him who made the deep; nor indeed could I get myself to think that He had brought me thus far to let me drown just at the end of my journey, and in so very unsatisfactory a way too; for had we then gone down, what news of the event off Sowādah would ever have reached home? or when?—so that altogether I felt confident of getting somehow or another on shore, though by what means I did not exactly know. The Mahometans on board (they were two)—so at least, poor fellows, their demeanour seemed to show,—prayed like men without hope, and as if fully convinced that their prayers would not have the smallest effect upon that inexorable Will which they worship under the name of God. The Biadeeyah mostly kept silence, or exchanged a few words relative to the management of the boat, while the young sailor already mentioned cracked jokes as coolly as though he had been in his cottage on shore, making the rest laugh in spite of themselves, and thus keeping up their spirits—the best thing just then to be done; for to lose heart would have been to lose all.

From an idea that so learned a man (in Arab estimation) as I, ought, among other acquirements, to be better acquainted with the chart than any one else, and perhaps, too, because I seemed less thrown out of my reckonings than most of our party, all referred to me for the direction of our hazardous course. By the stars, a few of which were dimly visible between mist and moonlight, I guessed the whereabouts of the shore. It lay almost due south; but the hurricane had now veered and blew from between west and north; hence we were obliged to follow a south-easterly line, in order to avoid the certain destruction of giving a broadside to the waves. Once sure of this point, I made the men keep our boat's head steady on the tack just explained, and for a long hour we pulled on, baling out the water every moment, and encouraging each other to keep up good heart; that land could not be far off. At last I saw by the milky moonlight a rock which I remembered sighting on the previous afternoon; it was the rock of Djeyn, an outlying point of the Sowādah group, and now at some distance on our leeboard. "Courage!" I cried out, there is Djeyn." "Say it again; say it again; God bless you!" they all exclaimed, as though the repetition of the good news would make it of yet better augury; but I perceived that none of them had his senses enough about him to see the black peak, which now loomed distinct over the sea. "Is it near?" asked he of Djebel-'Oḳdah. "Close by," I answered, with a slight inaccuracy, which the duty of cheering the crew might, I hope, excuse: "pull away; we shall soon pass it." But in my own individual thought I much doubted the while whether we ever should, so rapidly did the boat fill from the spray around, while a moment's mis-steerage would have sent us all to the bottom.

Another hour of struggle: it was past midnight, or thereabouts, and the storm, instead of abating, blew stronger and stronger. A passenger, one of the three on the beam astern, felt too numb and wearied out to retain his hold by the spar any longer; he left it, and swimming with a desperate effort up to the boat, begged in God's name to be taken in. Some were for granting his request, others for denying; at last two sailors, moved with pity, laid hold of his arms where he clung to the boat's side, and helped him in. We were now thirteen together, and the boat rode lower down in the water and with more danger than ever; it was literally a hand's breadth between life and death. Soon after another, Ibraheem by name, and also a passenger, made a similar attempt to gain admittance. To comply would have been sheer madness; but the poor wretch clung to the gunwale and struggled to clamber over, till the nearest of the crew, after vainly entreating him to quit hold and return to the beam, saying, "It is your only chance of life, you must keep to it," loosened his grasp by main force, and flung him back into the sea, where he disappeared for ever. "Has Ibraheem reached you?" called out the captain to the sailor now alone astride of the spar. "Ibraheem is drowned," came the answer across the waves. "Is drowned," all repeated in an undertone, adding, "and we too shall soon be drowned also." In fact such seemed the only probable end of all our endeavours. For the storm redoubled in violence; the baling could no longer keep up with the rate at which the waves entered, the boat became waterlogged; the water poured in hissing on every side; she was sinking, and we were yet far out in the open sea.

"Iḳḥamoo," "plunge for it," a second time shouted the captain. "Plunge who may, I will stay by the boat so long as she stays by me," thought I, and kept my place. Yoosef, fortunately for him, was lying like a corpse, past fear or motion; but four of our party, one a sailor, the other three passengers, thinking that all hope of the boat was now over, and that nothing remained them but the spar, or Heaven knows what, jumped into the sea. Their loss saved the remainder; the boat lightened and righted for a moment, the pilot and I baled away desperately, she rose clear once more of the water: those in her were now nine in all— eight men and a boy, the captain's nephew.

Meanwhile the sea was running mountains; and during the paroxysm of struggle, while the boat pitched heavily, the cord attached from her stern to the beam snapped asunder. One man was on the spar. Yet a minute or so the moonlight showed us the heads of the five swimmers as they strove to regain the boat; had they done it we were all lost; then a huge wave separated them from us. "May God have mercy on the poor drowning men," exclaimed the captain: their bodies were washed ashore off Seeb three or four days later. We now remained sole survivors—if indeed we were to prove so.

Our men rowed hard, and the night wore on; at last the coast came in full view. Before us was a high black rock, jutting out into the foaming sea, whence it rose sheer like the wall of a fortress; at some distance on the left a peculiar glimmer and a long white line of breakers assured me of the existence of an even and sandy beach. The three sailors now at the oars, and the man of 'Oḳdah who had taken the place of the fourth, grown reckless by long toil under the momentary expectation of death, and longing to see an end anyhow to this protracted misery, were for pushing the boat on the rocks, because the nearest land, and thus having it all over as soon as possible. This would have been certain destruction. The captain and pilot, well nigh stupefied by what they had undergone, offered no opposition. I saw that a vigorous effort must be made; so I laid hold of them both, shook them to arouse their attention, and bade them take heed to what the rowers were about, adding that it was sheer suicide, doubly inexcusable in men whom God had saved thus far, and that our only hope of life was to bear up for the sandy creek, which I pointed out to them at a certain distance.

Thus awakened from their lethargy, they started up, and joined me in expostulating with the sailors. But the men doggedly answered that they could hold out no more, that whatever land was nearest they would make for it, come what might; and with this they pulled on straight towards the cliff.

The captain hastily thrust the rudder into the pilot's hand, and springing on one of the sailors pushed him from the bench and seized his oar, while I did the same to another on the opposite side; and we now got the boat's head round towards the bay. The refractory sailors, ashamed of their own faint-heartedness, begged pardon, and promised to act henceforth according to our orders. We gave them back their oars, very glad to see a strife so dangerous, especially at such a moment, soon at an end; and the men pulled for the left, though full half an hour's rowing yet remained between us and the breakers, and the course which we had to hold was more hazardous than before, because it laid the boat almost parallel with the sweep of the water: but half an hour;— yet I thought we should never come opposite the desired spot.

At last we neared it, and then a new danger appeared. The first row of breakers, rolling like a cataract, was still far off shore, at least a hundred yards; and between it and the beach appeared a white yeast of raging waters, evidently ten or twelve feet deep, through which, weary as we all were, and benumbed with the night chill and the unceasing splash of the spray over us, I felt it to be very doubtful whether we should have strength to struggle. But there was no avoiding it; and when we drew near the long white line which glittered like witchfire in the night, I called out to Yoosef and the lad, both of whom lay plunged in deathlike stupor, to rise and get ready for the hard swim, now inevitable. They stood up, the sailors laid aside their oars, and a moment after the curling wave capsized the boat, and sent her down as though she had been struck by a cannon-shot, while we remained to fight for our lives in the sea.

Confident in my own swimming powers, but doubtful how far those of Yoosef might reach, I at once turned to look for him, and seeing him close by me in the water, I caught hold of him, telling him to hold fast on, and I would help him to land. But with much presence of mind he thrust back my grasp, exclaiming, "Save yourself, I am a good swimmer, never fear for me." The captain and the young sailor laid hold of the boy, the captain's nephew, one on either side, and struck out with him for the shore. It was a desperate effort, every wave overwhelmed us in its burst and carried us back in its eddy, while I drank much more salt water than was at all desirable. At last, after some minutes, long as hours, I touched land, and scrambled up the sandy beach, as though the avenger of blood had been behind me. One by one the rest came ashore—some stark naked, having cast off or lost their remaining clothes in the whirling eddies; others yet retaining some part of their dress. Every one looked around to see whether his companions arrived; and when all nine stood together on the beach, all cast themselves prostrate on the sands, to thank God for a new lease of life granted after much danger and so many comrades lost.

Then rising, they ran to embrace each other, laughed, cried, sobbed, danced. I never saw men so completely unnerved as they on this first moment of sudden safety. One grasped the ground with his hands, crying out, "Is this really land we are on?" another said, "And where are our companions?" a third, "God have mercy on the dead; let us now thank Him for our own lives;" a fourth stood bewildered; all their long and hard-stretched self-possession quite gave way. Yoosef had lost his last rag of dress; I had fortunately yet on two long shirts (one is still by me), reaching down to the feet, Arab fashion. I now gave my companion one, keeping the other for myself; my red scull-cap had also held firm on my head, so that I was as well off or better than any. "We may count this day for the day of our birth; it is a new life after death," said the young 'Omānee sailor. "There have been others praying for us at home, and for their sake God has saved us," added the pilot, thinking of his family and children. "True; and more so perhaps than you know of," replied I, remembering some yet further distant.

While we were thus conversing, and beginning to look around and wonder on what part of the coast we had landed, the distant sound of a gun was heard on the right. "That must be the morning gun of Seeb," said the captain. Seeb, being a fortified town, and often a royal residence, has the privilege of a garrison and artillery; now from the whereabouts of our wreck opposite Sowādah we could not be very far from thence. We were yet discussing this point, when another gun made itself heard from inland. "That must be from the palace at Baṭḥat-Farzah" (the valley of Farzah), said another. "Thoweynce is certainly there, for the palace guns never fire except when the sultan is in residence with his court."

It was now the first glimmer of doubtful dawn, and the wind sweeping furiously along the beach rendered some shelter necessary; for we were dripping and chilled to the bone. So we crept to leeward of a cluster of bushes, and there each dug out for himself a long trench in the sand; and after having thus put ourselves in some degree under cover, we waited for the morning, which seemed as though it would never come. At last the moonlight faded away, and the sun rose, though his rays did not reach us quite so soon as we should have desired, for the creek where we had landed was bordered on either side by high hills, shutting out the horizon. These hills ended in precipices towards the sea; on the left was the very rock on which the despairing impatience of the crew had almost driven us the night before; it looked horrible. The wind yet blew high, and we were shivering with cold in our scanty clothing. Those who, like myself, had come on shore with more than what was absolutely necessary for decency, had shared it with those who had nothing. When the sunbeams at last struck over the hill side on the right, we hastened to warm ourselves and to dry our apparel—a task speedily performed with so slender a wardrobe. Next we reconnoitred the position, with which some of the crew found themselves to be not wholly unacquainted; it was a little to the east of Seeb; but between us and that town was a high and broad range of rocks, on which our naked feet had no great disposition to venture; on the west we were hemmed in by a corresponding barrier. But landwards the valley ran up sandy between the hills, and in that direction appeared an easier path, leading ultimately, so the sailors averred, to the sultan's country palace—the same whence we had heard the night gun, nor could it be very far off. Once at the palace, all reckoned on the well-known liberality of Thoweynee for obtaining assistance. Thither we resolved to go; yet before setting out we turned back to look once more on the sea, still raging in mad fury. Not a trace of our saviour boat appeared, not a sail in sight, though the day before (a day that now seemed a year ago) there had been many. Ten large vessels, part belonging to the Persian coast, part to the 'Omānee, had gone down besides our own, close to the Sowādah rocks, that very night; three, as I afterwards learned, perished with every soul on board; from one alone the entire crew escaped; the rest lost some more, some less: we had at any rate companions in misfortune. Gazing on the ocean, every one made aloud the ordinary resolution of shipwrecked sailors never to attempt the faithless element again; a resolution kept, I doubt not, as steadily as most such—that is, for a fortnight or three weeks.

We then proceeded to toil southwards across sands and slopes in quest of the king's residence. "A sorry plight," said I to Yoosef, "for us to present ourselves in before his majesty; were the gifts along with us, our visit might be more to the purpose." Yoosef sighed; that part of our misadventure fell indeed mainly on him. For myself, I had of course lost every article retained since our parting from Aboo-'Eysa at Menāmah, besides some objects of local curiosity purchased on the way—amongst these a handsome dagger, a finely woven cloak, two pretty Persian carpets, and other remembrances of Linja and Sharjah. What annoyed me more seriously was the loss of all my notes, taken from January 23rd up to the present date, namely March 10th, and herein must lie my apology for a certain amount of omission and incompleteness during the part of my story included between those periods, perhaps even some involuntary inaccuracies. To the disappearance of my cash in hand I was less sensible, though in fact it was scarcely a joke to find oneself penniless with a penniless and nearly naked companion, in a strange land, and far from friends or resources. But all this was a trifle if compared to the mishap of the captain—deprived of ship, cargo, and everything except the shirt on his back; the rest of the crew were, in proportion, no better off. However, several had lost what was far more essential,—their lives, and in comparison with them we might well deem ourselves fortunate; so we cheered up, and agreed by common consent to thank God for the past, and to trust to Him for the future.

I could not but remark during these events (a fact which indeed I had often noticed before, but it now stood out in broader light) the great difference between Mahometans and non-Mahometans in their way of regarding that supreme Being whose name, as object of adoration, is common to all. Our Biadeeyah spoke of God much as sensible Christians might, as of an all-governing, all-directing Ruler indeed, but whose rule was for the good of men, and who willed not death but life, not suffering but relief and mercy; in this thought they went gaily and undoubtedly to do what was to be done, leaving the rest in the very best of hands, and with good hope for the result. The Mahometans, who, poor fellows, were all drowned but one, had a much less cheerful view of things, and seemed thoroughly convinced that they were in the hands of an absolute and arbitrary power, which might save them if it chose, or drown them if it chose, but on which their prayers and needs could have little or no effect. Not that such is the case with all Mahometans; I have seen myself numerous instances of a contrary phase of mind, the result of that happy inconsistency by which men do not always reason or act up to their theoretical principles. Besides, in mixed lands like Turkey, Syria, and Egypt, the Muslim often borrows much, even unconsciously, from the various creeds and systems around him. But Nejdeans, isolated from stranger influence, and truer in consequence to the idea on which their whole life and soul is modelled, have much the same God before them in action as in theory; and thus our luckless companions in the ship awaited their fate like beasts of slaughter, brought before the butcher with his knife ready in his hand.

My readers will, I hope, excuse this brief digression. It is not (so far as I can trust myself), through any theological, national, or personal animus, but through conviction arising from what I have seen in many lands and among many races of the natural workings of Islam, that I dwell upon this strange but natural result of that Azote of the East.

We walked on, half merry, half sad, and all very feeble, till an hour or so before noon. At last we crossed a ridge where trees began to mingle with the low bushes of the coast, and suddenly had the Baṭḥah full in view. It was a pretty and wooded hollow, amid high peaked granite hills; below all was green, save in one part of the valley, where a patch of clean sand spread out over some extent. By the side of this was the palace, strikingly resembling a château of Louis XIII's time, such as I have often seen in Central France. It consists of a central pavilion with side wings symmetrically arranged, open balconies running round the first storey, and steps leading up to the principal entrance; in short, it is the most European-looking construction that I have found in Arabia. This palace was erected by Sultan Sa'eed, and, I believe, by Western builders under his orders. Around stand long ranges of stables and outhouses. Here, beneath a wing of the edifice and close by a private entrance, sat Thoweynee himself, in the midst of his court, enjoying the morning air in the shade; before him about three hundred horsemen were engaged in the evolutions and caprices of a mock fight. Tents were pitched here and there among the trees; all was life, cheerfulness, and security; a very different scene from that which we had so lately beheld and shared in.

We halted awhile behind a screen of foliage, whence unseen we could ourselves see the king and his attendants. Before long the parade was over, and the cavaliers, after saluting their sultan, rode off to quarters at a little distance. We then advanced; after a few steps some of the bystanders perceived us, and came up. "Doubtless you belong to one of last night's wrecks," said they; "we had just been talking about the probable loss of many ships in the storm, and here you are to witness." After this greeting they led us without further preface before Thoweynee.

I could scarcely keep from laughing at the figure I made; but it was perhaps fortunate for my incognito with Thoweynee, whose royal eyes must have rested times out of number on Europeans of different categories, and who might have likely enough recognized the English traveller if under a better guise, and in more seemly circumstances. But to pick out an Englishman from amid our barelegged castaway band would have required a conjuror; and Thoweynee, whatever his mother may be, is not that himself. We now stood before him. He was handsomely, even gorgeously, dressed in fine white robes, lightly embroidered with a flowered pattern, and wearing a large and white Cachemire turban, surmounted by a diamond, with a magnificent golden dagger in his jewelled belt. His person is stout, and his face handsome; its expression clever but dissipated; he looks like what he is, a genuine follower of Epicurus, but one who might have been something much better had he chosen. Shrewdness, good nature, and love of enjoyment make up his whole face, manner, and, it appears, character too. By his side sat a boy of dusky features, but splendidly dressed, his cap set with precious stones; this youth is his eldest son by an Abyssinian concubine. Close by the king was the prime minister, whose name has escaped my memory, and several others of high rank and birth, all dressed in white and gold; while numerous attendants, armed with swords and daggers, stood or sat around.

Of course the captain acted for us the part of spokesman. The king received us with an air of compassion, enquired after the port to which our vessel had belonged, its cargo, its destination; how the ship had come to founder, how many had perished, how we ourselves had escaped; and then, after promising the unfortunate owner a compensation for his loss, gave orders that we should be lodged and taken care of in the palace.

I wished Yoosef to take the word next, and to say something about the presents which he had been charged with, and by whom. But my man wanted courage to come forward, and feared that under the present circumstances he might be held for an impostor, while for my part I thought it not prudent to draw too much notice on myself, especially as I had perceived some north-country looking faces among the attendants. So I kept in the background, and awaited the result. Meanwhile one of the guards came up to Yoosef and myself and offered to be our host; the sailors one after another were each claimed in the same hospitable way. We followed our conductor to his abode; it was among the outbuildings of the palace, a large apartment, and inhabited by half a dozen of the royal swordsmen.

Here all set about making us comfortable. I was soon provided with a pair of light trousers and a turban. Yoosef fared equally well; a blazing fire was lighted, and pipes and coffee prepared, while more substantial fare was getting ready. During these operations we had to relate our story over and over again; every one condoled, hoped, and what else is customary on such occasions. We made a very hearty meal of meat, rice, and saffron, along with raisins, dates, and whatever besides was at hand, and then laid down for a sound nap,—the first since our wreck, for the cold had not permitted us to close our eyes during the morning on the beach.

When I awoke the afternoon was far advanced. I found Yoosef already up, and he proposed a walk to see the palace and its neighbourhood. Close by the palace a copious hot spring gushes up, and supplies a natural warm bath to the monarch in his rural residence; the same waters, after cooling themselves in open plaster conduits, keep alive a large potherb garden, reaching broad and far in the valley; beyond its limits the rivulet irrigates intermingled plantations of date-palm and cocoa-nut. The entire valley swarmed at evening time with strollers, amongst whom cavalry and artillery officers in a half-European uniform made a conspicuous figure; none, however, of the Belooch guard were present in the Baṭḥah. A little before sunset we saw a large band of horsemen coming up the valley, till they halted at the palace door. Their leader was a broad-shouldered, bull-necked, large-headed, thickset man, clad in a red cloak, and mounted on a magnificent horse, one of the finest that I ever saw in Arabia, and alone sufficient to announce the importance of its rider. This was none other than the famous, or rather the infamous, Meṭeyree, the right hand of Khālid-ebn-Ṣaḳar in all his cruelties, and well known as the greatest brigand of his day. He cast around him a scowl of hatred while he alighted, and the palace servants hastened to escort him up the steps, and those who stood by our side a little withdrawn muttered curses and revilings. Thoweynee himself would, so men say, and I can well believe it, gladly see his dangerous ally at a greater distance, but policy obliges him to temporize; and the Meṭeyree remained three whole days the guest of the Sultan, after which he returned to his own immediate master Khālid at Sharjah. On what special business he came, or with what result, I could not learn; perhaps he had nothing in view but diversion.

Two of the sailors, with a curiosity nowise unnatural, made a return visit that very evening to the beach, where they found the broken planks of our boat, dashed to pieces by the surf. Of the ship we never heard or saw more—where sl e lay, not five but seventy or eighty fathoms deep, if the soundings of the Sowādah rocks be correct.

Yooscf and I loitered about the Baṭḥah till sunset, when one of the palace attendants presented us and our comrades with a small sum of money for immediate wants, and promise of more if we chose to abide for a day or two the Sultan's leisure. Ebn-Khamees and myself received in hand each a gold tomān, value somewhat under ten shillings English; this would hardly suffice for adventuring on an onward journey of any length, and we thought of waiting and trying the further extent of Ebn-Sa'eed's generosity, when a circumstance occurred which determined me on quitting the vicinity of the palace and the Baṭḥah without delay.

We had just finished our supper, night had closed in, and we were sitting guests and hosts round the fire at coffee, when a well-dressed negro came in, and, after due salutations, presented me with his master's compliments and invitation to honour him with my company. I rose and followed my black conductor, who led me to a neat tent pitched at some distance. There I found two ex-Turkish officers, for both had been in the great Sultan's service, till for reasons best known to themselves they had found the Ottoman army and territory too hot for them, and had, in plain English, deserted. The one had come straight to 'Omān; the other had roamed the world far as Bombay, Calcutta, and even Singapore and Malacca; his peregrinations had procured him a most extensive acquaintance with English, Indians, Malays, and all kind of people. He himself, though once holding a commission in the Ottoman troops, was not of Turkish but Albanian descent. "We noticed you," said he to me in the broken Arabic peculiar to that class of men, and by which they may readily be recognized, "and concluded from your appearance that you do not, like your companions, belong to this country." This was said with much politeness, and was accompanied by the offer of a silver-mounted Nargheelah, with other minutiæ of Eastern courtesy, so that I found myself extremely at ease, in spite of a remark evidently intended as a prologue to further enquiry. We next entered on a long and lively conversation, wherein I told him what I thought fit to tell, and my new acquaintance, animated by libations of something better than coffee, namely, good Cognac out of a black bottle, to which he and his friend made frequent applications, and which I must confess was not wholly declined by myself under the circumstances, recounted his own past history, his adventures by land and flood, how he had come into Thoweynee's service, and so on, with perhaps a little more fluency than exactness. "In vino veritas,"—sometimes also the reverse. According to his statements, the present Sultan of 'Omān had in his own garde-de-corps six hundred horsemen, besides a tolerable outfit of artillerymen, on whom he placed much reliance. That if war broke out he could reckon securely on levies from the local chiefs of Belad Ṣoor, Djailān, and Djebel-Akhdar, and even from most of the Bāṭinah, though some towns there were yet disaffected. That he had at his disposition above thirty ships of English build, some of which carried no less than fifty guns; that, in short, he might be looked on as equalling his father in strength and resources, would he but bestow a little more time on business, and a little less on court jesters and paramours.

In requital for such information, he wished to know more about my affairs, and was strongly disposed to opine that my voyage hither had other objects than herb gathering or medical investigation. But hereabouts the lateness of the hour and my own fatigue furnished me with a decent pretext for retiring, and I took my leave, while my entertainer assured me that next day he would not fail to return the visit, and that we would then have further conversation.

However, I was very far from ambitious of the proposed honour—not that I cared much at the moment whether Thoweynee, his minister (who, as I afterwards learnt, had really his doubts about me, and who had probably given the password of investigation to the Albanian), and all 'Omān too, from Cape Mesandum to Rās-el-Ḥadd, knew who and what I was, feeling sure from what I had already seen and heard, that such knowledge would breed no immediate harm or hindrance. But the Meṭeyree and his Nejdeans were just now at court, and I feared lest the news, with extensive Arab amplifications, might find its way to Bereymah, and thence to Nejed, and have ill results, at least for Aboo-'Eysa, who would in that case appear to have been all along, directly and indirectly, by himself and by his men, bear-leader and accomplice to that dreaded monster, a spy. Besides I had yet on hand the appointment to meet Aboo-'Eysa on the Persian coast; Barakāt was still with him, and the consequences of a premature detection might be very disagreeable. So, without explaining to Yoosef matters which nowise concerned him, I gave him to know that it was my high will and pleasure to leave the Sultan and his court to themselves, and to start the very next morning for Mascat, where doubtless something would turn up in our favour; adding many pertinent sayings about the vanity of putting one's trust in princes, and the like. Yoosef easily allowed himself to be persuaded; he was, in fact, so unhinged by the preceding night, that it cost no difficulty to lead him one way or another like a very child.

Accordingly next morning early we sought a pair of shoes, for my feet did not at all relish the angular pebbles thick-strewn over most of the ground in the Mascat district. But shoes were none to be found, so off we started barefoot, leaving our hosts engaged in their duties of morning parade, and Thoweynee probably asleep. A peasant from the neighbouring village of Farzah directed us into a track leading from the Baṭḥah to that locality. Crossing the mountain rim to the south-east, we threaded awhile a narrow footpath between reddish rocks, where evergreen oaks and acacias grew out of the crevices, till we came into a broad road, dividing off and going on the right to Farzah and on the left to Mascat. All around was a labyrinth of wild hills, I think chiefly granite, and between them pretty verdant valleys, with here and there a cluster of houses, a garden, or a few cultivated fields, where the crops already stood almost waist high, for the harvest of the land is reaped in April. Down the Farzah valley flows in the winter months a stream of some width, but it was already nearly dry, and must be entirely so in summer.

After a short halt we took the direction of Mascat, and walked courageously on in spite of pebbles and rock splinters, till before noon we passed the white castle of Khabb. This is a merely ornamental building—a villa, in short, rather than a fortress; the village lies close by in a deep valley, and is well supplied with water and surrounded with culture. But we were unwilling to delay, and continued our march without stopping, till three or four hours more brought us to Ri'ān, a hamlet smaller than Khabb, where sheer weariness and sore feet compelled us to sit down and rest awhile. Hither the villagers generously brought us a gift very acceptable to hungry men—namely, some sticks of sugarcane, with a lapful of Nabaķ, here plentiful and large as crab-apples; these delicacies we ate with some pieces of dry bread, taken by way of provision before leaving the Baţḥah.

While we recline by the well, my readers will allow me a few general remarks on the system of irrigation, differing here and in many parts of 'Omān from that adopted in Central Arabia. There, water is invariably drawn up by the labours of camels or asses, and often from a considerable depth, especially throughout Djebel Shomer. In Ḥasa, where springs abound, and where the wells are often brimful, "swipes," to borrow an east-country term, are not uncommon, and the hand of man suffices to draw for the watering of a field or for domestic uses. In 'Omān, camels and asses are still less required for this kind of work; water is plenty, and at or near the surface. Here too we occasionally meet with the long "swipe" levers, but more habitually with ropes and pulleys, like those employed at home where pumps happen to be wanting. No part of Arabia is better watered than 'Omān, nowhere are wells and fountains equally numerous—a fact partly explained by the presence of the lofty Akhdar range inland, and partly by the annual monsoon of the Indian Ocean along its shores. Yet here also the extreme porousness of the ground effectually hinders the formation of rivers; the torrents of Akhdar are soon absorbed in the ravines of the mountain chain, then reappear as fountains at its base, flow a little, and are reabsorbed by the soil, perhaps to break out once more nearer the coast, but never to maintain a steady course above ground. A last remark belonging to this subject is that the wells themselves are in general well constructed, guarded with masonry and kept in good repair.

From the hamlet where we had thus rested, the road split into two branches. The main one led to Mascat, at a distance of about fifteen miles; but it passes over rough and stony ground, on which I felt hardly inclined to venture unshod, especially that my feet were none the better for the way already travelled. The other path, on the left, conducts to Maṭraḥ, a seaport to the west of Mascat; in its course it traverses a level and sandy space. This now we determined to try; so, declining the reiterated invitations of the villagers to stop for the night in their dwellings, we pushed on, though extremely tired, till we came to a small group of houses just within the line of fortifications, which extend for about fifteen miles or rather more from east to west, and defend the immediate vicinity of Mascat on the land side. From height to height, from crag to crag, walls and round towers, strongly constructed, and capable of bearing heavy guns in their embrasures, run across the lines of approach to the great seaport; they are the work of the Portuguese, who while masters of this part of the coast fortified it somewhat as we ourselves have lately done for 'Aden; though the Mascat lines, if more picturesque, are also less in accordance with the principles of modern military defence. The towers and battlements, at times appearing white on the heights, at times half hidden among black ravines and fantastic cliffs, have a fantastic look, which all my fatigue could not hinder me from admiring. On the land side, whence the Portuguese were wholly excluded, the country is of a gentler character; the soil is covered with vegetation, but towards the sea-coast the rocks are equally barren in their surface and wild in their outline.

A narrow pass admitted us within the loop of fortifications; the entrance would be difficult were the deserted towers on either side suitably garrisoned. The sun set on the tops of the crags before we reached the houses, a long suburb of Maṭraḥ, or indeed Maṭraḥ itself; for so thickly are these valleys and gorges inhabited, that it would be hard to define the exact limits of each locality. Lines of cottages stretch from one to another, and connect them together, very unlike the compact and circumscribed hamlets of Shomer and Nejed. Once here we halted, and seeing before us a domicile of good appearance, stone built, two storeys high, and with a large entrance, we took leave to introduce ourselves under the title of two shipwrecked individuals on their way to Mascat. The master of the house, a wealthy merchant, saw in our attire an ample confirmation of our statements, readily afforded us the shelter which we asked, and moreover provided us with a good supper, after which we held conversation respecting the commerce of the place and its present condition. The negro trade is here in full vigour; and besides this half illicit though universal importation, rhinoceros horns and hides, ivory, and sweet-scented wood, are continually brought from the African coast; while India furnishes the articles already mentioned when describing the traffic of Ḥaṣa and Baḥreyn, but on an infinitely larger scale. In requital, horses, asses, camels, dates, weapons, cloaks, carpets, sweetmeats, copper and lead ore, are exported to different quarters. Our host was particularly anxious about a ship of his daily expected to arrive from Bombay, and much feared lest the storm fatal to so many vessels in the Gulf of 'Omān might have raged on the Indian Ocean also. And in fact we afterwards heard that many losses had taken place out there on the same night.

Early next morning we took leave of our host, and found our way down to Maṭraḥ proper. To judge after the account given by Niebuhr, who describes it as a small and dirty village, the town must have much improved of late years; it now presents many rows of houses equal in extent, regularity, and ornament, to those of the Anglo-Indian seaports; the market-place is spacious, yet more crowded by far than those of either Sharjah or Linja, while the dwellings of merchants, sea-captains, and wealthy proprietors, some perched like the Bastides of Marseilles on open rising ground, some lower down near the water's edge, and mixed with the cottages of sailors, fishermen, boatmen, negroes, and the like, extend round the entire bay, and reach far inland. I cannot reckon the actual population of Maṭraḥ at less than twenty-five thousand souls, and should rather incline to assign it a higher number. The harbour, secure, but somewhat shallow, is hemmed in to right and left by high volcanic-seeming rocks, crowned with guardian towers; no land path leads hence direct to Mascat, a circumstance highly advantageous to the countless ferrymen who ply round the eastern cape that runs far out between and separates the two ports. While Yoosef and I were walking about the market-place, and purchasing some articles of food and dress (for in addition to the royal boon bestowed on us at the Baṭḥah, our host of last night had given us a small alms on parting), we met the governor of the town, a very handsome young chief, arrayed in the white dress of the country, and well attended, but on foot. He belonged not to the Ghaferee family, or its Ebn-Sa'eed branch, which is far from numerous, but to the Yeleḳs of the Bāṭinah, a very ancient clan of Ḳaḥṭānee origin.

Maṭraḥ, even more than Mascat, is a mart for inland manufacture; and whoever desires a cloak of 'Omānee weaving, a dagger of 'Omānee make, a carpet of 'Omānee texture, has here no difficulty in getting his wants supplied. Every Monday a general rendezvous takes place of the countrymen and villagers from the interior, with fruits and vegetables, sweet potatoes, badinjans, melons, gourds, apricots, grapes, peaches, and mangoes, according to the season; the last-mentioned fruit is of what Indians term the "Junglee" variety. A very common article of sale is a large nut, two or three inches long, triangular in shape, and brown in colour; I could not identify the species. Dates in 'Omān hold a merely subordinate place on the list of eatables; they are much inferior in quality to those of Nejed, not to mention Ḥaṣa. Hence a considerable importation of Khalāṣ from the last-named province supplies the tables of the wealthy in 'Omān with a delicacy else unknown to the land. In the Indian merchandise of cloth and rice Maṭraḥ is inferior to Mascat.

After seeing what was to be seen, and making our purchases, we went down to the beach, where numerous canoes, each formed of a single trunk neatly shaped and hollowed out, double prowed, and capable of being rowed forwards or backwards, like Oxford skiffs, were ready for the conveyance of those whom business called to Mascat. These boats are clean within, and spread with light grass mats, of the kind usual in India, and there called "tatties." We embarked in one along with a Persian, two Banians, each furnished with a genuine "chatti," or Bombay umbrella, and four or five other passengers; the two oarsmen were negroes. I must plead guilty to the weakness of having felt a half reluctance on committing myself to the sea once more, even for so short a trip; Yoosef-ebn-Khamees looked as if he did not like it much either. However, we had no other practicable way of reaching Mascat, so we trimmed the boat, and our sturdy blacks pulled away till we rounded the first long cape to the east; behind it next appeared a small rocky bay, where nestled a few houses; and then came a second and longer granite promontory, far out into the sea; we passed it, and immediately afterwards entered the harbour of Mascat. The port was full of shipping, and all alive with boats and sailors; four good-sized frigates, provided with guns, bulwarks, and a complete European rigging-out, might have led me to suppose that European craft were here also; but the red pennon of Thoweynee, the ancestral banner of Yemen, fluttering from each masthead, showed the ships to be the property of the 'Omān government. We rowed up the harbour, and landed on a point of rock near the custom-house; but being without baggage, had no formalities to undergo there, and passports are not required in this territory.

Mascat, or at least its harbour, forts, and buildings, has been often and sufficiently described. Niebuhr, Welsted, and many others have made here, some a longer, and some a shorter stay; not to mention that English steamers on their backward and forward way between Bombay and Basrah, touch here regularly twice in every month, though their anchorage is only for a few hours. I may therefore be excused from several items of local detail, and intend describing the living and moving, rather than the brick and stone town, besides recording what incidents (they were not many) of general interest here befel me, with the particulars of a small excursion in the neighbourhood.

The hospitality of a Ḥaṣa merchant, Astar by name, and long since a settler in Mascat, provided Yoosef and myself with lodging, board, and raiment. For three days I was too tired to attempt much roaming about; and the businesslike way of our host and the friends who frequented his house, left less leisure than might elsewhere have occurred for general conversation. Besides Astar was a Mahometan, though fortunately not a Wahhabee, and we were now in the month of Ramadhan, when all good Mahometans are fasting and sulky, or at best silent. On the fourth day after our arrival, having been by this time provided with a decent upper garment of red cotton, 'Omân fashion, a large white girdle, a turban, shoes, and the Nebaa' walking-stick, indispensable for respectability, I began visiting the bazars, the port, and the other objects of curiosity which the town contains. In my first walk I fell in with an old acquaintance from Bombay, who rendered me many good services during my stay here, though motives of prudence obliged us to keep up a certain degree of secrecy in our interviews. Should chance ever open these pages to the perusal of my Indian friend, he may be assured that my gratitude is by no means equally restricted with the cursory allusion which is all that I have space for on this occasion.

The population of Mascat is a thorough Eastern Babel, in which the Banians of Western India bear, for their number, the chief commercial and monetary part. Some 'Omânees also are rich and enterprising merchants, on a footing with the traders of Bombay and Mangalore. The wealthiest native of the town is, I believe, one by name Seyf, who honoured me with his acquaintance during my stay here. His house, near the beach, might seem handsome, even at Breach-Candy or Malabar Point, and his excellent and copious table corresponds with the style of the dwelling. Here, even more than on the rest of the coast, the interior of the houses is in most respects after the Persian taste, though the Persians themselves are looked upon as strangers, and are even unpopular among the inhabitants, much as a high practical esteem for foreign fashions, foreign operas, and foreign cookery may coexist at home with a genuine John Bullish aversion for foreign races and lands.

In politeness of manner and general civilization, in elegance of furniture and dress, the townsmen of Mascat much surpass those of any other Arab seaport that I am acquainted with; nor is the peculiar Arab frankness and cordial hospitality wanting, though tempered by the reserve natural to men too much accustomed to the sight of strangers for taking the lively interest in a new comer which is naturally felt at Ḥâ'yel or Riaḍ. Yet it is curious to observe how much the different classes which compose the population—'Omânees, Arabs, Loothians, Persians, Jews, and Hindoos—form each a separate community, into which the rest are but sparingly admitted; and though market intercourse is universal, home intimacy is rare. Alone the men of Baḥreyn, here very numerous, seem to possess the hybrid privilege of mixing with all, while their easy-going, unnational, indistinctive character gives them facility of access where Persian narrow-heartedness, Indian oddness, Nejdean bigotry, and Jewish exclusiveness, do not find equally ready entrance:—Maltese of the East, yet more amiable and less hot-headed than the Mediterranean islanders, perhaps also more honest. The negro and mulatto tribe form one-fifth of the town population, but occupy only the lowest ranges of society; not that any special prejudice or pride in those around them excludes them from place or wealth, but their own idleness, incapacity, and licentiousness. This of the free negroes; those among them who have the advantage of owning a master, surpass in every respect their independent brethren, much as a well-trained schoolboy does a ragged runagates street urchin.

Religion is here of all kinds and denominations; but the golden calf counts, I think, more sincere worshippers at Mascat than any other divinity soever. However, since the first Wahhabee occupation, three or four mosques have been built, in which those who have leisure or inclination for five prayers a day may perform their devotions. These haunts of Islamitic piety are patronized more or less by Mahometan merchants from different parts of the Persian Gulf, from Basrah, from Yemen, and from Nejed itself, established here; but I never saw an 'Omānee proper within their walls. The Sonnee population of Mascat, taking it all together, may amount to about one-tenth of the town; the prevailing sect is the Shāfi'ee, though a few resolute Wahhabees maintain the peculiarities of Ḥanbelee observance. The Persians and the Baḥārinah keep to their Shiya'ee practices; but the so-called "Taḳeeyah," that is, an outward conformity with those from whom one inwardly dissents, a usage held by all Shiya'ees, Druses, Ismaileeyah, and their brethren included, as not only lawful but commendable, gives many of them a Sonnee appearance; often too they side, outwardly at least, with the Biaḍeeyah. Among the Sonnees we must reckon the natives of Beloochistan, those of Bokharah, Balkh, and the neighbouring provinces: Ḥaneefees in their own land, they are here Shafiy'aees, in compliance with the wealthier

Mahometans from Basrah and the West. Thus the Mahometan element in Mascat, Sonnees and Shiya'ees together, cannot be less than a fifth of the whole; another fifth is made up of Hindoos, Loothians, Sikhs, with a few Jews and Parsees; the remainder are Biadeeyah or negroes.

From these facts, my readers will perceive, what indeed analogy might alone suggest beforehand, that of all places wherein to study 'Omān, Mascat is the worst, being full half exotic, and the remainder under the daily action of exotic influence. No well-judging man would draw a picture of France from Boulogne-sur-Mer, of England from Southampton, of India from the fort of Bombay. But Mascat is even less a sample of the continent to which it belongs, than the above-mentioned places are of theirs; and he who knows this harbour and its immediate vicinity alone, is yet without the doors of 'Omān, and can form but a very imperfect idea of what lies beyond, whether men or things.

An English consul resides here, and seems to lead an isolated and discomfortable life; another European is a steam-boat agent, nor does his lot either appear a very enviable one. 'Aden is too near at hand to leave the Mascat government without a certain apprehension touching the possible designs of Europe on this coast; and of all Europe, England is just the quarter most likely to create alarm. Hence Englishmen are regarded at Mascat with a suspicion which scarce leaves margin for courtesy, though it does not hinder the dry transaction of business. Besides the climate of Mascat is ill-adapted to Europeans. Though this town stands only on the verge of the tropics, it is hotter than many places much nearer the line. The summer is said to be intolerable; and I can myself witness that the Mascat of March fully rivals in heat the Bombay of April, or even May. Among the indigenous population itself, none but those whom business of the most urgent character or poverty detains, and negroes, who here find a delicious resemblance to their own burning Africa, pass the summer within this circle of rocks. May has hardly set in, when the merchant commits his counting-office to some Banian clerk, the trader carries on his affairs by a distant correspondence, and the whole band of government and nobles, with numerous shopkeepers and artisans, set at liberty by the comparative emptiness of the town, hasten to their several country dwellings within the uplands of Sama'il, Nezwah, and Djebel-Akhdar, while Mascat is left half deserted till the month of October restores it to coolness and life. Some idea of what the heat must here be in July and August, may be gathered from the sale of ripe apricots (the first-fruits of which I myself witnessed) towards the end of March; while my 'Omānee friends earnestly pressed me to wait only one month more for the enjoyment of grapes, here too ripening about the latter part of April.

There is a striking resemblance in more than one respect between the two extreme corners of Arabia—Mascat and 'Aden. Both are evidently clusters of volcanic rocks, thrown up on the sea-coast by some old subterranean agency; both have much the likeness of huge hollow craters, girt by red-black peaks, rifted chasms, and perpendicular walls of crag; both by their heat would make one think that the underground conflagration which first gave them origin, had since shifted to the upper air; both have from the sea side an extremely barren and repulsive aspect. But in 'Aden the barrenness is real; in Mascat it is only apparent; for close behind these crags are the best and the most productive lands of Arabia—groves, running streams, populous villages, and green gardens. As to the town itself, it is far from healthy; indeed, while I was there, a typhoid fever, of which I was nearly a victim, prevailed among the inhabitants, and I was told that similar epidemics were of common occurrence. Commerce alone brings men to Mascat and its excellent harbour, procures it populousness and importance; in all other respects it merits to be the smallest among the many small fishing villages of the coast.

A favourable feature of this town, in a moral point of view, is the great security of its streets, and the excellent police here established; night and day one may traverse by-lanes and alleys unaccompanied, and without the least danger, though the ruins enclosed within its wide circuit of walls might seem a convenient harbouring place for ruffians and robbers. Such jail-birds are however very rare in Mascat, and the universal custom of dagger-wearing seems to have little result beyond that of show and ornament. Only if the townsmen do not often cut a purse, they know well how to empty it, for they are clever hands at driving a bargain.

Few towns in Arabia show greater marks of the vicissitudes of fortune than Mascat. The remains of a large church, now enclosed within the palace precincts, bear witness to Portuguese days, and to the same date are to be ascribed most of the fortifications which guard the harbour and crown the heights. Long rows of really good houses, many of them falling into decay, attest the Persian occupation and the days of Ṭakee-ed-Deen; while several khans and half-conventual seeming masses of building, equally neglected and ruinous, point out the quondam residence of Banians, Loothians, or other merchants of Hindoo or quasi-Hindoo origin, once attracted hither by the favourable rule of Sa'eed-es-Sultan, then diminishing and departing under the sinister influences now of Wahhabee intolerance, now of Thoweynee's own negligence, or the unchecked injustice of some subordinate harpy. The golden times of Mascat and its fullest population seem to have been between twenty and thirty years since; and the number of inhabitants at that period, negroes included, may well have reached sixty thousand or even more. At the epoch of my visit, forty thousand appeared about the total of inhabitants within the walls; the palm-leaf huts of the suburbs around contain a few thousand more. The great Ḳeysareeyah, a remarkably well-built and vaulted construction, consisting of several arcades, and containing shops worthy of Bombay or Madras, is now about one-third deserted; though the Sooḳs or market-places around, the resort of more ordinary shopkeepers and petty business, are still full and crowded. Sa'eed knew that, whatever might be the energy and enterprise of his own born subjects, their commercial transactions would never attain real importance, except by the co-operation and under the lead of Indian merchants, and accordingly used every means in his power to allure the Banians of Cutch, Guzerat, and the Concan to Mascat, and by absolute toleration, special immunities, and constant patronage rendered the port a half-Hindoo colony. Nor had ever a government more useful, more steady-working, and more inoffensive protégés than the Banians proved themselves to 'Omān: interfering with no one, seeking nothing beyond their direct line of business, unobtrusive, courteous, and above all far more skilled in the mysteries of the ledger and the counter than ever Arab was or will be, they made the good fortune of Mascat, and were its favourable genius. Banished during the years of Nejdean tyranny, under the Wahhabee princes, 'Abd-el-'Azeez and 'Abd-Allah, they reappeared on the removal of the hated yoke, and flourished more than ever. But since the accession of Thoweynee, and above all since the expedition conducted by 'Abd-Allah-ebn-Feyṣul, the tree of their prosperity, to borrow an Eastern simile, has been in part blighted, and with it the entire town of Mascat has fallen into "the sere, the yellow leaf," though with a little care and wisdom it might be made to blossom again and resume the freshness of its first spring.

My readers will, I think, have no objection to my inserting here a little story relative to a Mascat Banian; I heard it from a worthy Biaḍee, a shopkeeper in the Ḳeysareeyah, during a conversation occasioned by the purchase of a piece of Tanna-cloth, while we sat together and commented on the crowd of passers-by. Bālih, my merchant friend, recounted that during the moment of Nejdean ascendency which followed 'Abd-Allah's invasion, he was himself one day walking down the Ḳeysareeyah, accompanied by three or four acquaintances, and amongst them a zealous Wahhabee fresh arrived from Nejed. In the course of their walk they came before a magazine where sat a middle-aged Banian, whose corpulence, as is common with Hindoos, announced his wealth, diligently employed in conning over his account-book. The Nejdean, unaccustomed to the sight either of fat men or of Indians, stopped to gaze on the portly figure before them, and said in a tolerably loud tone to his companion, "What a log for hell-fire!" The Banian had been long enough resident in Mascat to understand Arabic, and to speak it too, though in the broken fashion common to Hindoos, who seem never to master that language except by halves and quarters. He raised his head, and looking at the Wahhabee said, "And why a log for hell-fire?" "Because you are an infidel," answered the Nejdean. "Indeed!" rejoined the Banian, "and so in your opinion all except yourselves are logs for hell-fire?" The Wahhabee answered with a decided affirmative. "That is out of your Coran," said the Hindoo, disregarding the winks of Bâliḥ and the Biaḍeeyah, who feared a bad result to the conversation from the irritated Muslim—"that is out of your Coran; but stop a little, and I will tell you how matters will really go at the day of judgment, and who are the logs for hell-fire. Will you hear quietly?" added he, for the Nejdean's hand was already on the hilt of his sword. The bystanders interposed to prevent violence, and the Banian went on in broken Arabic, but perfectly intelligible to those around: "I will tell you the truth of the judgment-day. God will sit on His throne, and then all men will be brought before Him by tribes and nations. 'Who are these?' will He say, as a troop of Wahhabees arrive. 'Muslims,' will be the answer. Whereon the Judge will say, 'See, some of them murdered, others plundered, others insulted their neighbours; this one is a thief, that one an adulterer: to hell with the guilty among them; if there are any innocent, let them enter my Paradise.' In the same manner Jews, Christians, Parsees, and all others, will be sifted each in turn; some will be sent to hell, some to heaven. Meanwhile we Banians will sit in a group on a little hill on one side, without troubling ourselves about the affairs of others. At last God will observe us, and will say to those near Him, 'Who are those quiet-looking men seated apart?' 'Banians,' will be the answer. 'Ah! very well,' the Judge will say; 'poor harmless Banians! they never killed, never plundered, never reviled their neighbours; let them all into Paradise together—free admittance!' Whereon we shall all, and I among the rest, enter heaven; as for you and your like, look out for your answer on that day." The Nejdean raved and cursed, the Biaḍee crowd assembled in the street laughed and applauded, and the Banian resumed his interrupted computations.

A maternal uncle of Thoweynee's, Ḥasan by name, if I remember right, acts as a kind of local governor in the town. I met him one day in the street—a venerable, white-bearded, white-garbed old man, thin and somewhat bent by age; his gold-hafted dagger alone, by the great richness of its ornament, announced his rank. He was on foot, accompanied by a few attendants; all made way for him, and saluted him with a respect amounting to reverence, for he has some peculiar religious authority among the Biaḍeeyah of the land. Thoweynee comes to Mascat according as business or fancy takes him, but is more often in some one of his coast or up-country residences at Seeb, Barka, or Nezwah. The English consul here stationed is supposed to be principally occupied in preventing the slave-trade, but the philanthropic exertions of our countrymen have in this respect met hitherto with but little success; however, the public negro mart has been courteously transferred from Mascat to Maṭraḥ, which answers just the same purpose.

Without the town, near the southern gate, a public fair is held daily, and there, among articles of 'Omānee and Persian manufacture, I saw many a blackwood chest and other genuine Indian wares exposed for auction. One evening, while sauntering about the booths of the fair, in quest of a more elegant dagger than that which at the time adorned my waist, I met our old shipmates, the captain and with him two of his crew, now well dressed and in good spirits, having received from the Sultan's liberality enough to render their past misfortune almost advantageous; they were about to return to Soweyk, and recommence afresh the gains and the hazards of a sea life; I trust under better auspices.

After about a week passed at Mascat I began to consider seriously with Yoosef what was next to be done. But my companion had now only one thought, namely, how to return without delay to his patron at Aboo-Shahr; the journey had no longer any attractions for him, either of profit or pleasure; while the terrors of the shipwreck and the hardships which followed had made him look ten years older than he had appeared a fortnight before. For myself also I began to think that we had done and suffered enough for this time, and that the rest might fairly be left to a future occasion; the more so since the mere return from Mascat to Bagdad, and thence to Syria, was a tolerably long prospect, above all in the summer season now drawing on. In addition an indescribable feeling of weariness and low spirits, for which I could not then account, but which was in reality the "incubation" (to use a medical term) of a bad typhoid fever, hung about me, and made me still more indisposed to additional excursions. Lastly, to all my proposals of an excursion to Bahilah, or even to Ṣoor, Ebn-Khamees had for sole and only reply a most decided negative, and refused to make even a single step out of the town. On the other hand he was unceasing in his researches after a ship bound for Aboo-Shahr. But the north wind blew strong and steady, nor seemed likely to change till after the new moon, that is the 21st or 22nd of the month.

Nothing was left for the moment but impatient patience; and I felt all the ennui of Mascat. This town, again like 'Aden, is somewhat of a prison, both physical and moral. Shut in by the sea in front, by iron-bound cliffs around and behind, under a stifling atmosphere, and amid a population who have borrowed too much of everything to be themselves anything, a stranger without special business and a present aim may well weary after a ten days' stay within its gates. To beguile the time I took daily walks of an hour or two without the walls, visiting the suburbs, and the little villages half lost amid the rocky scenery, till a chance occasion led me somewhat further into the country than my growing indisposition and feverish listlessness had allowed me to intend. This happened in the following manner.

On the 20th March I had gone on an early walk, leaving the town by the southern gate, and was slowly sauntering on between the gardens and wells at the roadside, where high rocks shut out the further view to right and left, when I fell in with three men, whose short kilt-like dress, leathern girdles, and small round targets slung on their backs, might almost have made them pass for Highlanders, had it not been for the white handkerchief knotted round each head, and the long black curls hanging down on either side of very swarthy but well-looking features. The handles of their daggers were encrusted with beautiful silver filigree work, except one which was ornamented with gold upon a hilt of giraffe-hoof, and of a rich amber colour.

We saluted each other; the owner of the golden dagger looked hard but good-humouredly at me, and asked me whence I came and whither I was going. On my answer that I came from the town, and that I was merely bound on a morning stroll, he entered into conversation, and I found that all three were in the service of a Ya'aribah chief, resident at Zakee in Djebel-Akhdar: they had been to Mascat on some business of their master's, and were now on their return home. He who had first addressed me, Zohām by name, invited me to accompany them on their way; the journey was, said he, a pleasant one, and the road thickly strewn with villages and halting-places. The desire of learning something from their conversation prompted me to accept the proposal, though with the intention of going no further than the nearest hamlet; for I had long since given up all idea of a serious visit to the interior. My new acquaintances were, like myself, pedestrians; the morning, though hot, was endurable, thanks to the northerly breeze.

During about two hours our way led across the rough hills which encircle Mascat from the land side, till we passed the last isolated forts on their heights, and began to descend by a narrow gorge on the level lands to the south. Foreground and landscape were worthy of a first-rate painter. Close in front dark and splintered rocks, crowned by white battlements and loopholed walls, the image of defiance and barrenness; then, opening out through the chasm, spread a large and verdant plain, where many groves lay scattered amid its undulations; and houses or cabins of palm-leaf, dispersed in little groups, as wont in 'Omān, without the precaution of walls or other formalities of defence. Beyond, to north, west, and south, stretched the huge chain of Djebel-Akhdar — dark green fading into blue; its first and lower ranges looked almost near; but my companions affirmed that three days of an ordinary travelling pace lay between Mascat and Zakee, a village situated near the highest part of the mountain; the distance is about forty miles in a straight line. Somewhat on our left, at about two hours off, stood Besheyr, a cluster of dusky roofs surrounded by a low circuit wall; no fort or castle overtopped its buildings. As the mountain peaks immediately opposite in the distance correspond to those sometimes called on the map "Djebel-Huther" and "Djebel-Fellah," I enquired after those names, but no one knew them; the general term of Akhdar, or "Green," was the only one recognized, except when some particular spot of the chain was designated by the town nearest to it, as "Djebel-Nezwah" and "Djebel-Samed."

We continued our path amid acacias and mango-trees, while peasants driving asses, riders on dromedaries, and groups of travellers like ourselves on foot, met or passed us every ten minutes. Most wayfarers were unarmed, others bore the short javelin-like spear, no longer the lance of Nejed, and a round target or "Yeleb," of leather stretched on a wooden framework and studded with metal heads; the sword is very commonly superseded by the dagger. Of firearms I saw comparatively few in 'Omān, except when carried by Beloochees, Ḥurrās, or the like; war is here an occurrence, not a business; and the inhabitants of the interior seldom come in contact with other tribes or people save peaceably and in the way of trade. Our road occasionally crossed some small watercourse, yet flowing, evidently destined to dry up in a few weeks or months later; but of wells there were plenty, and now and then a small tank, bordered with stone or plaster, and full of water. My readers will recall to mind that we were now at the end of the rainy season of 'Omān, and exactly at the time when moisture stands at its maximum in these countries; in summer and autumn the ground is comparatively dry. The fields around waved with the promise of a harvest scarce a month distant, while badinjans, gourds, melons, and the like, were already far advanced, much further than at a corresponding season even in Ḥasa. Still the Mascat district is in the main of inferior fertility to the Bāṭinah; a certain proportion of pasture-land for sheep, oxen, and camels mixes with the cultivation, which latter is allotted to distinct spots, not continuous, and most frequently is near some village or hamlet. The air is brisk, and the climate healthy; the prevailing type of the inhabitants more manly, more open, and less civilized than in the Bāṭinah; their complexion dark, their stature middle-sized, and their limbs well proportioned; altogether they might be compared with the better specimens of the Mahratta race, though even then a preference must be given to the 'Omānee, always endowed with a physical energy and power of endurance above that of the Indian.

In the afternoon we arrived at Besheyr, a large village, but mostly constructed of wood and thatch; the streets wide, clean, and irregular; an earth wall surrounds the whole, dividing the houses and the gardens; a weekly fair is held without the walls, on an open piece of ground amid the plantations. A few miles farther southwards is one of the pottery-grounds of 'Omān: the earthenware thence made is generally whitish in colour, somewhat resembling what we call "stone" in jugs and platters; it is very hard and waterproof, sometimes glazed. No potteries exist through the entire extent of Arabia between Djowf and 'Omān—Shomer, Nejed, and Ḥasa being alike unprovided with the materials for this kind of manufacture, and there all culinary and house utensils are of either wood or metal. In 'Omān alone we find earthenware in daily use, though metal is also not uncommon, perhaps because the carelessness of an Arab household would else render breakage too frequent for suitable domestic economy.

At Besheyr my companions sought out and found a friend's house, taking me along with them. The dwelling of our host, 'Oḳeyl-el-Dja'aferee by name, stood near the village walls; adjoining it was a garden, where mats and carpets had been spread alongside of a little tank, under the shade of some trees of the jujube species. We passed the hot hours of the afternoon pleasantly enough; a younger brother and some relatives or acquaintances came up to bear their share in the coffee and Nargheelahs; meanwhile apricots of the greenest, with cucumbers, Nabaḳ, and Nezwah sweetmeats were set before us by way of an anticipation of the supper. Had I myself been in what is sometimes termed a flourishing state of health, I should have much enjoyed the society of the family; nothing could be imagined more friendly and conversible. But I was tired out with the walk hither, and more disposed to sleep than chat; so after smoking a couple of huge clay Nargheelahs, I accepted 'Oḳeyl's offer of a red 'Omānee carpet and cushion, and lay down to doze till sunset, while our friends, from a motive of politeness, removed farther off in the garden to give me the benefit of quiet and rest.

At last one of the lads came and aroused me for supper. The dishes were many, and vermicelli abounded, besides a preparation known to my Syrian readers, should I have such, and ycleped "Kishk," a kind of blancmange with rose-water added thereunto for flavour, and by no means contemptible fare. The ewer and basin for hand-washing, with other copper implements, were of remarkably elegant pattern. No Bismillah preceded the meal, and no prayers were said at the stated time before or after; all present were Biaḍeeyah; in fact there was neither Mesjid nor Muṣalla in the whole village. At nightfall my Zaḳee companions declared their intention of paying a complimentary visit to the chief of the place, and the rest of the party agreed to accompany them. Accordingly we washed our hands, and proceeded in a body to his Excellency's residence, a low stone house, more of a dwelling than of a castle, but spacious. Here in a Ḳ'hăwah capable of containing sixty persons at least, sat the chief (I regret that I have lost his name), an elderly man dressed in the red cotton robe of the land, and over it a light cloak of home manufacture; his head was adorned with a Bengalee turban, and his waist with a gold-hilted dagger. Around him were the principal men of Besheyr, and several negroes, some belonging to the household, others as guests. The chief received us with the dignified courtesy which became the occasion, and paid great attention to my friends of Zaḳee, doubtless for their master's sake. For me, my quality of doctor, though without drugs, lancet, or diploma, obtained me a seat by the great man's own side, where I gravely felt his pulse, and gave him advice for the relief of "biliousness," to use his own term, but which being interpreted meant chronic rheumatism. Instead of coffee a spiced decoction of cinnamon was served round, and talk went on with the ease and decorum characteristic of good Eastern society, without the flippancy and excitement which occasionally mars it in some countries, no less than over-silence does in others. To my mind the Easterns are generally superior in the science of conversation to the inhabitants of the West; perhaps from a greater necessity of cultivating it, as the only means of general news and intercourse where newspapers and pamphlets are unknown.

The chief and village of Besheyr depend on Mascat, the head town of this province. But in matter of fact they and each other local chief depend more on their own selves than on any one else; and when I witnessed their offhand way of discussing the Sultan, his officers, and his ordinances, and came to understand how slight is the interference of the central government among them, I was almost reminded of the days when "there was no king in Israel," &c. Power of life and death indeed the village chiefs have not, but with this exception they are next door to autocrats, though after a familiar sort, and in concert with their local Mejlis. The very state dues are by them collected after their own estimation, and sent in accordingly; and it is seldom that questions are asked at Mascat why more arrives, or why less. In return, all are sincerely attached to Thoweynee, whose party is strong here, and are ready for war in his defence if required; in short it is an easy-going people, under easy-going chiefs, beneath an easy-going king, well contented with their condition in this world, and for the next rather inclined to "jump the thought" of it, at least in comparison with their Wahhabee neighbours.

The night wore on; the Ḳ'hâwah was lighted by a large five-wicked lamp of bronze placed in the centre, besides a smaller luminary in a niche at the farther end. The greatest speciality of the meeting was a dance, much to my satisfaction, as I had often heard of these performances in 'Omān but never yet witnessed them. On this occasion, while sweet cakes, pistachio-nuts, and the like "small gear" was being served round, twenty men appeared, in saffron-stained dresses and long braided hair, each a sword or buckler in his hand. On entering the Ḳ'hāwah they divided themselves into two bands of ten and ten, and went through a series of very pretty evolutions, something between a mock combat and a contredanse, beating time on their targets, and animating themselves into wild activity. Nabṭee songs followed, and we then broke up and returned home.

Next morning at an early hour my companions set themselves on their way for Zaḳee, and would fain have taken me with them, but I did not feel myself equal to an onward journey. Our host 'Oḳeyl, seeing me weary and weak, offered to procure me a donkey for the way to Kamlee, a village close by Mascat, and this I willingly accepted; while Zoḥām and his comrades bade me a hearty farewell, with hopes of meeting again, though I hardly know how or when that may be; and I mounted my noble beast, taking the northward road for Kamlee accompanied by a lad of Besheyr. Following our track across the undulating plain, jotted with little groves, and partly resembling some spots of the Deccan, in the neighbourhood of Poonah for example, we reached after about three hours the low rocky hills of the coast, and threaded their passes under a sun which though in March would have done honour to a Syrian July, so burning were its rays, reflected too by the naked rocks around; moreover my own ill state of health, which I vainly tried to disguise from myself, made the heat yet harder for me to bear. Above, around, were the fantastic forms of the cliffs, sharp as knives and pointed as lances, a strange framework to the quiet and fertile lands within. At last we crossed the crater-like rim seawards, and about noon reached the little village, for Kamlee is no more—a mere fishing-port and a suburb of Mascat, though hidden from it by the long promontory that forms the eastern horn of the great harbour. When at Kamlee I could bear no more; and seeing two negroes engaged in drawing water from a well close by the village, I procured myself an extemporary shower-bath by engaging them to pour a couple of bucketfuls over me as I reclined by the well side; this greatly refreshed me at the moment, though I doubt whether it was judicious. I then bade adieu to the young villager, who had entertained me with his lively talk all the way, and performed alone and on foot an hour's walk, sometimes close on the pebbly beach, sometimes behind the rocks and jutting promontories, till I re-entered Mascat and Astar's house, were Yoosef-ebn-Khamees had in my absence made an agreement with a sea-captain of Koweyt, whose vessel was to sail with the first fair wind, and who offered to take us to Aboo-Shahr, while he refused to receive any passage-money in requital, saying that it would be a sin to exact payment from men who had so lately suffered shipwreck.

But before we find ourselves on board of this hospitable cutter, I will give my reader some concluding details respecting the internal condition and the population of 'Omān—details partly collected from the men of Zaḳee just mentioned, partly from other local sources. I give them without that positive assurance which results from personal observation; however, the quiet unexaggerated character of the narrators, natives of the lands they described, added to what I myself was able to see of the country while coasting it from Rās Mesandum to Barḳa, or on land at Ṣoḥār, and in the Mascat district, induces me to think the following statements pretty near the truth. I should have much desired to verify everything with my own eyes; but the circumstances and mishaps already mentioned, which curtailed my explorations and abridged my stay, will I trust be accepted as a sufficient apology for my shortcomings in this respect.

The Arabian and Persian possessions of 'Omān, now under the sceptre of Thoweynee, are divided into thirteen distinct administrations, some of which are more immediately dependent on the central government, others less so. Those of the latter class are five in number: Baḥreyn, which at the period of my visit had scarcely any link with the Sultan of 'Omān except the payment of a slender tribute, and an ambiguous allegiance; Ḳaṭar and the territory of Benoo-Yass, whose union is a degree closer than that of Baḥreyn; and the three provinces of Sharjah, Ro'os-el-Djebal, and Ḳalḥooṭ, subject indeed to the Sultan, but through the unfriendly medium of Khālid-ebn-Ṣaḳar; this is the case especially with the province of Sharjah.

Eight provinces acknowledge a more absolute dependence and a stricter rule. The first is the Persian coast from Cape Bostanah to Djask, with the adjacent islands of Djishm, Larej, and Ormuz. This region is nearly two hundred miles in length, by a breadth varying from ten to thirty; a long strip of harbours, and valuable on their account alone.

Secondly, the Bāṭinah, or the entire plain comprehended between the gorge of Ḳaṭaa'-l-Loḥa to the north, Barḳa and the Mascat hills to the south, and the mountain-chain of Djebel-Akhdar to the west. This is a province of length equal to the former, but forty or fifty miles in breadth, and the most fertile and densely peopled in 'Omān.

Thirdly, Djebel-Akhdar. This commences at Ḳaṭaa'-l-Loḥa, and reaches to Ṣamad; the Bāṭinah bounds it on the north-east, the Ḍāhirah on the south-west. The entire district is mountainous, but well-inhabited; here lies the main political and military strength of the kingdom.

Fourthly, the Ḍāhirah, of which enough has already been said.

Fifthly, the province of Mascat from Barḳa to Rās Ḥeyrān; of this also enough has been related to convey a tolerable idea.

Sixthly, the Belad Ṣoor, from Rās Ḥeyrān to Rās-el-Ḥaḍḍ.

Seventhly, Djailān, which lies immediately behind it.

In the eighth place come the tracts extending from Rās-el-Ḥadd to Ḍofār—lands thinly peopled, and that principally by Bedouin or negro and African tribes: to the same category belong the Akḥāf between Ḳaṭar and Ḥareek. These eight provinces, with the exception of the last, constitute 'Omān in the strict geographical and political sense of the word.

The approximate population and military force of the several districts was given me as follows:—

	Villages	Population	Military Force
I Baḥreyn	60	70,000	3,000
II Ḳaṭar	40	135,000	6,000
III Sharjah	35	85,000	3,500
IV Ro'os-el-Djebal	20	10,000	500
V Kalhaṭ	40	60,000	2,000
VI Bāṭinah	80	700,000	30,000
VII Djebel-Akhdar	70	600,000	35,000
VIII Ḍāhirah	40	80,000	20,000
IX Belad-Ṣoor[1]	35	100,000	4,000
X Djailān	50	140,000	8,000
XI Persian coast, &c.	—	300,000	—
Total		2,280,000	112,000

To these must be added whatever inhabitants the adjoining desert and the south-eastern Arab coast may muster; an inconsiderable amount, judging by report. My readers may notice that the province of Mascat is omitted in the catalogue above; it was classified by my informants partly with that of the Bāṭinah, and partly with Djebel-Akhdar. Other remarks, made when I gave the list of Nejdean villages, population, and soldiery, are in their measure applicable here also.

The revenues of this kingdom are considerable and sure. When I applied myself to reckon up the sums afforded by the exactest valuation possible of the several sources of income, I was inclined to suspect either an error in my arithmetic, or some strange exaggeration in the data themselves. But on consulting in consequence the statement of travelled authors respecting some particular localities of 'Omān and the resources at the disposal of its government, besides the ratification afforded by official intelligence given me out of 'Omān itself, I found that my calculations fell considerably below those made by others within the limits specified; and hence I can hardly doubt that, taking all things together, my ciphering and summation may stand for a fair approach to the exact truth. Should there, however, be in this, no less than in the catalogue of the population just given, some error (nor dare I hope to have wholly avoided such), I have throughout aimed at ensuring the error a place on the side of under, not of over-statement. Time and further investigation will, I trust, correct all.

My readers should then know that the sources of public revenue in 'Omān are four: the pearl fishery; the commercial duties; the land taxes; and the monopolies and special trade in the hands of government. Each of these we will now consider separately, and then sum them up. Let us begin with the pearl fishery as the least important.

It would be very difficult to ascertain the exact number of boats which yearly ply on this trade from Ḳaṭeef to Sharjah, nor do I believe that the central government itself is over-accurately informed on this point, at least in its totality. However, registers more or less precise are kept in each village of the coast, and should any one take the pains of enquiring after them in the separate places, something near the mark might be reached. Now the total number of towns, villages, and hamlets which send out boats to the pearl fishery, is about one hundred and forty, including those of Baḥreyn; while the mean number of boats furnished by each, reckoning proportionally from those which I visited and counted in person, is about forty. The sum of fishing-vessels would thus equal five thousand six hundred in all. Secondly, each boat-owner has to pay, for every boat that he mans for the pearl season, a sum amounting to about thirty shillings of English money, besides a small percentage on the produce, seldom exceeding a rial and a half, or about eight shillings, taking the average; this added to the boat-tax gives thirty-eight shillings. Multiplying this sum into the number of boats, we get two hundred and twelve thousand eight hundred shillings, or ten thousand six hundred and forty pounds sterling for annual income, reserved to the exclusive profit of the central government · though in addition special and arbitrary exactions are not unfrequently made by the local chiefs, at least in Baḥreyn; in Ḳaṭar I did not hear from the beachmen any complaints on that score.

The second source of revenue consists in the port dues. Niebuhr, I find, states them to be five per cent on Christians, six on Mahometans, that is, on their respective cargoes, and so forth. Such may have been the case a hundred and twenty years ago, but now matters are much changed. Here I may claim the right of personal experience, since from the moment of leaving Menāmah up to the shipwreck off Sowādah, my companion and I had always along with us baggage and goods amenable to custom-house duties, and thus embarked and disembarked from and in no less than ten different harbours. Now the general rule followed in all the government custom-houses established upon the sea-line from Bahreyn to Ṣoor—namely, in Menāmah, Moḥarreḳ, Bedaa', Wokrah, Linja, Bander'-Abbas, Aboo-Ḍebee, Ḍobey', Sharjah, and the rest, making about thirty harbours of real activity and importance—is to exact a rial, that is, five shillings, for every full-sized bale disembarked, whatever its contents; a bale weighing on an average from sixty to seventy pounds avoirdupois. This method has certainly the advantage of abridging the trouble of the custom-house officers, but, as my readers will not fail to remark, bears a very unequal proportion to the value of the goods. Thus, for example's sake, the rial duty amounts to fourteen or fifteen per cent on dates, and scarce one per cent on cloth; on rice it would be between four and five per cent: after all, in the long run, one object balances another. This duty is on imports alone, for, contrary in this to Persian usage, the 'Omānee government takes nothing on exports—a wise system, at any rate in the East. Now, after daily observing the number of arrivals in the several ports where I made sufficient stay for calculation, I found that the average of disembarkments in any particular harbour is at least six per diem; at the large havens of Linja, Ṣoḥār, Maṭraḥ, Mascat, and their like, it is considerably greater; at some unimportant ports, less. Lastly, the medium quota of bales per cargo is about sixty, between large and small craft; the slightest bark brings ten or twelve, a good-sized ship six hundred or more. Multiplying all these different numbers together, and reducing the amount of trading days in the year from three hundred and sixty five to three hundred, in order to allow for foul weather and the like contingencies, we obtain sixteen millions two hundred thousand shillings, or eight hundred and ten thousand pounds sterling, for annual income derived from this source.

For the third item, namely, the land taxes, including those on live stock, produce, and the like, we have the following data. The tax, which, I should add, bears no longer in 'Omān the Islamitic name of "Zekah," but is simply entitled "Kharj," or "product," is lighter by about a third than in Wahhabee countries; nor did I hear of any extraordinary money levies, either for war or for other purposes. We must next consider that the population, and above all the fixed or landed population, is much more dense, amounting to almost double that of Nejed, taking the word in its political sense; thirdly, the ground is in general decidedly more fertile. Hence it comes that a better quality of dress, habitation, and living in 'Omān, bears witness to a standard of local wealth higher than what obtains in Central Arabia. Following this proportion, the revenue thus collected throughout the kingdom of 'Omān must be about double that which is poured into the treasury of Riad, and may reach from one hundred and eighty thousand to two hundred thousand pounds sterling a year. All my informants allowed that this source of income is on the one hand much inferior to the commercial; on the other, much superior to whatever other Arab states can draw by the utmost rigour of government dues. I should add that land rent, properly speaking, is here unknown; produce, cattle, and metal, under some circumstances, being the direct objects of taxation.

Fourth and last comes the commerce carried on by Thoweynee, his family, and his personal retainers in their own name; to this we should add certain monopolies such as those mentioned above, that is, of salt or other mines, and amber. Regarding these points I have no exacter information than that afforded by popular report, which assigns Thoweynee a private revenue of about two hundred thousand rials, or fifty thousand pounds, a year.

It may be well to remark that I have included the slave-trade in the second item of this list; every negro landed brings two rials, which I take here for about ten shillings, into the custom-house coffers—not a heavy sum. Hence, though the fear of foreign intervention may occasionally procure the poor blacks some additional inconvenience from close concealment under hatches, and the like, I never heard of any similar measures being taken by Arab sea captains in order to smuggle their living cargo through the port duties.

Let us now add together the different sums above specified; they give us a total of one million sixty-five thousand six hundred and forty pounds a year. No inconsiderable amount for an Eastern native government, though under a better rule and more genial circumstances it might admit of considerable augmentation. But taking it as it stands under the present system, it cannot be held as a burden on land and people; and if we consider the prosperity and well-being of a nation, high and low, artisans, traders, agriculturists, and proprietors, to be the one main end for which governments are instituted and taxes levied, we may, on the whole, congratulate the Sultan of 'Omān on having enough and to spare for all necessary and honourable ends, without overcharging his people or checking their industry and commerce.

About the revenues, whatever they may be, derived from the African possessions, from Socotra and from Zanjibar, I can say nothing precise. The current reports of wealth thence derived or there retained—of "gold and silver, ivory, apes, and peacocks"—no less vague than those of old times, are probably not better adapted to stand the test of statistics and mathematical computation.

My readers will perhaps enquire on what the government as such expends its yearly income. The official items run thus: Firstly, the maintenance of numerous forts still kept in repair, especially on the sea-coast, along with their Beloochee garrisons, artillery, ammunition, and whatever else is needed to that end. Secondly, the king's body-guard, consisting of the cavalry already described, and always on duty, besides a lesser number of foot retainers. Thirdly, the entire machinery of custom-houses and their officials, revenue collectors, police, and others of the like categories. Fourthly, the navy—large and effective, as we have already seen, and a continual source of expenditure much surpassing all the rest put together. Fifthly, the incomes of ministers, members of the royal family, and the pomp of office and state. Last, but not least, if report say true, Thoweynee's own personal luxury and extravagance; qualities wherein he copies only too faithfully his royal Ḳaḥṭânee predecessors, as history paints them, whether in Yemen or 'Omân. "No man can be blamed for being like his father," says the Arab proverb; and this may afford some kind of excuse for Thoweynee, if he tread in the steps of Ḍoo-Riash and the Tobaa's, with whom he claims so near an alliance.

It is time for us now to resume our narrative, fast drawing to a close. On my return to Astar's, Yoosef introduced me to his new sea friend, who repeated to me his proffer of free passage and board to Aboo-Shahr. During the two following days he was a constant guest at Astar's divan, whither he brought his mates and many other sons of Neptune. Among all the seamen who ply the Persian Gulf, the mariners of Koweyt hold the first rank in daring, in skill, and in solid trustworthiness of character. Fifty years since their harbour with its little town—I never visited it, but often heard it described by those who had—was a mere nothing; now it is the most active and the most important port of the northerly Gulf, Aboo-Shahr hardly or even not excepted. Its chief, 'Eysa by name, enjoys a high reputation both at home and abroad, thanks to good administration and prudent policy; the import duties are low, the climate healthy, the inhabitants friendly, and these circumstances, joined to a tolerable roadstead and a better anchorage than most in the neighbourhood, draw to Koweyt hundreds of small craft which else would enter the ports of Aboo-Shahr or Baṣrah. The inhabitants are Mahometans, Arab fashion, that is, tolerant to others and not over-rigid to themselves; Wahhabeeism is carefully proscribed, and all the efforts of Nejed have never succeeded in making one single proselyte at Koweyt. In its mercantile and political aspect this town forms a sea outlet, the only one, for Djebel Shomer, and in this respect like Trieste for Austria. Koweyt is only fifteen days' distance or thereabouts from Ḥâ'yel; hence the rulers of the Ebn-Rasheed family have constantly kept up the best possible relations with the chiefs of Koweyt, and these relations have been drawn even closer under the present reign of Ṭelâl. Perhaps, too, kindred blood has concurred to cement the political alliance, for the governors of Koweyt lay claim to ancestors of the Dja'afar clan, the same to which Ṭelāl himself belongs. But independently of this, the great advantages procured by this sea-port to Djebel Shomer, both for the commodious import of rice, cloth, and other wares, and for the export of horses, sheep, wool, and the like products of the uplands, would alone suffice to approve Ṭelāl's wisdom in this respect. Lastly, the Koweyt alliance aids Ṭelāl in keeping the balance even between himself and the encroaching Wahhabees on the south; while 'Eysa and his townsmen, strengthened by their union with Shomer, take courage and refuse the demands of tribute and submission made on them by the Mutasallim of Baṣrah and the Basha of Bagdad, thus escaping the decline and desolation almost inevitable for all sea-ports under Ottoman administration.

On the afternoon of the 22nd a southerly breeze sprang up, and our skipper announced his intention of sailing next morning; but Arabs are alike procrastinators by land and by sea, and when the morning came we found that there was no need to be on board till sunset at soonest. The ship meanwhile had moved out of the Mascat harbour, and was now lying at Maṭraḥ near the entrance of that port, opposite a huge rock called the Faḥl, or "stallion," a term generic among Arabs for whatever is bulky. The Faḥl of Maṭraḥ is a mass of black stones rising abruptly from the sea, like our old acquaintance Salāmah off Cape Mesandum.

At last, on March 23rd, towards evening, we took leave of our host Astar, and of other kind friends; and while I walked down to the harbour accompanied by Yoosef and by four or five particular acquaintances, I felt that my steps were finally homeward bound in good earnest. Nor was that feeling wholly unmixed with regret, nor without a hope, however distant, of once more revisiting these strange and pleasant lands. We embarked in a negro canoe, and pulled for about two hours round cape and headland till we sighted the ship's lantern and climbed up her dark sides long after nightfall. That same night, while we cleared out of the outmost harbour and stood for the open sea, I watched the Southern Cross, the lower limb of which is here four or five degrees above the horizon; though had it been down to the very water's edge, the clear atmosphere would have rendered every star visible. It was an old friend, seen again for a short space after an absence of many years, and soon to be hidden from sight, not from remembrance.

On the rest of our voyage I shall say very little. Our course lay across the Gulf to Bandar-'Abbas, where we stayed a day; thence we made for the little island of Hinjām or Hinyām, off Djishm, an excellent naval station, the very Pereem of the Persian Gulf for whoever may choose; thence to the quiet harbour of Chiro, just above Charak, and thence to Aboo-Shahr, amidst heavy storms and contrary gales which retarded our arrival till April 6th.

The captain and his crew kept up from first to last the same friendly and courteous ways of which they had given us a specimen at Mascat, nor was there reason for any complaint against our numerous fellow-passengers, mostly Indians from Lucknow and its neighbourhood. The ship was large, clean, and this time at least, watertight; well for us that she was so, for about half way up the Gulf we encountered a tempest, worse perhaps than that which sent our old 'Omānee craft to the bottom. But I was now taking very little notice of good or bad around; for the fever which I had contracted at Mascat here declared itself in full force. Nor was I the only sufferer in the ship; one of the Indians had taken it also while on shore, and died before we reached our destination. Sailors and captain did their best to nurse me; but beyond what relief sympathizing faces and kind words can give, an Arab ship has little wherewithal to meet the requirements of a sick man. At last we anchored before Aboo-Shahr; the crew carried me, for I could no longer move, on their shoulders, and Yoosef-ebn-Khamees led the way to the residence of Aboo-'Eysa, who had in his own mind put us down long since with the long catalogue of others, men and vessels, who had perished on the night of March 9th. Barakāt had already gone on to Basrah, and thence to Bagdad, where he was awaiting me; Aboo-'Eysa, with his Persian convoy of pilgrims, about a hundred and twenty in number, was in a few days to leave Aboo-Shahr for Baḥreyn, and so to Ḥasa.

Here I received the latest news regarding the fall of 'Oneyzah and the triumph of the Wahhabees in the West. But the fever, now at its height, left me small leisure to care for events near or far; in fact, I was constantly, with few and doubtful intervals, in that state of half-delirium so wearisome in typhoid illness. The Indian steamer arrived on April 10th, and took me to Basrah, where some sailors put me on board a river steamboat, then commanded by Captain Selby of the Indian Navy. Here generous and open-hearted kindness, that proper badge of an Englishman and a sailor, supplied me with good treatment and medical assistance of every sort, or my journey would probably have ended, like the wanderings of many another traveller, in quitting the world altogether. Our voyage up the Tigris, now swollen by spring inundations, lasted seven days; on the eighth we landed at Bagdad, where the hospitality of Captain Selby and other friends, English, Swiss, and French, went far to restore me, if not to perfect health, at least to a favourable convalescence. Here, after a few days, I met once more my old and faithful companion Barakāt; his joy on seeing me again after so many sinister reports, and fear outbalancing hope, may be easier imagined than described. I should notice that news of the March storm had reached Bagdad, where many enquiries awaited me regarding the loss or escape of sundry vessels in which the merchants of that town had a special interest.

Our return route lay by Kerkook, Mosoul, Mardeen, Diar-Bekr, Orfah, and thence round to Aleppo and Syria. It was a track new to me, and hence full of charm, but might be less so to my readers;—rendered, I doubt not, sufficiently familiar with that part of the world by numerous and better written narratives than mine. Indeed it is only the apology of novelty that can excuse to myself what, remembering the wealthy interest of the land, I must feel are at the best but imperfect outlines of Central and Eastern Arabia, from Ma'ān to Mascat. Much, how much! is left untold;—reserved, I trust, for some more fortunate traveller than he who now bids the reader a hearty Farewell.

INDEX.

'AARED, Wahhabee province of, i. 463; ii. 75
'Aaseer province, its position and inhabitants, ii. 49
'Abbas Basha, his policy, i. 189
'Abd-Allah-ebn-Rasheed, ruler of Djebel Shomer, i. 125; father of Telāl, 128
'Abd-Allah (son of Feysul), his treacherous conduct, i. 109; his qualities and campaigns, ii. 71, 109; interviews with him, 89; his endeavours to obtain strychnine, and our refusal, 112, 116
'Abd-el-Kereem a Riad Wahhabee patient, ii. 3; his statement of Wahhabee doctrines, 10; attempts to evade payment, 16
Aboo-'Eysa, his history, i. 288; our arrangements with him, 296; his assistance at Riad, 416, 420; his house at Hofhoof, ii. 141
Abyssinia, coffee from, i. 426; the Himyarites, Abyssinian colonists, ii. 240
Administration of law in Arabia: courts of justice, i. 79, 181; capital charges, 229; punishments, 136, 181; executions, ii. 25; rarity of, i. 134; the Kadee, 228
Aflāj, the province of, ii. 79; trade with Yemen, 81
'Akabah, Arabic for an ascent, i. 316
Arabia, object of author's journey into, i. 1; population, 117, 193; civilization, 75, 166; ethnology, 352, 453; habits and customs, 51, 73, 183, 268; commercial habits, 69, 263; national characteristics, 24, 35, 70, 175; envious character of, ii. 135; position of women among, i. 271; patriotism, 194; historical notices of, 117, 239; religious feelings, 68; early religion, 212; relics of Sabæanism, 250; traces of ancient Christianity in, 88; the Wahhabees, 363; mode of warfare, 306; external features of Central Arabia, 230-235; absence of rivers, 339; the water supply of, ii. 170; extent of cultivable land, i. 91; Christianity not a bar to travelling in, 264; Bedouin tribes, 30, 441; European accounts, 136, 425; inaccuracies, ii. 162; administration of justice, i. 134, 228; uncertainty of historical chronology, ii. 40; music, and general tone of Arab voices, i. 309; different races in, 453; confused nomenclature of towns and places, ii. 127; diseases, 27; absence of insects and snakes in, 355. (*See also* Architecture, Language)
Arab sailors, ii. 199; adoption of foreign words by, 298
— soldiers on the march, ii. 128
Arabs, not a nervous race, ii. 35
Architecture, description of an Arab house, i. 49; general characteristics, 283; dearth of inscriptions and carved work in Central Arabia, 301; tower and castle in the Djowf, 75; the Cyclopean arch, 176; ancient mosques, 444; house and castle in Bereydah, 280, 282; palace, &c. at Riad, 396; in Hofhoof, ii. 149; of Southern Arabia, 151, 167; the

palace at Kateef, 191; rib-vaulting in the Karmoot palace, 192; at Bahreyn, 209; tower at Sharjah, 308; 'Omânee architecture, 330
'Asr, a division of time in the East, i. 178
Assassination, approval of by all sects of Shiya'ees, ii. 41
Astronomy, in 'Omân, ii. 263
Awwâl (sharks) used as food, ii. 321; name misapplied to Bahreyn, 321

BAHREYN, the islands of, ii. 203; traces of Christianity among, 146; the rulers of, 201; its capital, 204; its population and government, 211; currency, 207; handicrafts, &c., 214; character of population, 366; voyage to Katar, 229
Banians in 'Omân, ii. 369; anecdote of a Banian and a Nejdean, 370
Barr-Fâris, Arab colony on the east coast of Persian Gulf, ii. 244; origin of, 245; description, 246; chief town of, 251
Bathah-Farzah, the 'Omânee king's palace, arrival at, after the shipwreck, ii. 351; our reception there, 355; conversation with officers, deserters from the Turkish army, 357; leave for Mascat, 359
Bâtinah, richest province of 'Omân, ii. 326; its produce, &c., 327
Bedaa', chief town of Katar, ii. 235; expeditions along the coast, 237; a hawking party, 238; leave for 'Omân, 243
Bedouins, a specimen of their conversation, i. 25; religion and morality of, 8, 32; slight impress of Mahometanism on, 9; characteristics of, 3, 33; precautions in use as guides, 41; mode of, dealing with, 93; customs, food, &c., of 23-30; condition of, in Central Arabia, 31, 193; tribe of Christian origin, 150; their forays in the lower Nejed, 223; the Bedouins under the Wahhabees, ii. 78, 84; in the Great Desert, ii. 133, 234; manners of the Bedouins in Hasa, 185; the pirate Bedouins on the Persian Gulf, 234; Ajmân Bedouins crushed by the Wahhabees, 71; Bedouins preceded in battle by a maiden, ib.
Bells, anathematized by Mahomet, i. 429
Benoo-Kahtân. See Kahtanic race
Bereydah, conquest of, by Feysul, i. 168; first view of, 270; described, 280; lodgings at, 281; difficulty of further advance from, 284; street scenes, 299; social life at, 309, 314; warfare, 306; journey from Bereydah to Riad, 323-388; the meeting with the Persian ambassador, 346
Biadeeyah, the name adopted by the 'Omânees, ii. 262; form of their religion, 263; Niebuhr's account, 265
Blacksmith's shop at Hâ'yel described, i. 165
Botany, notices of: colocynth, i. 12; samh, 29; mesaa', 30; ghada, 38; narcotic plants, 254; other plants, 232; cotton, 254; themâm, a grass, 332
Bread, forms of, in Arabia, i. 73; in the south-east portion, 355
Bushire, properly called Aboo-Shahr, i. 275

CAMELS, nature of, i. 39; milk, 29; price, 85, 451; difference between, and dromedaries, 324; the two-humped not an Arabian species, 325; the Nejed camels, 450
Carmathian sect, outbreak of, i. 245; origin of, ii. 145; their hatred to Mahometans, 203; present position, 748; a colony of them in the Wahhabee territory, 82
Christianity, traces of in Arabia, i. 61, 88; among the Bedouins, 119, 150; traces of on shores of Persian Gulf and islands, ii. 146; no bar to travel in Arabia, i. 264
Cisterns. See Water-supply
Coffee, preparation of, i. 51; Mokha, described, 424; other kinds of, 426

Coinage current in Arabia, ii. 178
Commerce in Arabia, system of, i. 67, 71; discouraged by Mahometanism, 435; fairs in Hasa, ii. 170
Copper, found in 'Omân, ii. 306
Cotton shrub, grown in Kaseem, i. 254

DAHIRAH, province of, ii. 340
Dahnâ, the. *See* Desert
Dârim, his history, i. 248
Darweeshes, described, sects, i. 257; assumption of disguise by Europeans, 258-260; fate of an English traveller in this disguise, 261; not popular among Wahhabees, i. 263; his mistake, ii. 152
Dates, staple food, i. 60; results of over use, *ib.*; different kinds of, 58; cultivation, 253; Khalâs dates, ii. 173
Derb-el-Hajj. *See* Pilgrims, route of
Derey'eeyah, ruins of, i. 386; fanaticism of inhabitants, 387; its former greatness, ii. 38; siege of, 56
Desert, journeying in, i. 12, 91; the sirocco, 17; ostriches, 43; the desert circles of Arabia, 19; general description of, 24; growth of samh plant in, 29; the ghada, 38; wells, 11, 28; sparrows, 95; crossing an arm of the Dahnâ, or Great Desert, 329; the Dahnâ, ii. 130; the stone heap, 131; attempt to sink well in, 135; Bedouins in, i. 9, 22; in the Great Desert, ii. 133. (*See* also Nefood)
Djebel Shomer, first sight of, i. 95; mountains of, 100; its history, 117; cause of increase, 161; population, revenue, and contingents, ii. 86
Djebel Toweyk, geology &c. of, i. 336; highest plateau, 352; pass, 358; second plateau, 351; termination of, ii. 128
Djelâjil, great antiquity of, i. 351; translated "bells," 352
Djereeschah (wheat), staple food in the Djowf, i. 73
Djowf, entrance into, i. 46; chief family in, 47; boundaries, 56; its capital, 57; villages and population, 60;

history of, 61; present government of, 65; architecture of palace, 75; manners, &c., 67; life at, 72; departure from, 85; not part of the Nejed, 102
Djowhar, treasurer of Feysul, patient at Riad, ii. 2; his gratitude, 194
Dromedaries frightened by locusts, ii. 137. (*See also* Camels)

EGYPT, influence of, in Arabia, i. 246; invasion of the Nejed, ii. 47; Nejdean view of, 100
El-Mukhzee, "the shameful," the Wahhabee name for tobacco, i. 350
Europeans, position of, in travelling through Arabia, i. 264. (*See also* Darweeshes)
'Eyn-Nejm, sulphurous springs, ii. 139
'Eyoon, the monument of Sabæan worship, &c., i. 250

FALCONRY, ii. 238
Feysul, prince of Nejed, i. 122; subdues Kaseem, 168; payment by Persian pilgrims to, 275; his palace, 393, 396; effect of our visit on, 402; his council, 417; his character, ii. 64; former history, 65; old age, 73; appearance in public, 109; his family, 74, 110
Fumigations, peculiar character of, ii. 6

G'HAWAH or K'hâwah, i. 49, 50
Ghât, i. 269, 341
Gold, stated to be found in 'Omân, ii. 306

HADEE'YAH a maiden who precedes the Bedouins in fight, ii. 71
Hamood, governor of the Djowf, i. 64, 74
Hareek, destroyed by Wahhabees, ii. 46; features of, 128

Hare's flesh, lawfulness of use, i. 360
Hasa, mountains of, ii. 136; inhabitants, 142; Kahtânic descent, 144; Wahhabee conquest, 147; alliance with Egypt, *ib.*; hot wells and volcanic symptoms, 154; products, 155; literature, 158; dialect, 164; education of women, 177; views of annexation, 217; agriculture, 178; emigration, 185; features of the country, 184; discontent against the Wahhabee government, 217
Hâtim-Tâ'i, the mythic model of Arab hospitality, i. 224; anecdote, 226
Hâ'yel, arrival at, 103; inconvenient recognitions at, 105, 152; its rise as capital of Djebel Shomer, 120; improvements by Telâl, 128; life at, 141; street scenes in, 162; pilgrim route through, 196; our dangers at, 201; departure from, 214
Hejâz, inhabitants of, i. 242
Himyarites, origin of, ii. 240
Hofhoof, the town, ii. 149; neighbourhood, 153; society, 166; feeling towards the Wahhabees, 168; weekly fairs, 170; excursions, 171, 176; departure, 180
Horeymelah, birth-place of Wahhâb, i. 362
Horses, sent to India, i. 221; of Central Arabia, at Riad, ii. 92; management, 93; colours, 94; exportation, 95; inferior in 'Omân, 97

IBRAHEEM BASHA, his fortresses in the Nejed, i. 362, 386; attempts the restoration of 'Eyânah, 381; heads the Egyptian expedition against the Nejed, ii. 48-60
Imâm, meaning of title, ii. 62, 285
India, language of, degree of affinity between it and Arabic, i. 341
Irrigation, system of, in 'Omân, ii. 300
Islam. *See* Mahometanism
Ismaelitic race, compared with the Kahtânic, i. 454; Mahomet sprung from, 455
Ithel tree, i. 153

JEKTAN. *See* Kahtânic

KADEREE sect, doctrines of, ii. 226; poetry, 227
Kahtânic race, linguistic variety of, i. 312, 465; described, 453
Kaseem, town of, revolt of from Wahhabee rule, i. 129; province of, a part of the Upper Nejed, 166; its inhabitants and politics, 167, 256; soil of Upper Kaseem, 222, 252; villages and external features of, 230; water supply of, 252; date-trees and other plants, 253; commerce, *ib.*; mosques, 256; southern Kaseem described, 238; evacuated by Egyptians, ii. 68
Katar, ii. 231, 235; pearl fishery, 232
Kateef, inhabitants, ii. 187; Feysul's navy, 188; our reception, 189; the town, 198; voyage to Bahreyn, from 199-202
Keysareeyah, the name of vaulted market-places, ii. 150
Khalâs dates (fruit), ii. 173; varieties of, *ib.*
Khâlid, the overthrower of Moseylemah, i. 383
Khodeyreeyah, mulattoes in Aflâj, ii. 80
Khowarij, free-thinkers, ii. 187
Koweyt, sailors of, ii. 386; rise of, and importance to Djebel Shomer, 387

LANGUAGE, Arabic, as used by Bedouins, i. 24; of the Coran, 311; as spoken out of Arabia, 310; localities where heard in greatest purity, 311; as spoken in 'Omân, 312; at Riad, 403; grammatical niceties of, not recent, 312; vagueness of expression and diminutives, 337; as affected by diversity of race, 459; the Kahtânic dialects, 464; not found in Yemen, 465; affinity between Arabic and Indian languages, 341
Linja, harbour and town, ii. 288, 289;

shipyards, 289; cisterns, ib.; commerce, 290
Locusts, swarm of, frightening dromedaries, ii. 137; the locust of inner Arabia, 138; used as food, 139

MA'AN, author's start from, i. 2; the town, 7
Mahometanism, slight effect of, on the Bedouins, i. 9, 243; its hold over the inhabitants of the Djowf, 68; in Ha'yel and Djebel Shomer, 179; over Arabia, 194; the revival by Wahhāb, 364; the Mahometan theory regarding God, 365; predestination, 367; effect of its teaching on medical science, 147; its principle of decay, 176; the principles on which wine was forbidden, 427; and bells and music, 429, 430; and commerce, 430; set in antagonism to Paganism and Christianity, 430; the objects and results of Mahometanism, 432; reaction against it, 436; as enforced by the Wahhabee Zelators, 408; the treatment by Mahometans of impostors, 260; the position of Christians among them, 264; Mahometan division of sins, ii. 7–15; future punishment, 8
Mahomet, sprung from Ismaelitic race, i. 454; visit of, to Damascus, ii. 19
Mārid, tower of, i. 60; described, 75
Mascat, Portuguese fortifications, ii. 361; harbour, 364; population, 365; climate, 367; police, 368; the town, 369; neighbourhood, 373; excursions, 376; an Arab dance, 378
Matrah, suburb of Mascat, ii. 361; Negro, and other trade, 362; population, ib.
Mebarras, village and fair, ii. 172
Mecca, profligacy of, i. 257
Meddey'yee or Zelators, the Wahhabee institution, i. 407
Menāmah, ii. 204; lodgings, 206; the town, 208; population, 211; politics, 217; departure, 224
Mesandum, Cape, ii. 317
Meshāree, the murderer of Turkee, i. 123
Metu'ab, brother of Telāl, his character, i. 132, 188; conversations with him, 189
Metow'waa', the Wahhabee clergymen, i. 79; act as spies, 201; exact contributions, 317
Mohammed-'Alee-esh-Shirāzee, the Persian ambassador to Riad, i. 275, 320; our journey in his company, 323; his reception at Riad, 400
Mohanna-el-'Anezee, the Wahhabee ruler over Bereydah, i. 277; his treachery to a Persian caravan, 278; our interview with him, 284
Moharrek, described, ii. 204
Moseylemah the liar, Mahomet's rival, i. 240; his history, 382
Mountains, Djebel Shomer, i. 95; Toweyk, 336; of Hasa, ii. 136; near Hofhoof, 165; Ro'os-el-Djebel, 315; Djebel-'Okdah, 339
Music, anathematized by Mahomet, i. 430; in Arabia, 309

NABATHÆANS, sect of, ii. 158
Nefood, or sand-passes in the desert, i. 90; in Kaseem, 329; crossing by night, 330
Negroes, their position in Arabia, i. 452; Negro colonies, ii. 242; in 'Omān, 272. (*See also* Slave Trade)
Nejed, the Arabian highlands, i. 91; upper and lower, 102; described, 230; danger to travellers, 284; the zephyr of, 231; mode of warfare, 306; the central point of, 326; character, 241; hospitality, &c., 343; provinces of, 361; sheep and cattle in, 450; the Nejdean of Riad, 459; language, 463; instruction, ii. 23
Nezār, tribes descended from, i. 455.

'OBEYD, "the Wolf," uncle of Telāl, ravages Kaseem, 126, 203; head of Wahhabee faction in Hâ'yel, 131, 203; his reception by Telâl, 205; attempted treachery to us, 208

'Omân, the kingdom of, and possessions in Arabia and Africa, 255; maritime character, *ib.*; history, 256; religions, 257; traces of Sabæanism, 257, 264; polygamy, 264; qualities of inhabitants, 267; negroes in 'Omân, 272; later history, 274; division of empire, 278; English intervention, and Wahhabees invasion, 278; form of government, 285; mineral produce of, 306; population, 379; the provinces, 380; population statistics, 381; revenue, 382; slave trade, 384; government expenditure, 385

'Omânee architecture, ii. 330; sailors, 340

'Oneyzah, the former capital of North-western Arabia, i. 170; attack on by Wahhabee government, 171; foray from, 307; preparations against, ii. 108; negotiations, 109; further account of siege and capture, 250, 388

Ormus, ii. 318; formerly Portuguese, 318; its decline, 319; harbour and castle, 320; voyage to Sowâdah islands from, 322

Ottoman government misrule, i. 30; money, not current in East and Central Arabia, 81

Oxen in Nejed, i. 451

PEARL fishery, ii. 213, 214, 232

Persia, influence of its literature, i. 175; caravan of, through Central Arabia, destroyed in the desert, 278; Persian ambassador, journey with, from Bereydah to Riad, 274

Persian Gulf, the, shallowness at Kateef, ii. 188; spring of fresh water in, 229; pirates, 234; tides in, 243; phosphoric, 252; marine monsters, *ib.*; storm off Cape Mesandum, 317; sharks, 321; language of sailors on, *ib.*; coast scenes, 328; shipwreck, 341

Pilgrims, route of, through Central Arabia, i. 102, 196; dangerous near Medinah, 208; payments exacted, 275

Pharmacy, medicines suited for desert travel, i. 5; practice of, in Arabia, 145; a rustic patient, 159; disease from over use of dates, 60; Arab diseases, 27; and treatment, 30; vaccination, 28

Phosphoric sea, Wahhabee ideas respecting, ii. 252

Planetary worship. *See* Sabæan worship

Pottery, Arab, made in 'Omân, ii. 275

RIAD, historical notices of, i. 123, 384; first sight of, 390; commencement of our stay, 393; our reception by Feysul's ministers, 404, 416; life at, 437; described, 442; morality, ii. 24; patients, 26; our position at court, 36, 89; different routes from, 82; invasion by Zelators, 104; difficulties of leaving, 113; position with 'Abd-Allah, 115; our flight, 122

Rivers, none in Arabia, i. 339. *See* Water-supply

Ro'os-el-Djebal, province of 'Omân, ii. 315; dialect and inhabitants, 315

Round towers in the Djowf, i. 58

SABÆAN worship, i. 250; circles of stones connected with, 251; described, ii. 258; influence of, in 'Omân, 262; connection with Egyptian pyramids, 264

Sa'ood family, history of, i. 376; advocates Wahhabeeism, 377; subdues Nejed, 378

Salt, rock, found in Djebel Toweyk, i. 340; in 'Omân, ii. 306

Sedeyr, a province of the Nejed, i. 338; inhabitants, 340

Seduction, Arab and Wahhabee feelings about, ii. 182

Seleem Abou-Mahmood-el-'Eys, name assumed by author at Hâ'yel, i. 152

Semoom, the, described, i. 17
Sharjah Harbour, ii. 301; town of, 304; commercial position, 305; the tower, 308; route from, to Ormuz, 312
Sharks, used as an article of food, ii. 321
Shejâh, the female impostor, married to Moseylemah, i. 383
Shiy'aees, the sect of, their doctrines, i. 163, 360
Shipwreck, the, in the Persian Gulf, ii. 343; the effect of the different religions in danger, 353
Slave trade in 'Omân, ii. 302. (*See also* Negroes)
Small-pox in Arabia, inoculation and vaccination, ii. 28
Sohâr, chief town of Bâtinah, ii. 329; social life and government, 330; the town, 332; trades, &c., 333; agriculture, 336; dialects, *ib.*; population, 336; ships, 337
Solibah Bedouins, i. 150
Sonnee sect, the, food prohibited under, i. 360
Sorcery, source of, in 'Omân, ii. 271; anecdote of, 267
Sowâdah islands, the ii. 341
Springs. *See* Water-supply
Stramonium Datura, growth of, i. 255
Sun, worship of by Bedouins, i. 8

TAHIR, the Carmathian chief, i. 245
Tâ'i, history of ancient tribe of, i. 117; alleged descendants of, 61
Tâj-Djehân, relict of 'Asaph Dowlah, on pilgrimage through Arabia, i. 274; cheated en route through Riad, 276; pillaged by Mohanna, 284
Tameem, familiar name in Nejed, i. 459
Telâl-ebn-Rasheed, his dominion and character, i. 14, 98; generosity, 126; ascends the throne, 128; his family, 135; government, 142; internal policy, 130, 228; foreign policy, 132, 195; his conquests, 63, 129; interviews with him, 110, 136; object of the journey revealed to him, 200; his passport, 211
Teymah, the Teman of Scripture, i. 97
Tides in Persian Gulf, ii. 243
Tobacco, sin of smoking, ii. 10, 12-15; anecdote of its punishment, 24
Turkee-ebn-Sa'ood, his history, ii. 57; assassination, 64
Turks, their religious principles, i. 69; influence on Eastern cultivation, 175

WAHHABEE sect, principles of their government, i. 316; the founder, 363; his views, 371; family, 379; the "Zelators," 407; peculiarities, 445; effect of, on the Arabic language, 463; not strict in outward Mahometan observances, 225; Wahhabeeism at Hâ'yel, 176, 202; hatred of Europeans, 113; of Darweeshes, 263; of Christians, 264; reaction from, 161; style of mosques, 256; Nejed, the genuine country of, 284; Wahhabee legend respecting the destruction of 'Eyânah, 377; the provinces of the empire, ii. 75; its tributaries and allies, 78; the Bedouins, 78, 84; general view of government and empire, 83; population and contingents, 84; reaction in 'Omân, 170
Wadi Farook, dangers of, ii. 136
Wadi Serhân, i. 14
Water-supply: wells in the desert, i. 28; the well of Shekeek, 87; hillocks and springs, 233; hydraulic machinery, 304; brackish water, 340; abundant in Nejed, 450; the hot spring near Hofhoof, ii. 174; at Hasa, 154, 176; cisterns at Linja, 289; irrigation in 'Omân, 360
Wâsit, village in the Nefood, i. 330
Wells. *See* Water-supply
Wine, the principles which led Mahomet to forbid its use, i. 427

YOOSEF-EBN-KHAMEES, guide to 'Omân, ii. 222

ZAMIL, treasurer to Telâl, his history, i. 111; assists us, 198
Zelators. *See* Meddey'yee
Zodiacal light, i. 314
Zoology: ostriches, i. 43; scorpions, 44; deer, peculiar varieties of, 334; hares, 360; scarcity of insects in Arabia, 355; snakes, Lamartine's account of, *ib.*; sheep in Nejed, 450; oxen, 451; game, 451. (*See also* Camels, Horses)

THE END.

LONDON
PRINTED BY SPOTTISWOODE AND CO.
NEW-STREET SQUARE

LIST OF BOOKS.

The Neutrality of England Vindicated.

A Letter to the President of the United States.
By Wm. Vernon Harcourt, of the Inner Temple ('Historicus').

By the same Author, 8vo. cloth, price 7s. 6d.

Letters on Some Questions of International Law.

By 'Historicus.'
Reprinted from 'The Times', with considerable Additions.
Also, ADDITIONAL LETTERS. 8vo. 2s. 6d.

Extra fcp. 8vo. cloth, 5s.

The Economic Position of the British Labourer.

By Henry Fawcett, M.P., M.A.,
Fellow of Trinity Hall, and Professor of Political Economy in the University of Cambridge.

By the same Author, Second Edition, crown 8vo. cloth, price 12s.

Manual of Political Economy.

'The clearness of Mr. Fawcett's treatment of an extensive and difficult subject will render his book a valuable companion to the mercantile and political student.'—Morning Post.

THE WAR IN NEW ZEALAND.

Crown 8vo. cloth, 10s. 6d.

The Maori King;

Or, The STORY of OUR QUARREL with the NATIVES of NEW ZEALAND.
By J. E. Gorst, M.A.
With a Portrait of William Thompson and a Map of the Seat of War.

General View of the Criminal Law of England.

By J. Fitzjames Stephen, Barrister-at-Law, Recorder of Newark-on-Trent.
8vo. cloth, price 18s.

'Readers feel in this book the confidence which attaches to the writing of a man who has great practical acquaintance with the matter of which he writes, and lawyers will agree that it fully satisfies the standard of professional accuracy.'—Saturday Review.

The Roman and the Teuton.

A SERIES of LECTURES delivered before the UNIVERSITY of CAMBRIDGE.
By the Rev. Charles Kingsley, M.A.,
Rector of Eversley, and Professor of Modern History in the University of Cambridge.
8vo. cloth, price 12s.

Plutology;

Or, The THEORY of the EFFORTS to SATISFY HUMAN WANTS.
By W. E. Hearn, LL.D.,
Professor of History and Political Economy in the University of Melbourne.
8vo. cl th, 14s.

The Coal Question;

An INQUIRY concerning the PROGRESS of the NATION and the PROBABLE EXHAUSTION of our COAL MINES.
By W. Stanley Jevons, M.A., Fellow of University College, London.
8vo. cloth, price 10s. 6d.

MACMILLAN & CO. London.

www.ingramcontent.com/pod-product-compliance
Lightning Source LLC
Chambersburg PA
CBHW022120290426
44112CB00008B/754
9783337011130